A GUIDE TO WELSH LITERATURE

A GUIDE TO WELSH LITERATURE 1282–*c.* 1550

VOLUME II

Edited by
A. O. H. JARMAN and
GWILYM REES HUGHES

Revised by
DAFYDD JOHNSTON

UNIVERSITY OF WALES PRESS
CARDIFF
1997

British Library Cataloguing in Publication Data

A catalogue record for this book is available from the British Library

ISBN 0-7083-1439-2

Published with the financial support of the Arts Council of Wales

Cover illustration: Poem by Lewis Glyn Cothi from Peniarth 109 C (f. 77) by permission of the National Library of Wales

Cover design by Olwen Fowler
Typeset at the University of Wales Press
Printed in Wales by Dinefwr Press, Llandybïe

For Saunders Lewis
who interpreted the tradition

CONTENTS

PREFACE TO THE 1979 EDITION

The first volume of this series surveyed the development of Welsh literature from its beginnings in the late sixth century to the end of the period of Welsh independence (*c.* 1300). The present volume continues the story to 1527 (although somewhat later in the case of prose), the year of the death of Tudur Aled, by common consent the last major medieval Welsh poet. During the greater part of the period discussed in Volume 1 verse predominated over prose, and this is an even more striking characteristic of the much shorter period dealt with in the present volume. Thus, twelve of the sixteen chapters which follow are concerned with the work of poets, and two with the functioning of the bardic system and the basic concepts which underlay it. One chapter illustrates the persistence of the modes of the *Gogynfeirdd* in the new era, but the main purport of the volume's central chapters is to show how the *awdlau* of the poets of the Princes were superseded in the fourteenth and fifteenth centuries by a vast corpus of verse composed in the new *cywydd* metre. The most outstanding poet using the *cywydd*, and the best-known outside the bounds of Wales, was Dafydd ap Gwilym, but six other *cywyddwyr* have also been selected as the subject of separate chapters. Others, whom many would regard as not being necessarily inferior to some of the six, have, it is hoped, received adequate discussion in chapters of a more general nature. Accounts of the Welsh metrical system in English are rare and the masterly elucidation of its intricacies contained in the ninth chapter will, we anticipate, meet a greatly felt need. The final chapter demonstrates that, although the creative period of medieval Welsh prose was over before the beginning of our period, the prose-writer's craft continued to flourish and the range of his interests was wider than has been realised by many.

As was the case with the first volume, we note the achievement of a remarkable consensus of opinion by ten different contributors working independently on the interpretation of a period of major importance in the history of Welsh literature. This serves to underline the degree of maturity by Welsh critical scholarship as a result of the endeavours of the past fifty or sixty years. As in the first volume again, a few instances of overlapping between chapters occur but their sum total will be found to be minimal in a volume of four hundred pages. Their suppression would have resulted in a distortion of the texts submitted by the contributors and their enumeration may with equanimity be left to those reviewers who prefer this mode of criticism to an appraisal of the substance of a book.

A. O. H. Jarman
Gwilym Rees Hughes

PREFACE TO THE 1997 EDITION

This volume is still the most thorough and authoritative survey of the Welsh literature of the later Middle Ages, and in this new edition changes have been kept to a minimum. Advances in scholarship made over the last two decades are reflected mainly in additions to the bibliographies. I would draw attention in particular to substantial new work on the two pioneers of the *cywydd* form, Dafydd ap Gwilym and Iolo Goch, and to the important project currently under way at the University of Wales Centre for Advanced Welsh and Celtic Studies at Aberystwyth, which is producing admirable editions of the remaining manuscript poetry of the period.

It is a pleasure to acknowledge the excellent work done by the volume's original editors, A. O. H. Jarman and Gwilym Rees Hughes, and also that of Mrs Eldra Jarman in preparing the index. I am most grateful to them for their encouragement and advice, and to the staff of the University of Wales Press for their efficient support in the preparation of this new edition.

Dafydd Johnston

Chapter 1

THE HISTORICAL BACKGROUND, 1282–1550

A. D. CARR

With the death of Llywelyn ap Gruffydd, prince of Wales, near Builth on 11 December 1282, and the execution of his brother Dafydd some months later the attempt of the thirteenth-century princes of Gwynedd to create a feudal principality in Wales came to an end. Their patrimony passed into the possession of Edward I to be divided into counties and brought under royal government. Castles were built to control the king's new territories, boroughs were founded around them as centres of English settlement, English criminal law was introduced, and English civil procedure made available.

However, it is all too easy to speak and write of the conquest of Wales in 1282. To a much later generation that year has seemed a traumatic one and with the benefit of hindsight we can see the elements of tragedy in it. But we have to remember that, even at the height of his power, Llywelyn's writ never ran in the whole of Wales as we understand it today. The poets of the thirteenth century might call for unity from Portskewet to Porth Wygyr but the reality never matched the vision and after the eleventh century no ruler of Gwynedd, even at the height of his power, ever succeeded in pushing his southern border beyond the Brecon Beacons. The line of Bleddyn ap Cynfyn continued to rule in Powys until it ended in an heiress in 1309. And the great change in the political geography of Wales had already occurred in the eleventh and twelfth centuries as a result of the initial advance of the Normans; from that time on Wales was divided between Pura Wallia, that is, those territories where Welsh dynasties continued to rule, and the March. The word *march* or *mark* meant a frontier zone; in Wales it was a band of territory in the south and east which comprised a number of independent lordships ruled by Anglo-Norman lords whose ancestors had won them by conquest and by doing so had inherited the rights and powers of the Welsh lords they had displaced.

The Principality recognized by the English Crown in 1267 remained as a constitutional entity, to be granted to successive heirs to the throne, beginning with the future Edward II in 1301. Although among the lands of the Crown, it was in no way a part of the English realm. Moreover, many Welshmen, both within Gwynedd and without, were already familiar with Anglo-Norman rule, with legal change, and with the castle and the borough; none of these were new phenomena in the Wales of 1282. Nor were there any profound social changes, any more than there had been in the March in the wake of the Norman invaders. There had been some English settlement in the lowlands of some lordships and in the boroughs that had grown up around the lords' castles; Pembroke can trace its origins to the eleventh century and Swansea, Neath and Carmarthen are among those boroughs established in the twelfth. But for most of the marcher lord's subjects there had been little change; the same rents and services were owed and it is significant that in the March the law of Hywel survived as a living jurisprudence down to the Union. Paradoxically the March was, on the whole, far more conservative than Pura Wallia; the Anglo-Norman lord was generally content with his traditional revenues but Welsh rulers had political reasons for encouraging change, which meant that in Gwynedd the great changes in law, administration, and economic activity had come about before 1282 in consequence of the state-building activities of the princes.

One result of these changes was the emergence of families of administrators who were among the executants of the princes' policies. The most famous of these families was that of the descendants of Llywelyn ab Iorwerth's seneschal Ednyfed Fychan who continued to enjoy great power and influence in the fourteenth-century Principality but there were numerous others who were often rewarded with grants of land on generous terms. Many of these men, finding Llywelyn's harsh rule increasingly hard to bear, may well have welcomed Edward in 1282 and he depended on them since he understood that the local community would only respond to its natural leaders. Marcher lords had long realized the necessity of governing Welshmen through Welshmen and in 1244 the officials of the earl of Pembroke made this very point to the royal justiciar in south Wales. The key men were the *uchelwyr*, free landed proprietors of good stock whose standing and influence in their localities stemmed from their position at the centre of a network of kinsmen and dependants and from the ties of blood and obligation. It has sometimes been fashionable to despise the *uchelwyr* on account of their attitude after 1282 and it is easy to bandy words like 'Quisling' and 'traitor'; the appeal to history in Welsh politics is all too often based on ignorance. One cannot apply modern concepts of politics and nationality to the thirteenth century since there was no real national consciousness; the tests of Welshness were linguistic and social. Loyalties were personal rather than national and those who went over to Edward I in 1282 did not feel they were betraying their inheritance. To accept Edward did not make them any less Welsh and they lost none of their influence; indeed, in some ways they were the gainers.

The basic structure of Welsh society was little different from that elsewhere in Europe; that much-abused adjective 'tribal' has long ago earned the right to a decent burial. In the words of the laws 'there are three kinds of persons, a king, a *breyr* (the southern term for *uchelwr*), and a bondman'. After 1282 it was the *uchelwyr* who dominated society and they went on doing so for a very long time; it was to take the combination of religious nonconformity and political radicalism to dislodge them in the nineteenth century. Wealth within this class might vary enormously but some of them could certainly put their hands on substantial sums of ready cash. Even before the end of the fourteenth century some had built up considerable estates by inheritance, marriage, or purchase and this process was to gather momentum in the next century. Not all of them were of pure Welsh descent; some, like the Stradlings in Glamorgan, the Salusburies and Thelwalls in Denbigh and the Bulkeleys in Anglesey were descended from some of the original Anglo-Norman invaders or from later settlers. Contemporary poets depict a society which laid considerable emphasis on conspicuous consumption; in the fifteenth century in particular they give us a picture of open-handed hospitality, of groaning tables, and of fine wines and exotic delicacies. Quite apart from what this tells us about their way of life, it also reflects the far-flung network of medieval trade; the spices from India and the wines from Cyprus and Gascony could find their way without any difficulty to the tables of *uchelwyr* in Eifionydd or Genau'r-glyn. When singing of the vanity of the world Siôn Cent could catalogue the things in which they delighted, among them the fine houses, the offices they held, the good things on their tables, their kitchens and cellars, their horses, hounds, and cattle, and their trips to England. Here were the leaders of Welsh society; they were a conscious and confident class, closely connected by marriage and dominant in their communities, and this dominance was strengthened by the tenure of office under king or lord.

As social leaders they fulfilled a further function. The poetry of the twelfth and thirteenth centuries was court poetry, dependent on the relationship of poet and prince. After 1282 the traditional patrons were gone and their place was taken by the *uchelwyr*. Some of the most important surviving manuscripts of medieval prose and poetry were written for them and the library of Llywelyn Bren, the leader of the Glamorgan revolt of 1315, included three Welsh books as well as a copy of one of the most popular French romances, the *Roman de la Rose*; several manuscripts from southern Ceredigion also reflect a flourishing cultural life there. Some *uchelwyr* were men of considerable culture; the fifteenth-century gentleman-poet Ieuan ap Rhydderch, for example, had attended one of the universities. Indeed, this was the class from which most of the poets came; Dafydd ap Gwilym's family held various offices in Dyfed, one ancestor having been constable of Cardigan, Iolo Goch's father held land in the lordship of Denbigh in 1334, Madog Benfras held land near Wrexham, and Gruffudd ap Maredudd ap Dafydd and Gruffudd Gryg were of Anglesey landowning stock.

Wives and daughters were as worthy of praise as the patrons themselves. Most marriages at this level of society were probably arranged and later evidence shows that a great deal of care and forethought went into choosing suitable spouses; marriage was far too important a matter to be left to the whim of young people and where land and status were concerned the head had to rule the heart. The history of some families shows the way in which the careful choice of partners could contribute to their rise; the great house of Mostyn, for example, owed much to a series of marriages in the fourteenth and fifteenth centuries that brought together estates in Chirkland, Flintshire, Caernarfonshire, and Anglesey. At the other end of Wales the Stradlings of St Donat's in Glamorgan were another family whose rise was helped by profitable matches and the marriage of Sir Edward Stradling and Gwenllian Berkerolles of Llanffa brought the family a share of one of the largest estates in medieval Glamorgan. These marriages were not always restricted to Wales; Sir Rhys ap Gruffydd, a descendant of Ednyfed Fychan, who was the outstanding Welshman in the southern counties of the Principality in the first half of the fourteenth century, married an English heiress who brought him lands in six counties. Some evidence from the March shows that the clash between the sacramental and contractual concepts of marriage was still unresolved; under Welsh law the making of the contract and the payment of the *amobr* or maiden-fee were sufficient to make a valid marriage and what was easily contracted was easily dissolved.

The third social category was that of the bondmen or *taeogion*; under various names this was the third great division of society throughout the world and its condition was basically much the same everywhere. The bondman was tied to the soil and could not leave it without his lord's licence. He owed his lord (who might be prince, bishop, religious house, or landed proprietor) food gifts and labour services, some all the year round and some at such special occasions as the harvest. He was allowed a small piece of land where he could grow what was needed to feed himself and his family. At Trallong in Brycheiniog in 1326 the bond tenants of the bishop of St David's owed carrying services, work on buildings and mills, ploughing and mowing, and the custody and execution of felons, and in 1352 the bondmen of Llanol in Anglesey were responsible for work on the prince's mill of Aberalaw and his manor of Cemais. In many bond communities the tenants held by a tenure called *tir cyfrif* whereby a fixed burden of rents and services was shared equally among them with the result that the fewer the tenants, the heavier was the individual burden. But the world was gradually changing and as time went on more and more dues and services were commuted to quit-rents. Although bondmen and their families could be bought and sold as were Madog ab Einion and his issue and Dafydd Chwith Bach of Bodedern in Anglesey in 1391, such transactions conveyed the rights and jurisdiction of the proprietor over the individuals concerned rather than their bodies. Indeed, bond status was becoming increasingly a device to raise revenue. A bondman could not live elsewhere, become a priest, a bard, or a smith, or make a will without his lord's consent but all these things were allowed on payment of a fine. Even the disparagement and forfeiture of a person of free status who married one who was unfree could be avoided in this way. The point that bondmen were a source of profit was made in the duke of Buckingham's lordships of Newport, Brecon, and

Huntington in 1500; bond status seems to have lapsed here but it was revived deliberately to force those who had been living as free-men for many years to pay large fines for enfranchisement.

There were other social classes. They included the avowry tenants who came into both Principality and lordships from elsewhere and who paid a fine to enjoy the lord's protection. There were the burgesses, some English and some Welsh. In Gwynedd, in particular, an English settler class had developed in the boroughs founded by Edward I and there was a degree of English settlement elsewhere. Some effort was made to keep the races apart but the attempt to distinguish between English and Welsh status and tenure often led to complicated situations and could not be sustained, especially since prosperous burgesses might marry local heiresses or buy property in the hinterland and found landed families which within a generation or two had become entirely Welsh. And not every borough was an English plantation; even in Beaumaris, always one of the most English towns in Gwynedd, the wealthiest burgess in 1305 was Welsh and in the fourteenth century its burgesses were in trouble for admitting too many Welshmen to municipal privileges. A number of boroughs, some of which had existed before 1282, were entirely Welsh; they included Nefyn, Pwllheli, Newborough, Llanrwst, Welshpool, and Lampeter. In Glamorgan there were Welsh burgesses at Neath and Llantrisant, if not at Cardiff and Swansea, and in the north-east English towns like Flint, Rhuddlan, and Denbigh were complemented by the Welsh boroughs of Caerwys and Chirk. Poets and people in this part of Wales were united in their hatred of the city of Chester and Tudur Penllyn berated the philistine burgesses of Flint, but Guto'r Glyn, Lewis Glyn Cothi, and Tudur Aled praised Oswestry and Dafydd ap Gwilym Newborough. The ranks of free and unfree obviously included traders, craftsmen, and some industrial workers; indeed, there were some self-contained communities of the last-named like the lead-miners of Flintshire who lived under their own laws and customs.

The Church was the one institution that recruited from all classes, high and low. In Bangor and St Asaph until the middle of the fourteenth century the bishops and higher clergy were drawn from the ranks of the *uchelwyr*; this kind of preferment seems, however, to have been extremely rare at Llandaff although a considerable number of dignitaries and prebendaries at St David's were Welsh. This class also enjoyed many of the most profitable benefices;

the rest were filled by the lower clergy, often men of little education and less remuneration. Rome might attempt to impose celibacy but the Welsh secular clergy tended to be married men even though the authorities might stigmatize their wives as concubines and their children as bastards. The hostility of Dafydd ap Gwilym and Iolo Goch to the friars may reflect a growing anticlericalism that was a European phenomenon but the Cistercians seem to have retained their popularity and in the fifteenth century several abbots were notable and respected patrons of the poets. Bishops were less notable in this respect and in the early fourteenth century Iorwerth Beli found fault with an unnamed bishop of Bangor who preferred English minstrels to Welsh poets; however, John Trefor II of St Asaph and some of his successors earned praise for their munificence as did other dignitaries like Ithel ap Robert, archdeacon of St Asaph and prebendary of Bangor, whose election to the latter see in 1357 was vetoed by the pope. The ranks of the patrons also included a number of the wealthier parish clergy, men like Hywel ap Dai, parson of Whitford, Dafydd ap Thomas of Faenor in Ceredigion, and Siôn Mechain, parson of Llandrinio in Powys.

The fourteenth century was an age of change and crisis. In the Principality the deposition of Edward II in 1327 seems to mark a turning-point in the relations of Crown and *uchelwyr*. Edward's Welsh birth may have had something to do with the loyalty of his Welsh subjects, though Welshmen generally followed the lead and espoused the cause of their own lords; Iorwerth ap Llywarch of Lleweni in the lordship of Denbigh rose to be the chamberlain of his lord, Thomas, earl of Lancaster, one of the king's greatest enemies, while Master Rhys ap Hywel, whose lands were in Herefordshire and the lordship of Brecon, followed Roger Mortimer and was one of those who captured the fugitive king near Neath in 1326. On the other hand Sir Gruffydd Llwyd of Tregarnedd in Anglesey was the leader of the royalist party in north Wales during the troubles of the reign. The next decade shows an increasing neglect of those Welshmen who had been the backbone of the royal administration under Edward I and Edward II; Edward III used offices in Wales to reward his servants and reimburse his creditors, the most blatant example being the grant of all the royal rights in Merioneth to Sir Walter de Mauny in 1341. The practice was continued by the Black Prince, by Richard II, and by the Lancastrian kings and the inevitable result was a deterioration in the maintenance of order and in administrative standards. The natural leaders of the community, neglected by the Crown, resented their position and this may have led to a heightening of racial tension, culminating in the assassination of the prince's attorney in north Wales, Henry de Shaldeford, in 1345. English burgesses were panic-stricken and some threatened to leave if more was not done to protect them. There were also problems in Flintshire where Welshmen oppressed Welshmen for their own profit but there seems to have been little trouble in the southern counties at this time.

Wales could not but be involved in the Hundred Years War which began in 1337. Troops were levied in the Principality and the March for the various royal campaigns and some Welshmen distinguished themselves, among them Sir Hywel ap Gruffydd from Eifionydd whose exploits with his battle-axe at Poitiers earned him the nickname Sir Hywel of the Axe and Sir Gregory Sais from Flintshire who became one of the circle of notable knights around the Black Prince. The tradition was continued by men like Matthew Gough and Sir Richard Gethin in the fifteenth century and poets like Guto'r Glyn praised their exploits. The level of recruitment led to a good deal of official concern about the security of Wales in view of French and Scottish activities in the Irish Sea and the authorities were warned from time to time of the dangers of denuding the maritime counties of able-bodied men. Welshmen also found their way into the service of the king of France; the best-known of these was Owain ap Thomas ap Rhodri or Owain Lawgoch, known to the French as Yvain de Galles, who was the grandson of one of the brothers of the last prince of Gwynedd and who played an active part in French service on both land and sea. In 1372 he sailed from Harfleur in a bid to recover his inheritance but was recalled by Charles V of France to go on a mission to Castile. A rising in his support was almost certainly being planned in Wales and a number of Welshmen in English service in France joined him; one of them, Ieuan Wyn, known as *le Poursuivant d'Amour* and probably a descendant of Ednyfed Fychan, took over command of Owain's company after his death. Owain Lawgoch was undoubtedly regarded by the English authorities as a serious threat and he was assassinated by an English agent in 1378. At least one poet mourned him in tones of deep disappointment and referred to the hopes which the expectation of his coming had aroused.

There was in Wales a long tradition of vaticinatory poetry, going back to *Armes Prydain* in the tenth century; it looked forward to the day when the Britons would come into their own again, honour would be restored, and a new messianic leader, an Owain or Cadwaladr, would lead them to victory. This *canu brud* or prophetic poetry is not easy to interpret and that of the fourteenth century is not so obviously harnessed to a particular political cause as is that of the fifteenth. Nevertheless, it may well have been harnessed to the hopes and ambitions of the *uchelwyr*; this was an age of messiahs and charismatic movements all over Europe although they tended to be social or religious rather than political. Owain Lawgoch and Owain Glyndŵr were both cast in the role of *mab darogan*, the son of prophecy, and in the fifteenth century the mantle finally fell on the grandson of another Owain in the person of Henry Tudor. The tradition survived his victory; one of the charges brought against Rhys ap Gruffydd of Dinefwr which led to his execution in 1531 was one of encouraging treasonable prophecies. These movements had more than a visionary appeal; experienced men of affairs did not become involved with either Owain in the hope of avenging Cadwallon ap Cadfan or of playing football with Saxon heads. It is possible to see them as a consequence of a growing disillusion with the house of Plantagenet leading to thoughts of restoring the old dynasty. The few surviving descendants of the Welsh dynasties did not count for much but the authorities generally viewed them with a certain degree of suspicion and it is significant that every outbreak before 1400 was led by a member of this class. It is not difficult, perhaps, indeed, deceptively easy, to see a rising national awareness (or, at least, a sense of grievance) against a background of plague, slump, and royal neglect.

Both royal and marcher government were certainly faced with problems, the more so since the Welsh had never been a particularly easy people to govern. The Shaldeford affair had its counterpart in south Wales in 1385 when the deputy-justice John Lawrence was murdered by a local *uchelwr* and there were disturbances elsewhere during the last decade of the fourteenth century. Every gentleman, being a leader of local society, had a body of men at his beck and call, his *plaid* or retinue of tenants, dependants, kinsmen, and retainers on whose services he could depend and by the end of the century many of these must have been old soldiers with experience in France or Scotland; their presence must have added considerably to the problems of keeping order. Nor was the Church without its tensions and grievances. Like all economic crises that of the fourteenth century hit those on fixed incomes the hardest and this applied particularly to the parish clergy, some of whose livings were very poor indeed. In 1381 several parishes in Llŷn had to be united because they were so poor that no one wanted them and a substantial share of the resources of the Welsh Church was drained off by wealthy pluralists and royal servants. The appropriation of parish churches by monastic houses also continued; even the Cistercians who, in their early days, had opposed the practice, now acted in this way. The grant of dignities and the more desirable livings to royal servants also caused resentment among the *uchelwyr* who had tended to regard them as the preserves of their clerical sons, brothers, and cousins, especially when educated and well-connected Welshmen were passed over in favour of royal clerks and confessors.

But behind all these problems lay the real source of tension, the great social and economic crisis of the fourteenth century. From the middle of the eleventh century to the end of the thirteenth the population of Europe had risen steadily, largely as a result of favourable climatic conditions. From the late thirteenth century onwards, however, the population began to decline, partly because the limit of land available for cultivation had been reached and partly because of the deterioration of the climate. The consequent colder and wetter weather led to worse harvests and then to regular famines. The worst of these was in 1315–17 when the harvest all over Europe failed for three successive years; the effect of such a sequence of disasters was cumulative since it meant that there was not only no food for the winter but no seed corn for the following spring. Then, in 1347, a greater catastrophe came upon Europe in the shape of bubonic plague—the Black Death. It has been estimated that about a third of a population already weakened by the changes of the previous half-century died and although the evidence from Wales is sparse and scattered there can be little doubt that the mortality was no less than it was elsewhere. The plague seems to have come in by way of the lower Severn valley; by March 1349, it had reached the lordship of Abergavenny, where even the lord's son was not spared, and it then moved northwards. In the town of Ruthin seventy-seven people died in the space of a fortnight in June 1349 and the lead-miners of Flintshire were almost wiped out; on the whole north Wales suffered more than the south. There were further visitations in 1361–2 and 1369, Glamorgan suffering a good deal in the former and Gwent in the latter.

The plague left serious social problems in its wake. Bond communities tended to live closer together than free ones which meant that they often suffered the most; the result was that royal and seigneurial taxation bore more heavily on the survivors, as both prince and lords sought to keep their revenue as much as possible at its earlier level. Although a recent study has suggested that the pestilence in north Wales could not have been bubonic plague because conditions were not suitable for its propagation, the fact remains that large numbers of people died of an epidemic disease. Consequently many bond tenements were now without tenants and there was a shortage of labour; the high incidence of avowry fines at this time indicates a good deal of mobility, perhaps in search of higher wages. However, the royal authorities soon made agreements with some marcher lords to secure the return of fugitive bondmen. The pace of social change was also accelerated. The custom of partible inheritance still applied, although some enterprising individuals were using the facilities offered by English law to find a way around it. Many inheritances were therefore becoming so small as to be unworkable and the fact that the cultivation of marginal land was now uneconomic made matters worse. Many sold out to their more fortunate neighbours; the Welsh legal device called *prid* which was, in effect, a mortgage that was never redeemed provided a way round the ban on the alienation of land and many took advantage of this conveyance to build up their estates. Often the prohibition was simply ignored and when the law caught up with it the community made fine for the retrospective sanction of its transactions. Enterprising proprietors who had money to spare took up leases of bond tenements which the authorities were only too glad to let and the acquisition of free land by outsiders led to the dilution of a tenurial pattern which was based on the rights of the kindred group. Some men therefore prospered but, as always, the weakest went to the wall and the other side of the coin was the growth of a class of landless labourers.

Here was a society in crisis; here, too, were the ingredients of an explosion and that explosion came in 1400. One can look at the revolt of Owain Glyndŵr from many angles; it was at once a national rising, a social protest, a feudal conspiracy, and a civil war. It is one of the most important events in the history of Wales, not so much for what it achieved as for what it represents; in the words of Gwyn A. Williams 'modern Wales begins in 1410'. Although not all Welshmen joined it this was the first nation-wide revolt and its effect on Welsh attitudes was profound. Owain himself, a descendant of the royal house of Powys, was lord of Glyndyfrdwy in Merioneth and Cynllaith Owain in the March; he was the wealthiest of the few surviving native aristocrats and had seen military service against the Scots and the French. He married the daughter of Sir David Hanmer, a Flintshire lawyer who became a judge. The traditional explanation of the revolt was that it was the result of a quarrel with his neighbour Reginald de Grey, lord of Ruthin; it has also been suggested that one of the motives was Welsh support for Richard II, deposed in 1399 but there is no evidence of Welsh backing for the fallen king, either during his reign or afterwards. Nor was it Glyndŵr's attack on Ruthin on 21 September 1400 that really began the revolt but his proclamation as prince of Wales at Glyndyfrdwy a few days earlier; this was a clear act of treason which suggests that there was nothing spontaneous about the rebellion. Glyndŵr was also descended through his mother from the royal house of Deheubarth and after the deaths of Owain Lawgoch and Roger Mortimer, earl of March, who had a tenuous descent from Llywelyn Fawr and who died in Ireland in 1398, this made him the natural leader of a national movement; it may be significant that Iolo Goch laid great stress on this double royal descent in his *cywydd* on his ancestry. He was also related to many of the leading families in north Wales, including the Anglesey descendants of Ednyfed Fychan who may have been among the prime movers of the revolt; the role of the *uchelwyr* was one of great importance in that it showed that this was a protest by the natural leaders of society.

It was also part of a European phenomenon; between the middle of the fourteenth century and the middle of the fifteenth practically every European country experienced one or more popular revolts, among them being those of the Jacquerie in France, the Ciompi in Florence, and the Peasants' Revolt in England. The one that most resembled the Welsh revolt was that of the Hussites in Bohemia which began as a religious protest and developed into a national war. All the tensions of the fourteenth century therefore erupted in the revolt of Owain Glyndŵr and his initial successes brought over to his side the men of affairs, the churchmen and lawyers like John Trefor, bishop of St Asaph, and the canonist Gruffydd Young who became his chancellor. These were the men who framed his foreign policy; he tried to make contact with Scotland and Ireland and made a treaty with Charles VI of France, and at Pennal in Merioneth in 1406 he set out his terms for transferring the spiritual allegiance of Wales from the Roman pope to his rival at Avignon. The conditions included an independent Welsh church with an archbishop at St David's and jurisdiction over several adjacent English dioceses and the establishment of two universities, one in north and one in south Wales. In 1403 Henry Percy, known as Hotspur, the justice of north Wales, rebelled against Henry IV and allied himself with Glyndŵr, but he was defeated and killed at the battle of Shrewsbury; two years later Glyndŵr made an agreement whereby Hotspur's father, the earl of Northumberland, was to have England north of the Trent, his own son-in-law Edmund Mortimer, the heir of Richard II, was to have the Crown and England south of the Trent, and he himself was to have an enlarged Wales. He held more than one parliament and took several castles, including Harlech, which he made his headquarters; in 1405 a French force landed at Milford Haven and advanced with him as far as Worcester, but then, with the road to London apparently open, he withdrew into Wales.

But there was another side to the story. Victories were won and castles taken but it was a vicious war. Crops and mills were destroyed by both sides and even churches were not safe; Bangor and St Asaph cathedrals were among the victims of the revolt. In a war of attrition the superior resources of the English Crown were bound to carry the day in the end and French aid was hamstrung by the rivalries of French domestic politics. Wales literally fought itself to a standstill; castles were retaken and royal control gradually restored. All over Wales whole communities made their peace with the king and were readmitted to his favour on payment of fines. Glyndŵr himself was never captured though some of his immediate family were; he disappeared and apparently died in 1415. Henry V offered him a pardon but there was no response.

Such a revolt could not but leave a legacy of bitterness. In 1400 and 1402 a series of penal statutes had been enacted which laid numerous disabilities on Welshmen. Inevitably there were repercussions in England, not only in the border counties which suffered at the hands of the Welsh but also throughout the kingdom where men saw Welsh labourers flocking home to join Glyndŵr and even the Welsh students at Oxford plotting in support of him. In Wales itself allegiance was sometimes determined by local rivalries which meant that not all men supported the cause and that even families might be divided. Yet in some ways recovery was surprisingly sudden. There was little victimization and Henry V, anxious to secure his kingdom in preparation for his campaign in France, took a conciliatory attitude on the whole. Communities had to pay heavy fines but Welshmen were not debarred from local office and some obtained grants of denizenship which exempted them from the penal laws. Even the damage was soon repaired; an agricultural society can recover far more quickly than an industrial one. Later poets have little to say about Owain Glyndŵr, whether of praise or blame, which may suggest a tacit agreement to forget. If any section of society can be said to have benefited from the revolt it was the *uchelwyr* who had been its leaders. Some families, like the house of Penmynydd, lost everything but others, like their Penrhyn kinsmen who changed sides at exactly the right moment, gained enormously. The fifteenth century was the age when the accumulation of landed estates, which had begun before the revolt, gathered momentum. In 1413 Gwilym ap Gruffydd of Penrhyn enjoyed an annual income of well over £100 from his lands in Anglesey and Caernarfonshire; the foundations of this estate were laid when his father inherited the lands of his maternal uncle in 1375. In the north-east the marriage of the heir of Pengwern in Chirkland and the heiress of Mostyn brought together two estates that had been built up in the fourteenth century. In Anglesey the century saw the rise of the Bulkeley family of Baron Hill that was to dominate the county for so long. All over Wales the process was repeated; in south-west Wales the great house of Dinefwr grew to dominate the southern counties of the Principality, and in Glamorgan families like the Stradlings and the Mathews strengthened their position. At a lower level many families added to their possessions and thus were laid the foundations of the class that was to come into its own under the Tudors. The prosperity of these families was reflected in the houses they built, some of which, like Cochwillan near Bangor and Bryndraenog in Radnorshire, the largest medieval timber building in Wales, still stand. Like the patronage of the poets, building could be described as a form of conspicuous consumption.

With land came power. Offices continued to be granted to absentees who had to discharge their duties through local deputies; thus, despite the penal laws, the influence of the leaders of local society was unbroken. But if they were the beneficiaries of the revolt, law and order was its principal casualty. The maintenance of order really depended on vigorous control at the centre and responsible behaviour on the part of the local communities but during the fifteenth century the Crown became less vigorous and the communities less responsible. The division between Principality and March was still there but many individual lordships, in particular those which belonged to the Duchy of Lancaster, were now in royal hands and there was no central machinery to govern them; the consequent diffusion of authority added to the government's problems. Those marcher lordships which remained out of the possession of the Crown were in little better condition since most lords by now were absentee magnates whose interests lay mainly in England and who were therefore unable to give their lordships the constant attention they required. The result was that all over Wales the responsibility for day-to-day administration and the maintenance of order was in the hands of the *uchelwyr* who were increasingly concerned with the pursuit of their own interests. The main preoccupation of both Crown and lords was the collection of revenue; this had fallen considerably and even in the late fourteenth century its level had only been maintained by constant pressure. This quest for money had a bad effect on administrative and judicial standards; in the southern counties of the Principality and in many marcher lordships the practice grew up of dissolving the sessions. When the royal or seigneurial justices came the community offered a lump sum equal to the expected profits of justice; this meant an assured income for the authorities and peace for the people but the effect of the practice on law and order can be imagined.

The effect of governmental weakness in both England and Wales at this time was the virtual autonomy of the local communities. In Merioneth royal authority collapsed completely and the career of Gruffydd ap Nicholas of Dinefwr in Carmarthenshire and Cardiganshire was only the most blatant example of the way in which a local landowner could dominate his area, ostensibly in the name of the king but in reality in his own interest. The result of political rivalries in England was the civil war known as the Wars of the Roses which was probably inevitable from the time that the duke of

York returned from Ireland and landed at Beaumaris in 1450; since both the Crown and many noblemen had lands in Wales the country could not but be drawn into the war. Men's allegiance still lay with their lords; on the whole the Principality and the Duchy lordships were Lancastrian while the rest of the March supported York but there were variations, generally in consequence of local rivalries. Needless to say, the effect of the war on public order was entirely negative; this was again true of both Principality and March and in the history he wrote of his family Sir John Wynn of Gwydir gave a graphic account of the disorder which caused his great-grandfather to move from Eifionydd to the Conwy valley.

After Edward IV won the Crown in 1461 some attempt was made to impose order. To control Wales he depended on his principal Welsh supporter William Herbert, whom he created earl of Pembroke, but Herbert, along with many other Welshmen, was killed at the battle of Banbury in 1469; when Edward regained power in 1471 he made his heir prince of Wales and sent him to Ludlow with a council to manage his affairs and it was this council, made a permanent body by Henry VII in 1502, that supervised Welsh affairs under the Tudors and early Stuarts. Herbert was a patron of the poets who saw in him, as they were to see in Henry Tudor, the personification of a new political ambition. Owain Glyndŵr's bid for independence had failed and ambitious Welshmen were now to seek to gain power within the English political system. But in spite of this ambition there was no lack of racial tension; between the castle boroughs of north Wales and the *uchelwyr* of their hinterland there was a complex relationship in which wealthy burgesses bought land and joined the ranks of the gentry while their colleagues petitioned parliament about the insolence and hostility of their Welsh neighbours. In Flintshire the local gentry squabbled with the citizens of Chester, a city where there was little love for Welshmen, and some of the poetry of the period is bitterly anti-English. But as the same time it was to men such as William Herbert, who stood high in the service and confidence of the Crown, that the poets addressed their appeals.

With Edward IV's victory at Tewkesbury in 1471 the Lancastrian cause seemed to be dead. There was, however, a new candidate in the person of Henry Tudor, earl of Richmond. His claim to the English throne was practically non-existent but he was the grandson of Owen Tudor of the house of Penmynydd and it was this descent that evoked a response in Wales, especially since he was born at Pembroke. After Tewkesbury he and his uncle Jasper Tudor fled to Brittany and it was from there that they maintained contact with their supporters and kept the Lancastrian party in being. It was to Henry that poets of Lancastrian sympathies, particularly Dafydd Llwyd of Mathafarn, addressed poetry that was at once apocalyptic and political, hailing him as the Swallow; Jasper, for his part, seems to have visited Wales from time to time and during this period he was very much the archetypal conspirator. The death of Edward IV in 1483 was followed by the mysterious death of his two sons and the accession of Richard III. As his brother had depended on Herbert, Richard turned to the greatest marcher lord, the duke of Buckingham, to control Wales but Buckingham was executed late in 1483. Henry's plotting went on and in August, 1485, he landed at Dale on Milford Haven. He was soon joined by Rhys ap Thomas of Dinefwr, the grandson of Gruffydd ap Nicholas and the leading figure in south-west Wales and he then advanced towards Shrewsbury, being joined by various *uchelwyr* on the way. The march ended at Bosworth with Henry's victory and his assumption of the Crown as Henry VII.

The accession of Henry VII had an electrifying effect on the Welsh imagination. Hitherto there had been a certain sense of alienation among the Welsh, a sense of being strangers in their own country. Now men felt that the prophecies were fulfilled, that Llywelyn was avenged, that a Welshman wore the crown of London, and that the son of prophecy had come to his people. The Elizabethan antiquary George Owen called Henry 'the Moses who delivered us from bondage' and, indeed, there was a feeling among Welshmen that a new world of opportunity was open to them. They flocked across the border in search of fame and fortune and many felt that Bosworth, where Henry had fought under the banner of the red dragon, was really a Welsh victory. The king's own attitude to his Welsh ancestry is another question. Welshmen like Rhys ap Thomas who had aided him were rewarded and in 1486 Jasper Tudor, now duke of Bedford, was given the oversight of Wales. The fact that Henry named his first-born son Arthur may not be without significance; Arthur was created prince of Wales in 1489.

Inevitably some were disappointed and some poets chided Henry for not doing enough for Wales. His campaign may have succeeded in harnessing anti-English sentiment but after 1485 he was king of England and his main concern was to remain so. There was no revolutionary change in Wales; the king's aim was to ensure order and strong government and to make the existing system work. Lawlessness remained; there was an insurrection in the lordship of Brecon in 1486 and another in Merioneth in 1498. And there were other problems, the origins of which lay in the Glyndŵr revolt or even earlier. One feature of the early fifteenth century which was particularly evident in Gwynedd was the depopulation of bond townships and the consequent loss of revenue. This led, after 1485, to a thorough investigation and overhaul of the north Wales administration and then, in the early sixteenth century, to the grant of a series of charters to the northern marcher lordships and Principality. They cost their recipients large sums of money but they removed the restrictions imposed by the penal laws and earlier enactments and abolished many customary dues; they also emancipated the bondmen and made English tenures generally available. The problems which arose from social and economic change had been dealt with in the fifteenth century by a series of short-term expedients but now something positive was being done to solve them.

The lack of any new departure in the king's Welsh policy meant that the division between Principality and March remained although by the early sixteenth century only two real marcher magnates were left, the duke of Buckingham and the earl of Worcester. The former owed his position as lord of Newport and Brecon to inheritance and the latter as lord of Gower, Raglan, and several other lordships to marriage and service to the Crown. But both of them had so many interests elsewhere that they could not manage their lordships efficiently; Buckingham, moreover, in constant search of revenue, tried to exercise his rights to the limit and made himself extremely unpopular by doing so. In 1521 Buckingham, who had become the object of royal suspicion as an over-mighty subject, was executed and his lands were forfeit to the Crown; this was followed in 1531 by the fall of Rhys ap Gruffydd of Dinefwr, partly in consequence of his quarrel with Lord Ferrers. In addition to this the problem of order was becoming increasingly acute and many now realized that something would have to be done about Wales. This was the period of the 'Tudor revolution in government' associated with the name of Thomas Cromwell and in 1534

Rowland Lee, one of Cromwell's servants and bishop of Coventry and Lichfield, was appointed lord president of the Council in the Marches of Wales. Lee had few attractive qualities but he was competent; his task was to put down crime and restore order and this he did, without worrying unduly about the methods he used.

The next step came in 1536. In that year was passed 'An Act for laws and justice to be ministered in Wales in like form as it is in this realm', commonly known as the first Act of Union. The marcher lordships were brought under royal control and divided up into counties. Wales was to be represented in Parliament and brought within the ambit of the English legal system and Welshmen were to enjoy the same rights and status as Englishmen. A knowledge of English was to be required of those holding office in Wales. It was followed in 1542 by a further act which established a system of courts throughout Wales and gave a statutory basis to the Council in the Marches; it also provided for the appointment of justices of the peace in all the counties and abolished partible succession. Together these acts made up what has become known as the Union of England and Wales. What lay behind the Union was the growing awareness of Thomas Cromwell and men like him that legal and administrative uniformity was vital to the effective functioning of a modern state. Wales, with its division between Principality and March and its diversity of jurisdictions, was an anomaly for which there was no longer any place. This attitude was not restricted to England; the same thing was happening in France and Spain at this time and the concept of the nation-state required that all the national territory be subject to a single government. This would help to solve the problem of law and order and there was also the question of security. Henry VIII's breach with Rome and his divorce of Katherine of Aragon might lead to war and Wales was particularly vulnerable to invasion; indeed, the very presence of the Tudors on the throne bore witness to the strategic advantages of a landing in Wales and Sir Richard Bulkeley was only one of those who warned Cromwell of this danger.

Thus a comprehensive attempt had now been made to deal with the Welsh problem. Although the Union made Wales a part of the English realm its real significance may lie in the fact that it united the country within itself by doing away with the distinction between Principality and March. As usual, the gentry were the principal beneficiaries; their appointment as justices of the peace set the final seal of royal approval on their local power and influence and like their counterparts in England they became the rulers of their counties. The representation of the Welsh counties in Parliament gave them yet more opportunities for advancement and the final abolition of partible succession facilitated the growth and transmission of their estates. Now Wales had a coherent system of local government supervised by the Council at Ludlow and the effects were to be seen over the next half-century as standards of public order gradually improved and disputes were settled by litigation rather than violence. It is less than fair to lay blame for Wales's later problems, particularly the Anglicization of its social leaders, at the door of the Union; whatever the language clause of the first Act might say, English must have been used at the higher levels of administration long before 1536 and neither local government nor the courts could have functioned in a largely monoglot society without the use of Welsh for a long time afterwards. Although the bardic tradition was in decline in the sixteenth century and the golden age of Guto'r Glyn and Tudur Aled was over, the *uchelwyr* continued to patronize the poets and it was to them that the authorities looked to regulate the order at the two Caerwys *eisteddfodau* in 1523 and 1567. In the sixteenth century the gentry managed to reconcile their Welshness and the new fashions coming across the border as they had done since 1282; the dilution of their inheritance came later.

One of the causes of the Union was the king's break with Rome; this was followed by the dissolution of the monasteries and the successive phases of the Reformation. It was a long time before the Reformation took root in Wales; by the second half of the fifteenth century the Church seems to have recovered from the material damage wrought by the Glyndŵr revolt and much of the best ecclesiastical architecture in Wales, especially among the parish churches, dates from this period. But church building and embellishment tended to be manifestations of civic, aristocratic, or institutional pride rather than of religious fervour. Of the Church as an institution the best that can be said is that it existed, neither militant nor triumphant but functioning. Men worshipped as their fathers and grandfathers had done and for the same reasons but there was no great depth of spirituality, and religion to most people was a matter of pilgrimages, saints, and images; there were few in Wales who would have gone to the scaffold for pope or mass. The monasteries were in a poor state; the praise of the poets of the previous century for the hospitality of Cistercian abbots is a telling comment on the decline of the ideals of that particular order and when the abbacy of Basingwerk could become hereditary and the abbot of Valle Crucis be imprisoned for highway robbery there could be little hope of amendment. When dissolution came the gentry, often already enjoying leases of monastic property and managing the affairs of houses as stewards, obtained a good deal of land. If there was little enthusiasm for the old religion, there was little for Protestantism either; the changes were neither accepted nor rejected and the substitution of English for Latin in the services could have little effect. It was not until the Bible and the Prayer Book were translated into Welsh that the Anglican Church made any headway in Wales.

Since Wales was a nation but not a state, its history after 1282 is not political history in the generally accepted sense of that term. But politics is the art of governing and managing men and in that sense the political history of medieval Wales is to be seen in the activities of the various families and individuals who were the leaders of the local community; national politics, if such a concept existed, were the politics of London. Thus Welsh political history is an integral part of the general history of Welsh society and its leaders. The dominant class in Wales was that of the *uchelwyr* and their importance to the student of Welsh literature lies in the fact they were at once the patrons and nourishers of the native literary tradition and the class from which the poets themselves came. Gruffydd ap Nicholas could send a royal messenger packing, drunk and wearing his livery; he also presided over the *eisteddfod* which revised the traditional metres of classical Welsh poetry. Owain Glyndŵr appealed to one of the Dwnn family of Cydweli for aid; another, in the same century, commissioned a painting from no less an artist than Hans Memlinc. One cannot say that the history of medieval Wales is the history of this one class or the sum of the histories of the various local communities but the historian of the period neglects them at his peril; the history of the period cannot be written without them.

BIBLIOGRAPHY

Critical Studies

A. D. Carr, 'Welshmen and the Hundred Years War', *Welsh History Review*, iv (1968).

Idem, *Owen of Wales: the End of the House of Gwynedd* (Cardiff, 1991).

R. R. Davies, 'Race Relations in Post-Conquest Wales: Confrontation and Compromise', *Transactions of the Honourable Society of Cymmrodorion*, 1974–5.

Idem, 'Colonial Wales', *Past and Present*, No. 65 (1974).

Idem, 'Cymru yn Oes Dafydd ap Gwilym' in J. Rowlands (ed.), *Dafydd ap Gwilym a Chanu Serch yr Oesoedd Canol* (Caerdydd, 1975).

Idem, *Conquest, Coexistence and Change: Wales 1063–1415* (Oxford, 1987).

Idem, *The Revolt of Owain Glyn Dŵr* (Oxford, 1995).

H. T. Evans, *Wales and the Wars of the Roses* (Cambridge, 1915; reprinted Stroud, 1995).

Ralph A. Griffiths, 'Wales and the Marches' in S. B. Chrimes, C. D. Ross and R. A. Griffiths (eds), *Fifteenth-century England, 1399–1509: studies in politics and society* (Manchester, 1972).

Idem, 'Patronage, Politics and the Principality of Wales, 1413–1461' in H. Hearder and H. Loyn (eds), *British Government and Administration: Studies presented to S. B. Chrimes* (Cardiff, 1974).

Idem, *Conquerors and Conquered in Medieval Wales* (Stroud, 1994).

T. Jones Pierce, 'Landlords in Wales: the nobility and gentry' in J. Thirsk (ed.), *The Agrarian History of England and Wales, Volume IV, 1500–1640* (Cambridge, 1967).

Idem, *Medieval Welsh Society* (Cardiff, 1972).

W. Garmon Jones, 'Welsh Nationalism and Henry Tudor', *Transactions of the Honourable Society of Cymmrodorion*, 1917–18.

J. E. Lloyd, *Owen Glendower* (Oxford, 1931).

T. B. Pugh (ed.), *Glamorgan County History, Volume III: The Middle Ages* (Cardiff, 1971).

William Rees, *South Wales and the March, 1284–1415: a Social and Agrarian Study* (Oxford, 1924).

Idem, 'The Black Death in Wales' in R. W. Southern (ed.), *Essays in Medieval History* (London, 1968).

Glyn Roberts, *Aspects of Welsh History* (Cardiff, 1969), 179–239, 295–318.

P. R. Roberts, 'The "Act of Union" in Welsh History', *Transactions of the Honourable Society of Cymmrodorion*, 1972–3.

E. I. Rowlands, 'Nodiadau ar y Traddodiad Moliant a'r Cywydd', *Llên Cymru*, 7 (1963).

J. Beverley Smith, 'Einion Offeiriad', *Bulletin of the Board of Celtic Studies*, xx (1964).

Idem, 'Crown and Community in the Principality of North Wales in the Reign of Henry Tudor', *Welsh History Review*, iii (1966).
Peter Smith, *Houses of the Welsh Countryside* (London, 1975).
Glanmor Williams, *The Welsh Church from Conquest to Reformation* (Cardiff, 1963).
Idem, *Owen Glendower* (Oxford, 1966; new edition Cardiff, 1993).
Idem, 'Landlords in Wales: the Church' in J. Thirsk (ed.), *The Agrarian History of England and Wales, Volume IV, 1500–1640* (Cambridge, 1967).
Idem, *Welsh Reformation Essays* (Cardiff, 1968).
Idem, 'Prophecy, Poetry and Politics in Medieval and Tudor Wales' in H. Hearder and H. Loyn (eds) *British Government and Administration: Studies presented to S. B. Chrimes* (Cardiff, 1974).
Idem, *Recovery, Reorientation and Reformation: Wales c.1415–1642* (Oxford, 1987).
W. Ogwen Williams, *Tudor Gwynedd: The Tudor Age in the Principality of North Wales* (Caernarfon, 1958).
Idem, 'The Social Order in Tudor Wales', *Transactions of the Honourable Society of Cymmrodorion*, 1967.
Sir John Wynn, *The History of the Gwydir Family*, ed. J. Gwynfor Jones (Llandysul, 1990).

Translations

Joseph Clancy, *Medieval Welsh Lyrics* (London, 1965).
Tony Conran, *Welsh Verse* (Bridgend, 1986).

CHAPTER 2

THE LATER GOGYNFEIRDD

D. MYRDDIN LLOYD

'Why are we left to linger?' The anguish and dismay expressed by Gruffudd ab yr Ynad Coch (Son of the Red Judge) in these words must have been shared by other court-poets at the collapse of Gwynedd in 1282, and is easy to understand. What had given meaning to their lives and their art seemed to have received a mortal blow. They were learned and highly trained professional poets, dependent on the patronage of princes. Years of preparation had been spent in mastering the complexities of their art, and in acquiring the vast store of essential traditional background knowledge. Furthermore, the whole object of their profession was, by panegyric, to extol the patron-prince, to make his reign and the collective life of the community meaningful by presenting it, in verse, in terms of a long-accepted ideal. Now the whole basis had been shattered.

However, man cannot long survive in the depths of despair, and during the next hundred years or so, to say nothing of subsequent periods, the art of learned Welsh poetry did far more than merely survive. New patrons were sought, and not always found where most expected. Iorwerth Beli, for instance, appealed to a bishop of Bangor to assume the role of a patron-*pendefig* (nobleman), and to preserve the standing of the *pencerdd*, the learned court-poet, as had been maintained by the princes in Gwynedd from the days of Maelgwn Gwynedd in the sixth century. He mentions Cynddelw and other master poets of the previous two centuries who had been thus honoured and clothed in fine raiment. But, alas, their kind were now ignored by the bishop in favour of crowthers whose scraping noises resembled the squeals of piglets, drummers, and young lads honoured for knowing English.

Patrons, however, were found, and panegyric much in the old style continued as the prevailing mode of verse. In the elegy to Trahaearn, by Gwilym Ddu o Arfon, the dead poet is extolled for his bardic learning, and there is a very conscious effort to place him in the tradition stemming from Taliesin and Myrddin and later maintained by court-poets, several of whom are named. For example, Trahaearn was like Einion ap Gwalchmai 'whose song prevailed like the gushing forth of a spring', or Cnepyn of Gwerthryniawn 'correct by Latin standards', presumably the accepted rhetorical standards of the time. Like that of their predecessors the verse of the post-Conquest poets consisted of *awdlau* and *englynion*, although with a wider range of metres of the former category and a higher proportion of *englynion*. The rules of alliteration and internal rhyme are gradually tightened to approach the standards of full *cynghanedd* as practised in the next century, but there is the same pursuit of perfecting the individual line of verse as a unit of expression that marked the pre-Conquest *Gogynfeirdd*. There were clerical and lay patrons. All the bishops of Bangor were not, as we shall see, like the subject of Iorwerth Beli's dispraise; the long support of the Cistercians by the Welsh princes was bearing fruit as is evident from Rhisierdyn's eulogy of Ieuan, abbot of Aberconwy. Lay patrons arose among leading families widespread throughout the land from Anglesey to Dyfed, from Maelor Saesneg to Glamorgan and Gwent. Among these, a few are very prominent, such as the Penmynydd family (Tudors) in Anglesey, Sir Gruffudd Llwyd and his wife in Arfon, the Gogerddan family in Ceredigion, and another in the Aeron valley, and in south Wales, above all, Hopcyn ap Tomas of Ynystawe and his son, Tomas. Poems in praise of Hopcyn by five poets have survived, and there are other instances which also suggest that, as in Ireland, certain patrons might have kept a *duanaire*, or family album of panegyrics sung in their honour.

Some poets, like Gruffudd ap Maredudd ap Dafydd, tended to confine their panegyrics to members of one family, but the practice of travel throughout the country by poets was on the increase. The term *clêr* (cf. *clerici* and *clerici vagantes*) appears to be one of opprobrium to Casnodyn, and it is not to be wondered at if he had in mind the perpetrators of scurrilous abuse poured on him and on Trahaearn by base rhymesters, but very soon it became an acceptable appellation of more reputable poets who, as is evident from their compositions, were moving freely on visits to patrons throughout the country. References to taverns and towns begin to appear, and although archaic vocabulary derived from the heroic tradition of the old court-poets continues to predominate, it gradually becomes interspersed with words indicative of new surroundings, and more English words such as *baril* creep in. The two main themes of praise had always been prowess in battle and hospitality in the hall, but now with the pacification of the country the balance changed in favour of the domestic virtues of hospitality and the gentler qualities. Military prowess, however, is not entirely ignored, and although now patrons fought alongside English troops, poets were loath to abandon the vocabulary and attitudes derived from the earliest Welsh poets and they even continued to describe the opponents as *Lloegrwys* (Lloegrians; *Lloegr* meaning England), *Brynaich* (Bernicians) and *Gwŷr Deifr* (Men of Deira). The *reductio ad absurdum* is achieved by Hillyn, in sounding the praises of an Is-aeron patron: 'most honoured under the Crown is he . . . The Bernicians of England with his arm he fed to the ravens'.

The relationship between poet and patron now has a different quality. It is no longer defined by law, and there is no longer the same compulsion to resort to *dadolwch* or intercessionary poems. The basis is more personal, and the patron oftener addressed as *cyfaill* (friend), or even *brawd* (brother) and even *fy mrawd cyfannedd* (my brother under the same roof). Part of this new intimacy is the increasing evidence of patrons sharing a technical understanding of the verse, and of their being readers and collectors of the manuals of the art of poetry that began to appear. *Deallu barddlyfr da a ellynt* (Well could they understand a book on poetry), states Llywelyn Goch at the end of our period of two of his patrons. Far greater knowledge than heretofore is shown by these poets of Arthurian romances, and of the *matières de Rome* and *de France*. The experiences of patrons who had served in the French wars were beginning to have effect, and are seen for example in passing references to songs of that country.

With the growth of a more settled society, more is heard of strongly built houses and increasing comforts and embellishments of domesticity. The place of the lady as hostess figures more in the poetry. There is an increase too, at least in the verse that has survived, of compositions to young women, tender and lyrical as a rule, with delight in the freshness and beauty of youth, the attractiveness of dress, the fine materials and the adornments of gold and precious stones. There are several references to the elegant Welsh spoken in a quiet voice by these young ladies. The period, however, saw the Black Death, and the tragedy of early life being cut off in the bud was a frequent occurrence. Some of the most touching references consist of stark contrasts, succinctly phrased with vivid visual imagery, between the charm of youth followed with cruel rapidity by the putrefaction of the grave. In a different mood poets find themselves pierced by the shafts of love, and Gruffudd Gryg's taunt at the 'sufferings' of Dafydd ap Gwilym as expressed in his *cywyddau* could with equal justice be directed at some poets of the older school.

Religion provides the themes of a good deal of the verse of our period. There is variety, and there are features that distinguish much of it from that of the previous two centuries. The trend set in the religious verse attributed, rightly or wrongly, to Gruffudd ab yr Ynad Coch, of dwelling at length on the horrors of death, the grave, judgement and hell, is continued, particularly by Casnodyn, and recurs at times throughout our period. 'It is strange that we do not consider,' says Dafydd Ddu o Hiraddug, a priest-poet, in the opening line of his ruthlessly grim and detailed portrayal of the 'rancid stinking sack of a corpse infested with maggots and worms'. Time and again, however, the poets resort to intense meditation on the Passion of Christ and the Resurrection, together with the Harrowing of Hell. We know that there was a great increase in the production of popular religious prose throughout western Europe, and much of it in Welsh has survived. With the coming of the friars there was more preaching, including the use of *exempla*, and also there was much activity in the field of religious art, such as the setting up of crucifixes. These trends are reflected in the religious verse by far greater detailing of individual sins and virtues, of the circumstances of the Passion and other theological points. The growth of the cult of the Blessed Virgin, and the closer defining of doctrine regarding her led to a far greater place being given to her in religious poetry; devotion to Mary expressing itself at its best in an intense and tender lyricism.

Every coin has two faces. The prevailing mode of Welsh verse of standing had always been panegyric, the life of mortals being rendered meaningful and ennobled by its presentation in relation to an ideal expressed in universal qualities of perfection. The opposite pole would be its portrayal in terms of utter depravity. A body of such verse appears in our period. It is called *dychan*, which is usually translated 'satire', but the verse in question would be better described as lampooning. Every device is employed to degrade, men and women are presented as foul beasts and vile creatures. Filth, physical and moral deformity and curmudgeonly behaviour (as opposed to hospitality) are dwelt on pitilessly and *ad nauseam*. Rare indeed in the portrayal is the saving grace of humour. In the same way as the perusal of many of the popular dramatic 'interludes' of the early eighteenth century makes the extreme reaction of Methodist reformers easy to understand, the prohibition of descent to *dychan* by poets of standing, as expressed in the Welsh fourteenth-century *ars poetica*, composed by priests, is not to be wondered at, although it was not always observed by even the best poets.

Following the fall of Gwynedd in 1282, most of the patronage of learned poets came from members of leading families who had come to terms with the new political order, but who also saw themselves as custodians of the native culture. Prominent among the earliest of them was Sir Gruffudd Llwyd, descendant of Ednyfed Fychan, seneschal of Llywelyn the Great. His career, however, was no unbroken success, and at one time he found himself a prisoner in Rhuddlan Castle. This was the occasion of two of the four extant poems of Gwilym Ddu o Arfon, who portrayed graphically the sad deprivation to poets that Gruffudd's imprisonment entailed. 'Pining, that ravager of the mind, has left me reeling'. 'No fine horses, or trappings, or delightful amiability . . . Without thy coming, of what use is the world? . . . All of May is at ebb-tide, great the sadness; lo the month of June is deprived, an oppressive appearance.' References to the great days of Welsh history and their heroes are numerous, the poet endeavouring to present Gruffudd's significance through these linkages. In spite of all disasters and setbacks this practice is maintained throughout the *Gogynfeirdd* and *cywydd* periods. Mention has already been made of Gwilym's elegy to the poet Trahaearn, where there is similar desire to heighten the present by relating the subject of his poem to the great poets of the past, whom he mentions by name.

Continuity is sought by the late *Gogynfeirdd*, but new notes are heard. Often it is not easy to decide what is new as so much has been lost. It is a moot point, on which there is some disagreement, for example, how many of the new traits that appear in love poetry about this time are due to foreign influences. Three love-poems by Gruffudd ap Dafydd ap Tudur have survived. They are very varied. The first is a thank-offering for a belt of gold and precious stone and silk given him by a maid. Delight in detailed description of an artefact is a new feature that was to be much developed in the polished work of the great *cywydd* poets of the fifteenth century. 'Hard it is to converse with a mute.' Thus, in a second poem, does Gruffudd reproach the maid whom he addresses. In a typical piece of medieval word-play he muses on the fate of his 'two souls' of which the maid is one, and concludes the poem in a vein soon to be magnificently exploited by Dafydd ap Gwilym: he invites her to share with him a 'bed of leaves', and harks back to the days before the 'Pope's law', when as in the time of Adam love brought no rebuke. Alas, she is, although 'demure, modest, shapely', his enemy and he cannot sleep. The similarity to Continental conventions is more apparent in the third poem, describing a court of love with a use of legal jargon and word-play, long familiar enough in France and Provence in verse of this kind. Gruffudd's other two poems also have a newness. One is in praise of St Cedig and the other is the sole instance by a pre-*cywydd* poet of a *genre* that was to acquire major importance in the fifteenth century—a begging poem. It is a request for a yellow bow, of which Hywel, the owner, is associated with Prestatyn and Overton. The poet makes the dire threat that a refusal would turn him into an object of derision among the maidens of Gwynedd.

The less formal and more personal relationship between poet and patron is well exemplified in the case of Llywelyn Brydydd Hoddnant's *awdl* and *englyn* poems to the mid-Cardigan Ieuan ap Gruffudd Foel. He reiterates many times the phrase 'I have a powerful friend', and justifies the relationship in consecutive lines: 'I am a friend to my leader, and my leader is a friend to me.' He informs us that he has spared him from a long outlawry. Freer of restraints by patrons the poets may have been, but, if we credit their professions, they were as enslaved as ever to their lady-loves. So one gathers, for instance, from Iorwerth Fychan's poems to his Gweirfyl and his Gwenllïant, where he displays mastery of the *rhieingerdd* (maid-poem) as fashioned by his great twelfth-century predecessors. Their phrasing and imagery occur again, together with their ideal of a bright young maiden, genial, of quiet cultivated speech. Swift touches of imagery are a part of the tradition, yet the observation is clear and fresh, whether it be of the girl, 'the lovely whiteness of her skin above her shoe', or of the natural scene, such as the play of sunlight on the waters of an estuary, or on a hillside by the blue sea. The poet draws on the age-old tradition, with his reference to Myrddin and his sister Gwenddydd, but other influences are encroaching, and he regrets he is not an Ovid, not a love-poet of his surpassing excellence.

The verses attributed to Trahaearn Brydydd Mawr hardly seem to warrant the title *Mawr* (Great) on grounds of bardic excellence, and in lampoons at his expense there are references to his size; so, like Cynddelw Brydydd Mawr, who however grew to merit the title on the quality of his verse, it would appear in both cases that mastery over the muse was not the initial reason for the appellation. He is also called a 'high-lipped camel', so an air of self-importance may also have been contributory. There remains of Trahaearn's work a very conventional elegy to a patron, Hywel, of Llandingad in the Tywi valley, and a satirical attack on his fellow poet Casnodyn. His religious *awdl* opens with mention of the four posts of a hall built by God. Its final section is partly macaronic, containing Latin phrases which may echo the mass. It has striking lines such as, 'Christ, eloquent-creator, the ocean's fetter', but it is hard to find anything outstanding enough to win for the author of any of these verses the title *Mawr*.

For vigorous scatological abuse, a *per contra* to the eulogistic poetry with a vengeance, it is hard to beat Hywel Ystorym, and all the features of this kind of composition, which emerges in plenty about this period, are found in his extensive diatribe on Addaf (Adam) the gelder. He has the effrontery to preface his scurrilous abuse by invoking the aid of the Deity in the manner of the praise-poets, and immediately goes on to wish poor Addaf such misfortunes as 'hunger without fail'. He mocks him for his bodily defects and disabilities, blemishes of character ('a venomous petty thief and clipper of coins') in the coarsest of terms, his bodily uncleanliness, his paltry attempts at rhyming, and above all, and at great length, his miserliness, the cardinal sin for poets dependent on patronage. In a lengthy tirade, with each line beginning with *lle* . . . (where . . .) a powerful cumulative impression is created of a foul verminous 'court' bare of good food and drink even at the feasts of Christmas and New Year, where the beard of a goat is boiled for sustenance!

There follow this poem in the *Red Book of Hergest* ten columns of anonymous verse on the same pattern. Place-names from Maelor to Glamorgan reveal how widespread was its vogue. The work of these poetasters is clearly parasitic on that of the panegyrists, not only in metre and diction, but also in allusions, except that they turned them upside-down. Their victims are 'unlike Hiriell' (an ancient hero of Gwynedd), and 'Is it true that a descendant of Merfyn Frych . . . stole an ox?' The far more serious and artistic satire of Siôn Cent is foreshadowed in the contrasting of mead and whey at feastings, and at one feast, in Chester, the rhymester had to subsist on gnawing a 'sharp back-bone'. References to taverns indicate where verse of this kind was appreciated. Dafydd ap Gwilym was only around the corner, and he would bring together strands that previously existed, but generally separate.

Problems of establishing the canon of his works are difficult in the case of Casnodyn, but there is a core of some quite long poems that can be ascribed to him with considerable confidence, and they supply a basis for establishing his significance. He is the earliest of the Glamorgan poets whose works have survived, and references by him to Llangynwyd and Coetref associate him with Tir Iarll, a lordship of that county that was to remain a nest of poets for many a long day. He was a poet of the 'old school', which led to the mutual abuse between him and lower orders of poets. Nevertheless his own work marks an advance in the direction of *cynghanedd* as fully developed in the next century, although subsequent poets broke away from the cluttering of their lines with over-frequent internal rhyme repetition, cumbersome alliteration and excessive compounding of words, somewhat mechanical in effect. Even his best-known line is not entirely free from some of these tendencies: 'M*ain* fir*ain* ri*ain* g*ain* Gymraeg'. In this closely wrought style he laments, in *englyn* and *awdl* forms, the death of Madog Fychan, steward of Tir Iarll, praising his prowess in battle (against the English!) and his hospitality. He furthers the tendency that became far more marked at this period, and which persists through that of the *cywydd* poets, of drawing many references indiscriminately from several sources, including Welsh historical tradition, the ancient classical world, Arthurian romance and Holy Writ. Caesar, Macsen, Urien, Arthur, Roland and Abraham are here cheek by jowl to a far greater extent than in former days.

Another tendency he shares, and which was getting more marked in his day, was to take the whole of Wales as his parish. He sings not only to Madog, but also to Ieuan Llwyd, of Gogerddan, a Ceredigion house that was to produce both patrons in plenty and poets. It was there he learned, he tells us, to achieve perfection of verse, unlike the 'Caeo rubbish', Gogerddan being a 'court of high quality'. Further afield again he travelled to Gwynedd to sing the praises of Gwenllïan, wife of Sir Gruffudd Llwyd, and herself sprung from the Lord Rhys, and thus a link between north and south. In this poem one finds an early reference to a distinction between the Welsh of Gwynedd and of Gwent, both of which he claims to excel in, although his own verse is very much in the standard literary language of all the court-poets and, in essentials, of their successors throughout the *cywydd* period. His praise of Gwenllïan is well in the tradition of Gwalchmai, Cynddelw and Hywel ab Owain Gwynedd. Her skin is white like foam when the oar breaks the water, or when the tip of a wild wave dresses a rock in white, and her father, Cynan, was an eagle commanding hawks (stalwarts) who knew no English, but the references, as will become more frequent from his day onwards, are drawn from a wider field than in earlier times: Gwenllïan is like Indeg, a figure from Arthurian romance, and the steed on which the poet is privileged to approach her has the vigour of Bugethal (Bucephalus).

Casnodyn's powerful sequence of monorhyming *awdlau* to the Trinity represent in several features the religious poetry of the late *Gogynfeirdd* at its best. In the opening lines of six of these *awdlau* the 'Sinless Trinity' is invoked. In the same vein as in the religious verse attributed to Gruffudd ab yr Ynad Coch, Casnodyn gives extensive portrayals in stark imagery of the physical torments of hell: in the first of them we see, *inter alia*, the brimstone fire, the ice-covered pit full of flinty ruts, the horrible cauldron, the hard scaly worms with bony and prickly bristles, 'and all means of destruction spread by melting flames'. It is small wonder that the poet throws out an anguished plea to the 'Lord of light and lovely day to admit him to His well-sheltered court of eternal feasting'. The appeal for mercy is continued in the second *awdl*. There is no end to the bliss of heaven, so unlike the fate of over-reachers and oppressors who tomorrow will lose all except their share of the torments of Lucifer. Thus it has been decreed by Him who 'arranged' the stars and the sea, the great earth and all that is on it. Likewise, it was He who 'arranged the swamp of hell, Satan's place, the abode of worms where they will find their relish'. But immediately following his Cross, Christ was hard on the Satanic host, hence the poet is emboldened to utter another appeal for mercy, invoking this time, Christ, Mary and John the Apostle. The third *awdl* opens with the 'eternal sadness' of losing heaven, followed by a powerful repetition of 'woes', such as 'woe to the man whose mind is set on a world that drowns him . . . woe to him who snatches his due share from the weak . . . woe to the oppressive angry one whose plan will be put to confusion . . . woe to the disparager of saints and the destructive, wilful thief . . . He whose blood streamed from his scourgings invites us to his good land, so let us venture over the brine and the waves, and draw towards our Lord'. The poem moves rapidly, and with a wealth of concrete detail. One *awdl* contains a meditation on the Passion, followed by a series of brief references to the life of Christ, back to the Nativity scenes, and ending in a eulogy of the Creator who 'made learning and the Mass and priests, the wine from water, and all weathers and seeds, night and day, grass and trees, wild and tame things, sea and land, and the ten grades of heaven'. In another of the *awdlau* there is a sequence of seventeen lines, all beginning with the word *Gŵr* (best translated in this context as 'The One'), listing the merits of the Deity including the inspiring of writers, being a candle to the blind, and being the One who does not hide his secrets from men of medicine. 'Yet it was He who bore the nails in his hands and feet and the suffering in his heart'. 'God, Mary's Son, is the Christian's treasure.' Having risen to these heights, and thus showing what sublimity the muse is capable of expressing, Casnodyn goes on to pour scorn on the 'appalling emptiness of vain poetasters'. This sequence of *awdlau* to the Trinity in content, diction and imagery and intense conciseness is a peak of Welsh religious poetry of the fourteenth century.

Among other Cistercian houses Maenan was known for its patronage of poets. Gutun Owain in the fifteenth century referred to this house as a model of hospitality, and as a standard by which he judged the homes of secular patrons. It had evidently assumed this role in the previous century, as can be learned from an *awdl* in praise of Ieuan, its abbot by Rhisierdyn. Ieuan is for long the poet's great hope and support, his 'brother in the Faith'. A new note is struck, that will be frequently heard in the next century, for the poet refers to the 'fine buildings' at Maenan, a fore-note of the pride in householdership that was to become a prevailing theme in Dafydd Nanmor's day and beyond it. There is further evidence in this poem too of the wider field of reference now becoming apparent in Welsh poetry. Not only are greater numbers mentioned of ancient native saints, such as Beuno, Machreth and Dyfrig, but the Venerable Bede, Saint Bernard and Pope Gregory also appear, a new feature in *Gogynfeirdd* poetry, and indicative of widening horizons.

Manuscripts disagree in their attributions of poems to Goronwy Gyriog, but mention may be made of two that may well be his, a eulogy of Madog ab Iorwerth, bishop of Bangor, and an elegy in the form of a series of *englynion* to Gwenhwyfar, wife of a scion of the house of Penmynydd. Madog was evidently better disposed towards the learned poets than the bishop of whom Iorwerth Beli sang. Goronwy's poem is an enthusiastic monorhyme of forty-eight lines. Although passing mention is made of the cleric's role as a 'physician of souls', that aspect is quickly brushed aside to give him ample place, in intricately woven verse, as a provider of a good table. More agreeable to our taste is the other far simpler poem, the elegy. The death of a warrior in battle had been portrayed during the period of Welsh freedom as glorious, but now our mortality is seen in a different light in the century of the Black Death and other pestilences, when the young, and among them beautiful ladies, are with awful frequency and suddenness cut down in the prime of life. Several of the poets of the period are haunted by such scenes, and the touching lyricism and poignancy of this short poem are very moving. A covering of stone in the Franciscan house at Llanfaes hides her, and the poet finds that the shock clings long to him. He even accuses the Deity of an act of aggression (an example of the 'Titanism' that Matthew Arnold noticed in medieval Welsh verse). 'How ugly to have put a floor over one fair as the moon. Gravel (*gro*) today imprisons her whose cheek had worn fine fur (*gra*).'

Hywel ab Einion Llygliw's love-poem to Myfanwy, of Dinas Brân Castle, by Llangollen, is best known as the inspiration of Ceiriog's famous nineteenth-century poem to the same Myfanwy. Hywel ab Einion was an uncle to Gruffudd Llwyd, who has a far greater place in Welsh literature. Hywel writes competently, but with little distinction, in the tradition of the *rhieingerdd* (poem to a young lady) as practised by the *Gogynfeirdd*. Dwelling on his suffering as a rejected lover is in the vein that won for Dafydd ap Gwilym the scorn of Gruffudd Gryg, and like Dafydd he claims to have spread the maid's fame far and wide, but to no avail, and it is hard to know her mind.

Our understanding and appreciation of several of the leading poets of the mid-fourteenth century are impeded by the considerable confusion, textual and ascriptive, in the manuscripts. In the case of Rhisierdyn and Gruffudd ap Maredudd ap Dafydd, however, some of it was skilfully unravelled by the late Professor Henry Lewis in 1923. One can now confidently ascribe to Rhisierdyn an *awdl* to Goronwy ap Tudur of Penmynydd, an early member of what became the famous house of Tudor, one to Myfanwy, his wife, and another to Sir Hywel y Fwyall (of the Battle-Axe), a doughty warrior created knight-banneret on the field of Crécy. Both of these men, Rhisierdyn's main patrons, had fought in France, and are both acclaimed for their military prowess, but there is a different emphasis noticeable in the poems. A corner of the white chancel of Beuno's great church, at Clynnog, hides Hywel, the gory armed leader of his fair countryside. The prowess of this 'Perceval' as the crusher of the young shoots of France is proclaimed, but only alongside his role as a proud Welshman, the support of his district of Eifionydd and its poets, where he is loved for his wisdom and gentleness. The conflict of loyalties is stretched to the extent of describing this faithful servant of Edward III as a 'disturber of Bernicians'! It was the dilemma of the age in Wales, to remain unresolved from 1282 to 1485. Goronwy is portrayed to a marked degree as the intelligent patron, [*g*]*air ynad ieithfydr* (a judge of words and metre), one who well understood the technicalities of the poems sung in his praise. This feature remains in many of the panegyrics from this period onward, as for example in those addressed to Hopcyn ap Tomas, and which will be discussed below. It was part of the new relationship between poet and patron, and was furthered by books in Welsh on the art of poetry, which are first mentioned about this time, and which as we learn from the poems to Hopcyn were treasured and studied by some of the patrons.

The increased prominence given to the patron's lady is seen in Rhisierdyn's poem in praise of the Powysian Myfanwy, wife of Goronwy and lady of Penmynydd. It is a forerunner of many of its kind. She is lovable, wise, of unfeigning nobility, of high-born stock, proud but courteous, a gem of ladies, fair as the snowdrift on a hill slope, refined and delightful in her patronage of poets. 'Not halting her praise throughout the North': praise that Rhisierdyn fittingly provides with a fluidity and dignity of diction that creates the right atmosphere.

Now we come to the finest of all the late *Gogynfeirdd* poets, Gruffudd ap Maredudd ap Dafydd, contemporary with Dafydd ap

Gwilym, but unlike him an adherent of the older school, confining himself to *englyn* and *awdl* metres, and eschewing the *cywydd* which was to become the prevailing metre of the new age. However, in the use of alliteration and internal rhyme, he was to approach nearer than did his predecessors to the new standards. A good deal of the work of this major Anglesey poet has survived, and its range of subject-matter is very wide. Unlike a growing number of bards in his day he appears to have been a stay-at-home, for with one notable exception his panegyrics to patrons are all to members of the Penmynydd family and their kinsman, Sir Hywel of the Battle-Axe. Among his several poems to ladies is his finest composition, in praise of Gwenhwyfar, of Anglesey. His religious verse is most varied, and very different from his indulgences in satire of a scabrous kind, written obviously in defiance of the *ars poetica* produced by clerics during his day. He was a poet of considerable learning, and in the range of his references to names and topics in literary tradition, romance, Scripture, and other fields of knowledge he is foremost among any of the *Gogynfeirdd*, late or early.

In his day he was a forerunner of Dafydd Nanmor in his devotion to the members of one family; in his case Tudur ap Gronwy, of Penmynydd, his son Goronwy in health, sickness and death, Hywel who was Tudur's brother, and to a remoter kinsman the aforementioned Sir Hywel of the Battle-Axe. They were all descended from Ednyfed Fychan, seneschal to Llywelyn the Great, but had all accepted the new order, much to their enrichment and advance, had served in the king's wars in Scotland and France and held various offices. At the same time they had used their influences and prestige in their homeland not only to maintain the king's peace and order, but also the native culture and the feasts where poets and musicians practised their ancient arts. A figure of speech used by Gruffudd several times is that of comparing these patrons to oak-trees—strong, lasting, far-spreading and giving shelter to those around. Grief at their demise is expressed with strength and terseness, and the poet is intensely aware of their significance as custodians of order and the Welsh way of life. The conciseness of expression is somewhat eased in the elegy to Hywel ap Gronwy, Tudur's brother. Here is found a fuller description than usual of a 'gathering of poets, of lovely rhymes, proud young men and their sports, the admirable winning of fame in the true feats of Nudd (i.e. in hospitality), fine red gems, streams of wine in gold and glass, soaring songs and harp music in the fine hall. The splendid hero of elegant manners and the carousal of bards—woe to the loss!' With great intensity he gives play to his grief, execrates 'vile death', remembers the 'good books' including those of the Venerable Bede of 'great knowledge'. Great also was the love in which Hywel was held in Gwynedd whose people will pray for him, and for the sake of His gory Cross Christ will bring Hywel without delay to God's beautiful palaces, to the full freedom of heaven.

For a short while around the year 1370 expectations of the restoration of Welsh rule ran high. All members of the leading families were not so resigned to the new order that they would ignore the call of a returned scion of the House of Gwynedd, and Owain Lawgoch, Froissart's Yevain de Galles, whom he described as a flower of chivalry, was awaited by many, prior to his expected return from France, as the long prophesied deliverer. We know that there were expectations in Anglesey that he would arrive at the head of an army of liberation, and the brief *élan* is powerfully expressed in an altogether unique poem attributed to Gruffudd ap Maredudd in which the spirit of pre-Conquest *Gogynfeirdd* poetry is well caught. There will be carnage, the huge losses to be inflicted on the enemy are recounted with relish, the allusions to Welsh heroes from the days of Owain ab Urien and Arthur are revived. Wales is to have secure borders, and the rightful ruling line restored. The spirit of this rousing poem, and it was obviously meant to rouse, is quite different from that of the panegyrics already mentioned, and it reveals how easily reawakened were the old hopes and loyalties when it was thought that the true leader was coming and that there was a chance of success.

Gruffudd was not above exercising his considerable gifts of abuse also, but in a very different vein, when there was no patriotic incentive, and he could rival the meanest poetaster in his portrayal of filth, and in jeering at the physical ugliness and defects of his hapless victims. Among even less savoury comments one of these is described as 'a sackful of coughing, mouth a gap stuffed with holly (jagged teeth presumably), a cur's heart'.

No one familiar with Chaucer should be surprised on encountering in the work of the same medieval poet the extremes of grossness and delicacy, and in his verse to ladies, Gruffudd excels in the latter quality. They also have a lyrical lightness and simplicity. He can sing the agonies of unrequited love: 'It is high time I spoke, dumb with longing; unavailing love destroys a man.' The daughter of Garwy the Tall is 'beautiful, long-fingered and discreet, of the hue of driven snow, golden her hand, and she is generous, bright her glance, of superior stock is she'. No *Gogynfardd* heaped together more profusely the names of heroes and ladies of romance and tradition, and his unresponding maid is a Luned, an Enid, a Fflur (the Brythonic maid sought by Julius Caesar), and an Esyllt (Iseult). Her poet cannot sleep for the spear in his bosom, his love is a long-lasting wound, while hers is like the liveliness of a northern wave on the Anglesey shore, as the Gwynedd dawn. In happier mood he can sing the joy of mutual love, of a 'gem of beauty' who rules his life, for his soul is alive within him, and he does not cease singing the praises of his tranquil one. They have made love under a covering of fine material, with beaten gold above her eyebrows. The poet luxuriates in naming rare things—fine linen and cloth, silk, enamel, silver, gold, and azure. One is well on the way to the delight in rich surroundings that reached its peak in the poetry of Lewis Glyn Cothi.

Gruffudd ap Maredudd ap Dafydd was closely attached to his native isle, and in singing from Chester of his longing for his modest beloved in Anglesey, his Venus whose cheeks are like the rose, he longs too for the 'bright waves that encircle the curves of the rocks where my thoughts stay, myriads of green waves from Ireland, the sea that bathes the gentle compass of Anglesey'. In his poem to Awd (Aude), also, much as separation from her is breaking his heart, despite love's wound, his island's hold on him is the stronger: 'Abandon the Anglesey shore—that I cannot.' All these poems to ladies, however, pale into insignificance when set against the elegy to Gwenhwyfar, a maiden cut down at the height of her youth and beauty. No translation or comment can begin to convey the surpassing quality of the diction, the smoothness and simplicity attained by expert control of intricate metrical patterns, suffused by intense feeling. Seldom has the horror of early death been expressed with such skill and anguish combined, and this poem ranks high among the finest achievements of Welsh verse. It is a poem of considerable length, but unity of tone is perfectly maintained throughout. The stark contrast of the opening line sets the tone: 'Gwynedd's shining sun a grave, the lady no longer lives, and we gain not her like; the much-loved one is perished; the brightness of the moon is a cold sleep tonight'. Attention is held fast by a series of antitheses expressed with great economy of words. 'The shapely slender form wore a covering of stone, the pressure of the church floor after fine furs.' 'Where there was fur and green raiment, red and blue, lo the pallor of sickness unto death; where there was gold around her cheeks, where purple was, the chancel hides.' The poet sings his own grief and the general sorrow after 'the light of Pentraeth'. It was a crooked world, and Gruffudd makes bold even to reproach the Mother of God, but among his antitheses is to be found a contrast between the insecurity of earth and the 'land of the father of peace' where she has gone, where there is 'feasting and a life that knows not sickness'. One can hardly fail to be moved even today by this poem, but how much stronger the effect must have been in an age when early death was a daily occurrence, and a great weight on the mind.

Gruffudd ap Maredudd ap Dafydd's religious poetry is notable for its freshness of imagery. The beauty of the creation meant much to him and he observed it in detail with a loving eye. In the longest of his poems to God he dwells on His role as Lord of the created world, of the ebb and flow of the tide, the wild wind and the onrush of the sea, the brilliance of the stars. He is creator and ruler of the waves of the sea, the land, and sliding-down limits of the sky; likewise Lord of learning and books, 'Thou once sold for thirty pieces of silver who art Lord of all good qualities and intentions every hour'. There follows with an onrush of words and rhyme a lyrical description of heaven, followed by an earnest plea that before the grave, and before the loss of his reason and mental faculties, he might through his appeal to Christ be loved in that desirable abode. In a passage of great rhythmic and rhetorical power he enumerates ('through . . . through . . . through . . .') a long list of the means of grace in which he places his trust. In another poem also God is presented as the creator of the clear depths of water, of fire, wild and tame birds, the sky, streams and stars, and he is overawed by the wisdom that this entails. 'God is my leader, with his great wisdom. Let us consider with strong faith that without Him there is no strength, and no beginning or end to beautiful words. Woe to him who puts his faith in the land of brittle life, for like a salmon his back is caught in the trident.'

The cult of Mary, though of course very much older in origin, was much advanced in the thirteenth and fourteenth centuries, the doctrine of the Immaculate Conception having been formalized, the great scholastic thinker Duns Scotus having given her greater place, and these new developments having their effect on popular religion. They are reflected in the work of Gruffudd ap Maredudd ap Dafydd more than in any other of the *Gogynfeirdd*, for he refers to Mary far oftener than any of them, and he composed several poems to her in particular. They give scope to that lyrical warmth, freshness and enthusiasm which are marked features of his verse. She is a star, the zenith of light, and is mother of peace and mercy. He pleads for her help in overcoming his failings, which, and not for the only time, he lists at length, including this time 'deep sloth, hatefulness and angry covetousness'. The longest of these poems ends with the telling of the Nativity story. In other poems he dwells on the joys of Mary, a popular late medieval theme, contrasting them with the sadness of the world, and in another poem, again in typical late medieval fashion, on the contrast between her and our first mother, playing on the letters EVA/AVE.

A large Cross set up in Chester, 'an image of Heaven's Emperor by the lovely river-mouth', must have made a deep impression. Other Welsh poets also refer to it, but Gruffudd makes it the subject of a long poem in which he makes use of the legend that the wood of Christ's Cross could be traced back to the days of Adam and Moses, and refers to its rediscovery by Helen. The Chester Cross, he states, had been carried by the waves from Eastern waters to 'Deirian' shores, and now stood by the Dee at the extremity of their land. Its sanctity must have been very effective, for it induced *Gogynfeirdd* not only to speak kindly of Chester, but, *mirabile dictu*, the Cross has been brought to 'the bright, fine city *in the fair land of England*'.

Other religious poems by Gruffudd include a series of *englynion* in which many Scriptural events are, unscripturally in most cases, held to have taken place on a Sunday, a poem to the four Evangelists where John is an eagle, Mark a lion, Luke an ox, and Matthew in the form of a man, a confession poem much like the death-couch (*marwysgafn*) poems of earlier *Gogynfeirdd*, and a series of *englynion* comprising a touching prayer for his native Gwynedd: 'the grainland of saints, may it not become escheat'.

The *Red Book of Hergest* contains eulogies to Hopcyn ap Tomas, of Ynystawe, the most distinguished of the patrons of the late *Gogynfeirdd* in south Wales, by five poets, and one to his son, Tomas, by a sixth. Hopcyn is acclaimed as patron, warrior, scholar and collector of manuscripts, and as seer. He was versed in the technique of Welsh poetry, and possessed copies of treatises on the poetic art which were a new feature of his day. For Dafydd y Coed he was 'the spear and sword of Gower', and 'the tower of Tawe land', his home staunchly true to Welsh culture and free of Irish or English influences, 'the treasure house of poets from Glamorgan to Anglesey'. He was 'the gentle and brave one whom I love entirely'. The white house and the fare earn this poet's praise, but no more so than his books—law books of all kinds, the *Elucidarium* (that stand-by of popular medieval theology), the *Grail*, and the *Annales*. The reference to the *Elucidarium* is confirmed by another poet who claims also that Tomas knew it well, and that he was a king of the *clêr*, a term now used with greater respect than by Casnodyn. For Meurug ab Iorwerth, he was 'father' to the art of poetry, and he refers several times to his *myfyrdawd* (reflectiveness). For the wisdom of his replies he compares him to Bede and Cato the Wise. This student of *Bruts* and *Annales* is compared to Camber, and among all these compliments the reference to French manners is not insignificant, for houses like his, particularly in Glamorgan, could be channels for the advance of French influences. It was the enlightened patronage of men of standing, wealth and influence, such as the Penmynydd family, Hopcyn ap Tomas and their like at Gogerddan, Glyn Aeron and Basaleg that restored to the learned Welsh poets that status and patronage they had lost with the fall of the princes, and which was to enable them to continue as professionals trained in their bardic schools throughout the *grand siècle* of Welsh verse (the fifteenth century) and later.

Indeed the latter half of the fourteenth century too, and this without mentioning the rise of *cywydd* poetry, was a prolific period of Welsh verse of high quality and variety, of which the main features can be seen in the work of poets already mentioned. There is much religious contemplation, revealing an increasing knowledge of the Scriptures. The themes may be commonplace orthodoxy but the phrasing is often powerful, and the feeling bears all the marks of reality: 'How wretched is the pride of man in a dirty miserable world,' cries Bleddyn Ddu, who also forces us to see in Judea's court 'the verdict of Pilate, a graceless judge, a maimed soul.' In intense contemplation of the Passion, Gruffudd Fychan feels we are all involved in the Betrayal, for 'Judas is our kinsman'. Small wonder in an age when kin were expected to seek retribution for the death of kin that Iorwerth ab y Cyriog pleads with God the Father not to be moved to avenge the death of Christ on mankind. No poets have sought harder than the *Gogynfeirdd* to perfect the individual line of verse. An example of the range of late *Gogynfeirdd* poetry is seen in ab y Cyriog who can lilt a love-song with a mellifluous lightness suggestive of Dafydd ab Edmwnd, and who can also reveal a keen religious sensibility and intensity of devotion.

Mention was made above of Dafydd y Coed's praise of Hopcyn ap Tomas. In the same strain he sings of patrons at Glyn Aeron, where English was resisted, and Gogerddan, but he descends elsewhere to the grossest of lampoons, and among them is found the earliest of the very few instances in Welsh of the abuse of Jews (other than those involved in the Crucifixion). There are the same two sides to Madog Dwygraig. His poems on the Passion are intense, and in our day, when so much is said of life's meaninglessness, one can appreciate his remark that the sinner laboriously carries 'a load of emptiness'. His panegyrics are also admirable but he is primarily remembered for his satiric verse. He revels in horrible descriptions of disease, such as leprosy, bodily filth and deformity, and reaches the depths of cruel insensitivity in his account of an unfortunate 'hag'. His descriptions, however, are powerful, and occasionally relieved by touches of humour: his account of the wretched Deicyn is styled a *Historia*, and he is a master of juxtaposing dignified and base words for comic effect.

Dryden towards the end of his days wrote: ' 'Tis well the old age is past and time to begin anew.' It was not so in the latter half of the fourteenth century for the new school had already reached great splendour in the *cywyddau* of Dafydd ap Gwilym, Iolo Goch, Gruffudd Gryg, and Llywelyn Goch and others. The two last mentioned wrote well in both styles. Only a very partial appreciation of Llywelyn is possible without regard to both. It is hard to find another elegy in *cywydd* metre on a young woman to compare with his *Lleucu Llwyd*, where his feeling of loss is superbly expressed. But in an *awdl* he recounts what God has done as creator and as redeemer, interspersed with confessions of his own shortcomings and sins. Listing of one's sins was common in the *awdlau* of the period, but in general terms. Llywelyn provides an exception. In confessing his adultery he names his partner—and that name is Lleucu.

BIBLIOGRAPHY

Editions

Edward Anwyl (ed.), *The Poetry of the Gogynfeirdd from the Myvyrian Archaiology of Wales* (Denbigh, 1909).

N. G. Costigan, R. Iestyn Daniel and Dafydd Johnston (eds), *Gwaith Gruffudd ap Dafydd ap Tudur, Gwilym Ddu o Arfon, Trahaearn Brydydd Mawr ac Iorwerth Beli* (Aberystwyth, 1995).

R. Iestyn Daniel (ed.), *Gwaith Bleddyn Ddu* (Aberystwyth, 1994).

Dafydd H. Evans, 'Yr Ustus Llwyd a'r Swrcod', in J. E. Caerwyn Williams (ed.), *Ysgrifau Beirniadol XVII* (Dinbych, 1990), 63–92.

J. Gwenogvryn Evans (ed.), *The Poetry in the Red Book of Hergest* (Llanbedrog, 1911).

Dafydd Johnston (ed.), *Blodeugerdd Barddas o'r Bedwaredd Ganrif ar Ddeg* (Llandybïe, 1989).

Nerys Ann Jones and Erwain Haf Rheinallt (eds), *Gwaith Sefnyn, Rhisierdyn ac Eraill* (Aberystwyth, 1995).

Owen Jones and others, *The Myvyrian Archaiology of Wales*, 2nd edn, (Denbigh, 1870).

Ann Parry Owen (ed.), *Gwaith Llywelyn Brydydd Hoddnant, Dafydd ap Gwilym, Hillyn ac Eraill* (Aberystwyth, 1996).

Translations

J. P. Clancy, *Medieval Welsh Lyrics* (London, 1965).

Tony Conran, *Welsh Verse* (Bridgend, 1986).

Gwyn Williams, *The Burning Tree* (London, 1956).

Critical Studies

Dylan Foster Evans, *'Goganwr am Gig Ynyd': The Poet as Satirist in Medieval Wales* (Aberystwyth, 1996).

T. Gwynn Jones, *Rhieingerddi'r Gogynfeirdd* (Denbigh, 1915).

Ceri Lewis, 'The Literary Tradition of Morgannwg . . .' *Glamorgan County History III. The Middle Ages* (Cardiff, 1971), 480–9.

Henry Lewis, 'Gruffudd ab Maredudd ab Dafydd a Rhisierdyn', *Bulletin of the Board of Celtic Studies*, i (1922), 123–33.

Tom Parry, 'Twf y Gynghanedd', *Transactions of the Honourable Society of Cymmrodorion*, 1936, 143–60.

Chapter 3

EINION OFFEIRIAD AND THE BARDIC GRAMMAR

CERI W. LEWIS

Medieval Welsh bardic poetry, regarded by some Celtic scholars as Wales's most distinctive contribution to the European literary heritage, was pre-eminently social in function, formal and conventional in both theme and treatment, archaic and polished in diction, impressively dignified in style, and generally conservative in metrical patterns. Poetry that consistently and triumphantly exhibits, as does this substantial corpus of verse, such a high degree of artistic refinement and technical accomplishment, was obviously the product of a long and rich tradition, which must have been devotedly fostered throughout the centuries in bardic schools.

For a craft as difficult as that practised by the medieval Welsh bards, a craft that demanded, *inter alia*, a complete mastery of the complicated strict metres and a detailed knowledge of archaic vocabulary and syntactical constructions, could only have been acquired after many years of detailed instruction, which, in early days, was probably imparted orally. Moreover, a long and rigorous system of training helped to preserve and enhance the essentially esoteric nature of the bardic craft and was, therefore, one highly effective means of safeguarding the exalted status of the bards, for it prevented unskilled rhymesters and other undesirable elements from entering the profession and ultimately undermining the bards' privileged position. The bardic poetry composed in Ireland from approximately the end of the twelfth century to the middle of the seventeenth contains many features similar to those found in its Welsh counterpart and was obviously the product of a long and rigorous training in the bardic schools of that country. The activities of those schools and the methods of instruction regularly adopted there have been described in some detail in *The Memoirs of the Right Honourable The Marquis of Clanricarde*, which, though not published until 1722, is nevertheless considered to be a fairly reliable portrayal, so markedly conservative were the manners of the professional classes and the general structure of Irish society, of the conditions that prevailed several centuries earlier. A careful analysis of medieval Irish syllabic verse reveals quite clearly that, in addition to acquiring a thorough knowledge of the literature, history, mythological and genealogical lore of his country, the young bardic novitiate in Ireland was required, as a vital part of his professional training, to make a detailed study of the language itself and of the intricate metrical patterns he would eventually employ in his compositions.

This training could not have been substantially dissimilar to that given to the Welsh bardic aspirants. According to the short English tract preserved in Llanstephan MS. 144, 1–19, in the autograph of the celebrated seventeenth-century scribe and calligrapher, John Jones of Gellilyfdy, the 'Office and functione of the Bruttish or Cambrian Bards was to keepe and preserve *Tri chof ynys Brydain*: That is the Three Records of Memorialls of Bryttaen, which otherwise is called the Bruttish antiquitie which consisteth of three parts and is called *Tri chof*.' The first of these, we are told, was 'the History of the notable Acts of the Kings & princes of this land of Bruttaen and Cambria.' The second was 'the language of the Bruttons for which thee Bards ought to giue accompt for every word and sillable therein when they are demaunded thereof.' And the third was 'to keepe the genealogies or Descents of the Nobi[li]tie, there Division of lands and there Armes'. A detailed examination of the works of the bards who belonged to the classical Welsh tradition shows beyond any doubt that this short tract, as far as it goes, gives a fairly accurate summary of some of the training given in the bardic schools in medieval Wales. One must not be misled, however, by the use of the word 'school' in this connection, for young aspirants were undoubtedly instructed in the mysteries of the bardic craft by being apprenticed to a 'chief-of-song' (*pencerdd*), who had acquired considerable renown in his profession. And it is clear from the Laws of Hywel Dda that only a *pencerdd* could properly discharge the functions of a bardic teacher. Nevertheless, the use of the word 'school' in this context is not altogether inappropriate, for extremely accomplished *penceirddiaid* would naturally tend to attract more than one pupil, as Gruffudd Hiraethog (d. 1564), unquestionably the most talented and important practitioner of the art of heraldry in his day, instructed some of the foremost bards of the second half of the sixteenth century, such as Simwnt Fychan, Wiliam Llŷn, Wiliam Cynwal, Siôn Tudur and Raff ap Robert, or as Lewis Morgannwg (*fl.* 1520–65) instructed Gruffudd Hiraethog and the two late sixteenth-century Glamorgan bards, Meurug Dafydd and Dafydd Benwyn.

Undoubtedly, it was this close and intimately creative contact, repeated from generation to generation, between a young novice and an acknowledged master in the art that ensured the continuity of the native bardic tradition and created the solid basis for the great technical accomplishment and the sustained dignity of style that characterizes the majestic corpus of verse composed in the strict metres between the middle of the twelfth century and the mid-sixteenth. It was mainly as a result of this personal tuition that bardic aspirants ultimately mastered the intricate rules relating to the strict metres, the complicated pattern of consonantal alliteration and internal rhyme known as *cynghanedd* in Welsh, the various *cymeriadau* (or correspondences) at the beginning of successive lines, and the exact technical classification of the Welsh syllables and diphthongs, so that they could be used correctly and effectively in their compositions. Included also in the long and rigorous training they were required to undergo was a detailed study of the themes, the archaic vocabulary, the figures of speech and various syntactical constructions found in the works of the older bards, which they regularly took as their exemplars. It is obvious, too, that they studied the ancient Welsh tales and various aspects of the history of Wales and Britain, according to the ideas that were then popular. And in the late medieval period the genealogies of the nobles and gentry, their estates and coats-of-arms were accorded a prominent place in the bardic curriculum. The attention given to these subjects accounts for the substantial manuscript collections that have survived of the work of Lewis Morgannwg, Gruffudd Hiraethog, Wiliam Llŷn, Wiliam Cynwal, Simwnt Fychan, Edwart ap Roger, and various other heraldic bards containing detailed and extremely valuable collections of genealogies drawn from many different areas of Wales.

Some examples of literary exercises by young bardic aspirants have survived, it has been suggested, in the compositions known as 'Rhetorics' or 'Orations' (*Areithiau*), which are comparatively brief passages of prose written in a distinctly ornate style. Most of these compositions occur in manuscripts that are ascribed to the sixteenth century, or later, and are obviously literary exercises in rhetoric, for they contain a plethora of compound nouns and adjectives, common collocations, stereotyped expressions, and various other rhetorical tropes. In a number of respects they resemble the rhetorical device called a 'run' in Irish folk tales. Written on some manifestly contrived themes, such as things liked or disliked, praise of a woman, or parodies of parts of the old tales, many of these prose passages are connected with the names of famous poets, such as 'Things Hated by Owain Cyfeiliog', 'Iolo Goch's Oration (or Rhetoric)', 'Dafydd ap Gwilym's Favourite Sight', or 'The Dream of Gruffudd ab Adda ap Dafydd'. It must not be assumed, however, that any real connection existed between these particular poets and the rhetorical passages that are linked with their names in the manuscripts. Nevertheless, these literary exercises may well derive from a bardic milieu and they have reasonably been interpreted as stylistic flourishes in which the bards demonstrated their abundant command of the Welsh language and their astonishing verbal dexterity. For Mr Gwenallt Jones, who edited an interesting selection of these prose passages, was firmly convinced that they were 'the lessons of bardic aspirants beginning to acquire an acquaintance with the language, rhetorical exercises, and the *declamationes* of novices in the bardic schools'. Whatever the final verdict may be on the particular milieu from which these *Areithiau* are derived, the carefully contrived alliteration, the stylized syntax, and the rhythmically modulated passages they contain are unquestionably characteristics that reflect the influence of Welsh oral techniques.

Not surprisingly, when it is remembered that the instruction was probably imparted orally in early days, no detailed contemporary accounts of the activities of the medieval Welsh bardic schools or of the teaching methods employed by the various *penceirddiaid* have come down to us, and the surest method of deducing what constituted the major part of the comprehensive bardic curriculum is to become intimately acquainted with both the content and the craft of the strict-metre verse itself. A Statute linked with the names of Gruffudd ap Cynan (*c.* 1055–1137) purports to set out the rules for the efficient government of the bards and musicians, with the clear implication that they are based on various regulations drawn up by the king of Gwynedd in the early twelfth century. The Statute refers explicitly to poets, musicians, and declaimers (*atgeiniaid* or *datgeiniaid*), the name given to those who recited poetry, frequently to musical accompaniment, and it is clear that there were various grades of qualifications within the craft of the poets and musicians. The bardic aspirants are classified as follows: licensed disciple without degree (*disgybl ysbas heb radd*); licensed disciple with degree (*disgybl ysbas graddol*); disciplined disciple (*disgybl disgyblaidd*); disciple of the degree of chief-of-song (*disgybl pencerddaidd*); chief-of-song (*pencerdd*), and teacher. The poetic requirements of the various classifications are noted, the gifts, or payments for compositions, to which they are entitled are fixed, and clear regulations are laid down for the bards' good conduct. From the details contained in various copies of the Statute it has been reckoned that it took nine years before a bardic aspirant could reach the grade of *pencerdd*. The Statute also sets out the rules to be followed in the practice of circuiting, that is the wandering of accredited bards from the house of one nobleman to another.

No reference, however, occurs in *The History of Gruffudd ap Cynan* to any changes that may have been introduced by him in the organization of the bards, and it is generally agreed that the Statute, the earliest copy of which dates from the sixteenth century, cannot be connected with any regulations promulgated by this twelfth-century king of Gwynedd with a view to establishing some degree of order and discipline in the crafts of poetry and music. It seems to have been drawn up in connection with the famous *eisteddfod* held at Caerwys in 1523, the primary purpose of which was to rid the accredited poets and musicians of the so-called 'useless weeds' that had spread amongst them by that time.

Nevertheless, parts of the Statute do reflect the bardic practices of the fifteenth century, and earlier. For example, it is stated in the Statute that a bard could receive a degree at a royal wedding feast, by which is meant the wedding feast of a person who was descended from the royal line of the Welsh. There is plenty of independent testimony to show that this was a well-established practice among the professional bards. It was at a wedding feast that Gruffudd Hiraethog received the degree of *disgybl pencerddaidd* in 1545/6, and the licence (or certificate) given to him on that particular occasion, permitting him to go on bardic circuits, still exists. Nor was this practice confined to the sixteenth century, for in an elegy to Ieuan ap Dafydd ab Ithel Fychan of Tegeingl, and his wife, the famous poet Tudur Aled (*fl.* 1480–1526) refers explicitly to the fact that a bardic degree had been conferred upon him there for his knowledge of the 'three memorials' or 'memories' mentioned above:

> The first hall where I received a degree
> Was the outskirts of the court of my grey eagle;
> For three memorials he elevated me
> At his wedding feast, with three gifts.

Again, in an elegy on Ieuan ap Hywel Swrdwal, written *c.* 1470 by Hywel ap Dafydd ab Ieuan ap Rhys (*fl.* c. 1450–80), of Brycheiniog, it was claimed that there was no bard from south Wales who could suitably replace the deceased, and to this end the author of the elegy felt constrained to look in the direction of Gwynedd. The studied insult implicit in Hywel ap Dafydd's remarks prompted Gruffudd ap Dafydd Fychan, one of the bards of Tir Iarll in Glamorgan, to compose a *cywydd* in reply. In this composition the Glamorgan bard stated unequivocally that it was quite unnecessary to seek any one from north Wales to replace Ieuan, for Tir Iarll had every reason to be proud of the wealth of its bardic traditions and could boast of poets 'of three degrees'. There is, therefore, irrefutable evidence in the strict-metre verse itself to show that different degrees of bards—and hence different levels or standards of professional attainment—existed. Moreover, the Laws of Hywel Dda mention three classes of bards, namely, chief-of-song (*pencerdd*), household bard (*bardd teulu*)—or bard of the bodyguard, as he is sometimes called—and minstrel (*cerddor*), and the first two classes, or grades, were accorded recognition and authority under the law. The fourteenth-century bardic grammar, which is discussed below, again refers to three distinct classes of bards, called *prydydd* (poet), *teuluwr* (man of the household), and *clerwr* (low-grade itinerant bard or minstrel), although this may be nothing more than an echo of the older classification found in the Laws and, possibly, a further example of that marked predilection for triple groupings that is discernible from a very early period in both Welsh and Irish literature. Even so, it is beyond doubt that there were different grades of bards in the medieval period and that there is some basis for a number of the statements made in the so-called Statute of Gruffudd ap Cynan. But this is no way alters the fact that the Statute in its present form cannot possibly be ascribed to a date earlier than the sixteenth century, and it has appropriately been described as 'pseudo-antique'.

There is, nevertheless, one incontrovertibly authentic medieval tract that has long been regarded as a source of great importance for the understanding of both the content and the background of Welsh bardic poetry. This is the earliest extant bardic treatise traditionally associated with the names of two clerics, Einion Offeiriad ('Einion the Priest') and Dafydd Ddu of Hiraddug. Detailed studies of various sections of this treatise, although sometimes differing in emphasis or even interpretation, have done much to enlarge and deepen our appreciation of that rich and complex corpus of poetry composed in the strict metres, which has authoritatively been described as 'the major glory of Welsh literature'. The work, however, bristles with difficulties, and these can occasionally make the task of interpretation and evaluation extremely hazardous.

There are, to begin with, some tantalizing obscurities in the manuscript stemma. Professor G. J. Williams, to whom we are indebted for a scholarly edition of the texts of the bardic grammar preserved in various manuscripts, was firmly convinced, as was Sir John Morris-Jones before him, that the oldest extant copy occurs in the *Red Book of Hergest*, the most important single manuscript compilation of medieval Welsh literature, which was written in the late fourteenth century, while a slightly later copy is preserved in Llanstephan MS. 3. Two other important copies of the treatise occur in Bangor MS. 1, which is incomplete, and Peniarth MS. 20, an important copy, though very difficult to read at the end, which differs in a number of significant respects from the other texts mentioned. Both of these were ascribed by Professor G. J. Williams to approximately the end of the first half of the fifteenth century. On the other hand, Mr Saunders Lewis has cogently argued, partly on orthographical evidence, that the earliest extant text is that preserved in Peniarth MS. 20, which, in his view, cannot reasonably be ascribed to a date much later than the mid-fourteenth century. This revision, it has been argued, is of crucial importance, for it vitally affects our interpretation of the motives that prompted the compilation of the bardic grammar and helps us better to understand the particular milieu from which the work is derived. For these four early copies, it must be emphasized, are not identical in every respect. Although there is not, on the whole, any great divergence in the subject-matter, there are nevertheless some significant differences in places in the phraseology and terminology, in the precise order in which various items are occasionally arranged, and, more particularly, in the examples of the different metres quoted in the important section on prosody, so that it is difficult to believe that any three of these early sources are direct transcriptions of the fourth or, indeed, that all four are transcriptions of a common original that is now lost.

Nor, it must be emphasized, does any one of these early sources give any firm indication of authorship, and it was not until the early years of the seventeenth century that the composition of the bardic grammar was attributed to a specific author. Sir Thomas Wiliems (1545/6–1622?) of Trefriw, who was throughout his life an assiduous collector and transcriber of old manuscripts and an enthusiastic student of Welsh literature, included two copies of the treatise in a manuscript collection of prose he compiled in 1609, now known as Mostyn MS. 110. One of these was attributed by him to 'Dafydd Ddu Athro o Degeingl', and the other which Wiliems claimed he had transcribed from a source written more than a hundred years previously, to 'Einion Offeiriad o Wynedd'. Very little is known of Dafydd Ddu. According to tradition, he was considerably renowned in his day for his learning, and the period usually suggested for his *floruit* is the second half of the fourteenth century. As Moel Hiraddug is the name of a hill near Rhuddlan, Sir Thomas Wiliems may not have been very wide of the mark when he suggested that Dafydd Ddu came from Tegeingl, i.e. Englefield, in the old county of Flint. Furthermore, in a deed, dated 1605, concerning a gift of land, Hiraddug is clearly located in the county of Flint: *de huriathuke in com. fflint*. In Peniarth MS. 49 Dr John Davies (d. 1644), of Mallwyd, claimed that Dafydd Ddu had been 'archdeacon of Diserth', and as the title '*Athro*', to wit, 'teacher, tutor, instructor', which is regularly associated with his name, can denote, on the evidence of the bardic grammar itself, a particular type of cleric, it has been suggested that Dr John Davies was recording a tradition that had been current in the Vale of Clwyd in his youth. But this is highly speculative. Some compositions on the *cywydd* measure are attributed to him, but undoubtedly one of the most interesting works to be linked with his name is *Gwasanaeth Mair*, the Middle Welsh metrical version of the *Officium Parvum Beatae Mariae Virginis*, a liturgical devotion to the Blessed Virgin which developed during the twelfth and thirteenth centuries, especially in England, first of all as a private devotion and later as part of the daily obligation of the secular clergy. Since the seventeenth century, on the strength of a suggestion made by Dr John Davies of Mallwyd in 1631, the Welsh version of this *officium* has often been attributed to Dafydd Ddu of Hiraddug. The work is composed partly in the strict metres, which were used for translating the hymns, and partly in the free metres, which were employed for translating the psalms, although it is clear that the author was considerably more at ease when he sang on some of the traditional strict metres, in which he must have received a rigorous training.

Einion Offeiriad, obviously another cleric, is an equally enigmatic figure, although not quite as obscure as Dafydd Ddu. He sang an *awdl* to Rhys ap Gruffudd ap Hywel ap Gruffudd ab Ednyfed Fychan (d. 1356), a figure of considerable wealth and influence among the Welsh gentry of the fourteenth century, whose career, it has been claimed, 'crystallized the attitude and aspirations of those members of his class who lent support to the Angevin cause in Wales during the first century of the English settlement'. The composition of this *awdl* has been ascribed, on internal evidence, to the period between 1314 and 1322. References to a person—or persons—called Einion Offeiriad occur in a number of official entries between 1344 and 1354–5. The first of these is found in the records of the session held in Ceredigion in 1344. Under the heading *deliberacio gaole* a certain Lleucu daughter of Morgan is charged with being an accessory when Gruffudd ap Morgan ab Einion was accused of killing Iorwerth ap Iau. The following entry then occurs:

> Eynon Effeyrad was accused of feloniously helping the aforesaid [Griffith] ap Morgan ap Eynon to kill the aforesaid Iorverth ap Iau.

In another section, where the *presentaciones* of the commotes of Mabwynion and Caerwedros are recorded, it is stated that Gruffudd ap Morgan had slain Iorwerth Ddu and that he had been assisted in the commission of this crime by Rhys ap Rhys Foel. Although Einion Offeiriad is not explicitly mentioned in this particular section, the entry is important, for it locates the crime recorded in either the commote of Mabwynion or the commote of Caerwedros, in the *cantref* of Is-aeron in Ceredigion. A possible connection with this region is further established by the fact that the name 'Eygnon Yfferat' also occurs in the Ministers' Accounts for the year 1352–3, and it is clear from this entry that he had formerly been the owner of an acre of land in the commote of Mabwynion, which had subsequently escheated to the Crown. And it can safely be implied from the nature of the entry that this Einion Offeiriad was by that date deceased. There are two other entries which must be considered, one relating to the old county of Carmarthen, the other to the old county of Caernarfon. In the official accounts of the chamberlain of south Wales for the financial year 1354–5 an entry occurs that establishes beyond any doubt that a certain 'Eynon Effeyrat' had owned lands in Gwidigada, one of the southern commotes of Cantref Mawr, in the old county of Carmarthen. It appears that this person had died by January 1354. Finally, a reference to a person bearing the same name occurs in the records of an inquest held in Caernarfon in 1349, when Wales was ravaged by the first of the series of great epidemics or pestilences known generally as the Black Death, on three clerics from Is-gwyrfai in the *cantref* of Arfon. This person is explicitly identified as the parson of the church of Llanrug in the commote of Is-gwyrfai in Gwynedd.

Four references occur, therefore, as Mr J. Beverley Smith has shown, to a person—or persons—bearing the name Einion Offeiriad in three different parts of Wales between the years 1344 and 1354–5. The Einion who is firmly located in the northern commote of Is-gwyrfai died in 1349; it appears that the Einion who owned lands in Mabwynion had died by the financial year 1352–3 and that the Einion who held lands in Gwidigada had died by January 1354. Clearly, there is not a huge gap between these dates, and as the lands in south Wales referred to in the aforementioned entries are situated fairly near one another, it is possible that the properties named in the two southern commotes were held by one and the same man, although it is obviously impossible to prove this conclusively from the surviving evidence. In Mostyn MS. 110 Sir Thomas Wiliems claims that Einion Offeiriad was '*o Wynedd*', which can reasonably be interpreted to mean that he was a native of that region. He may, therefore, have been the parson of the church of Llanrug in the commote of Is-gwyrfai in north-west Wales, and if this identification is correct, it is unlikely, at first sight, that he can be connected with the person bearing the same name who once held lands in Mabwynion. On the other hand, it must not be overlooked that his patron, Sir Rhys ap Gruffudd, not only held a number of important offices under the Crown in Cardiganshire and Carmarthenshire, and very extensive properties in those regions, but was also bailiff of the forest of Snowdon and a member of the influential Penmynydd family. Furthermore, as a result of his marriage to the wealthy heiress, Joan de Somerville, he had acquired lands in as many as six English counties. Therefore, even if Einion Offeiriad was really a native of Gwynedd, as has been claimed, there would be nothing surprising in the fact that he owned lands in southern regions where his wealthy patron exercised such influence and power. Moreover, there is evidence to show that another important cleric, Ieuan ap Gruffudd Llwyd, who was archdeacon of Anglesey, owned lands in both Gwynedd and south Wales in exactly the same period. However, it is by no means certain that the Einion Offeiriad whose name occurs in the official entries mentioned above was one and the same person, for 'Einion' is far from being an uncommon personal name; nor was it unusual for the title *Offeiriad* (Priest) to be linked with a personal name in medieval Wales.

According to Sir Thomas Wiliems, the medieval Welsh bardic grammar was compiled by Einion Offeiriad in 'honour and praise' of Sir Rhys ap Gruffudd, to whom, as we have already seen, he also addressed a panegyric *awdl*. In considering the date when the grammar was most likely to have been compiled, Sir Ifor Williams drew attention to the important fact that the text contains an example of the *toddaid* measure taken from one of the two odes Gwilym Ddu o Arfon (*fl. c.* 1280–1320) sang in praise of Sir Gruffydd Llwyd of Tregarnedd. Obviously, the grammar, in the form in which it has been preserved in the earliest extant copies, cannot be ascribed to a date earlier than the composition of the *awdl* from which the example of the *toddaid* measure has been taken, and this ode was written while Sir Gruffudd Llwyd was incarcerated in Rhuddlan castle. His imprisonment was assigned by Sir Ifor Williams to the year 1322, when Sir Gruffudd Llwyd was supposed to have participated in a Welsh revolt against the Crown. However, as Sir Goronwy Edwards has convincingly demonstrated, the view that Sir Gruffudd Llwyd revolted directly against the Crown is based on a fundamental misunderstanding of the events of that period, and there can be no doubt that Gruffudd, in reality, acted in the closest co-operation with the king. It is equally beyond doubt, even after the hypothesis of his leading an anti-royalist rebel lion has been rejected, that Gruffudd Llwyd was imprisoned on at least two occasions in his life, first of all during the reign of Edward I, and, on the second occasion, at the beginning of Edward III's reign. His second imprisonment, which began shortly before late October 1327, lasted eighteen months, and Sir Goronwy Edwards was firmly convinced that it is to this period that the odes composed by Gwilym Ddu refer. If this argument is accepted, it follows that the compilation of the grammar in the earliest form in which it has been preserved for us cannot be earlier, therefore, than this period, and Sir Ifor Williams believed that the most likely period was sometime after 1335. Obviously, this does not conflict in any way with the traditional attribution of the authorship to Einion Offeiriad.

This attribution is further strengthened, it has been argued, by one feature in the metrical pattern of the *awdl* Einion Offeiriad sang to his patron, Sir Rhys ap Gruffudd. In the interesting section of the grammar which deals with various aspects of Welsh prosody it is claimed in the copies preserved in the *Red Book of Hergest* and Llanstephan MS. 3 that three of the Welsh metres, namely, *hir-a-thoddaid, cyrch-a-chwta*, and *tawddgyrch cadwynog*, were devised by Einion himself. The first two of the metres mentioned occur in the *awdl*, and some missing lines may well account for the absence of an example of *tawddgyrch cadwynog*. It is significant that the example quoted of this particular metre in the bardic grammar ends with the name Rhys ap Gruffudd, as though it had originally been composed to complete the *awdl*. If this was the case, the ending of the *awdl* would then correspond closely with its beginning, according to the rule laid down in the bardic treatise itself. It seems probable, therefore, so the argument runs, that the poet who composed the *awdl*, the inventor of the three metres referred to above, and the author of the grammar were really one and the same person. Furthermore, the personal names Einion and Rhys are closely linked in a statement in the text preserved in the *Red Book of Hergest* that attempts to justify grammatically the use of the plural verbal form *carant* (love) when two singular nouns form the subject: 'Two singular nouns are equivalent to one plural [noun], as in *Rhys ac Einawn a garant Oleuddydd*'. It would have been perfectly natural, some scholars have claimed, for Einion

Offeiriad to use his own name and that of his influential patron in formulating a sentence to illustrate a particular grammatical rule. This is not at all unlikely, and we find that in the modified and expanded versions of the bardic grammar that were transcribed by Simwnt Fychan (*c.* 1530–1606) and Wiliam Cynwal (d. 1587 or 1588) these two sixteenth-century *penceirddiaid* sometimes included their own names in the examples quoted to illustrate particular rules. Against this view, however, the argument has been advanced that the occurrence of Einion's name in the example quoted above does not necessarily imply that he was the original author of the grammar, but merely that he may have transcribed the text, as the practice of the sixteenth-century *penceirddiaid* clearly shows. Moreover, in the text preserved in Peniarth MS. 20 the three new metres mentioned above are attributed to the inventive genius of Dafydd Ddu, whose original contribution to the development of Welsh prosody is also briefly mentioned by Sir John Prys (1502?–1555) in his celebrated work, *Historiae Brytannicae Defensio* (1573). And it is interesting in this connection that in *Gwasanaeth Mair*, a work whose authorship, as we have already seen, has often been attributed to the learned cleric from Hiraddug, the metre employed for the translation of the hymn *Ave Maris Stella* is the *hir-a-thoddaid*, one of the new measures. Clearly, the argument used in connection with Einion Offeiriad and the *awdl* he addressed to Rhys ap Gruffudd can be applied with equal force and validity to Dafydd Ddu and *Gwasanaeth Mair*, for it can reasonably be maintained that it would have been perfectly natural for him to introduce into one of his own works a metre he himself had invented. The fact that Dafydd Ddu may have been associated in some way with the compilation of the grammar could account for the fact that it was he, rather than Einion Offeiriad, who was highly esteemed by a number of the leading *penceirddiaid* of the fifteenth and sixteenth centuries as an authority on the indigenous bardic tradition and lore. Some scholars have suggested that Dafydd Ddu revised a treatise originally compiled by Einion Offeiriad. There is nothing inherently improbable in this from the chronological standpoint, for such scanty information as we possess concerning these two rather nebulous figures suggests that Einion Offeiriad lived in the first half of the fourteenth century and Dafydd Ddu in the second. However, as Professor G. J. Williams conclusively demonstrated in his masterly introduction to *Gramadegau'r Penceirddiaid*, a detailed analysis and careful comparison of the earliest extant versions of the work hardly supports the hypothesis that any of these copies represent either Einion Offeiriad's original compilation or the later revision Dafydd Ddu may have made.

References occur in some sixteenth-century copies, transcribed by poets who were manifestly well versed in the native bardic tradition, to another poet-grammarian named Cnepyn Gwerthrynion, who flourished in the early thirteenth century, although not one of his compositions seems to have survived. The earliest known reference to him occurs in an elegy by Gwilym Ddu o Arfon to Trahaearn Brydydd ap Goronwy (or Trahaearn Brydydd Mawr, as he was sometimes called). In this elegy Cnepyn is included among a number of the leading poets of the thirteenth century and it is maintained that he belonged to their tradition. From this reference we may gather that he hailed from Gwerthrynion, later included in Radnorshire, and that his verse was regarded as being 'correct by Latin standards', which may mean that he had acquired a firm grasp of the rhetorical standards of his period. Moreover, in the copy of the 'Five Books of Poetic Art' (*Pum Llyfr Cerddwriaeth*), the expanded version of the bardic grammar containing five parts or sections, which occurs in Cardiff MS. 38 in the hand of Wiliam Cynwal, and also in other transcripts of this work made during the sixteenth century, Cnepyn Gwerthrynion is referred to as a grammarian and, significantly, his name invariably precedes that of Dafydd Ddu. As parts of the Welsh bardic grammar were undoubtedly based on the Latin grammatical treatises of Donatus (mid-fourth century) and Priscian (*fl. c.* 500), whose works were widely studied in medieval schools and universities, the reference that occurs in Gwilym Ddu's elegy is of exceptional interest, for it suggests that the leading bardic teachers already possessed a written Welsh grammar as early as the thirteenth century, at least, and certainly much earlier than the period to which Einion Offeiriad and Dafydd Ddu are ascribed. And it is of great interest in this connection that Mr Saunders Lewis has suggested that the three earliest extant copies of the bardic grammar evolved gradually between the twelfth century and the second half of the fourteenth.

Turning from the intractable problem of authorship to the bardic treatise itself, we find that its contents can conveniently be divided into two main sections, the first dealing with the science of grammar, the second with certain features of Welsh prosody and the bardic craft. There is no serious divergence of opinion regarding either the intent or the significance of the grammatical section of the bardic treatise. It is generally agreed that this is largely an abridged translation of some version of the Latin grammar associated with the names of Donatus and Priscian. A reference in the Life of St Cadog, who lived in the sixth century, shows that their works were in common use in the medieval Welsh monastic schools, as they were throughout the whole of western Christendom. One published edition of the *Vita Cadoci*—a composite version consisting not only of the original Life, as written *c.* 1090 by Lifris, son of Bishop Herewald (d. 1104) of Llandaff, but also of substantial additions made by different scribes at various periods—depicts its subject in a distinctly Roman setting and states that Cadog had been assiduously instructed from an early age in the works of Donatus and Priscian, as well as in other arts. The influence of their works is clearly reflected in those sections of the bardic treatise that are devoted to a discussion of the alphabet, syntax, and the parts of speech. It must be emphasized that these sections were not intended to be a grammar as that word is usually understood today, that is, a detailed analysis and description of a particular language in its written and spoken form, but rather the study of grammar as a science unconnected with the distinctive features of a particular language. These sections are really only an abridged translation into Welsh of Latin grammar and they undoubtedly reflect the influence of the monastic schools. It is hardly likely that the whole of this information was imparted orally to the bardic aspirants, but rather from a book; it may well have been committed to writing quite early and it was perhaps translated into Welsh some centuries before the oldest extant copy of the bardic treatise.

The reason for such a translation is not difficult to understand. No evidence exists to prove that prior to the fourteenth century the Welsh professional bards, in general, had more than a very superficial knowledge of Latin and its literature, acquired mainly from the Church service and from some familiarity with the life of the monasteries. There could well have been exceptions, of course, to the general rule, and Mr Gwenallt Jones has argued that the influence of the rhetorical instruction given in the monastic schools can be detected in the works of the twelfth-century bards. The latter seem also to have been acquainted with the names, at least, of the most famous classical heroes. Nor should one overlook the connection between secular and ecclesiastical learning in medieval Wales, as evidenced by the fact that the earliest manuscripts containing secular verse were almost certainly transcribed by clerics. Nevertheless, in spite of these facts, it is fairly certain that such knowledge as the bards may have acquired of the Latin language itself was, in general, far too imperfect to enable them to study the grammatical treatises of Donatus and Priscian in the language in which they had originally been written. Hence the need arose for an abridged translation of these works into Welsh. The influence of the Latin original is clearly reflected in the technical terms used in this part of the Welsh bardic treatise, for most of these have been borrowed directly from Latin or have been consciously modelled on Latin technical terms.

In all the early copies it is stated that there are two parts of speech, namely, noun and verb, a classification that unquestionably reflects the influence of those medieval dialecticians who maintained a similar view. As Mr Saunders Lewis has emphasized, the study of grammar was treated in the medieval schools as a branch of dialectic, the influence of which permeates the entire section devoted to a discussion of syntax and the parts of speech. As a result, the distinctive idioms and syntactical constructions of the Welsh language are generally disregarded. For example, the adjectival numerals are usually followed by the singular form of a noun in Welsh: *saith marchog* (seven knights, literally 'seven knight'). Nevertheless, the Welsh grammar books state unequivocally:

> It is a fault in a poem when singular and plural are brought together, as when one says *pedwar gŵr* [i.e., 'four man'], when one should say *pedwar gwŷr* [i.e., 'four men'].

Based as it is on some of the salient features of Latin grammar and on the prevailing concept of the period that the study of grammar was essentially a branch of dialectic, the greater part of this section of the bardic treatise bears little relevance to Welsh and could not possibly have contributed to the firm command the strict-metre bards had manifestly acquired over their medium. It was not by acquainting themselves with the matter contained in this section of the treatise but rather by a minute analysis of the works of their predecessors that the Welsh professional bards came to acquire the linguistic expertise they triumphantly exhibit in their compositions.

The grammatical section is of some historical importance, nevertheless, for it shows that Welsh bards were acquainted with some of the great currents of thought of the twelfth and thirteenth centuries, and it has been suggested, albeit tentatively, that the ancient kingdom of Powys in north-east Wales, which had long-standing political and cultural links with Mercia, was one vital intermediate channel for the transmission of some of the learning of the medieval monastic centres to the Welsh bardic schools. This part of the bardic treatise also reflects the concept, which was popular in the Middle Ages, that grammar, described by Dante as *la prima arte*, was an extremely important and worthwhile study in itself. A knowledge of the general principles of grammar, 'the mother of all the arts', as Peniarth MS. 147 confidently asserts, was considered to be an indispensable part of the intellectual equipment of any reputable bard, a vital acquisition whose cultural value was not to be assessed by the practical use to which it might be put. For grammar was traditionally the first of the seven 'liberal arts', which from late Roman times onwards constituted the solid basis of the educational curriculum. Nor should it be forgotten that in the Middle Ages poetry was sometimes regarded as a part of grammar, for the exegesis of the works of the poets was considered in some circles to be the responsibility of grammarians. This conception had obviously influenced Walter of Châtillon, who wrote: 'Among the *artes* which are called the *trivium*, grammar takes precedence as the first foundation. Under her serves the troop of those who write in verse.' No Welsh poet, therefore, if he seriously aspired to be a man of culture and earnestly wished to elevate himself above the level of the common *jongleur*, could possibly disregard the *trivium* of grammar, rhetoric, and logic, which formed the solid basis of education throughout the Middle Ages. Although it may have had no real practical value, a study of the science of grammar constituted, therefore, an important part of the instruction imparted in the bardic schools, and it is clear from the many references in the elegies that were addressed to various poets from the mid-fifteenth century onwards that mastery of the bardic grammar, or *dwned* as it was frequently called in Welsh, was considered to be one of the major cultural achievements of a bard. (The form *dwned* is a borrowing from Middle English *donet, donat*, the elementary grammatical treatise [*Ars Grammatica*] of Aelius Donatus, the fourth-century grammarian.) Not surprisingly, therefore, new and more comprehensive grammatical treatises were later translated into Welsh. One copy, which was transcribed—and, possibly, first translated—in 1455, has preserved many of the examples contained in the Latin original, which suggests that the copyist was quite ignorant of that language. The scribe who expressed in a long note appended to this copy of the *dwned*, preserved in Llanstephan MS. 28, his considered justification for the study of grammar—'for it is an excellent thing, and in it lie the roots of all learning in other languages'—must have been keenly aware of the intrinsic value of grammar as a purely intellectual discipline.

Included in the grammatical section of the bardic treatise, however, is information that was demonstrably of more practical value for the bardic aspirants. This information is contained in the detailed discussion of the different kinds of syllables and diphthongs in the Welsh language, which are minutely classified according to the way they are used in Welsh poetry for purposes of rhyme and *cynghanedd*. This section, which is placed between the discussion of the letters of the alphabet and the analysis of syntax and the parts of speech, undoubtedly summarizes a vitally important part of the practical instruction given to the young bardic novitiates, a mastery of which was absolutely essential before they could seriously undertake the composition of verse in the strict metres. As the length of each metrical line in Welsh strict-metre verse is determined not by its accentual beats, but rather by the precise number of syllables it contains, the syllable is appropriately described in the bardic grammar as the poet's 'measuring rod'.

First of all, the syllables are classified as 'heavy' (*trwm*), i.e., those ending in two consonants or in a consonant originally double, and 'light' (*ysgafn*), i.e., those ending in a single consonant, and after the pupil had mastered this basic distinction, he was shown how to avoid the prohibited fault, called *trwm ac ysgafn*, of rhyming a short (or 'heavy') syllable with a long (or 'light') one. The rules given in the bardic grammar are extremely interesting, for they are derived from an earlier period in the history of the language when the accent fell regularly on the ultima in words of more than one syllable. Thus, it is shown in the section devoted to the prohibited faults that the final *-on* in the word *kallon*, modern *calon* (heart), is a 'heavy' or short syllable, for the final consonant was originally double, and it is shown that the syllable is short in the plural form *kallonneu*, modern *calonnau*. The same is true for the final syllable of *gwinllan* (vineyard), as can be seen from the plural form *gwinllannoedd*. On the other hand, the final *-an* in *amkan*, modern *amcan* (purpose, intention), is known to be a long or 'light' syllable, for it ends in a single consonant, and the syllable is long, it is emphasized, in the plural form *amkaneu*, modern *amcanau*. The final *-on* in *afon* (river) (< British **abonā*) is likewise a long or 'light' syllable, as can be seen from the plural form *afonydd* in Modern Welsh. Therefore, during the period when the accent fell regularly on the ultima in Welsh words of more than one syllable there was a distinct difference between the length of the final syllables in such words as *kallonn* and *afôn*, or *gwinllann* and *amkân*, and attempts to rhyme pairs such as these were unreservedly condemned as a fault, called *trwm ac ysgafn* by the bardic teachers. Later, however, after the accent had moved back, sometime in the Old Welsh period, to the penultimate, where it still regularly falls in words of two syllables or more, this distinction was lost, for the long *a* in *amkân* and the long *o* in *afôn* were shortened, and the *nn* of *kallŏnn* and *gwinllănn* was simplified; hence the Modern Welsh forms *cálon* and *gwínllan*. As the bard's ear could no longer detect any clear difference in the length of the unaccented ultima in such words as these, he is advised in the grammar to add a syllable in order to ascertain whether a certain syllable is 'heavy' or 'light', as explained above. The early medieval bards tended to preserve this distinction, and the rules contained in the bardic grammar probably constituted an important part of the instruction given to bardic pupils in the period of the *Gogynfeirdd*. In the works of the later *Gogynfeirdd*, however, examples occur which show beyond any doubt that the old distinction between *trwm ac ysgafn* in final syllables was being gradually abandoned by that period. Thus, for example, we find in the work of the Glamorgan bard, Casnodyn (*fl. c.* 1320–40), the rhymes *bychan / glan (=glân) / kyvan(n) / diflan(n) / darogan / . . . kalan(n) / kan (=cân) / Ieuan(n)*. Although the rule to determine the length of final syllables was included in the bardic grammar in the fourteenth century and consistently repeated in the new and expanded copies that were compiled at various times down to the sixteenth, the Poets of the Nobility, on the whole, disregarded the old distinction, and we find, for example, in the work of the fifteenth-century bard, Dafydd Nanmor, such rhymes as *afon / hon* and *arian / glân*.

Later on, the grammar proceeds to classify the various diphthongs in considerable detail and with a wealth of technical terms for which there are frequently no exact English equivalents. Here, again, the nature of the classification is determined by the use of the diphthongs in poetry, especially for purposes of *proest*, a kind of 'half rhyme' or 'mute rhyme' which consisted in the repetition of the same consonant (where one occurred at the end of a word), but with a change of vowel or diphthong; e.g. *llaeth, doeth, ffrwyth; saer, oer; Pyll, toll, gwall.* According to the bardic grammar, the diphthongs could appropriately be divided into three main classes:

(*a*) *dipton dalgron* (literally 'compact or neat diphthong'), one of the diphthongs *aw, ew, iw, yw,* or *uw.*
(*b*) *dipton wib* (lit. 'straying diphthong'), a kind of *dipton dalgron,* namely *eu,* which cannot form a *proest* correspondence with the diphthongs *aw, ew, iw,* etc.
(*c*) *dipton leddf* (lit. 'inclining diphthong'), one of the diphthongs *ae, oe, ei (ai), ŵy.*

The significance of this classification becomes obvious when it is borne in mind that consonantal *i̭* and *w̭* (or the semi-vowels, as they are frequently called) play an important part in the correspondences in *proest*. For example, in order to form a correct *proest* with the word *iawn* one must have a word such as *mewn*: the vowel *a* changes, but the semi-vowel *w̭* and the final *n* are both retained, exactly as they would have been in rhyme. When, therefore, a syllable contains a diphthong, great care must be taken that the word used in the *proest* correspondence contains in the answering syllable a diphthong whose second element is phonetically similar. To this end, each diphthong was carefully classified in the bardic grammar as either *dipton leddf* or *dipton dalgron*. The description of each of the diphthongs *ae, oe, ei (ai)* and *ŵy* as *dipton leddf* becomes immediately clear when it is realized that these all ended in the semi-vowel *i̭* in Old Welsh; thus, for example, the Modern Welsh forms *llaeth, doeth, rhaith,* and *ffrwyth* would all be written as *laith, doith, reith,* and *fruith* in Old Welsh, and as these are derived ultimately from the forms *lact-* (Latin *lactis*), *doct-* (Latin *doctus*), *rect-* (from Celtic and Indo-European), *fruct-* (Latin *fructus*), each of which contained, it will be noted, the consonantal combination *ct*, it appears that the intricate rules governing the use of *proest* in the works of the medieval strict-metre bards are very old, indeed, and may ultimately derive from the bardic traditions of the Brythonic period.

In this particular connection the syllables were divided into two main classes, described in the grammar as *talgrwn* (fem. *talgron*) and *lleddf*. The former was defined as one that contained a vowel without a final consonant, or, alternatively, one in which the vowel contained in the syllable came immediately before the final consonant; the words *glan* (Mod. Welsh *glân*) and *glut* (Mod. Welsh *glud*) are quoted as examples of the latter type in one of the texts. A syllable that contained a *dipton dalgron*, as defined above, was also included under this heading. A syllable could be described as *lleddf*:

(*a*) when it contained a *dipton leddf*, as in the word *glwys*; this particular syllable was called *pengamleddf* in the grammar;
(*b*) when it ended in two liquids, or in a mute and a liquid, e.g. *torf, tarf, cerdd, mygr, mydr*; this particular type of syllable was called *cadarnleddf*;
(*c*) when it ended in a non-syllabic *y* or *w*, as in the words *eiry* and *berw*, which were originally monosyllables; this type of syllable was called *tawddleddf*.

The bardic teachers must have devoted a great deal of time and attention to the classification of the syllables and diphthongs, and it was in the bardic schools, most probably, that many of the technical terms used in the grammar were first coined. Once the pupils had mastered this important part of their training, they were able to avoid the fault called *lleddf a thalgron*, which is discussed elsewhere in the treatise, i.e., rhyming a syllable classified as *lleddf* with one classified as *talgron*, such as *ŵy* and *wŷ*, or incorrectly using the two different classes of syllables in a *proest* correspondence, such as *hwyr / câr*. In spite of the variations that undoubtedly existed in the local dialects, it is significant that there are no striking differences in the language of the strict-metre bards who hailed from Gwynedd, or Powys, and the language of those who came from south Wales. Final *-ai* had been levelled with *-e* in the local dialects before the sixteenth century, as some of the early free-metre verse and miracle plays convincingly prove. But one searches in vain in the works of the leading *penceirddiaid* for any evidence of this dialectal development, for the bards had been assiduously trained to regard rhymes such as *camre / gwelai* as an example of the forbidden error called *lleddf a thalgron* by the bardic teachers.

The discussion of the syllables reveals also quite clearly that the teachers gave detailed attention, when instructing their pupils, to such words as *barf, coffr, mydr, cabl,* etc., which ended in two consonants. There is ample evidence in the prose works written in the medieval period to show that an epenthetic vowel had developed between certain groups of consonants at the end of a word and, furthermore, such forms as *marw* and *enw*, which were originally monosyllabic, as they ended in the semi-vowel *w̯*, had later become disyllabic, exactly as they are in Modern Welsh, for the final sound later became vocalic. Nevertheless, the bardic novitiates were instructed to treat these as monosyllables in the literary language, and the bardic grammar gives rules for determining the precise number of syllables contained in such words as *mydyr (<mydr), mygyr (<mygr),* or *bagyl (<bagl)*, where, owing to the development of an epenthetic vowel between the two final consonants, they had become disyllabic in the spoken language. The bardic novitiates were probably required by their teachers to compose poems containing words of this kind, and it has been suggested that a poem on the *cywydd* measure which the Cardiganshire bard, Ieuan ap Rhydderch (*fl.* 1430–70), wrote in praise of a girl's hair may well provide us with an instructive example of such an exercise; for the author has included such words as *sathr, dwbl, sofl, nobl, cabl, crwybr, clastr, saffr,* and *copr* in his rhyme scheme. It was also emphasized in the bardic grammar that *ey* in the word *teyrn* or *ae* in the word *Cymraeg*, for example, were not to be treated as diphthongs in the strict-metre syllabic verse, for they were comparatively late contractions from *e-y* and *a-e*. Hence *tëyrn* was treated as a disyllabic word (rhyming with *cyrn* or *chwyrn*), and *Cymräeg* as trisyllabic (rhyming with *teg*), although the contractions referred to had occurred many centuries earlier in the spoken language.

Few sections of the bardic treatise have been analysed in greater detail by Welsh scholars than the one that deals with various features of Welsh prosody and includes a discussion of the twenty-four strict metres, of the metrical errors, and faults in language and matter, which the bards were strictly enjoined to avoid, and of other aspects of the poet's craft. Sir John Morris-Jones regarded this part of the grammar as 'an authoritative work, the basis of all we know about the bardic craft'. The analysis of the so-called 'prohibited faults', such as *trwm ac ysgafn, lleddf a thalgron*, excessive rhymes in the *englyn* measure, and faulty accentuation, undoubtedly incorporates an extremely important part of the instruction imparted in the bardic schools. Nevertheless, the view that the detailed description of the Welsh metrical system contained in this part of the work is an accurate reflection of contemporary bardic practice is, beyond any doubt, very misguided, for material that was largely extraneous to the bardic craft was given considerable prominence, while other elements that were quite essential to that craft were completely ignored. One surprising characteristic of this section is the absence of a detailed discussion of *cynghanedd*, one of the outstanding features of Welsh strict-metre verse. This intricate pattern of consonantal alliteration and internal rhyme had developed gradually in the works of the professional bards between approximately 1100 and 1350. Beginning as a comparatively simple repetition of consonants and internal rhyme, it had evolved into a fairly elaborate and well-defined system by the middle of the fourteenth century. By the end of the first quarter of that century this intricate pattern of metrical adornment had become almost as complex as the system that emerges in the works of the Poets of the Nobility from the late fourteenth century onwards, and *cynghanedd* was manifestly considered to be an indispensable feature of the compositions of the professional bards. Another notable feature of the verse written in this period was the device known as *cymeriad llythrennol*, which involved the repetition of the same consonant at the beginning of a series of lines. It is remarkable, therefore, that the only reference to these two conspicuous metrical features in all the early versions of the bardic grammar is contained in the bald statement: 'Errors can occur in three places in a poem, namely, in the *cymeriadau* and the *cynghanedd* and the rhymes . . . The *cymeriadau* are at the beginning of the lines, the *cynghanedd* in the middle, and the rhymes at the end.' The statement that *cynghanedd* is found in the middle of the line does not accurately reflect the practice of the bards who sang in this period, for in their works the system of *cynghanedd* had evolved to such an extent that it virtually filled the line, apart from a few syllables at the end. Einion Offeiriad, to whom, as we have seen, the authorship of the bardic grammar has been attributed by some authorities, was fully aware of these metrical developments, for he employed them with telling effect in the *awdl* he addressed to his influential patron, Rhys ap Gruffudd.

The detailed account of the twenty-four metres included in this part of the grammar is extremely important, for the classification there given has been regarded for centuries as the authoritative account of the intricate rules governing compositions in the strict metres. This is not to imply that comparatively small changes or innovations in the metrical system were not recognized. Between the middle of the fourteenth century and the mid-fifteenth one type of *englyn* had been omitted from the classification and the measure called *rhupunt hir* included, and at the famous *eisteddfod* held at Carmarthen *c.* 1451 a further change was made by the *pencerdd*, Dafydd ab Edmwnd (*fl.* 1450–90), who dropped two more *englyn* forms from the system and introduced in their place two new metres of extreme complexity, the *cadwynfyr* (short chain) and *gorchest y beirdd* (bards' masterpiece), which he himself had invented. But it is significant that, whatever changes were made in the metrical system, great care was always taken not to deviate from the total of twenty-four. This figure, which was rigidly adhered to throughout the centuries, had a powerful symbolic significance in the Middle Ages, and it is interesting that the author of the bardic grammar lists twenty-four letters in the Welsh alphabet, although these do not represent all the sounds of the language. This figure occurs also in many other connections. For example, there were twenty-four measures of instrumental music, while the officers of the king's court (in the Laws of Hywel Dda), the great physical feats, the noblest ancestors, the wonders of the island of Britain, the best knights in Arthur's court, the kings traditionally considered to be most powerful, and the prime virtues all numbered twenty-four, on the evidence of medieval Welsh manuscripts.

A careful analysis of the detailed classification of the twenty-four metres contained in the grammar reveals that the author often disregarded contemporary bardic practice and that, in order to arrive at the number twenty-four, he deliberately proceeded to double the twelve metres found in the works of the *Gogynfeirdd*. He achieved this feat by an astute manipulation of established metres, by his own resourceful ingenuity, for he is acclaimed in one copy of the grammar as the inventor of three of the twenty-four, and by including in his description a borrowing from a medieval Latin verse form, the so-called *cywydd llosgyrnog* which does not seem to have been employed by any bard before the middle of the fifteenth century. The author included in his classification not only the metres that were popular with the contemporary *penceirddiaid*, but also some old measures rarely used in that period, such as two *englyn* measures from the 'old poetry', as they are called in the grammar. The inclusion of these early *englyn* measures in the system is hardly surprising when we remember that a detailed study of early Welsh verse constituted an important part of the instruction given to novitiates in the medieval bardic schools. And it is significant, in this connection, that a number of the 'prohibited errors' only pertained to the *englyn* measures. Some metres, however, were taken over from the works of the lower class of itinerant bards and minstrels known usually in Welsh as *y glêr*. Notable examples of this are the metres called *englyn unodl cyrch, cywydd deuair fyrion*, and *awdl-gywydd*, which, significantly, were never popular with the professional bards even after they had been included in the Welsh strict-metre system. The more accomplished bards only used them, as a rule, when they composed an 'exemplifying ode' (*awdl enghreifftiol*), in which they sought to demonstrate their virtuosity in handling all the metres included in the strict-metre classification. But the three measures referred to were probably very popular with the lower-grade itinerant bards and minstrels all through the centuries, and it is significant that when these metres occur in free verse they are not drastically dissimilar to the corresponding metrical patterns that occur, albeit rarely, in the strict-metre compositions, except that the more skilled professional bards have purposely made them much more intricate and ornate by introducing *cynghanedd*, by defining with greater precision the rules of accentuation, and by prescribing an exact number of syllables for each line according to the particular measure involved. It is also interesting that the example quoted in the grammar of the important measure called *cywydd deuair hirion*, which consisted of rhymed couplets with seven syllables in each line, does not conform to the rules of accentuation that later became compulsory in this measure. This metre had developed from the less ornate measure called *traethodl*, and when the latter was taken over into the strict-metre system, it was deliberately made more polished and complicated by introducing *cynghanedd* into each line and by applying the rule that an accented syllable at the end of one line in each couplet should rhyme with an unaccented syllable at the end of the other. It appears, therefore, that this part of the bardic grammar had been written before the rule governing accentuation had been formulated and generally accepted by the professional bards. The accentuation is regular in the *cywyddau* composed by Dafydd ap Gwilym (*fl.* 1340–70), and it is generally assumed that it was under his inspired influence that the *cywydd deuair hirion* assumed its final form.

In many respects, therefore, the classification of the twenty-four strict metres contained in the bardic grammar is a distinctly personal and arbitrary one. Moreover, it represents an amalgam of two essentially contrasting principles, for although the author, who was probably acquainted with the main features of medieval Latin rhymed verse, had an unmistakable predilection for the stanza form, which, with the obvious exception of the *englyn*, was a feature originally alien to Welsh prosody, he was nevertheless constrained on a number of occasions to adopt in his classification the basic line-unit, which was an essential feature of the bardic craft. That he completely overlooked some interesting metrical forms that were popular with the professional poets of the period—such as the *toddaid byr* and a variant of the latter, consisting of a triple division of the six-beat line—is yet another indication of his ignorance of some of the essential features of contemporary bardic practice. If he had been more intimately acquainted with certain metrical developments in the works of the bards, he might have found various divisions and combinations that could reasonably have been regarded as stanza forms. All this evidence strongly suggests that the author was not an initiate of the professional guild of bards, and this, in turn, tends to confirm the traditional view that he was either Einion Offeiriad or Dafydd Ddu, both of whom were probably trained in one or other of the monastic schools of their day and so approached the contemporary bardic craft from an essentially scholastic standpoint.

Nevertheless, although the classification of the metres is largely a reflection of the author's personal predilections, the copy of the treatise contained in the *Red Book of Hergest* seems to be a skilful adaptation of much older traditional material, for Dr Thomas Parry, with characteristic acumen, has drawn attention to three traces of antiquity in the important section on prosody. First of all, the puzzling statement that *cynghanedd* occurs in the middle of a line seems to represent an appreciably earlier and more primitive stage in the development of this art of metrical adornment than that attained in the works of those bards who sang in the first half of the fourteenth century. It is hard to explain satisfactorily why the author made no attempt to change or amplify this statement in order to reflect more accurately that stage reached in the development of *cynghanedd* in the fourteenth century. This suggests that he had taken some of his material from an earlier work that had been written at a time when *cynghanedd* was a less stable and less complex feature of Welsh bardic verse. But the earliest extant copies of the grammar unquestionably incorporate modifications of the original work, for some of the examples quoted therein to illustrate particular metres have been taken from the compositions of fourteenth-century bards. Secondly, although the example quoted of the *cywydd deuair hirion* does not conform to the rules of accentuation and *cynghanedd* that characterize this measure in the works of those poets who sang from the late fourteenth century onwards, it is nevertheless written in a distinctly ornate style. This suggests that it is a comparatively early version of this metre, which may have been used at one time by the higher ranks of the bardic order. Thirdly, the names of some of the metres discussed in this section of the treatise—*rhupunt, toddaid, gwawdodyn, englyn, cywydd, clogyrnach*—have an unmistakably archaic ring, and the etymological derivation of a number of these terms is far from clear. All this strongly suggests that, in compiling the bardic grammar, the author sometimes used older traditional material, including some of the expert tuition given to young pupils in the bardic schools, which he adapted and cleverly manipulated according to his own personal whims and predilections.

BIBLIOGRAPHY

H. I. Bell, 'The Literary Tradition of Wales', *The Welsh Review*, vi, No. 4 (Winter, 1947), 233–8.

D. J. Bowen, 'The Bardic Functions' in D. M. and E. M. Lloyd (eds), *A Book of Wales* (London and Glasgow, 1953), 104–8.

Iestyn Daniel, 'Awduriaeth y Gramadeg a briodolir i Einion Offeiriad a Dafydd Ddu Hiraddug', in J. E. Caerwyn Williams (ed.), *Ysgrifau Beirniadol XIII* (Dinbych, 1985), 178–208.

J. Goronwy Edwards, 'Sir Gruffydd Llwyd', *English Historical Review*, xxx (1915), 589–601.

R. Geraint Gruffydd, 'Dafydd Ddu o Hiraddug', *Llên Cymru*, 18 (1994–5), 205–20.

Idem, 'Wales's Second Grammarian: Dafydd Ddu o Hiraddug', *Proceedings of the British Academy*, xc (1995), 1–28.

J. T. Jones, 'Gramadeg Einion Offeiriad', *Bulletin of the Board of Celtic Studies*, ii (1924), 184–200. This contains the text of Bangor MS.1.

D. Gwenallt Jones, *Yr Areithiau Pros* (Caerdydd, 1934).

T. Gwynn Jones, 'Bardism and Romance: A Study of the Welsh Literary Tradition', *Transactions of the Honourable Society of Cymmrodorion*, 1913–14, 205–310.

Saunders Lewis, *Gramadegau'r Penceirddiaid*, Darlith Goffa G. J. Williams (Cardiff, 1967).

J. Loth, *La Métrique galloise du IXe à la fin du XIVe siècle* (2 vols., Paris, 1901–2).

A. T. E. Matonis, 'The Welsh Bardic Grammars and Western Grammatical Tradition', *Modern Philology*, 79 (1981), 121–45.

Eadem, 'The Concept of Poetry in the Middle Ages: The Welsh Evidence from the Bardic Grammars', *Bulletin of the Board of Celtic Studies*, xxxvi (1989), 1–12.

John Morris-Jones, *Cerdd Dafod* (Oxford, 1925; 2nd edn, 1930).

Thomas Parry, 'Twf y Gynghanedd', *Transactions of the Honourable Society of Cymmrodorion*, 1936, 143–60.

Idem, 'Datblygiad y Cywydd', ibid. 1939, 209–31.

Idem, *A History of Welsh Literature*, translated from the Welsh by H. Idris Bell (Oxford, 1955), 127–63.

Idem, 'The Welsh Metrical Treatise Attributed to Einion Offeiriad', The Sir John Rhys Memorial Lecture, 1961. *Proceedings of the British Academy*, xlvii (1961), 177–95.

Idem, 'Statud Gruffudd ap Cynan', *Bulletin of the Board of Celtic Studies*, v (1929), 25–33.

Idem, 'Y Gorcheston', ibid., v (1929), 138–40.

T. H. Parry-Williams, 'The Bardic Tradition', *The Welsh Review*, vi, No. 4 (Winter, 1947), 249–53.

Brynley F. Roberts, *Gwassanaeth Meir* (Caerdydd, 1961).

Gwyn Thomas, *Y Traddodiad Barddol* (Caerdydd, 1976).

G. J. Williams, 'Tri Chof Ynys Brydain', *Llên Cymru*, 3 (1954–5), 234–9.

G. J. Williams and E. J. Jones (eds), *Gramadegau'r Penceirddiaid* (Caerdydd, 1934). This volume contains most of the essential texts and a masterly introduction by Professor G. J. Williams.

Ifor Williams, 'Rhys ap Gruffudd', *Transactions of the Honourable Society of Cymmrodorion*, 1913–14, 193–203.

Idem, 'Awdl i Rys ap Gruffudd gan Einion Offeiriad: Dosbarth Einion ar Ramadeg a'i Ddyled i Ddonatus', *Y Cymmrodor*, xxvi (1916), 115–46.

Idem, 'Dosbarth Einion Offeiriad', *Y Beirniad*, v (1915), 129–34.

J. Beverley Smith, 'Einion Offeiriad', *Bulletin of the Board of Celtic Studies*, xx (1962–4), 339–47.

CHAPTER 4

THE CONTENT OF POETRY AND THE CRISIS IN THE BARDIC TRADITION

CERI W. LEWIS

Few parts of the bardic grammar have aroused greater interest among historians of medieval Welsh literature, and none reflects more clearly the major crisis confronting the native bardic tradition during the closing years of the thirteenth century and the beginning of the fourteenth, than the section that is devoted to a discussion of those manifold attributes of the Godhead, Our Lady, the saints, and the various categories of men, both lay and clerical, that it was considered to be the duty of the poet to eulogize. Mr Saunders Lewis, in a penetrating and percipient analysis, has drawn attention to the markedly Platonic nature of this section, which, it is argued, constituted the philosophic basis of the panegyric verse composed by the bards of the classical Welsh tradition from approximately the mid-fourteenth century onwards. The significance of this important section becomes immediately clear when it is remembered that the Middle Ages pictured the structure of the universe as a great chain or ladder of degrees of being, which, according to the principle of linear descent, extended from the very throne of God, the *ens perfectissimum*, through all possible grades, including the Virgin Mary, the angels, the saints, man, animals, the vegetative class, down to the meanest of inanimate objects. This concept served to give expression to the infinite plenitude of God's creation, its unfailing order, and its ultimate unity. Every part of creation, however small or seemingly insignificant, formed a vital link in the chain, and each link therein, with the obvious exception of those at the two extremities, was at once larger and smaller than another: there could be no gap. The idea originated with Plato's *Timaeus*, was developed by Aristotle, was taken over by the Hellenizing Jews of Alexandria, and was later disseminated by the Neo-Platonists. Throughout the Middle Ages and down to the eighteenth century the image of the chain of being, as Professor A. O. Lovejoy has shown in a penetrating and detailed study, was one of the great notions about the creation and the cosmic order that made a deep impression on the collective thinking of the people who lived during that time. Not surprisingly, therefore, it exercised a powerful influence on the creative literature of the period.

A singularly charming feature of the concept of the great chain of being was that it permitted each class to excel in a single particular. For example, plants, though devoid of sense, excel in their faculty to assimilate nourishment, while beasts are generally more powerful than man in both their physical energy and their natural desires. Another form of excellence associated with this influential image was that within every class there existed a primate, such as the oak among the trees of the forest, the eagle among the birds, the lion among beasts, the emperor among men, the sun among stars, etc., although opinion sometimes varied on this matter. References to the primacies abound in medieval Welsh bardic poetry, especially from the late fourteenth century onwards, but these references lose much of their deeper significance if it is not realized that they arise from the concept of an ordered and carefully graded universe. The image of the great chain of being enhanced the inherent dignity of all creation, even the smallest part of it, and it also effectively highlighted the idea of a closely interrelated universe, in which no part was considered to be superfluous. *Natura nihil agit frustra.* Inherent in the image was also the principle of plenitude, which held that the universe exhibited the maximal diversity of all kinds of existences. But with the principle of plenitude went also that of continuity, for although the universe was composed of an innumerable variety of forms, it was held that each shared with its neighbour in the chain at least one attribute. All forms, therefore, were indissolubly linked to the base of God's throne. Hence there was ultimate unity in infinite diversity: the medieval conception of the universe was solidly theocentric.

The most detailed Welsh discussion of the great chain of being occurs in a sixteenth-century treatise called the *Graduelys*. This influential medieval concept can also be clearly detected in the very interesting section of the grammar-book of the poets that discusses how all things are to be praised and lists, with the detailed apparatus of classification derived by the medieval schoolmen from Aristotle, the appropriate virtues and excellences of each grade:

> Furthermore, one must know in what way each thing to which it may be desired to compose poetry is to be praised. There are two

> kinds of things to which poetry ought to be written, namely, a spiritual thing and a corporeal thing: a spiritual thing, such as God and the saints; a corporeal thing, such as a man, or a beast, or a place.

Detailed instructions are then given for each class in each category; for example, among spiritual things:

> God should be praised for divine quality, and strength, and almightiness, and supreme wisdom, and complete goodness, and entire mercy, and truth, and righteous judgements, and generosity, and majesty, and glory, and heavenliness, and righteous love, and purity, and holiness, and creative power, and fatherliness, and spirituality, and honour, and heavenly beauty, and every honourable spiritual quality.
>
> Mary is praised for her maidenhood, and her virginity, and chastity, and her purity, and sanctity, and her heavenly beauty, and her compassion, and her glory, and her bounty, and her honour, and her [saintly] life, and her tenderness, and for every other honourable thing for which her Lord Son is praised.

The author then proceeds to classify the varieties of man:

> There are two kinds of human beings who ought to be praised, man and woman. There are two kinds of men, a man of religion and a man of the world. There are two sorts of men of the world, laymen and clerics. There are two sorts of clerics, prelates and subordinates. Prelates, such as bishops and archbishops, are praised for their wisdom, and their prudence, and the skilful accomplishment of their church government, and their firmness in maintaining the laws of the Church, and their mercy to the poor, and their deeds of charity, and their prayers, and their spiritual works, and their righteous generosity, and the maintenance of their courts, and their meekness, and other honourable ecclesiastical attributes . . .
>
> There are two kinds of laymen, a lord and a nobleman. A lord is praised for power, and ability, and military prowess, and courage, and strength, and pride, and meekness, and wisdom, and accomplishment, and generosity, and gentleness, and amiability towards his men and his friends, and beauty of countenance, and a dignified bearing, and magnanimity of mind, and nobleness of actions, and other honourable and kindly qualities . . .
>
> Three kinds of women are praised, a noblewoman, a maiden, and a woman of religion. A noblewoman is praised for wisdom, and propriety, and chastity, and generosity, and beauty of countenance,

> complexion and form, and guilelessness of speech and actions. And it is not fitting to praise a noblewoman for prowess in love-making or dalliance, for amatory verse is not seemly to her.

The emphasis is constantly on praise; the master-poet of high grade, called *prydydd* in the text, is strictly enjoined to avoid satire, which was regarded as one of the base activities of the *clerwr*, the low-grade itinerant bard or minstrel; and we are reminded that 'the eulogy of the *prydydd* ought to be more potent than the satire of the *clerwr*'. For the art of the *prydydd*, it is proudly asserted, 'is a portion of natural wisdom, and is derived from the Holy Spirit . . .' This statement is only one of a number of interesting and highly significant indications in this section of the treatise of the extent to which the Church succeeded in leaving its *imprimatur* on the bardic grammar. For although the author's minute classification with regard to panegyric clearly belongs to the main stream of medieval rhetoric, it also has distinct affinities with the methods and philosophy of the great medieval schoolmen. Moreover, holy or intercessory poetry, called *gwengerdd* in one text, is given clear precedence over verse composed in praise of maidens (*rhieingerdd*) or chieftains (*unbengerdd*). And in listing the particular attributes for which the various classes of human beings are to be praised, the writer invariably gives pride of place to clerics over laymen. The original author of the copy preserved in Peniarth MS. 20 was unquestionably familiar with certain aspects of theological doctrine and with the Latin liturgy. It has been shown, for example, that the section on the Godhead echoes the opening paragraph on God in the Nicene Creed, while the paragraph on the Virgin Mary joins together lines from Latin prayers and hymns that were sung as part of the daily life of the monasteries: *mam y drugaredd* (mother of mercy) = *mater misericordiae; brenhines nef a daear ac uffern* (queen of heaven and earth and hell) = *regina caeli et terrae; a bod yn wyry cyn esgor ac wedi esgor* (and being a virgin before giving birth and after giving birth) = *virgo prius et posterius*, etc. There is also evidence to suggest that the author was familiar with monastic vows, with certain aspects of university life, and with the contemporary ecclesiastical hierarchies. All this evidence had led Mr Saunders Lewis to conclude that the original author of the copy preserved in Peniarth MS. 20 had received a university education and had subsequently been appointed a teacher in one of the Welsh monastic schools. It is quite possible, therefore, that this part of the grammar-book was the work of Einion Offeiriad, and it is well to remember that the late sixteenth-century bard, Robert ab Ifan (*fl.c.* 1572–1603), who hailed from Brynsiencyn, Anglesey, states at the end of his copy of this section preserved in Peniarth MS. 158, a copy he himself transcribed in 1587, that it had been written by Einion Offeiriad for Rhys ap Gruffudd.

At the end of the grammar-book there occurs a list of triads, which, it is generally agreed, incorporate some of the instruction imparted to pupils in the bardic schools on various matters relating to their craft and general moral behaviour. Originating simply as mnemonic devices, these poetic triads were probably fashioned by the bardic teachers. Welsh literature, from a very early period, shows a marked predilection for triple groupings, or triads, as a convenient means of cataloguing a variety of technical information: in addition to those contained in the bardic treatise, triads are used extensively in the legal codes, especially those belonging to the Blegywryd tradition, in the medieval medical tracts, where they are employed as a convenient device for classifying various ailments and the recommended remedies, and in the early poetry, where the predilection for triadic groupings is clearly reflected in the way subtle variations of mood and manner are conveyed with a high degree of technical accomplishment in the three-line *englyn* from the 'old poetry' (*englyn o'r hen ganiad*). And in many manuscripts we find short collections of triads incorporating general moral, gnomic, and proverbial statements.

There can be no doubt that the bards were required, as part of their professional training, to memorize many of the numerous triad sequences that have been preserved in various manuscripts, for down to the final disintegration of the bardic order in the late sixteenth and early seventeenth centuries much of the instruction continued to be imparted orally, and the extant copies of the *dwned*, or bardic grammar, were only a comparatively late supplementary aid to the traditional bardic teaching. An important part of that process of instruction was devoted to preserving the national inheritance of ancient tradition. It is generally agreed that the prose narrative literature that has survived from the medieval period in both Wales and Ireland represents only a very small part of the great corpus of oral literature that was carefully preserved and transmitted throughout the centuries by a skilled and highly trained class of men of learning. The original nucleus of the Triads of the Island of Britain (*Trioedd Ynys Prydain*), as Dr Rachel Bromwich has shown, served as an index to this rich corpus of orally transmitted narrative literature, an index that had been created for the use of that learned class of bards who considered it one of their primary professional obligations to preserve, foster, and transmit the numerous tales that incorporated the oldest surviving traditions of the Britons about themselves in this island. Those tales embraced the national past of the native inhabitants of Wales and of those Britons who had formerly occupied the northern territories that were subsequently lost to the Anglo-Saxon invaders. The Triads of the Island of Britain, which are in effect a kind of catalogue of the names of the traditional heroes, classified in groups of three, originated as mnemonic devices to help the young bardic novitiates recollect the wide repertoire of early history, legend, and traditional narrative material they were actively engaged in mastering. And these Triads were also a convenient source of reference which the bards could use for the standards of comparison regularly required by their craft. The bardic grammar, as we have seen, lists the particular virtues and qualities to be attributed to men and women according to their fixed status in the social hierarchy. It was perfectly natural, therefore, for a bard to attribute to his patron the unstinting generosity of Rhydderch Hael, or the fearless valour of a formidable warrior such as Arthur or Alexander, for these figures—and many others like them who are listed in the Triads—were traditionally regarded as the outstanding exemplars of the particular virtues with which they had been endowed. Unquestionably, it is from the same milieu that we have derived such lists as 'The Names of the Island of Britain', 'The Twenty-four Kings adjudged most powerful', 'The Names of the Kings of Wales before the Saxons took possession of the Island', 'The Twenty-four Wonders of the Island of Britain', and many more besides, for these lists or catalogues were all transmitted as an essential part of the rich bardic heritage, although in origin they are not as old as *Trioedd Ynys Prydain*.

In Ireland, as in Wales, the professional bards were obliged to master a large repertoire of stories and verse that preserved the mythology, native oral record, and traditional history of Ireland (*seanchas*); and, with regard to the narrative material, the classification of the tales in saga lists, according to their basic themes, has appropriately been compared to the classification in Welsh literature by means of triads. It is significant that the same basic conception of classifying according to subject matter, rather than according to cycle or period, can be detected quite early in both Welsh and Irish sources, and it seems that the Irish bards were able, when so requested by their patrons, to deliver a spontaneous recitation of these detailed catalogues. Some idea of the rigorous and exacting nature of the training the professional bards were required to undergo is provided by the fact that the Irish *ollam*, who corresponds broadly to the Welsh *pencerdd*, spent a period of twelve to fourteen years mastering the intricate details of his craft. As part of his training he was required, *inter alia*, to have a wide and intimate knowledge of the native saga, for he was expected not only to know two hundred and fifty *primscéla* 'primary stories' and a hundred *fo-scéla* 'subsidiary tales' or 'anecdotes' (classified according to their main themes, such as cattle-raids, adventures, battles, feasts, visions, invasions, births, deaths, voyages, elopements, etc), but also to be able to blend different tales with one another in a skilful manner.

That the medieval Welsh bards, like their learned counterparts in Ireland, were also required to master an extensive repertoire of tales, and thereby familiarize themselves with the national inheritance of ancient tradition and legend, is demonstrated by one of the poetic triads in the bardic grammar, which states that there are 'Three things that give amplitude to a poet: knowledge of stories, the poetic art, and old verse (*hengerdd*).' It is clear that the references contained in the compositions of the Welsh court-poets—especially those who sang in the twelfth century—to the ancient tales and legends are firmly based on a detailed knowledge of the stories themselves, not merely on a vague and rather superficial acquaintance with the various proper names that occur in them. The impressively wide range of reference to the characters of the early stories and old Welsh verse contained in the work of Cynddelw Brydydd Mawr (*fl.* 1155–1200) clearly testifies to the strength and richness of the oral traditions still current in the kingdom of Powys in his day. However, from the thirteenth century onwards the bards' knowledge of this great repertoire of national tradition and legend seems to be constantly diminishing, although the compositions of the later court-poets, as well as the works of the *cywyddwyr* who succeeded them, still contain numerous references to characters from the tales. Throughout the thirteenth and fourteenth centuries, with the progressive decline in knowledge of the early Welsh narrative tradition, the bards tended to draw more frequently on literary sources of mainly foreign origin for their allusions and comparisons.

The bard may also have been a story-teller (*cyfarwydd*) at one time, although this is far from certain. If this was the case, it would help to explain why the words *bardd a chyfarwydd* are closely linked in some references. Nor should it be overlooked that some tales were told in a combination of verse and prose. In most instances only the verse sections have been preserved, as in the celebrated Llywarch Hen and Heledd cycles, the dialogues in the *Black Book of Carmarthen*, or some of the verses contained in the *Book of Taliesin*, which seem to derive from an early Taliesin saga. The *locus classicus* for a bard fulfilling the function of a story-teller is the Fourth Branch of the Mabinogi, where Gwydion, 'the best story-teller in the world', and his travelling companions are described as bards from Glamorgan who are asked to entertain the royal court of Pryderi with a tale. This reference can obviously be interpreted to mean that story-telling was, at one time, one of the acknowledged functions of the bards, or, at least, of a particular grade of bard. However, it is by no means certain that these entertainers were official members of the professional guild of bards, nor is there any substantial body of evidence to prove that the twelfth-century court-poets, however detailed their knowledge may have been of the immense corpus of native traditional material to which the Triads of the Island of Britain provided a convenient index, ever narrated tales in the halls of their regal patrons. It is possible, nevertheless, that the oft-quoted reference in the Fourth Branch of the Mabinogi reflects the practice of a very early period, although, in that case, it is difficult to account satisfactorily for any change that may later have taken place in this particular aspect of bardic routine.

There can be no doubt, however, that a detailed study of early Welsh verse, as the poetic triad quoted above clearly indicates, also formed an important part of the syllabus of the bardic schools. A careful reading of the strict-metre verse itself reveals that the works of the earliest Welsh poets were analysed in considerable detail, and it is significant that there are commendatory references to a number of the *Cynfeirdd* in the compositions of the twelfth- and thirteenth-century court-poets. When the different metrical patterns, the various rules governing rhyme and alliteration, as well as other technical aspects of the bardic craft were being discussed, the teachers probably chose illustrative examples from the early verse. The basic themes of the late sixth-century bards, Aneirin and Taliesin, recur with unfailing regularity in the works of the *Gogynfeirdd*, and there is also a striking similarity in the way in which these topics are treated. No less marked is the resemblance between some of their metaphors and similes. Obsolete words and archaic constructions were also diligently culled from the works of the earliest poets, and we find that bardic vocabularies have been included in the manuscripts of a number of *cywyddwyr* who lived in the fifteenth and sixteenth centuries. For example, in Peniarth MS. 51, which is mostly in his autograph, we find the Glamorgan *pencerdd*, Gwilym Tew (*fl.c.* 1460–80), attempting to interpret the meaning of some of the difficult words he had discovered in the *Book of Aneirin* during the period when that famous manuscript had been in his possession. An Old Welsh vocabulary, transcribed from an original that was, inferentially, in the autograph of Gruffudd Hiraethog (d. 1564), also occurs in one section of Peniarth MS. 155, while in Peniarth MS. 230 the same bard compiled a Welsh dictionary with quotations, chiefly from the poets, illustrating throughout the use of the words listed. This compilation was later copied by Wiliam Llŷn (1534 or 1535–80), and the admirable practice followed by the *penceirddiaid* in this matter was later adopted by such celebrated scholars and antiquarians as Sir Thomas Wiliems (1545 or 1546–1622?), of Trefriw, and Dr John Davies (*c.* 1567–1644), of Mallwyd. Some bards, such as Simwnt Fychan (*c.* 1530–1606), who was granted the grade of *pencerdd* at the famous *eisteddfod* held in Caerwys in 1567, compiled detailed collections of synonyms for God, king, queen, lord, battle, shield, sword, spear, armour, feast, etc., words that recur with considerable frequency in the panegyric and elegiac verse composed by the medieval Welsh bards. It was in this way that the leading professional poets came ultimately to acquire that remarkable verbal dexterity and abundant command of language (*amlder Cymraeg*) that is so highly commended in another of the triads at the end of the early copies of the bardic treatise as an essential ingredient of the poet's craft.

The bardic grammar, therefore, in the earliest form in which it has been preserved for us, is a clever amalgam of some of the instruction imparted to pupils in the bardic schools and material compiled by the author himself. To the first category may safely be ascribed the discussion of the way in which the Welsh syllables and diphthongs are to be classified, the analysis of the various 'prohibited errors' in rhyme, metre, and *proest*-correspondences, and the matter contained in the poetic triads; to the second category belong the interesting section on praise-poetry and parts of the section devoted to a discussion of Welsh prosody, which clearly reflect the author's personal whims and predilections. The work, taken as a whole, cannot legitimately be regarded either as a product of the bardic schools or as a manual of instruction for bardic aspirants. It is clearly the work of a man of considerable learning, a cleric who had been educated at a university or one of the monastic schools, who had sufficient grasp of the bardic lore and culture of his day to enable him to present a fairly accurate description of certain aspects of it, but who allowed his own personal predilections to guide him to such an extent that the treatise cannot be regarded as an accurate description of contemporary bardic practices and usages. The motives that prompted the compilation of the grammar are probably to be sought in the confused and uncertain conditions that followed the loss of Welsh independence in the closing years of the thirteenth century. From the late sixth century onwards the tradition of heroic panegyric had formed the main stream of Welsh verse, and the Norman incursions into Wales that began in the closing years of the eleventh century had given that time-honoured tradition a renewed impulse and an added significance. But the destruction of the Venedotian dynasty and, as an inevitable corollary, the complete collapse of the independent Welsh principality that had been, beyond any doubt, that dynasty's most magnificent achievement, created a crisis of major proportions for that highly-trained professional class of bards that had made heroic praise of the defending Welsh princes the prime function of its poetic activity. For, to all appearances, that activity had finally lost its *raison d'être*, and in the magnificent elegy he addressed to Llywelyn ap Gruffudd, effectively the last native independent prince of Wales, who was slain on 11 December 1282, Gruffudd ab yr Ynad Coch gave eloquent expression to the feeling of intense despair and foreboding the bards must generally have experienced during that period of doubt and uncertainty.

That the first quarter of the fourteenth century produced no poet of great repute is one significant indication of the changing circumstances of the period: such figures as Iorwerth Beli, Llywelyn Brydydd Hoddnant, Iorwerth Fychan, Goronwy Gyriog, and Gwilym Ddu o Arfon can hardly be regarded as bards of the first order, and only a few compositions by them occur in each case. Nor was the verse produced by Casnodyn and Gruffudd ap Dafydd ap Tudur, possibly the two best poets to emerge in this period, by any means prolific. No less significant is the manifest dearth of the kind of panegyric verse that characterized the poetic output of the twelfth and thirteenth centuries. This is replaced in the early fourteenth century by love-poetry and verse composed on religious themes. The poetry produced in this period stands, therefore, in sharp contrast, not only in bulk but also in subject matter, to the verse composed during the previous hundred and fifity years.

A few of the poems composed in the early fourteenth century provide us with some indication of the agonizing predicament in which the bards found themselves during that period of gloom and despondency. In an *awdl* he addressed to the bishop of Bangor—probably Anian Sais, whose tenure of the episcopate extended from 1309 to 1327—the Venedotian bard, Iorwerth Beli, declared that those poets who still continued to cherish the old court tradition were anxiously looking to the bishop in the hope that he would undertake the obligations of patronage that had formerly been discharged by the independent Welsh prince, and he further reminded the bishop of the status and dignity conferred on the poet in the court of Maelgwn Gwynedd in the sixth century. The bishop, however, seemed to be singularly reluctant to discharge those duties. Furthermore, not only did he choose to neglect the Welsh poets, but he even extended a generous hospitality and gave fine raiment to alien usurpers, whom Iorwerth Beli contemptuously described as the very 'dregs of art', to English youths with their 'earsplitting cacophonies', whose song was not unlike the squealing of piglets (*perchyllson debyg*). These foreigners, with their horns and drums, had even won the bishop's respect for their knowledge of English!

Not surprisingly, when we bear in mind the historical background, a broadly similar note of unease and criticism is struck in the work of the Glamorgan bard, Casnodyn (*fl.* 1320–40), who, if one may safely judge from his extant verse, represented the more traditional and conservative school of his period and was deeply scornful of the aspiring lower orders of poets that were coming increasingly into prominence during this period of political uncertainty and social upheaval. Casnodyn's view of the new society he saw being gradually shaped around him in the early fourteenth century was predominantly one of disapprobation, and one clear indication of his strong contempt for the alien influences he genuinely believed were undermining the indigenous society in post-Conquest colonial Wales, thereby destroying many of the traditional values the *Gogynfeirdd* had long fostered and cherished, was the fact that he took as his ideal the old-type Welsh gentleman who had no knowledge of English.

There is, therefore, some evidence to suggest that the end of the thirteenth century and the first quarter of the fourteenth was a period of considerable uncertainty and confusion in the history of Welsh bardism, when the status and time-honoured panegyric function of the *prydydd* (or high-grade bard) were in grave danger of being inextricably merged with those of the less genteel *ioculatorum turba.* This is not to imply, however, that it was only in the exceptionally disturbed conditions of the early post-Conquest period that an element of friction or tension existed between the various grades of bards, for the master-poets, as many statements in their majestic odes amply confirm, had always been extremely proud of their exalted status and had naturally viewed with some alarm any attempt to usurp their special function and to encroach on their long-established rights and privileges. It is clear from a number of statements contained in their works that the court-poets tended to look disdainfully on the activities and effusions of the low-grade minstrels and rhymesters of their day. For example, in the stately elegy he addressed to his patron, Gruffudd ap Cynan (d.1137), king of Gwynedd, Meilyr Brydydd (*fl.c.*1100– 37), who is regarded as the earliest of the *Gogynfeirdd*, refers disparagingly to the *manfeirdd* (minor rhymesters) of his period, and it is obvious that this bard, who was privileged to sit next to his regal patron at feastings, was most anxious not to be confused with one of their number. No less contemptuous is the reference to inferior poetasters (*beirdd ysbyddaid*) in the ode the court-poet, Llywelyn Fardd, addressed to Llywelyn ab Iorwerth (or Llywelyn the Great, 1173–1240), prince of Gwynedd. Of even greater interest, however, are the two odes in which Phylip Brydydd (*fl.c.* 1222) claimed priority over rhymesters of lower degree. One of these compositions, which was sung in the court of Rhys Ieuanc in Llanbadarn Fawr, refers to the bard's contest with the *gofeirdd*, or inferior poets, who were in the habit of visiting that court, and this reference proves conclusively that the poets of the classical Welsh tradition were being forced in some of the courts of south Wales, even as early as Phylip Brydydd's day, to oppose the activities of the so-called 'vain bards', 'poetasters', and 'unskilled dabblers' who seriously threatened to undermine the professional bards' position. But this deep-rooted tension and professional antagonism must have been sharply exacerbated by the exceptionally disturbed conditions that prevailed in the period immediately following the loss of Welsh independence, when interest in Welsh bardism had sunk, it would appear, to an unprecedentedly low level and when the Anglo-Norman influences that were then flooding with ever-increasing momentum into both lay and ecclesiastical centres in Wales, including even those situated in the heartland of Gwynedd and Deheubarth, constituted a threat of major proportions to the very existence of the professional guild of bards. This crisis and the feeling of great anxiety experienced by the bards during this period are reflected in some of the early copies of the grammar-book in the final paragraph of the section that discusses how all things are to be praised:

> It is not becoming for a *prydydd* to dabble in *clerwriaeth* [i.e., the practices of low-grade poets, cf. *clerici vagantes*], for such base matters are contrary to the arts of the *prydydd*. For it is the habit of the *clerwr* to mock and to disparage, and to arouse feelings of shame and disgrace, whereas it behoves the *prydydd* to praise and compliment, and to procure fame and joy and glorification. And, moreover, *clerwriaeth* is not reducible to rule, for it is a disorderly art, and for that reason may it be avoided by the *prydydd* . . . Wherever the *prydydd* practises his art, it is not right to credit the disparaging productions of the *clerwr*, for the eulogy of the *prydydd* ought to be more potent than the satire of the *clerwr*. Incantations, sorcery, and magical practices are not worthy of the *prydydd*'s art, and he should not meddle with them. Old verse (*Hengerdd*), and tales preserved in writing, questions reflecting honour on those who asked them, and replies rendered excellent by art and truth—these are the things that are good for the *prydydd* to know when called upon to converse with wise men, to delight young maidens, and to entertain gentlemen and ladies of breeding. For the *prydydd*'s art is a portion of natural wisdom, and is derived from the Holy Spirit, and its inspiration is a fruit of genius mated to artistic assiduity . . .

Such vigorous protestations would hardly have been necessary were it not for the fact that the bards of the classical Welsh tradition were rapidly losing much of their erstwhile status and respect.

It may well have been in response to this crisis that Einion Offeiriad—if he really was the author—compiled his grammatical and metrical treatise. It was no accident, according to some scholars, that he should thus have endeavoured, sometime towards the end of the first quarter of the fourteenth century or, perhaps, a little later, to blend the ancient Welsh bardic lore with the broader European culture that he, by virtue of his clerical background and training, had acquired, possibly in one of the monastic schools of his day. Einion Offeiriad's reaction to the debilitating effect the loss of Welsh independence apparently had, for a while, on the activities of the professional guild of bards was to compose, in Dr Thomas Parry's words, 'a charter for the bardic schools, meant, not to supplant the oral instruction given by the poets to their pupils, but rather to supplement it, and to widen the horizons of those who were concerned with the native Welsh culture'. The work seems to have been very favourably received by the master-poets for well over a century after it had first been written. As we have already seen, the four earliest extant manuscript copies of the work are not identical in every respect, for although there is no marked divergence in either the subject matter or the general framework, there are occasionally some significant differences in the phraseology, in some of the definitions, in the order in which various items are sometimes arranged and, more particularly, in the examples of the different metres quoted in the important section on prosody. These variations suggest that the grammar-book had been used by persons who took an intelligent interest in Welsh bardism and that, in order to meet their particular requirements, slight modifications had been made from time to time in the various copies. But the fact that no major changes were introduced into the material contained in the treatise strongly suggests that the work, as a whole, was held in considerable esteem. It is clear, therefore, that the four earliest extant copies of the grammar cannot represent Einion Offeiriad's original compilation, but rather the slightly modified versions used by fourteenth-century bards. This doubtless explains why some of the original metrical examples were replaced by illustrative quotations from the compositions of contemporary, or near-contemporary, poets. That some of the metres devised by Einion

Offeiriad occur in poems composed towards the end of the century is another firm indication that the treatise was highly esteemed by the bards. For example, the metre called *tawddgyrch cadwynog* was employed by both Ieuan Llwyd and Y Proll. Furthermore, the occurrence of a figurative reference to the 'grammar book' (*llyfr dwned*) in the panegyric ode Dafydd ap Gwilym addressed to his uncle, Llywelyn ap Gwilym, who was constable of Newcastle Emlyn in 1343, shows that a knowledge of Einion's work was already current in some circles, at least, not long after it had been written. The influence of the section on praise-poetry, which is frequently called the *prydlyfr* in Welsh, can also be detected in parts of the famous bardic contention between Dafydd ap Gwilym and Gruffudd Gryg, while the former's work unmistakably echoes in places a number of the examples quoted to illustrate particular metres in the section that is devoted to a discussion of prosody.

In the fifteenth century a number of important changes were made in the content of the bardic grammar. At the famous *eisteddfod* held in Carmarthen *c.* 1451 certain modifications were made in the metres, for two *englyn* forms were excluded from the classification and were replaced, as we have already seen, by two new metres of extreme complexity devised by Dafydd ab Edmwnd (*fl.* 1450–90). The latter also added to the difficulties of other measures by decreeing that double rhymes should be used in the metres *rhupunt hir a byr* and *tawddgyrch cadwynog*, and that the metre called *awdl-gywydd* should contain regular *cynghanedd*. He also made the rules governing *cynghanedd* even stricter. The basic purpose of all these innovations was to make the examinations for bardic degrees appreciably more difficult and thereby protect the professional bards against the encroachment of the inferior poetasters who would not have scrupled to usurp their privileges. Nevertheless, in spite of these changes in the strict metres, the total number of twenty-four, which had been arbitrarily fixed by Einion Offeiriad, was steadfastly adhered to, although this did not significantly affect the bards' choice of metres during the succeeding centuries. However, Einion Offeiriad's most valuable contribution to the development of Welsh prosody was, possibly, the invention of the metre called *hir-a-thoddaid*, for this became extremely popular with many of the poets who sang in the nineteenth century, while some of the greatest and most memorable verse composed in our own period has been written in this particular stanza form.

Another important result of Einion's work was that the concept of a written curriculum for the bardic schools—to supplement the main instruction, which was still imparted orally—continued down to the end of the sixteenth century, by which time the professional guild of bards was in marked decline. More and more of the bardic lore was, therefore, committed to writing, and in the expanded versions of the bardic grammar that were transcribed by such leading *penceirddiaid* as Gwilym Tew and Gutun Owain in the fifteenth century, or Wiliam Llŷn, Wiliam Cynwal, and Simwnt Fychan in the sixteenth, we can observe a steady growth in the content of the treatise. In Simwnt Fychan's great work, the 'Five Books of Poetic Art' (*Pum Llyfr Cerddwriaeth*), compiled about the year 1570, we find the bardic grammar in its definitive form. The material it contains is basically similar to that found in Einion Offeiriad's work, except that each section is fuller, and that it contains a long dissertation on *cynghanedd.* Even this detailed work, however, does not contain the sum total of bardic teaching, for the greater part of the instruction given in the bardic schools was still imparted orally, as we have seen. And it is significant that even after an increasingly large part of the bardic lore had been committed to writing, the bardic craft continued to be regarded as a secret—the 'Secret of the Bards of the Island of Britain' (*Cyfrinach Beirdd Ynys Prydain*)—which the disciples and those cultured members of the gentry who were themselves skilled exponents of this intricate art were under a strict obligation to keep. This rule was later to be roundly condemned by sixteenth-century humanists, who strongly urged the bards to renounce the secretiveness for which their profession had been so long renowned and explain the mysteries of their craft to all who wished to understand them. Throughout the expanded copies of the treatise that were compiled in the fifteenth and sixteenth centuries we find the idea persisting that the study of grammar as a subject in itself—that is, grammar regarded as a science, devoid of any vital connection with a particular language as such—should constitute an essential part of the bardic curriculum. Not surprisingly, therefore, the grammatical section of the treatise was considerably expanded and increasingly 'latinized', the examples quoted being left sometimes in the original Latin, which again proves that the leading bards who transcribed the various copies had very little knowledge of that language.

But perhaps the most important aspect of Einion Offeiriad's

work is the contribution it may have made to the preservation of the centuries-old Welsh bardic tradition. For, according to Mr Saunders Lewis, the reorganization of the bardic order and the poetical resurgence that can clearly be detected from about the mid-fourteenth century onwards in the works of such notable figures as Dafydd ap Gwilym, Gruffudd ap Maredudd ap Dafydd (*fl.c.* 1350–80), Llywelyn Goch Amheurig Hen (*fl.c.* 1360–90), and Iolo Goch (*c.* 1320–98) can be attributed to the slightly earlier efforts of Einion Offeiriad, who, approaching the bardic craft of his period from a distinctly scholastic standpoint, redefined and creatively widened the ancient tradition of panegyric by investing it with a new philosophic content, as evidenced by those parts of the grammar-book that demonstrate how all things are to be praised, and so gave it a wider significance and a new *raison d'être*. This reorganization, which drew a clear moral distinction between the work of the noble panegyrist and the less edifying antics of the mimicking and reviling buffoon or *jongleur*, was not drastically dissimilar, it has been claimed, to the near-contemporary movement of poetic reform in France, as witnessed by the work of Watriquet de Couvin and Jean de Condé. The tradition of heroic panegyric, which was thus reorientated as a result of Einion Offeiriad's work, formed the solid basis of the substantial corpus of *cywydd* and *awdl* poetry of the next two centuries, which is generally considered to be one of the outstanding achievements of Welsh literature.

By destroying the native political superstructure on which Welsh bardism then rested the Edwardian conquest had obviously created a serious crisis of patronage for the professional bards. Fortunately, however, the economic foundations that were quite indispensable if the poets were to continue their creative literary activities were soon relaid. For a class of numerous small property owners, the *uchelwyr*, as they are known in Welsh, who had been deeply imbued with many of the cultural ideals of the native princes, gradually undertook the duties of literary patronage. Not surprisingly, the bards came to recognize in them many of the attributes they had previously extolled in the independent princes. Moreover, the staunch support given by generations of Welsh princes to the monastic houses, especially those of the Cistercian Order, was richly repaid, for these monasteries gave their assistance and encouragement for centuries to the professional bards and played a notable part in fostering Welsh literature and scholarship. The patronage generously provided by the gentry and by many ecclesiastical dignitaries, which became quite marked by the late fourteenth century, proved to be a factor of crucial importance in the continuation of the native bardic tradition; indeed, it even provided that tradition with a fresh and potent impetus. One prominent feature of the succeeding period was the keen and intelligent interest taken in the bardic craft by some members of the gentry, and a number of the outstanding poets of the period, such as Dafydd ap Gwilym, Madog Benfras (*fl.c.* 1320–60), Llywelyn Goch Amheurig Hen, and Ieuan ap Rhydderch (*fl.c.* 1430–70), were men who enjoyed some social status and prestige in their day.

With the disappearance of the princely courts, as a result of the Edwardian conquest, there no longer existed an appropriately responsive audience for the distinctive type of stately panegyric verse that had been composed by the *Gogynfeirdd.* Their *awdlau* had been closely linked with some of the ceremonial activities of the independent ruling dynasties, and it was naturally difficult for the professional bards, who became increasingly dependent on the *uchelwyr* from the mid-fourteenth century onwards for their patronage, to perpetuate indefinitely in their compositions the ceremonial pomp and stately dignity of the *awdlau* composed by the court-poets. The Edwardian conquest, therefore, provided an opportunity for innovations in the bardic craft, and one of the most important of these from the metrical standpoint was the emergence in the work of Dafydd ap Gwilym and his contemporaries of the *cywydd deuair hirion.* This was the measure employed most frequently by the strict-metre bards for about two and a half centuries, until their professional guild finally disintegrated under the combined pressure of the far-reaching changes that manifested themselves in the sixteenth century—the union of Wales with England, the progressive Anglicization of the gentry, the dissolution of the monasteries, the invention of printing, the new learning, and the intellectual milieu of the modern age, which generally proved to be distinctly inimical to the native bardic tradition. The *cywydd deuair hirion*, as we have seen, developed from an older metre, the *traethodl*, consisting of seven-syllable rhymed couplets and formerly used by the inferior grades of poets. An interesting example of this older metre occurs in the work of Dafydd ap Gwilym. When it was taken over into the strict system, it was deliberately made into something far more intricate and polished by introducing *cynghanedd* into each line and by applying the rule that an accented syllable at the end of one line in each couplet rhymed with an unaccented syllable in the other.

The *cywydd deuair hirion* became, therefore, a most exacting metre, which demanded a great deal of skill and artistic accomplishment on the part of those who used it. Nevertheless, it was better adapted to a more personal and more readily comprehensible mode of expression, although it would be quite misleading to exaggerate the differences between the traditional poetry of the *Gogynfeirdd* and that composed by the leading *cywyddwyr*. Some of the more prominent bards were equally adept in both styles, and even Dafydd ap Gwilym, who is generally regarded as the most accomplished master of the new style, did not entirely forsake the earlier mode, for in a great number of his *cywyddau* we find the compound expressions, the recurring parentheses, the archaic vocabulary and syntactical constructions that were regarded, according to the prevailing bardic theory, as indispensable to an elevated poetic style. The theme of love, which occurred occasionally in the works of the court-poets, but mainly in poems that paid compliment to ladies of high rank, loomed larger in the poetry composed after the loss of Welsh independence and this, together with nature, became the dominant theme in the poetry of Dafydd ap Gwilym. His work, therefore, is a vital link between the songs of the household bard *(bardd teulu)* in the queen's chamber and the strict-metre verse composed on the lighter and more popular themes of love and nature in the later Middle Ages. Dafydd ap Gwilym, however, was not averse to addressing some panegyric *cywyddau* to his patrons in the comparatively simple style of the love and nature poems. In this way the *cywydd* metre and style became an acceptable medium for panegyric verse, an extremely important stage in the development of the native bardic tradition. In the work of Iolo Goch, another important figure in the history of Welsh bardism, we find some of the diction, style, traditional imagery and technique of the earlier court *awdlau* being transferred to this new metre, which he used as the normal medium for his panegyric verse. The works of Dafydd ap Gwilym and Iolo Goch represent, therefore, the crucial stages in the evolution from the stately court-poetry of the *Gogynfeirdd* to the less formal panegyric poetry of the fifteenth century, the great age of bardic poetry, when the verse composed by the great masters who sang in that period reached its highest pitch of artistic refinement and elegance. It was no doubt inevitable, when we consider the great artistry and verve displayed by Dafydd ap Gwilym in his treatment of the appealing themes of love and nature, that some poets attempted to imitate him. But even a bard of his undisputed genius and artistic accomplishment failed to deflect appreciably the main stream of the Welsh bardic tradition: panegyric and elegy for aristocratic patrons still remained the central theme, and the bards were still subjected to a fairly rigorous discipline, which clearly manifested itself in both metre and style.

The classical tradition of the Welsh bards successfully recovered, therefore, after a comparatively short period of floundering and uncertainty, from the shock of the Edwardian conquest and the momentous political, social and economic changes that came in its wake. That the fourteenth century was a period of crucial importance in that process of recovery and in the general evolution of Welsh bardism is undeniable. However, it is extremely difficult to determine whether the poetical resurgence that can clearly be detected from about the mid-fourteenth century onwards is to be attributed directly to Einion Offeiriad's inspired efforts or whether his work was itself a product of that movement of reorganization and reform by which the bardic order eventually achieved a measure of stability or equilibrium. Nor should it be overlooked that Einion, far from attempting to introduce changes of fundamental importance in the poetic practice of his day, was really reaffirming with greater emphasis and conviction vital principles and assumptions that had long lain at the root of Welsh bardic verse. Convincing proof of this is provided by the religious poetry composed by the *Gogynfeirdd* during the twelfth and thirteenth centuries. Although this majestic corpus of verse had been written long before Einion himself was born, it nevertheless adheres fairly closely to the general dicta he laid down—so it is traditionally assumed—in the bardic grammar. This suggests that the Church had long exercised some influence on the standards adopted by the Welsh bards. Furthermore, even if it could be firmly established that it was Einion's work that really gave the vital initial impetus to the poetical resurgence that began about the middle of the fourteenth century, it would still be incontestable that there is a clear tendency in the verse composed later in the century to reject his scholastically dominated schema and to assert the manifold claims of secular life and all the delights and pleasures of earthly existence. The ribald satires of a bard like Madog Dwygraig (*fl.c.* 1370) were obviously as firm a repudiation of Einion Offeiriad's most exalted dicta as the decidedly more artistic compositions of Dafydd ap Gwilym. The criteria so clearly enunciated in the grammar were probably accepted or rejected by each bard as it suited his individual purpose. And it is significant that the copyists who transcribed the earliest extant texts of the work could not completely ignore the existence of love and nature poetry, even though the original author had accorded it a rather inferior position, for some of the illustrative examples quoted in the grammar have been taken from verse written on these lighter and more appealing themes. Verse of this kind became increasingly popular with the new-style patrons, especially in south Wales, which had long been exposed to powerful Norman-French influences. Some patrons, it is true, like Hopcyn ap Tomas (*c.* 1330–after 1403), of Ynystawe, who was described by the poet Meurug ab Iorwerth (*fl.c.* 1320–70) as 'the father of the great good art of poetry', or Ieuan Llwyd and his son, Rhydderch, pointedly eschewed the lighter, more secularly orientated verse. But their number was constantly decreasing from the mid-fourteenth century onwards, and it is difficult to escape the conclusion that, despite Einion Offeiriad's elevated canons, the influence exerted by the Church on Welsh bardic verse, though by no means completely eradicated, was henceforward considerably diminished. Nor is it in the least surprising that this attenuation of ecclesiastical influence becomes increasingly evident during the second half of the fourteenth century, for during that period there was unquestionably a marked decline in the general standard of clerical scholarship and a significant increase in the strength of anti-clerical trends.

BIBLIOGRAPHY

Texts and Critical Studies

D. J. Bowen, 'Dafydd ap Gwilym a Datblygiad y Cywydd', *Llên Cymru*, 8 (1964), 1–32.

Rachel Bromwich, *Trioedd Ynys Prydein* (Cardiff, 1961; 2nd edn, Cardiff, 1978).

Eadem, 'Gwaith Einion Offeiriad a Barddoniaeth Dafydd ap Gwilym', in J. E. Caerwyn Williams (ed.), *Ysgrifau Beirniadol X* (Dinbych, 1977), 157–80.

Eadem, *Tradition and Innovation in the Poetry of Dafydd ap Gwilym* (Cardiff, 1967; reprinted 1972).

Eadem, *'Trioedd Ynys Prydein' in Welsh Literature and Scholarship*. The G. J. Williams Memorial Lecture (Cardiff, 1969).

D. Gwenallt Jones, 'Rhethreg yng Nghyfundrefn y Beirdd', *Y Llenor*, xii (1933), 158–72.

Saunders Lewis, *Braslun o Hanes Llenyddiaeth Gymraeg . . . hyd at 1535* (Caerdydd, 1932), 51–69.

Idem, *Gramadegau'r Penceirddiaid*. Darlith Goffa G. J. Williams (Caerdydd, 1967).

Idem, 'The Essence of Welsh Literature' and 'Dafydd ap Gwilym' in Alun R. Jones and Gwyn Thomas (eds), *Presenting Saunders Lewis* (Cardiff, 1973), 154–8 and 159–63 respectively.

D. Myrddin Lloyd, 'How to Praise Each Other', in D. M. and E. M. Lloyd (eds), *A Book of Wales* (London and Glasgow, 1953), 102–4.

A. T. E. Matonis, 'Traditions of Panegyric in Welsh Poetry: the Heroic and the Chivalric', *Speculum*, 53 (1978), 667–87.

Thomas Parry, 'Datblygiad y Cywydd', *Transactions of the Honourable Society of Cymmrodorion*, 1939, 209–31.

Idem, 'The Welsh Metrical Treatise Attributed to Einion Offeiriad', The Sir John Rhys Memorial Lecture, 1961. *Proceedings of the British Academy*, xlvii (1961), 177–95.

E. I. Rowlands, 'Iolo Goch', in James Carney and David Greene (eds), *Celtic Studies: Essays in Memory of Angus Matheson, 1912–62*, (London, 1968; 2nd edn, 1969), 124–46.

Idem, 'Bardic Lore and Education', *Bulletin of the Board of Celtic Studies*, xxxii (1985), 143–55.

Gwyn Thomas, *Y Traddodiad Barddol* (Caerdydd, 1976).

G. J. Williams, 'Gramadeg Gutun Owain', *Bulletin of the Board of Celtic Studies*, iv (1928), 207–21.

G. J. Williams and E. J. Jones (eds), *Gramadegau'r Penceirddiaid* (Caerdydd, 1934), especially pp. 15–18, 34–7, 55–8, 131–6, 147–8, 150–1 and 198–203.

Historical and Intellectual Background

E. Bréhier, *La Philosophie du Moyen Âge* (Paris, 1937).

E. R. Curtius, *European Literature and the Latin Middle Ages*, translated from the German by W. R. Trask (London-New York, 1953).

R. R. Davies, 'Colonial Wales', *Past and Present*, No. 65 (1974), 3–23.

Edgar de Bruyne, *Etudes d'esthétique mediévale* (3 vols., Ghent, 1964).

E. Gilson, *La Philosophie au Moyen Âge* (Paris, 1944).

Idem, *A History of Christian Philosophy in the Middle Ages* (London, 1955).

Friedrich Heer, *The Intellectual History of Europe*, translated from the German by Jonathan Steinberg (London, 1966).

Idem, *The Medieval World*, translated from the German by Janet Sondheimer (London, 1962).

Gordon Leff, *Medieval Thought* (Pelican, 1958).

D. Myrddin Lloyd, 'Estheteg yr Oesoedd Canol', *Llên Cymru*, i (1950), 153–68 and 220–38.

Arthur O. Lovejoy, *The Great Chain of Being: A Study of the History of an Idea* (Harvard University Press, Cambridge, Massachusetts, 1936; sixth reprinting, 1957).

Glyn Roberts, 'The Significance of 1284', *Aspects of Welsh History* (Cardiff, 1969, 281–7.

Idem, 'Wales and England: Antipathy and Sympathy, 1282–1485', ibid., 259–318.

E. M. W. Tillyard, *The Elizabethan World Picture* (London, 1943), chapter 4 on 'The Chain of Being'.

Glanmor Williams, *The Welsh Church from Conquest to Reformation* (Cardiff, 1962), especially 106–13 and 183–200.

Chapter 5

DAFYDD AP GWILYM

RACHEL BROMWICH

Poeta nascitur, non fit it has been said; 'a poet is born, not made.' One is tempted, however, to speculate as to how far genius may not receive its initial stimulus from a rare combination of circumstances peculiarly congenial to its flowering. In Dafydd ap Gwilym the birth of a poetic genius who is acknowledged to have been the greatest that Wales has known coincided miraculously in both time and place with an unprecedented opportunity to mate the new with the old, the foreign with the national idiom, and to draw the Welsh poetic tradition, if only briefly, into the mainstream of contemporary European literature. It is because of Dafydd ap Gwilym that we look back upon the fourteenth century as a major turning-point and a fresh beginning in Welsh poetry, just as it is because of Chaucer that we regard the fourteenth century in England in much the same way.

Paradoxically, the circumstances which were so auspicious for the nurture of Dafydd's exotic genius arose from that very state of traumatic flux in society and in politics, with all their disruptive implications for the ancient culture of Wales, which followed upon the conquest of 1282, and which have already been described in Chapter I. The traditional bonds of poetic patronage became loosened at the very time that ideas and influences from the outside world were flooding into Wales as never before: this was a time, to adapt the words of R. T. Jenkins, when Wales held her windows wide open to the outside world, and yet retained, in spite of all, an assured confidence in her individual national identity. For the poet, the post-conquest atmosphere was one which proved more stimulating than it was depressing (though deeper undertones of personal sadness and national frustration are from time to time explicit in his work), enabling him to achieve a highly original and personal synthesis between the new modes and the metrical and linguistic expertise which he had inherited in full measure from his poetic forebears. Here again, fortune favoured Dafydd's birth, for Dyfed on the western sea-board where he was born and which had been the home of his ancestors, and Morgannwg in the south-east which was the home of his later patron Ifor ap Llywelyn, were just those areas where assimilation of Norman-French cultural influences had been implanted since the early years of the Norman conquest of England, and had thus been gaining ground for more than two centuries before Dafydd's birth, and to a degree quite unparalleled in independent and culturally conservative Gwynedd. In the south there existed a society which was more than ready for a poet or poets who could give fitting expression to a perplexingly altered world, with its new ideas and widened horizons. The traditional maxim that in Wales 'the South initiates and the North conserves' has in no instance been more fully realized than in the unique phenomenon of Dafydd ap Gwilym.

Since the datable elements in Dafydd's poetry point to the 1340s and 50s as his period of maximum production, it has been estimated that the poet may have been born about 1320. We have no certain knowledge as to the date of his death: he may have died at a relatively early age, and in any case there is no evidence which suggests that he was still active as a poet in the final quarter of the century. On the basis of his contemporary Gruffudd Gryg's poem to the yew tree above Dafydd's grave 'by the monastery wall of Ystrad Fflur' it is generally believed that he was buried at Strata Florida Abbey, not many miles away from his early home. An ancient tradition gives Dafydd's birth-place as 'Bro Gynin'—a *plasty* or substantial homestead (now destroyed) whose site has been identified as lying beside a ford on the little river Stewi, close to the modern farm-house of Bro Gynin Fach, and in the parish of Llanbadarn Fawr, just outside the castle and chartered borough which was later to be called Aberystwyth. His family was one of *uchelwyr* (descendants of the native landed nobility: there is no exact English equivalent for the term) who had held powerful and lucrative offices under the English Crown in south-west Wales for at least a century and a half previously. The family traced descent from a certain 'Gwynfardd Dyfed' and his son 'Cuhelyn Fardd'—progenitors from whom a number of other families in south and west Wales also claimed to be descended. Dr Geraint Gruffydd has drawn attention to the fact that the name of 'Cuhelyn Fardd' is to be found as that of the recipient to whom a praise-poem in the *Black Book of Carmarthen* is addressed—a poem which probably dates from the early years of the twelfth century. Since the family were not professional bards, but were *uchelwyr* of noble descent, there is in the existence of this poem a suggestion, which is borne out by the epithet *Gerdd Gymell* or *Gerdd Gynnil* ('song-imposing' or 'song-accomplished') which the genealogy attaches to yet another of his forebears, that Dafydd may have inherited from his ancestors a long tradition of practising poetry in the role of 'gifted amateurs', unbound by the relatively rigid bardic conventions with respect to subject-matter and mode of treatment which had bound professional poets throughout the intervening centuries. He may thus have enjoyed as a part of his natural inheritance a freedom to make innovations in the tradition such as had been enjoyed in twelfth-century Gwynedd and Powys by the poet-princes Hywel ab Owain Gwynedd and Owain Cyfeiliog.

Whether or not it is true that Dafydd's assured mastery of the traditional techniques of bardic verse as practised by the court-poets of the preceding centuries came to him as a family legacy, handed down over the intervening generations from these ancestors, it seems certain that a more immediate cultural influence upon the poet in his early years was that of an uncle, Llywelyn ap Gwilym. Like his forebears already mentioned, Llywelyn was an official in the service of the English Crown, being constable of Newcastle Emlyn in Dyfed. He was also the owner of substantial properties, both in Emlyn itself and in the adjoining *cantref* of Cemais; these were at Dôl Goch beside the river Teifi and at Llystyn in Cemais. Llywelyn is recorded as having been one of a group of south Wales *uchelwyr* who swore allegiance to the Black Prince when he came to Wales in 1343. In two *awdlau* (odes), which the poet addressed to his uncle, Dafydd extols Llywelyn's wide learning and culture, describes him as a poet and a linguist (*prydydd* and *ieithydd*), and says that he 'knew all knowledge', and comprised within himself a complete *llyfr dwned* or 'book of Donatus' (this is a reference to the Bardic Grammar, discussed in Chapter III above). *Ys difai y'm dysgud* (faultlessly you instructed me) are Dafydd's words of his uncle. Bearing in mind the official position and high-level external contacts with which Llywelyn ap Gwilym is credited, it is reasonable to conclude that the wide culture which his nephew attributed to him must have ranged much further afield than the contents of the *llyfr dwned* alone, and that he is likely to have been proficient and at ease in both French and English. Not only was Llywelyn

Dafydd's bardic teacher to all appearance, therefore, but he was also in a position to have been a likely intermediary in introducing his nephew to literary influences which originated far beyond the borders of Wales—to new poetry, new stories, and by no means least important, to a new vocabulary. Of the very many French loan-words which were taken into Welsh during this period, and which were borrowed either directly from French or indirectly through the medium of medieval English, the earliest recorded instances cited in the dictionaries are quoted with impressive frequency from the works of Dafydd ap Gwilym. How many of these words were the poet's individual borrowings, and how many were already acclimatized in the colloquial Welsh spoken about him in Dyfed, we can never know for certain; but we can be sure that a widespread knowledge of French—if not also of English—could be relied upon on the part of the intimate and familiar audiences whom Dafydd primarily addressed; and this would in itself have greatly facilitated such extemporary borrowings by the poet, in which each word would have carried its individual nuance of meaning, the associations of which it is virtually impossible for us who live today to recapture. This seminal relationship between uncle and nephew may however have been short-lived: Dafydd's second *awdl* to Llywelyn is a *marwnad* (elegy) in which he clearly indicates that his uncle was killed by the violent hand of an assassin:

> Dyfed has been bereaved of its pride
> by the loss of the eagle of the enchanted land;
> today he is speechless
> who for many yesterdays was a gifted speaker.
>
> Till now, Llywelyn—wealth, territory, and home
> you never closed against me;
> you who were the supreme lord of all arts—
> open now to me, I ask you, silent one.
>
> Woe to the sad nephew who remains to see it
> —awakening the deep abyss of memory—
> yonder motley court in ruins
> and the Llystyn a home of desolation.

Since a new constable was appointed at Newcastle Emlyn in 1346, Llywelyn's death may be presumed to have occurred shortly before —or, possibly, shortly after—that date.

Here then, on the banks of the Teifi, and in fruitful and sympathetic communion with his uncle, it is indeed most likely, as Mr Dafydd Bowen has indicated, that Dafydd ap Gwilym first began to compose poetry which treated of new and lighter themes in a new and more personal vein than had hitherto been customary, and in the newly-developed metrical form of the *cywydd*: couplets of seven-syllabled lines, rhyming asymetrically, which in the verse of Dafydd ap Gwilym and his contemporaries became endowed with full *cynghanedd* (see Chapter IX below). Dafydd's *cywyddau* are normally between thirty and sixty lines in length; only rarely do they exceed this length by a small amount. Just what may have been the part played by Dafydd ap Gwilym himself in extending the use of the *cywydd* and in winning popularity for it, is a matter on which we can have no certainty, and can do little more than speculate: some considerations affecting the problem will be discussed in the following chapter. Before the middle of the fourteenth century *cywyddau* were being composed by Dafydd ap Gwilym, and in all probability by some at least of his contemporaries, notably by Iolo Goch; the *cywydd* gained rapidly in popularity among their successors, so that by the end of the century it had won a secure and lasting prestige which it was never again to lose, having become an accepted medium for *canu mawl* or traditional praise-poetry no less than for the new *canu serch*—the poetry of love and nature which is associated above all with the name of Dafydd ap Gwilym. This is not to say, however, that Dafydd ever rejected the older *awdlau* metres as the most fitting mode of expression for certain specified subjects which were to be treated in a special manner; indeed, it is highly probable that he composed *awdlau* as occasion demanded throughout the whole course of his life.

We do not know when it was that Dafydd left Dyfed and took to wandering; the departure from his early home, it has been suggested, may have followed closely upon his uncle's death, and may well have occurred as a direct consequence of it. Nor do we know when it was that there first began the poet's close association with Ifor ap Llywelyn, or Ifor *Hael* (Ifor the Generous), the patron who was to play a part fully as important in his poetic development as had Llywelyn ap Gwilym in his early years. To Ifor, as to Llywelyn, Dafydd addressed both *awdlau* (two in each case), and a sequence of *englynion*. There are also extant two *awdlau* addressed by him to other patrons—Hywel ap Goronwy, dean of Bangor, and Ieuan

Llwyd of Genau'r Glyn, an *awdl farwnad* to 'Angharad', a satire of a rival poet, Rhys Meigen, a devotional *awdl* to Christ, and some *englynion* of contrition, linked to the words of a fourteenth-century Latin hymn sung after the Mass. These *awdlau* all in their different ways exhibit in full measure the metrical techniques of the *Gogynfeirdd*, together with their rich stores of vocabulary and of traditional metaphor. For instance, Dafydd refers to Llywelyn, perhaps surprisingly, as *Deifr helgud* (pursuer of the men of Deira), and to Ifor as *Einglgrwydr* (scatterer of the Angles), and as *yn rhoi Deifr ar esyth* (putting the men of Deira on biers)—phrases which bear witness to a traditional memory of the *Gododdin* and of the poetry of the 'Old North', which had come down through generations of poets: such phrases as these, even after their exact significance had become forgotten, would still have struck some chord of recognition in the poet's audience, as symbols which were loaded with evocative power. The *marwnad* for Llywelyn reiterates the recurrent Celtic elegiac theme of the lament for the deserted home, and the manner in which the poet addresses his dead uncle directly, calling upon him to rise up and answer, is another recurrent feature of elegies both in Welsh and in Irish, and is therefore a feature of high antiquity among the Celtic peoples. Here too is the imagery characteristic of the praise-poetry of preceding generations: Llywelyn and Ifor are in turn referred to metaphorically as a stag, a hawk, a lion, an eagle. Dafydd's abusive satire of Rhys Meigen presents the opposite side of the traditional bardic coin, and serves to remind us that in Wales, as in Ireland, satire and eulogy were the two complementary facets of the bardic art, and that the deadly effects attributed to satire help to emphasize the great social significance traditionally attached to praise-poetry.

Whatever the precise nature of the relation between Dafydd and Ifor ap Llywelyn may have been—and there can be little doubt but that it was one which was highly fruitful in the intellectual stimulus which it provided for the poet—it was in the terms of one of the *penceirddiaid*, or poets of the highest grade in the old society, that Dafydd envisaged his position with regard to Ifor in the poems which he addressed to him. He compares his privileges in Ifor's home with those enjoyed by Taliesin from the favour of his patron Urien Rheged. In similar vein, the epithet *Hael* (the Generous) which Dafydd bestowed in gratitude upon him, and which has clung to Ifor ever since, derives from an implicit comparison of

Ifor's generosity with that of the legendary heroes Nudd, Rhydderch, and Mordaf, who are grouped together in the triad of the *Tri Hael* or 'Three Generous Men': a triad which for obvious reasons was the most popular of all triads among the bards at all times. As Dafydd puts it:

> You have given me treasure, a pledge of love:
> I bestow on you the great name of Rhydderch.

This quotation comes, in fact, from one of the four extant *cywyddau* in which, in addition to his two *awdlau* and his *englynion*, Dafydd sang the praise of Ifor. This group of four poems is of the very greatest importance, not only as illustrating the poet's concept of his independent and mutually beneficial relationship with his friend and patron, but also because the forms effectively demonstrate the fusing and blending of two traditions. We can observe how elements from the familiar imagery of praise-poetry are transferred into the new *cywydd* metre; and in addition, as Mr Dafydd Bowen has aptly pointed out, these *cywyddau* bear the indubitable stamp of their maker in the highly characteristic manner in which the imagery employed elsewhere by Dafydd in his *cywyddau* of love and nature is here adapted to the purposes of praise-poetry. Essential to early bardic verse in both Wales and Ireland had always been the concept that all Nature reflects the qualities and fortunes of the lord of the land. So here, in a *cywydd* to Ifor, Nature's luxuriance is shown to reflect the genial prosperity associated with his home at Basaleg, just as in his *awdl* on his patron's death, the accompanying storms and swollen rivers reflect Nature's sorrow at the event. And just as, on another occasion, in a poem of greeting to summer, Dafydd says that he 'laughed' at seeing the leafy 'hair' on the birch-tree, so here he characteristically personifies the trees in their summer foliage in a copse near Ifor's home (its name, Y Wennallt, survives to this day):

> There is no tree in Y Wennallt
> whose head-dress is not green
> and her branches interwoven,
> her gown and her petticoat hedge her in.
> Is it not a joyful sight
> for a poet to see this fair assemblage?

Finally, Dafydd crowns his gratitude and praise of Ifor with a memorable hyperbole:

> As far as man may travel furthest,
> as far as summer sun revolves on its course,
> as far as wheat is sown
> and fair dew-fall moistens,
> as far as the unclouded eye may see
> —strong he is—and as far as ear may hear,
> as far as the Welsh language is known
> and as far as fair crops grow:
> Splendid Ifor, of sprightly ways
> —long thy sword—will thy praise be sown.

Ifor's praise is 'sown' just as in other poems Dafydd claims to have 'sown' the praise of his chosen sweetheart throughout the length and breadth of Wales. The poems to Ifor fully substantiate Mr Eurys Rowlands's assertion that 'Ifor Hael's patronage of Dafydd ap Gwilym is one of the most important facts in Welsh poetry' because of the manner in which they give to the theme of praise not only a new metrical form but also a completely new style, making it more personal and more informal than it had ever been before, by introducing overt and recognizable elements evocative of *cywyddau serch*—the poetry of love and nature for which we may conclude that Dafydd ap Gwilym had already won a name for himself. The purpose for which Dafydd employed *awdl* and *englyn* was a different one: for his religious poems and for his serious elegies to dead friends and patrons (his uncle, the joint elegy on Ifor and his wife Nest, and on Angharad), while he employed the emerging medium of the *cywydd* for themes which were themselves new and which were essentially different from the traditional themes of serious praise-poetry—for his relaxed, informal, and at times even 'playful' poems to Ifor, and for his addresses, in the form of 'fictitious' *marwnadau* to friends and fellow-poets who were in fact still living at the time. (This *genre* of poems will be discussed more fully in the following chapter.) It is true that both Dafydd and his contemporaries employed the form of the *cywydd* as well as that of the *awdl* for poems of serious religious devotion: indeed, the evidence suggests that, of the various established themes of traditional praise-poetry, it may have been devotional rather than conventional secular praise which became first transferred into the new medium of the *cywydd*. In the event it was this new verse-form which Dafydd moulded into the medium for his most inspired creations: for the poems which express his most extensive imaginative range, his greatest metrical and verbal resilience, depth of experience and sensitivity, and his near mystic insight into the marvels of Nature—poems whose significance rises immeasurably high above and beyond what might legitimately be expected of the intellectual concepts to be enshrined in so deliberately 'frivolous' a framework as that which he devised for them—the light poetry of love and of love's intrigues.

However long, or however short-lived, may have been the period of Dafydd's close association with Ifor ap Llywelyn (living, apparently, as a member of his household), it is clear that during the span of his life-time the poet travelled widely over the length and breadth of Wales, and that he appears to have known Gwynedd as intimately as he knew Dyfed and Glamorgan. There is no reliable evidence that he ever crossed the English border. We may assume that he would have been a welcome guest in the houses of hospitable *uchelwyr* over wide areas of the Principality, in homes where he might expect to meet with small and sympathetic audiences of familiar friends, before whom he could recite his *cywyddau*, often accompanying his own recital on the harp; and knowing that he could depend on his listeners to appreciate his art and his technical *finesse*, to understand his hidden allusions, his jokes, his subtle innuendos and his double meanings. A chief reason, probably, why we have no manuscript of Dafydd's poems written for nearly a century after his own life-time is that his *cywyddau* must have circulated originally among such audiences by oral, word-of-mouth channels, both in his own day and among more widely-dispersed audiences for many years afterwards. There can be no doubt but that the poet's life was rich in human relationships, and some of his friendships are recorded in his poems—with the poets who were his contemporaries, Madog Benfras, Gruffudd ab Adda, and Gruffudd Gryg, with the *uchelwr* Rhydderch ab Ieuan Llwyd of Glyn Aeron (renowned for his ownership of the famous *White Book of Rhydderch*), with Hywel ap Goronwy, the dean of Bangor. In one poem Dafydd says that he is *gŵr â chorun* (a man with a tonsure), which must imply that he had qualified at some time of his life for minor religious orders—a not uncommon proceeding. Certainly Dafydd described himself in a number of passages as a member of the *clêr*—a term which in Welsh is used as the equivalent of the *clerici vagantes*, the 'wandering scholars' or *joculatores* of other countries. But the word is also capable of retaining an older meaning, in which it is a comprehensive and entirely non-committal term for poets in general, and it is occasionally confusing that Dafydd is capable of using *clêr* and *clerwr* in both senses: positively, when he speaks of himself as one of a body of honourable practitioners of the craft of poetry, and negatively and disparagingly when he contrasts himself with the *clêr ofer* or 'vain versifiers' (such as the unfortunate Rhys Meigen whom he satirized)—poets who lacked his own high qualifications.

In the course of his wanderings over Wales, Dafydd evidently became well acquainted with the life of both the newly-founded Norman boroughs, as well as with those which had been more long-established—with Rhosyr, or Newborough in Anglesey, with Caernarfon and Aberystwyth. He was familiar with their streets and taverns and ware-houses. He knew also the cathedral city of Bangor. The boroughs, with their mixed populations, commercial interests, and generally bustling life, provide a likely setting for one or two of Dafydd's most riotous poems of amatory escapade. But it was in the wilderness of the intervening countryside, the dense and indeed partially uncharted woodland which must in the fourteenth century have extended over much of Wales, that Dafydd found the characteristically congenial setting for those *cywyddau* of love and nature which were the really new development in Welsh poetry for which he is primarily responsible, and on the quality of which his exalted reputation must ultimately stand or fall. The forest with all the varied life which it shelters is the focus for his most significant verse; ostensibly it is the setting for the poet's *oed* or tryst with 'Morfudd' or with some other sweetheart, but on occasion the forest scene is described for its own sake, at its spring awakening or at its summer meridian, and always as the setting for the busy activities of its natural inhabitants, in particular of the birds. *Gwell yw ystafell os tyf* means literally 'a room is better if it grows', and Dafydd employs the phrase in speaking of the *deildy* or house of leaves and branches which he has constructed to be a shelter for himself with his beloved. The *deildy* is the antithesis of the conventional man-made dwelling; its life, untrammelled by convention, is the calculated opposite of normal gregarious human society. It is thus that Dafydd reports the advice which the Cock-Thrush has given him:

I would give you good counsel
for the long days of May: do it, if you will.
Sit beneath the birch-tree castle
—God knows there was never a better house—
and beneath thy head a pillow
of leaves, the comely feathers of the forest;
and let my birch-tree be above your head,
a fair, gleaming fortress of coverlets.

At the symbolic centre of the forest life are the birds, Nature's own poets and priests, in whose activities Dafydd discerns the implicit counterpart of his own activity as a poet. Their essential concern, like that of the poet, is to offer thanks and praise to God for His miraculous creation. Thus it is that Dafydd fancies the Thrush and the Nightingale as celebrating the Mass in the forest:

I heard in perfect utterance
prolonged, unfailing chanting;
and the Gospel read to the parish
clearly—no unseemly haste.
There was lifted above the ash-tree mound
a fair leaf as a wafer.
And the Nightingale, slender, fair, and eloquent
from the corner of the thicket, close by,
the poetess of the valley, rang out the Sanctus bell
to the assembly, with sharp whistle,
and lifted the consecrated Host
to the sky above the copse
with devotion to our Lord the Father,
a chalice of ecstasy and love.

The individual characteristics of different birds are apprehended with exact and loving detail. Of the Thrush he says:

What composition could be sweeter than his little whistle?
Far across the land his voice is heard from the thicket and his loud shout.

Leaving the woods for the sea-shore, the Seagull is

Of the hue of snow or of the white moon,
unpolluted is your beauty,
a patch of sunlight, gauntlet of the salt sea.

You ride lightly on the wave,
swift, proud, fish-eating bird.

He observes the birds with a wondering admiration, which comes closest to mysticism in describing the Skylark's upward flight:

Man sees you up aloft
truly, when day is at its longest.
When you come thus to worship
God Three-in-One has bestowed on you the gift to do so.
No branch of tree high above the world supports you
—you have your own language—
but the grace of the righteous Father,
His abundant miracles and his design.

Such descriptions as these, and others like them, in which the poet's deepest feelings of beauty, awe, and reverence are focused with astonishing clarity of detail upon particular birds or other creatures, occur in his verse but as the prologue to a transition into a world of fantasy, in which the creature described is imaginatively dispatched by the poet with a message of love to the girl he is addressing. Significantly, it is birds alone whom Dafydd endows with the power of speech, imagining them as entering into dialogue with him, and occasionally, indeed, as responding tartly enough to the poet's requested embassy; as does the Woodcock, who refuses the poet's mission both on the grounds of bad weather and because, according to him, the girl whom he is wooing has already chosen another companion. In 'The Magpie's Counsel' the busy, nest-building bird is imagined as turning upon the poet and rebuking him for his impotent and unproductive love-longing—and she receives from the poet in return a heady stream of vituperation which echoes closely the style and rich vocabulary of satirical invective practised by the bards over many previous generations:

The Magpie said—an indictment of (my) anguish—
proud, sharp-beaked upon the thorn-bush:
'Great is thy fuss, a vain and bitter chant,
Old Man, all by thyself;
it were better for thee, by Mary, garrulous of speech,
beside the fire, you old grey man,
rather than here, amid the dew and rain
in the greenwood, in a chilly shower . . .'

'As for you, black-beaked Magpie,
hellish, very savage bird . . .
your nest is like a gorse-bush,
a thick creel of withered sticks.
You have speckled black plumage, precious, perfect,
your looks are ugly, and you have a raven's head,
motley-hued, with ugly home and raucous voice,
and every sort of far-fetched forceful speech
you have learned, black speckled wing',

—and the poet undertakes, if ever again he sees a magpie's nest, to destroy both eggs and nestlings. In the poems to the Woodcock and the Magpie, the love-messenger theme is effectively turned inside-out by the poet.

The convention of these *llatai* or 'love-messenger' poems (the word appears to be derived from *llad* meaning a gift) would seem to have been Dafydd's individual creation: not, indeed, by virtue of the initial idea of sending a bird or animal as a messenger of love —for this device can be paralleled in many other literatures, and certain of the *Gogynfeirdd* had previously played upon the fantasy of dispatching their horses upon such amatory errands—but because of the poet's preliminary invocation of his messenger and the elaborate and admiring detail with which the messenger is described. In one of the greatest of all his poems it is the Wind itself, characteristically personified as a living creature, whom the poet dispatches as his ambassador of love:

Sky Wind with hardy tumult
that journeys yonder with powerful clamour,
strange, rough-voiced creature,
most venturesome of all, though without foot or wing.
Amazing how marvellously you were sent
out footless from the sky's pantry,
and how swiftly you run now across the slope above.
No need for a swift horse to carry you
nor bridge nor boat at river-crossing.
You will not drown, you have been forewarned,
nor be entangled, being without corners.
Nest-seizing, no one indicts you
(even) though you were to winnow leaves.
Neither swift troop nor governor's hand restrains you,
nor blue blade nor flood nor rain.
Neither officer nor body-guard can hold you

to your day, scatterer of the feathers of the tree-tops.
No mother's son can strike you, a false mention (i.e. 'spare the thought')
no fire burns you, nor deception weakens you.
No eye sees you in your great empty lair;
a thousand hear you, nest of the great rain;
swift-natured annotator of the clouds,
fair leaper across nine fallow lands . . .
You fly the length of the world
bold on the slope, be above tonight;
ah, man, go to Uwch Aeron
clear and fair, with audible voice.
Do not stop, nor falter,
nor fear the Bwa Bach,
that complaining accuser, jealousy-serving.
That land, which nourished her, is closed to me.
Woe is me that I placed serious love
on Morfudd, my golden girl,
the maid who has locked me to the land
—Run forth, above, to her father's home.

'Morfudd' is named in a number of Dafydd's *cywyddau* as the poet's most favoured sweetheart, and according to Dafydd's own statement, he composed 'seven and seven score' *cywyddau* to her (though nothing like this number has come down) and had caused her praises to be sung by the *clêr* to the uttermost bounds of Wales. Morfudd's home, like that of Dafydd, seems to have lain in the *cantref* of Uwch Aeron in Ceredigion; the *Bwa Bach* ('Little Bow' of 'Little Hunchback') was apparently the epithet by which her husband—and hence Dafydd's hated rival—was known (his real name is given once as 'Cynfrig Cynin'). Behind Dafydd's many allusions to Morfudd and to her elusiveness and tantalizing treatment of him it seems likely enough that there lies a genuine story of deep and passionate love on the side of the poet, culminating in the final bitter frustration caused to him by Morfudd's marriage to his rival. Yet the reference to the girl's parental home in the final line of the above quotation suggests that 'The Wind' was inspired by circumstances before Morfudd's marriage, at a time when the poet had stirred up so much hostility by his attentions to her that his own homeland was henceforth debarred to him. In so far as it is either possible or legitimate to draw conclusions about the poet's real experiences from the internal evidence of the poems it would seem that Morfudd was the single object of the poet's lasting love, and that in spite of passing adventures and attachments to a number of other girls to whom he addressed poems ('Dyddgu' is the most prominent of these, a contrast to Morfudd in every characteristic, remote and aristocratic, and it would seem, for ever unattainable)—he brought considerable trouble upon himself by continuing to pursue her with his unremitting attentions even after she had become married to the 'Little Hunchback' and had become a mother.

Descriptions such as we have in 'The Wind' of Dafydd's various imaginary love-messengers, descriptions of the inhabitants of the forest, and above all of such natural forces or material objects as in one way or another acted as impediments to his assignations, are all made occasions for the poet's use of the technical device known as *dyfalu*. This consists in a prolonged description of the object or creature concerned, by means of a string of imaginative comparisons and hyperbolical similes, which draw upon the full range of the poet's resources in vocabulary and inspired imagery. It is thus that he describes the Star which leads him on his way to Morfudd's home:

> Radiantly from God on high
> she is a candle in the cloudless sky,
> a candle whose beauty will not fade
> and which may not by deceit be stolen.
> The wind of autumn will not quench her:
> she is the consecrated wafer of Heaven's roof.
> The cowardly water of torrents will not drown her—
> she is the waiting-woman of the meal-platter of the saints.
> No thief's hands can reach towards her—
> (in) yonder base of the Trinity's bowl.
> It is useless for any man from his dwelling (here)
> to chase after this pearl of Mary.
> She shines over all lands
> a golden coin of refined yellow gold,
> a true buckler of light
> she is the image of the shining sun in the sky.

The starry heavens represented for Dafydd the supreme example of the perfect order of God's creation; as indeed they did for his contemporary Chaucer, and for a number of other medieval poets.

There are indications that *dyfalu* was closely bound up with the emergence of the *cywydd* in the fourteenth century; but in fact the ultimate origins of the device are much older than this in both Welsh and Irish, and they exhibit an even closer alignment with the richly figurative and elaborately compounded language of bardic satire and vituperation than they do with riddles. It is indeed noticeable that Dafydd ap Gwilym employs the device 'pejoratively' for satire, far more frequently than he does 'positively' for praise (as in the above quotation); he employs it most frequently of all when he abuses some object or creature, or some natural force which has acted as an obstruction to his love-making. Ice is described as 'thick plate-armour of the breast of the valleys'; the Mist is

> a thick, grey, weakly-trailing fleece,
> like smoke, hooded cowl of the plain,
> a hedge of rain, impeding progress:
> coat-armour of the oppressive shower.

The Hare (whose hunt is but a symbol of the poet's own love-pursuit) is described with rich invective:

> Hermaphrodite who on the clean loam
> would give muscular pains to a slow feeble hound.
> Short-of-jaw, bob-tailed, fed on young shoots,
> I know the fate of the grey, white-trousered one.

In 'The Wave on the River Dyfi' Dafydd pleads with the river in spate to allow him to cross to Llanbadarn so that he may visit Morfudd: the *dyfalu* here is skilfully inverted, so that the poet becomes the butt of his own wide-ranging comparisons:

> Did anyone's lips ever sing
> so much praise as I of your masterly tumult,
> sail's companion, gem of the waves, loop of the sea?
> There is no wind sent by the planet's signs
> nor sudden grievous onset between two resisting banks,
> nor swift battle, nor strong branch,
> nor shoulder of horse or man,
> that I have not compared (well do I know the anguish),
> strong forceful wave, to your own strength.
> There was never organ nor harp,
> nor man's tongue with faultless praise
> that I have not adjudged as strong,
> grey flood, as is your splendid voice.

It is evident from this passage that in Dafydd's theory of poetry the art of *dyfalu* was among the most essential of poetic skills: it was in fact for him the very essence of poetry, and by no means the least of the means through which he expressed his personal vision of creation.

The extracts from Dafydd's poems which I have quoted in the above pages in unadorned prose translation, will at least have given the reader some idea of the linear movement of the poet's verse, with its parallel images and comparisons (*dyfalu*) and its frequent interjected and parenthetical phrases. *Sangiadau* (a name originally bestowed by Sir John Morris-Jones) has won the acceptance of long usage for these interjected phrases, which are usually of an exclamatory or descriptive kind. As a poetic device, they have their origin far back in the earliest Welsh poetry that has come down, but they hold a very important place in the technique of the *cywydd* as this was developed in the fourteenth century, and it is as essential to understand their function in the poetry of Dafydd ap Gwilym and his contemporaries as it is to understand the use by them of the device of *dyfalu.* In their simplest form such phrases occupy part of a line only, but in Dafydd's poetry they are sometimes continued over one or more lines at a time; running parallel to the poet's main statement, yet always subordinated to it. The linguistic constituents of the *sangiadau* are conditioned by the requirements of *cynghanedd* and rhyme, to which they give obvious assistance; yet as Dafydd employs the device, his *sangiadau* very rarely, if at all, fail to make an essential contribution to his total meaning, and therefore—however difficult they may often be—they can never safely be ignored.

Any attempt to translate Dafydd ap Gwilym's poetry, therefore, must take account alike of the complex requirements of *cynghanedd* and of the parallel but subordinated statements in his *sangiadau*, as well as of the depths of meaning which may at any time underlie his use of particular words and phrases. By intricate innuendo, and frequently by an intentional ambiguity attained by a complex play upon the richly varied nuances both of his traditional vocabulary and of the new words of French origin which were at his disposal, Dafydd evolved for himself a poetic medium of a degree of complexity which had never previously been envisaged in Welsh, and which at times by its very nature defies all attempts at adequate paraphrase or transposition into another language. It frequently happens that only a very restricted part of his meaning can be conveyed by translation: too often it becomes a matter of opting for a single meaning out of a wide choice of equally valid but never completely adequate alternatives. The task of the would-be translator of Dafydd's poetry is therefore from the outset virtually self-defeating: accuracy of meaning must necessarily give place to metrical effect, or *vice versa*. This is why the ingenious and praiseworthy attempts of a succession of verse-translators, most recently of Professor Clancy and Mr Conran, to convey something of the movement of their originals without falling too far short of offering the best equivalent in English for the poet's actual words, can encompass what at best can only be, as they would admit, a very qualified success. The fact that poetry is untranslatable was never more true than in the case of Dafydd ap Gwilym: there can be no substitute for acquaintance with the original poems.

It is for these reasons, coupled with the fact that Dafydd composed in a language which has, on the whole, not been widely known outside the borders of his own country, that Dafydd's status as one of the major poets of the European Middle Ages has very rarely received anything like its due recognition. Yet even on the basis of reading the poet's works in translation alone, Mr Peter Dronke has remarked with amazement in a recent article, which is of considerable importance from the comparative standpoint, on the breadth and versatility of Dafydd's poetic *repertoire*. We have his authority for the statement that Dafydd's subject-matter covers the complete span of the types of verse practised by the court-poets of medieval Europe, whether in Latin or in the vernaculars; that is to say: (i) religious verse; (ii) secular praise-poems (i.e. formal elegies and greetings to patrons); (iii) satire and controversy with rival poets (for Dafydd's poetic contest with Gruffudd Gryg see the following chapter); (iv) informal addresses to friends and fellow-poets (these would include the 'fictitious' *marwnadau*); and the whole range of love-poetry, comprising (v) subjective verse (i.e. reflections on love and addresses to the loved one); and (vi) objective verse (i.e. poems of dialogue and incident: these would include the *llatai* poems). Of course the first three categories listed above represent Dafydd's indigenous inheritance from his own native tradition: it is in the final three categories that he added to Welsh poetry a new dimension, which had only been foreshadowed in quite minor ways by any of the poets who were his predecessors.

As a poet of love, Dafydd asserts that Ovid was his master and his instructor; he describes himself as *dyn Ofydd* (Ovid's man), and for him *ofyddiaeth* and *cerdd Ofydd* were comprehensive terms which described love-poetry in general. From Ovid, by way of the Troubadours, derived ultimately the concepts found commonly among medieval poets, of love as a sickness, as an obsession, and as a form of warfare, as well as that of a science which was to be taught and learned. Dafydd asserts that:

> Wherever there may be fresh green trees
> I am no coward in the work of Ovid's book.

His avowed allegiance to Ovid—who is in fact the only foreign poet he ever so much as mentions—is an allegiance which was almost invariably claimed in his day by poets in other lands when treating of the love-theme: one may instance Dafydd's contemporary Geoffrey Chaucer, with his reverence for 'Venus' clerk Ovyde. 'This claim by Dafydd implies a significant recognition on his part of the existence of a literary tradition beyond that of Wales and differing markedly from it. But the real validity of the comparison with Ovid is limited to certain aspects only of Dafydd's poetry: that is to say, to the poems of incident and situation, composed in his lightest manner, which fall within the sixth category noted above, in which the poet recounts his amatory adventures (whether real or imaginary) in a relaxed, even 'conversational' and self-deprecatory style, and with a light irony which recalls not only Ovid, but more immediately, perhaps, the stance adopted by Chaucer when he, too, presents himself as an actor-observer in his own poems. 'The Girls of Llanbadarn' is an example; a poem in which Dafydd describes his distracted attention during Sunday Mass in Llanbadarn church, on overhearing the whispered comments on his personal appearance passed between two girls in the congregation. 'Trouble at a Tavern', the most vivid of these poems of incident, recounts the poet's chance encounter at an inn with a girl whom he entertains lavishly with food and wine; in attempting later at night to reach her room, he encounters a series of impediments, and noisily arouses the three sleeping English tinkers, Hickyn and Jenkin and Jack, who fear for the safety of their packs and immediately raise the hue-and-cry after the supposed Welsh thief: in the resultant confusion the poet escapes safely into the outer darkness. The excited, jerky movement of the verse, with its interjections and inverted *sangiadau* reflects admirably the anecdotal character of the poem: one can well imagine that the adventure (real or imaginary) would have lost nothing in the telling, as the poet recited it to his chosen circle of friends:

I got a wretched fall and made a noise
—it was by no means clever—
easier to rise (costly mischief)
clumsily than swiftly.
I struck my skin above the ankle,
woe to my shank—not jumping safely—
against the edge of a stupid noisy stool
—ostler's work.
Getting up, a sorry tale (Welshmen love me)
I struck—too much eagerness is bad—
my brow on the table's edge,
where there was placed for me
—I could not jump free—
a common snare, madness to strike it,
a loose standing basin
with the clatter of a brass bowl.
The table fell, a mighty piece of gear,
with its two trestles and all the furniture,
the bowl cried out after me
—it could be heard afar—
I was an idiot, with the basin resounding
and the hounds baying after me.

In 'Defaming his Servant', which is located in the Anglesey borough of Rhosyr (later to be called Newborough), the poet sends a present of wine to a girl who rejects his advances out-of-hand, throwing the wine at his messenger's head. 'The Goose-Shed' tells how Dafydd took refuge from the fury of the 'Jealous Husband' in a goose-shed where he was set upon by an irate mother-goose, defending her young. This poem comes even closer than 'Trouble at a Tavern' to the stock pattern of the medieval *fabliaux*, belonging as they do to the timeless literature of jest and anecdote, which typically present the triangle situation of old husband (*Yr Eiddig, Le Jaloux*, 'The Jealous Husband'), young wife, and clerk-lover. It is as the latter that Dafydd consistently presents himself in his frustrated attempts to outwit *Yr Eiddig*—a pseudonym which is frequently, though perhaps not invariably, used to denote Morfudd's husband. He chooses for himself the clerk's role in a poem which echoes another popular medieval *genre*, the 'Clerk versus Knight' controversy, in which the relative advantages of members of the two professions to make satisfactory lovers are compared. Here the poet replies to a girl who reproaches him for cowardice by pointing out to her the advantages which his affectionate care for her could provide over the behaviour of a soldier-lover, who at the first rumour of war would make off for France or Scotland, and come back all covered with scars—if indeed he came back at all.

Others of Dafydd's poems of incident and situation echo unmistakably certain Continental themes and modes: in 'Under the Eaves' the would-be serenading poet is frustrated by torrential rain and snow; on another similar occasion, it is the icicles, hanging sharp as a harrow from the eaves of the girl's house, which torment him so that he abuses them in elaborate *dyfalu*. Yet another poem offers what can only be interpreted as a parody of the Continental *alba* or poem celebrating the dawn-parting of lovers: in lively colloquial dialogue the poet disputes his lady's assertion that dawn has come; the light, he says, is that of the moon and stars. She contradicts him:

'A likely tale; if it were true
why is the raven croaking up above?'

He: 'Vermin are attempting there
to kill her—keeping her from sleep.'

She: 'Hounds are barking yonder in the township,
and others too are fighting with each other.'

He: 'Believe me, my denial nears the mark:
it is the Hounds of Night cause this distress.'

(The allusion is to the *cŵn Annwn*, or fairy-pack of the legendary Gwyn ap Nudd).

Another poem apparently reiterates remotely the theme of the Continental *pastourelle,* or chance meeting of a poet with a country-girl, who after a dialogue rejects him; while 'The Magpie's Counsel' recalls those French and Provençal (and English) poems of greeting to spring, in which the poet contrasts his frustrated love-longing with the happy singing and mating of birds. Yet it would be fruitless to search for exact prototypes for these poems, either in Continental *fabliaux*, or in specific examples of the *alba, pastourelle*, or *sérénade*. They merely echo poems or songs that Dafydd had at some time heard recited, sung, or read: perhaps in the cultured homes of his aristocratic friends, perhaps in the less-exalted company of the taverns he may have frequented in the densely populated boroughs. Such poems and songs would have acted as catalysts in his mind, suggesting wholly new and original variants of his own making, in which native and foreign traditions were triumphantly blended. Nor can we ever be certain to what extent such themes had not already become acclimatized in the popular unrecorded verse of the *clêr*, so that Dafydd may even have come to know of them through the medium of Welsh. Dafydd ap Gwilym's supreme achievement was the integration and synthesizing in his poetry of multiple streams of tradition of disparate origin.

The task of establishing a reliable canon of Dafydd ap Gwilym's poems is one which presents enormous difficulties, and Dr Thomas Parry, who studied the problem in all the complexities presented by the innumerable manuscripts, regards it in its final details as virtually insoluble. This is partly because of the scarcity of early manuscripts of the poet's work: the earliest we have is a fragment dating from *circa* 1450, and containing only seven *cywyddau*; and there are no more than eight collections which date from a period earlier than 1500: presumably a number of others have been lost. From the fifteenth century onwards, scribes engaged in copying *cywyddau* were tempted to append the name of 'Dafydd ap Gwilym' to an increasingly large number of poems, which cannot by any means all have been the poet's work. The preservation and transmission of these over a long period of time, subsequently to their original composition, by purely oral channels, facilitated these false attributions to Dafydd of any *cywyddau* of doubtful authorship which chanced to be concerned with the twin subjects of love and nature. Previous oral transmission also inevitably increases the probability of textual contamination: there is more than one instance in Dr Parry's edition of couplets which are to be found elsewhere in compositions attributed to other poets; together with instances of identical lines and couplets which occur in more than one poem which has been accredited to Dafydd ap Gwilym himself.

The pioneer edition of the poet's work, *Barddoniaeth Dafydd ap*

Gwilym, edited by the scholars Owain Myfyr, William Owen Pughe, and Edward Williams (Iolo Morganwg), and published in 1789, contained 246 poems attributed to Dafydd, together with an 'Appendix' containing sixteen others, which in a brilliant study (in 1926) Professor G. J. Williams proved to be clever imitations of the poet's work by Iolo Morganwg. Of the poems in the body of the volume, Dr Parry rejected about 100 as spurious. In the introduction to the first edition of his *Gwaith Dafydd ap Gwilym*, he provided a valuable series of notes in which he explained his reasons for denying the authenticity of each one of these rejected poems, together with others attributed to the poet in various of the manuscript collections. These notes are very helpful as laying down some guidelines by which we may be helped to distinguish *cywyddau* composed in the fourteenth century from those of the fifteenth; though within the fourteenth century itself we still lack anything approaching secure criteria by which we may in all instances distinguish Dafydd's own work from that of some gifted contemporary. Briefly, Dr Parry's criteria for dating may be summarized as follows: (i) linguistic archaisms showing affinities with Middle Welsh grammatical and syntactical forms may be taken as evidence pointing to the earlier period, and hence favouring authenticity, as also does the occurrence of numerous compound words; (ii) certain indications provided by the *cynghanedd*, in particular a preponderance of *cynghanedd sain*, also favour a fourteenth-century date; (iii) in the earlier period, again, metrical requirements are dove-tailed into the sentence-structure in the movement of the *cywyddau*, so that in place of the neat self-contained couplets of the later centuries, we have sentences carried over many lines, the loose syntactical structure being assisted by the use of parenthetical *sangiadau* and by the device of tmesis or *torymadrodd*. Dr Parry would give weight to each one of these features, combined with the internal indications provided by the subject-matter, in assessing the claim of any individual poem to be regarded as authentic.

Nevertheless, as Dr Parry is the first to admit, the conclusions reached by him on this basis cannot be regarded as final in every case; and it is at once apparent that the so-called 'apocrypha' of rejected poems (now partly edited by Helen Fulton) contains a number of *cywyddau* of high quality which were previously attributed without question to Dafydd, and were thus included by Sir Ifor Williams in his volume of selections from the poet's work (1914;

1935). Seven of these poems, comprising the *cywyddau* on 'The Stars' and on 'The Snow', 'The Poet's Burial for Love', 'The Grove of Broom', 'A Girl's Cruelty' and a couple of poems urging a nun to forsake her calling in the interests of love, were subsequently included by Dr Parry in the *Oxford Book of Welsh Verse*, where they are assigned as a group to the fifteenth century, and printed under the caption 'Anonymous'. But the rejection of *Cywydd y Sêr* (The Stars) from the canon in Dr Parry's *magnum opus* called forth an early and vigorous protest from Mr Saunders Lewis; and Mr Dafydd Bowen has since added powerful and detailed arguments in favour of the authenticity both of this poem and of *Cywydd yr Eira* (The Snow). Neither scholar called in question the validity of Dr Parry's first two criteria for fourteenth-century dating as these are listed above (and it has never been claimed that either of these criteria can stand alone, unsupported by other evidence), but both emphasize that Dafydd himself practised the 'couplet-style' in a number of his accepted poems. Mr Bowen has shown that this style is particularly characteristic of Dafydd's passages of *dyfalu* (for instance in 'The Skylark' and 'The Mist')—a device which by its very nature does not admit of 'sentence-structured' lines with interpolated *sangiad* and *torymadrodd*. The excellence of both these poems consists in the intricacy of the passages of *dyfalu*, which on the one hand is 'positive' (a kind which is indeed rare except in Dafydd's own *cywyddau*) in the description of the Stars which appear to succour and guide the poet on his love-errand when he is lost on the moor at night:

> God was good, and lighted for me
> the rush-lights of the zodiac;
> in a dense shower, to cast out fear
> swift and proud appeared to us
> the Stars, the night-time's cherries.
> Shining was their brilliant host:
> bonfire-sparks of seven saints,
> flaming plums of the loveless moon,
> cheerful berries of her coldness

—and on the other hand initially 'negative' in the description of the snow-covered landscape which prevents the poet from sallying forth (the Snow is a *pla*, a 'plague'), but which manifestly changes its nature as the poem proceeds, to become an expression of wonder and astonishment at the beauty of the Snow:

White bees from Heaven
they pierce their way through Gwynedd;
whence does God send such a plague on us?
whence so many goose-feathers of the saints?
. . . Does anybody know in January
what is the host that is spitting down?
it is no less than the holy angels
busy with their carpentry in Heaven;
you see the trap-door of the flour-loft
has been drawn away from underneath.

Mr Dafydd Bowen has pointed out pertinently that these swiftly-changing piled-up metaphors must have depended for their effect upon the quick comprehension of a listening audience, together with its thorough familiarity with the convention of *dyfalu*. He has also shown that a number of poems accepted as authentic in *Gwaith Dafydd ap Gwilym* exhibit a similar structural development: a coloquial 'sentence-structured' opening, followed by a passage of 'couplet-structured' *dyfalu*, and frequently drawing to a close with a short group of simpler couplets. Of the two poems, 'The Stars' has undoubtedly the greater claims to be regarded as authentic, since on Dr Parry's own showing, its language, style, and craftsmanship assign it without doubt to the fourteenth century. Indeed, in a final published lecture in *Y Traethodydd*, Dr Parry indicated his readiness to accept the authenticity of these two poems.

Summarizing the present position of scholarship with regard to the poems of the 'apocrypha', I would suggest that stylistic analysis along lines similar to those so auspiciously started by Dafydd Bowen and Eurys Rowlands, including the close study of *cynghanedd*, vocabulary and imagery, offers the most fruitful method advocated so far for assessing the claims to authenticity of any one of the poems of doubtful authorship, and that such methods could profitably be extended to others of the rejected poems. Other kinds of evidence offer a much less convincing guide: owing to the unpredictable vagaries of scribes, it is obvious that little reliance can be placed upon manuscript attributions which depart from the general consensus in favour of Dafydd, to name as author some other poet, and frequently a poet who is very little-known, and whose known work may be of indifferent quality. And again, since our deductions as to the main events of Dafydd's life are based entirely on inference from the internal evidence of his poems, and since we are in total ignorance as to the details alike of his movements and of his personal relationships, since also we are quite in the dark as to how far fantasy prevails over actuality in his allusions to his various adventures of love, it is obviously fruitless to depend in any way upon the evidence of the names and place he alludes to in his episodic poems to support any argument for or against their authenticity. For instance, it is immaterial whether or not in *Cywydd y Sêr* the poet is describing a real journey to woo a girl whose home was in Anglesey, or whether he is merely expressing a wish to invoke the help of St Dwynwen in his love-affairs, since Dafydd is as likely as not to have invented the whole, and would surely have felt under no obligation to provide consistent clues as to his real life in his *cywyddau*. Of all the criteria for judging authenticity, that which in the last resort may well be the most reliable is that intuitive 'sixth sense' of a poet's individual style and personality which can only come as the hard-won result of years of study and familiarity.

Yet it is now possible, on the basis of such studies as have been made, to propose certain features as characteristic, and even in some cases as distinctive of the poetry of Dafydd ap Gwilym. His quite surprisingly wide range of types of poem has already been alluded to: this in itself places him in a class apart among medieval Welsh poets. Distinctive too, and unprecedented in Welsh, is the manner in which Dafydd constantly imbues his poems with his own personality: in his wonder, which has in the best sense been compared with the wonder of a child, at the great and small miracles of Creation; distinctive too, is his way of constantly presenting himself with ironic self-deprecation as an actor in all his episodic poems (and wherever in these he may hint at an awareness of some foreign convention, in creatively adapting it to his own purposes); and so also are his intricate passages of *dyfalu*, which tend to be subjective and self-revelatory in their symbolism, rather than merely exercises in fancy and metrical ingenuity. He endows birds and animals and the very forces of nature—even a haystack and a ruined dwelling—with their individual capacity to feel and to live. Imagery of this kind springs from an attitude in the poet's mind which transcends any conventional use of personification, for it emanates from an impulse to reach out and encounter sentient life in all created things, both animate and inanimate: in the Wind, in the mist and snow and rain, and in the very seasons of the year themselves. The birds who are the poet's most congenial companions are the small musicians and poets of the woodland: the Stag is a 'tall baron', but equally the Haystack is a 'burgess' and has a soul which the poet commends to Heaven, and the Ruin is credited implicitly with a personal capacity to mourn the warm human life which has departed from it. Summer is 'a fair wood-ward', the month of May is 'a strong horseman' and 'a generous nobleman'. Above all, the Wind is a *gŵr eres* (a marvellous being), whose essential nature is most fully described by reference to the human restrictions from which its cosmic freedom renders it exempt—and yet the Wind, like the Skylark (who enjoys a similar franchise) is nevertheless tamed in imagination to do the poet's bidding, and to act as his messenger. Indeed (as Mr Dafydd Bowen has pointed out) these poems in which Dafydd expresses awed reverence before the wonders of the firmament and of the cosmic forces are unmatched in their kind among contemporary poets (that is, if we may give the benefit of the doubt to *Cywydd y Sêr*, which has already been discussed). In all these poems, the poet's reverence for the Creator as artist and craftsman is all-pervasive.

Dafydd's imagery is instinctive and penetrates every aspect of his work; not least, as Dr Thomas Parry and Mr Eurys Rowlands have demonstrated by a close analysis of individual poems, in the subtle nuances, suggestions, and deliberate ambiguities of his vocabulary. One aspect of his predilection for gaining surprise effects by his choice of words is to be found in the ways in which he employs borrowed words of Romance origin. These borrowed words, whether they are taken directly from French, or indirectly through the medium of medieval English, consist almost invariably of nouns denoting concrete things. They are words for buildings and furnishings of all kinds (in terms of which he describes his woodland retreat in his *deildy* or house of leaves); for different kinds of weapons, especially the cross-bow or *arblastr* and its adjuncts; and words for various types of currency—*coron* 'crown', *fflwring* 'florin', *copr* 'copper coin', *mwnai* 'money' and so on. There is also a less concrete series of words dealing with the law and official administration—*ustus* 'justice', *seiler* 'jailer', *fforffed* 'forfeit', *ceisbwl* 'catchpoll', *corodyn* 'pensioner'. And when these borrowed words are used, they are employed almost without exception in a figurative sense, in that they are used right out of their normal prosaic context, to give the shock and stimulus of the unexpected. The leaves of May are florins on the tops of the branches, they are *iawn fwnai* 'true currency'; the Stars are golden pieces of wrought metal—*goldyn o aur melyn mâl*; ears are (surprisingly) *ceiniogau cof* 'the pennies of memory'; everyone is only a copper coin compared with his friend the poet Madog Benfras, *copr pawb wrthaw*. In addition to the employment of metaphor implicit in his use of *dyfalu*, there are poems in which Dafydd elaborates a metaphor throughout a number of lines or even throughout a whole poem, as in 'Morfudd like the Sun' or 'Love like a Hare'; or in a passage in which he compares the growth of his love and his final loss of Morfudd to the action of a farmer who sows his grain and watches it grow, only to find it destroyed at the last by a storm at the moment when it is ready to be harvested. His extended images may occur in triple groups: for instance, in aspiring after Dyddgu, he compares his temerity firstly to some small climbing creature (he seems to be referring to a marten, a pole-cat, or a squirrel) who ascends from branch to branch, but on reaching the top of the tree does not find it so easy to come down again; next, to the audacity of sailors who venture on the sea with only a thin plank between them and the deep (he, like them, cannot easily turn back); and, finally, to the marksman who, after many random shots, finally scores a bull's eye: may not Dafydd also aim successfully at last and win the girl with his poems of praise? In another *cywydd*, he cites a very different set of images in alluding to his persistency in the pursuit of Morfudd: he is like the flexible branch of an apple-tree which bends easily and yet does not break; like a starved old cat, long accustomed to being kicked and knocked about, who in spite of ill-treatment, nevertheless survives; and, finally, like one who reaches his destination by walking while others run. His protest against girls putting on ornaments to go to the fair is elaborated by reference to the Sun, which can have no need of additional brightness; then to an old broken bow, which is not to be mended merely by gilding it externally; and lastly, to a lime-washed wall which he says is as good as one which is painted with coats-of-arms. In another poem, he compares his fruitless efforts to please a heedless young girl to the efforts of those who try to tame wild animals, and describes in turn a hare, a squirrel and a roebuck; in each case, in spite of their fostering, their wild natures will cause them to make off to the wilds at the first opportunity. More cynically, he compares his position in relation to Morfudd's husband to that of two oxen in a yoke, to a ball which is tossed from one hand to another, and to a rejected empty barrel. Morfudd's beauty, polluted as a result of her marriage, is compared to a splendid varnished carving in negligent keeping, to a valuable English fur destroyed by peat-smoke, and to an oaken palisade warped by the salt water of the sea.

These are some of the ways in which Dafydd ap Gwilym introduced a new dimension into Welsh poetry. The full extent of his achievement can only be apprehended against the background of the contemporary literary scene in Wales, and it is the poets who were Dafydd's near contemporaries who must be considered in the next chapter.

BIBLIOGRAPHY

Editions

R. Geraint Gruffydd, '*Englynion y Cusan* by Dafydd ap Gwilym', *Cambridge Medieval Celtic Studies*, 23 (Summer 1992), 1–6.

David Johnston, '*Cywydd y Gal* by Dafydd ap Gwilym', *Cambridge Medieval Celtic Studies*, 9 (Summer 1985), 71–89.

Owen Jones (Myfyr), William Owen (Pughe) and Edward Williams (Iolo Morganwg), *Barddoniaeth Dafydd ap Gwilym* (London, 1789).

Thomas Parry, *Gwaith Dafydd ap Gwilym* (Cardiff, 1952: second edition, 1963).

Idem (ed.), *The Oxford Book of Welsh Verse* (Oxford, 1962).

Ann Parry Owen, 'Englynion Dafydd ap Gwilym i'r Grog o Gaer', in *Gwaith Llywelyn Brydydd Hoddnant, Dafydd ap Gwilym, Hillyn ac Eraill* (Aberystwyth, 1996), 51–91.

Ifor Williams and Thomas Roberts, *Cywyddau Dafydd ap Gwilym a'i Gyfoeswyr* (Bangor, 1914; second edn, Cardiff, 1935).

Translations

Rachel Bromwich, *Dafydd ap Gwilym: A Selection of Poems* (Llandysul, 1982; revised edn 1993).

J. P. Clancy, *Medieval Welsh Lyrics* (London, 1965).

Tony Conran, *Welsh Verse* (Bridgend, 1986).

Nigel Heseltine, *Twenty-five Poems by Dafydd ap Gwilym* (Dublin, 1944; reprinted Banbury, 1968). With a Preface by Frank O'Connor.

Richard Morgan Loomis, *Dafydd ap Gwilym: The Poems* (Binghamton, New York, 1982).

Gwyn Williams, *The Burning Tree* (London, 1956). Text with facing translations.

Critical Studies

Dafydd Bowen, 'Dafydd ap Gwilym a Morgannwg', *Llên Cymru*, 5 (1958–9), 164–73.

Idem, 'Awduriaeth y Cywyddau i'r Eira a'r Ser', *Llên Cymru*, 7 (1962–3), 193–205.

Idem, 'Dafydd ap Gwilym a Datblygiad y Cywydd', *Llên Cymru*, 8 (1964–5), 1–32.

Idem, 'Nodiadau ar Gywydd y Gwynt', *Llên Cymru*, 10 (1968–9), 113–15 (reprinted in J. E. Caerwyn Williams (ed.), *Ysgrifau Beirniadol IX* (Dinbych, 1976), 57–60).

Idem, 'Bardd Glyn Teifi', *Y Traethodydd*, cxxxi (1976), 132–48.

Rachel Bromwich, *Tradition and Innovation in the Poetry of Dafydd ap Gwilym* (Cardiff, 1967), reprinted, with additions, from *Transactions of the Honourable Society of Cymmrodorion*, 1964, 9–40.

Eadem, *Dafydd ap Gwilym* ('Writers of Wales' series; Cardiff, 1974). (With bibliography).

Eadem, 'Gwaith Einion Offeiriad a Barddoniaeth Dafydd ap Gwilym', in J. E. Caerwyn Williams (ed.), *Ysgrifau Beirniadol X* (Dinbych, 1977), 157–80.

Eadem, *Aspects of the Poetry of Dafydd ap Gwilym* (Cardiff, 1986).

Theodore Max Chotzen, *Récherches sur la Poésie de Dafydd ap Gwilym* (Amsterdam, 1927).

Anthony Conran, 'Translating Welsh Metres', *Poetry Wales: Special Issue on Translation*, Winter, 1976, 88–106.

Huw M. Edwards, *Dafydd ap Gwilym: Influences and Analogues* (Oxford, 1996).

Helen Fulton, *Dafydd ap Gwilym and the European Context* (Cardiff, 1989).

R. Geraint Gruffydd, 'A Poem in Praise of Cuhelyn Fardd from the Black Book of Carmarthen', *Studia Celtica*, x/xi (1975–6), 198–209.

Idem, *Dafydd ap Gwilym* (Caernarfon, 1987).

David Johnston, 'The Serenade and the Image of the House in the Poems of Dafydd ap Gwilym', *Cambridge Medieval Celtic Studies*, 5 (Summer 1983), 1–19.

Saunders Lewis, 'Dafydd ap Gwilym', chapter v in *Braslun o Hanes Llenyddiaeth Gymraeg* (Caerdydd, 1932).

Idem, 'Dafydd ap Gwilym', *Llên Cymru*, ii (1952–3), 199–208; reprinted in Geraint Gruffydd (ed.), *Meistri'r Canrifoedd* (Cardiff, 1973), 41–55.

Idem, 'Dafydd ap Gwilym', *Blackfriars*, March 1953, 131–15; reprinted in A. R. Jones and Gwyn Thomas (eds), *Presenting Saunders Lewis* (Cardiff, 1973), 159–63.

Idem, 'Sangiad, *tropus* a chywydd', *Trivium*, i (1966), 1–4.

Thomas Parry, 'Datblygiad y Cywydd', *Transactions of the Honourable Society of Cymmrodorion*, 1939, 209–31.

Idem, 'Dafydd ap Gwilym', *Yorkshire Celtic Studies* 5 (1949–52), 19–31.

Idem, 'Dafydd ap Gwilym', *Lleufer*, xii (1956), 55–61, 119–26 (reprinted in J. E. Caerwyn Williams (ed.), *Ysgrifau Beirniadol IX* (Dinbych, 1976), 41–56).

Idem, 'Dafydd ap Gwilym' in A. J. Roderick (ed.), *Wales Through the Ages: from the Earliest Times to 1485* (Aberystwyth, 1959; reprinted Llandybïe, 1965), 168–75.

Idem, 'Dafydd ap Gwilym', *Y Traethodydd*, 133 (1978), 64–79.

Eurys I. Rowlands, 'Cywydd Dafydd ap Gwilym i fis Mai', *Llên Cymru*, 5 (1958–9), 1–25, 143–5.

Idem, 'Nodiadau ar y Traddodiad Moliant a'r Cywydd', *Llên Cymru*, 7 (1962–3), 217–43.

Idem, 'Arddull y Cywydd', in J. E. Caerwyn Williams (ed.), *Ysgrifau Beirniadol II* (Dinbych, 1966), 36–57.

Idem, 'Rhamant Hanes y Beirdd', in J. E. Caerwyn Williams (ed.), *Ysgrifau Beirniadol III* (Dinbych, 1967), 28–33 (for *Cywydd y Rhew*).

Idem, 'Dafydd ap Gwilym', *Y Traethodydd*, cxxii (1967), 15–35.

John Rowlands, 'Delweddau Serch Dafydd ap Gwilym', in J. E. Caerwyn Williams (ed.), *Ysgrifau Beirniadol II* (Dinbych, 1966), 158–76.

Idem (ed.), *Dafydd ap Gwilym a Chanu Serch yr Oesoedd Canol* (Cardiff, 1975: Cyhoeddiadau Arbennig *Trivium*); contains articles by Peter Dronke, Sean O'Tuama, Rachel Bromwich, Rees Davies, Dafydd Elis Thomas and Gilbert Ruddock.

Meic Stephens and Gwilym Rees Hughes (eds), *Poetry Wales: Special Dafydd ap Gwilym Number*, Spring, 1973; articles by A. D. Carr, Gwyn Williams, Gwyn Thomas, Thomas Parry, Rachel Bromwich, R. Geraint Gruffydd and translations by J. P. Clancy. With bibliography of recent critical studies.

Gwyn Thomas, 'Dafydd ap Gwilym ac Ifor Hael', *Llên Cymru*, 7 (1962–3), 249–51.

Idem, 'Golwg ar y Sangiad yng Ngwaith Dafydd ap Gwilym', *Llên Cymru*, 10 (1968–9), 224–30.

G. J. Williams, *Iolo Morganwg a Chywyddau'r Ychwanegiad* (London: Cymdeithas yr Eisteddfod Genedlaethol, 1926).

Ifor Williams, 'Dafydd ap Gwilym a'r Glêr', *Transactions of the Honourable Society of Cymmrodorion*, 1913–14.

Documentary

J. E. Lloyd, 'Hynafiaid Dafydd ap Gwilym', *Bulletin of the Board of Celtic Studies*, viii (1953), 1–3.

Chapter 6

THE EARLIER *CYWYDDWYR*: POETS CONTEMPORARY WITH DAFYDD AP GWILYM

RACHEL BROMWICH

The following lively fragment describing a horse is quoted in each of the four early versions of the bardic grammar (Chapter III above) as an example of the metre *cywydd deuair hirion*, which was to become the increasingly favoured medium of fourteenth-century poets:

Breichffyrf, archgrwn, byr ei flew,	Strong of foreleg, round-chested, short-haired,
Llyfn, llygadrwth, pedreindew,	Sleek, keen-eyed, thick-haunched,
Cyflwydd coflaid, cyrch amcaff,	Victorious darling, greedy for oats,
Cyflym, cefnfyr, carn geugraff,	Swift, short-backed, firm and hollow-hoofed,
Cyflawn o galon a chig,	Fulfilled in spirit and in flesh,
Cyfliw blodau'r banadlfrig.	One hue with the flower-tips of the broom.

This is evidently an excerpt from a poem of request or thanks for the gift of a horse, but beyond this the authorship and provenance of the fragment are equally unknown. If we knew by whom and at what time the lines were composed, this knowledge would be of the greatest value towards elucidating the origin of the *cywydd*. Metrically, these lines are a crude and inadequate illustration of the metre as it came to be developed by Dafydd ap Gwilym and his contemporaries. Only the first and the third of the three couplets of which it is composed have end-rhyme between accented and unaccented syllables, such as later became obligatory, and *cynghanedd* appears only in an incipient or rudimentary form most evident in the alliterating initial words of the last four lines. Apart from the predilection for compound words in describing the horse, there is little that can be related to the art of *dyfalu* as this was developed in the poetry of Dafydd ap Gwilym.

Yet the lines are a fair example of the verse-type known as the *traethodl*, which was practised by the poets of subordinate status called the *clêr* (the *clerici vagantes*), to whom Dafydd ap Gwilym, as has been seen, acknowledged a somewhat ambivalent allegiance. The *cywydd* came into being in direct descent from the *traethodl*, by the endowment of the latter with full *cynghanedd*, and the tightening up of the rule as to the asymmetrical final rhymes. Except in occasional instances, such as his dialogue with the Grey Friar, which is composed in the looser form of the *traethodl*, the *cywydd deuair hirion* was Dafydd's choice for all those kinds of verse which departed radically in their subject-matter from the older tradition of praise-poetry—for verses of familiar personal address to friends and to his patron Ifor Hael, and above all for poetry concerned with the love-theme in its various aspects, most characteristically set against a background of wild woodland scenery. Yet with hindsight we can see that the literary development in fourteenth-century Wales, which was at least as far-reaching in its consequences as were Dafydd's thematic innovations, was this very transference into the medium of the *cywydd* of all the traditional apparatus of praise-poetry, as this had been practised by previous generations. Without this development, which secured lasting prestige for the *cywydd*, the poetry of love and nature might not itself have persisted, in the way that it did, to remain a lasting and recognizable constituent in the poetic tradition of Wales.

Since Dafydd ap Gwilym adhered to the traditional *awdl* for his 'genuine' praise-poems and elegies, he cannot with any probability be regarded as the innovator responsible for the adaptation of the *cywydd* to *canu mawl*. Some other powerful influence must be postulated as having lain behind the emergence, in the middle years of the fourteenth century, of *cywyddau* paying tribute to patrons, and recreating within the new medium all the inherited concepts of the *awdlau* of the *Gogynfeirdd*. The verse of five poets needs to be considered in relation to that of Dafydd ap Gwilym, if we are to obtain anything approaching to a correct perspective of his achievement. These were Iolo Goch, Llywelyn Goch ap Meurig Hen, Gruffudd Gryg, Madog Benfras and Gruffudd ab Adda, all of whom appear to have been closely contemporary with each other and also with Dafydd himself. References in contemporary legal documents place this beyond reasonable doubt in the case of Madog Benfras and Gruffudd Gryg, showing that they may be presumed to have reached man's estate by the year 1340: these two, in addition to Gruffudd ab Adda, were certainly known personally to Dafydd. It is a significant and striking fact that all five of these pioneer poets of the *cywydd* belonged to north or to north-east Wales: not one of them, like Dafydd himself, belonged to the south. Iolo Goch came from the Vale of Clwyd, Gruffudd Gryg from Anglesey, Llywelyn Goch ap Meurig Hen from Meirionnydd, Madog Benfras from Marchwiail near Wrexham in Powys, and Gruffudd ab Adda also from Powys. The likelihood that all five were closely contemporary with Dafydd himself has been obscured by the fact that whereas there are no certainly datable poems by Dafydd composed after the 1350s, Gruffudd Gryg was still composing in the 1370s, and probably later, while Iolo Goch and Llywelyn Goch, whose earliest *cywyddau mawl* of certain date belong to the 1350s, were still active in the final decades of the century: both speaking of themselves in their last poems as being very old men. These two, it would seem, may actually have survived to reach their eighties—a remarkable attainment in the fourteenth century. All five had passed away before the end of the century, and did not live to witness Glyndŵr's revolt.

All of these poets composed love-poems in the *cywydd* form. Indeed, all the main types of *cywyddau* composed by Dafydd ap Gwilym are represented in the work of one or other of them: by all there are *cywyddau* of love and of love-complaint addressed to girls; there are poems showing affinity with the Continental *fabliaux* (Madog Benfras and Iolo Goch), *llatai* or love-messenger poems (Gruffudd Gryg and—probably—Llywelyn Goch) and poems abusing friars (Iolo Goch), besides religious *cywyddau* (all of them but Madog Benfras and Gruffudd ab Adda). The poetry that has been preserved in the name of each of these poets is very much smaller in quantity than is the accepted canon of Dafydd ap Gwilym. Of the five, Iolo Goch has by far the largest number of poems ascribed to him, and is second in stature only to Dafydd himself, though very different from him in the main features of his verse. On the existing evidence, Madog Benfras is the least distinguished of the five, though it is he who is the most plainly under the influence of Dafydd ap Gwilym, without distinctive inspiration of his own. But much of his verse, and indeed of that of the others, may be presumed to have been lost, or may perhaps in a few instances be recoverable among the 'apocryphal' *cywyddau*, rejected by Dr Parry from the canon of Dafydd ap Gwilym's own work. There exists in the manuscripts the same kind of confusion with regard to the authorship of individual poems by these poets as is the case with Dafydd himself, and their verse—again like his—has in the main survived only in late copies which have suffered all the vagaries of both scribal and earlier oral corruption.

Yet among the poems which may with confidence be ascribed to these poets there have come down a handful of highly original and exceptional *cywyddau* which deserve to be placed on a par with Dafydd's finest work: Gruffudd Gryg's *cywyddau* 'To the Moon' and 'To the Wave', Gruffudd ab Adda's poem to the Birch-tree uprooted and placed as a may-pole in the town of Llanidloes, Iolo Goch's praise of the labourer or ploughman, his dialogue between the Soul and Body (which effectively burlesques the old convention of such dialogues, to describe a *taith clera* or bardic circuit between the homes of his patrons), and his vivid description of the miseries of a sea-journey in his satiric *dyfalu* of a ship. There is also Llywelyn Goch's celebrated *marwnad* or lament for his beloved Lleucu Llwyd, to which I shall return later. Mutual influences are discernible in a marginal degree between all these poets, yet all but the one mentioned show strong and impressive originality. In addition to these poems, which may indeed, like Dafydd's *cywyddau*, be classified as 'personal poetry', three of the five poets composed *cywyddau* of a kind which is quite unparalleled in Dafydd's work: that is, *cywyddau mawl* and *marwnad*, or formal praise-poems addressed to patrons, including also a *dadolwch* or placatory poem asking forgiveness for offence from patrons who were also relatives (Gruffudd Gryg), and poems of asking and thanks for the gift of a horse, a dagger, and for generous hospitality (Iolo Goch). These are all verse-types which are attested at an earlier date in the *awdlau* of the *Gogynfeirdd*. Metrically, the verse of these poets tends to be 'couplet-structured' more often than it is 'sentence-structured' with tmesis (*torymadrodd*—with *sangiadau*), in the manner favoured by Dafydd ap Gwilym. Where the device of *dyfalu* occurs, it is almost always used 'pejoratively' rather than 'positively' by these poets (whereas Dafydd ap Gwilym employs it in both ways), and mainly with the purpose of satirizing the various impediments to love's game. A notable exception, however, is Iolo Goch's remarkable 'positive' *dyfalu* of the Plough in his *cywydd* to the Labourer:

> A cradle which tears the trailing broom,
> a gentle creel which yet can shred the plain.

Dear is his praise, a holy relic,
a heron who opens a quick furrow.
A basket of the wild land, which will now be cultivated
with a coulter in wisely-ordered state.
A gander of the untamed acres,
true it is that grain will be had from his skill.
He drives forth crops from the heavy tilth,
a splendid creature, biting the ground.
He must have his knife and his food
and his table under his thigh.
He goes unwillingly over small stones—
a lad who flays with leg outstretched.
His snout is active daily
in a fair hollow beneath the oxen's feet.
He would often sing his hymn—
his wish is to follow the plough-chain.

But this is in every respect a remarkable poem: the fact that it is unmatched in the work of any other of the early *cywyddwyr*—except by Dafydd ap Gwilym himself—in its 'positive', rather than negative and 'pejorative', use of the device of *dyfalu*, lends force to my earlier suggestion that the main origin of this device is to be found in the elaborately figurative language of bardic satire—witness, for instance, Dafydd ap Gwilym's satire of Rhys Meigen. Iolo Goch was apparently inspired to compose his praise of the Labourer by the words of the *Elucidarium*, a popular twelfth-century theological treatise, which was translated into Welsh in the *Book of the Anchorite of Llanddewifrefi* and appeared in 1346. In a well-known passage of this work the author assigns the *clêr* (meaning, in this case, poets in general) to perdition, and contrasts them with the humble tillers of the soil, who shall be blessed because they feed the populace by the sweat of their brows. Iolo paraphrases the text of the *Elucidarium (Lusudarus hwylus hen* or 'fortunate old Lucidarius' is for him a person) when he quotes this authority as saying: 'Blessed is he who from boyhood holds the plough with his hands'—and he goes on to expand upon the virtues of the Labourer —he trusts in God, he pays his tithes and receives God's bounty in recompense; he is hospitable and generous to all; he does not utter an opinion on any subject but one which concerns his own craft; he dislikes all disputation and all warfare; he does not rob anyone or claim the least thing unjustly; he prefers humbly to follow the plough, rather than to be an 'Arthur' despoiling castle towers. And yet *nid bywyd, nid byd heb ef* (there is no life, nor world without him). As in Dafydd ap Gwilym's *cywydd* to the Wind, the picture of the Labourer is built up by a series of negative statements: the Labourer's virtues are expressed mainly by a list of the things he does *not* do. In both poems the catalogue of negatives indicates a deftly implied criticism of their opposites: in The Wind this is aimed against the 'restrictive practices' of the alien officers who administer the foreign legal system; in Iolo's poem it is obviously directed against those in high places who rob and persecute, pursue unjust claims, fail to dispense charity and hospitality, are too ready with their opinions—or interference—in matters which do not concern them, and above all, who prosecute warfare. These are the sins which are proper to the great and powerful ones of the earth, and it is surprising to find such a minutely detailed list in the work of a poet who was a pioneer in composing *cywyddau mawl* to just such temporal magnates as might in some cases with some justice be accused of committing them. Yet no doubt Iolo's idealized portrait of a character who embodied the opposite of all these sins was intended for a clerical rather than for a secular audience. The poem 'Piers Plowman' by the English poet Langland invites an obvious comparison; it appeared about 1370, but we have no means of knowing whether or not Iolo's *cywydd* preceded it in date of composition. The social upheavals consequent upon the Black Death are likely to have been a contributory cause behind both poems.

Another characteristic of the verse of these poets which is also significantly characteristic of Dafydd ap Gwilym's poetry is their use of personification. In the passage which has been quoted from Iolo's *cywydd* to the Labourer the plough is personified as *gŵr* and *gwas*, 'a man' and 'a lad', and 'he must have his knife and his food, and his table under his thigh'. For Gruffudd Gryg the Moon is *mursen* (a coy wench), while Gruffudd ab Adda's Birch-tree is poignantly addressed as if it were a sentient and suffering creature:

> Green birch-tree with bedraggled tresses, you have been long exiled from the hill-side; a lovely tree in the forest where you were reared, green-mantled, you are now a traitress to the grove. Your enclosure made a lodging for me with my darling in the short nights of May . . . Now no longer do you meditate on love, and your branches up aloft stay dumb. In your entirety, and at whatever cost,

> you have gone from the green slopes where you were once a miracle, to the town—a swift exchange. Though your favoured monument may seem good, in Llanidloes town, where crowds assemble, yet may I not approve, my birch-tree either your abduction, or your present company, or your home; it is no good place for you, with long face, to bear forth new leaves. Every town-garden is able to have feathery green—was it not rash, birch-tree, to bring about your fading there—a wretched pole, beside the pillory? Have you not come, at the very time of putting forth leaves, to stand at the barren centre of the cross-roads? Although they say that your station is pleasant, birch-tree, yet it were better by far to be a roof above the brook. No bird sleeps or sings, with slender voice, in the fair precinct of your topmost branches, owing to the great clamour of the people about your tent, sister of the shady trees . . . You have been made over to bartering, and you have the look of a selling-woman; everyone will point his finger at your suffering, with joyful chatter, as you stand in your grey dress and your worn fur, amidst the trivial merchandise of the fair. . . You will no longer shelter the April primroses; no more will you have thought or care for the valley's birds, though once their fair protector . . . Choose one of the two, captive branches—your burgess-hood is a folly—either to return home to the woodland, or to wither yonder in the town.

Here again, as in Iolo Goch's *cywydd* to the Labourer, the undertones are all but audible: beneath the sensitive evocation of the birch-tree's beauty in its natural woodland setting, which is rarely matched even by Dafydd ap Gwilym, lies a general suspicion and rejection of the crowded life of the boroughs, with their often predominantly alien population ('your burgess-hood is a folly'), and again at an even deeper level there is the poignant realization of beauty's frailty and life's transitoriness.

Another characteristic which more than one of these early *cywyddwyr* share with Dafydd ap Gwilym is an expertise in the embodiment of colloquial dialogue in their verse, undaunted by the restrictions imposed by *cynghanedd* and by the *cywydd's* obligatory rhyme-scheme: good examples are Iolo Goch's 'Dialogue between the Soul and the Body' or the poem in which he abuses his beard ('like a hedge-hog's coat') for acting as an impediment to his love-making. Yet a third feature which is also characteristic of Dafydd is their manner of presenting themselves as leading actors in their poems of incident, as does Madog Benfras in his *fabliau* poem 'The Saltman' and Iolo Goch when—again like Dafydd—he tells how he was pursued by *Yr Eiddig*, the stock figure of the 'Jealous Husband' as the result of a game of fortune-telling with the man's wife, played with nuts.

A critic of the contemporary literary scene in England has pointed out that a relaxed and 'un-grand' style, tending to irony and humour and self-deprecation—and therefore very obviously comparable with these features in the style of Dafydd and his contemporaries—is a characteristic of the informal manner shared in common by Chaucer and other late fourteenth-century English poets, who as a group have been designated the 'Ricardian' poets.

We do not know how these poets stood in relation to each other with respect to the early development of the *cywydd*. Any conclusions which are to be reached concerning this must be based upon the poets' own statements, and in particular upon what they have to tell us concerning their own attitudes towards Dafydd ap Gwilym. Some indication of these may perhaps be deduced from the 'elegies' composed for Dafydd by Gruffudd Gryg, Iolo Goch, and Madog Benfras, and—more importantly—from the eight *cywyddau* of the *ymryson* or poetic controversy which took place between Dafydd ap Gwilym and Gruffudd Gryg. This poet came from the commote of Llifon in the west of Anglesey. Evidence brought to light from a legal document some years ago by Mr E. D. Jones would place the probable date of Gruffudd's birth several years earlier than was hitherto supposed, and this earlier dating puts a somewhat different light upon the controversy between the two poets than that in which it had been regarded previously. No longer do we have a young poet from Gwynedd, the stronghold of the poetic 'establishment', challenging the poetic innovations made by his senior from the more volatile south; but instead an argument between two contemporaries relating to differences in the basic assumptions of each concerning the subjects proper to be celebrated in poetry. There can be no mistaking the import of Gruffudd Gryg's initial attack upon Dafydd's verse: he accuses him of monotony of theme and of obvious and blatant 'untruth' by his exaggeration of the plight to which the spears and arrows of his love for Morfudd have reduced him over the last ten years. Such exaggeration would have outraged the conventional standards of truth as recognized hitherto in bardic praise-poetry, and Gruffudd claims that missiles of this kind would have been quite sufficient to kill any other man, even the great Arthur himself. Implicit in this charge is an even deeper one: that of departing from the formal restraints imposed by the *rhieingerdd* convention, in order to introduce improper and irrelevant personal feelings into his poetry. Dafydd retorts with a much-discussed couplet in which he defends the new kind of verse practised by him as being at least equal in value with that which belonged to the familiar old tradition: *Nid llai urddas, heb ras rydd / No gwawd, geuwawd o gywydd* (No less the honour (though) without free favour / Than a praise-poem, a *cywydd* of false praise). A '*cywydd* of false praise' means Dafydd's own love-poetry: the phrase is employed with similar meaning by Llywelyn Goch (p. 145 below). He asserts that Gruffudd is merely *cynnydd cerdd bun unflwydd* (the product of a maiden-song of a single year)—which is as much as to say that he is a newcomer to the practice of love-poetry, compared with Dafydd himself. In obscure and even cryptic language but with striking imagery, Dafydd then asserts that the mature technical accomplishment of his own *cywyddau* is such that it would give distinction even to the meanest of antiquated worn-out harps; if such a one were to accompany it, or to the tattered pages of the most ragged song-book in which such verses as his own might be written: without the harp's accompaniment of song, or the barely legible love-poetry inscribed in the book, both of these would by themselves be valueless. Adopting attack as the most satisfactory form of defence, Dafydd then introduces another issue into the argument: he claims that Gruffudd lacks originality, that he takes his subject-matter from the verse of others, including Dafydd's own poetry, and that in doing so he debases it—*gwyrodd â'i ben gerdd y byd* (his mouth has distorted everyone's song). Gruffudd replies by hotly denying that Dafydd is his teacher with respect to the content of his verse, and he asserts confidently that his own high attainments are fully recognized in his own country: 'Though my voice may stammer (*cryg*), by Mary, there is no stammering in any word of my verse.' Nevertheless, he concedes that in the past Dafydd's poetry had introduced a major novelty into Gwynedd: *Hoff oedd yng Ngwynedd, meddynt / Yn newydd ei gywydd gynt* (A favoured novelty in Gwynedd, they say / his *cywydd* was when new)—it was a short-lived wonder which caused as much stir at the time as did two other similar marvels: the wooden hobby-horse (an adjunct of the morris-dance) and the new organ in Bangor cathedral—but these too have long since become familiar and are no longer of particular remark.

In his second *cywydd*, Dafydd refuses to withdraw his charge of plagiarism and issues a challenge: since both contestants are *prifeirdd*, or established and qualified poets, let them grapple together in a word-contest in the traditional manner of their craft —a fitting test, indeed, as to the high degree of technical accomplishment to which each laid claim. The last two *cywyddau* by both poets consist of a series of charges and counter-charges, elaborated with richly vituperative invective. There is much obscure allusion and innuendo in the argument which inevitably escapes us, but the scurrilous claim made by both contestants to be the 'father' who has begotten the other is perhaps no more than a crude metaphor reverting to their basic difference: the argument as to the real parentage of the *cywydd bun* or new love-poetry, in whose composition Dafydd was plainly acknowledged by his opponent to be pre-eminent. The controversy breaks off without any clear decision having been reached either as to Gruffudd's charge of exaggeration, or Dafydd's of imitation. Clearly there was a serious and important issue underlying the *ymryson*, in so far as it concerned the clash between the older established poetic modes and Dafydd's thematic innovations—though from the point of view of metrics, the major poetic innovation of the fourteenth century is completely left aside from the argument, both poets tacitly accepting the *cywydd* as the natural medium for their discussion; as indeed it was for them for all kinds of personal and 'untraditional' poetry.

An 'elegy' composed by Gruffudd Gryg to Dafydd ap Gwilym regularly follows the *ymryson* in nearly all the manuscripts, and is best regarded as a poem composed to form a gracious termination to the controversy. Gruffudd forgives Dafydd for his harsh words, expresses regret for their dissension, admits that he himself has been partly in the wrong, and acknowledges his debt to Dafydd—*Disgybl wyf, ef a'm dysgawdd* (I am his pupil, he instructed me). Dafydd is *paun Dyfed* (the peacock of Dyfed); he is in the direct line of descent from Taliesin, Myrddin, Aneirin, and the most famous of the *Gogynfeirdd*; and Gruffudd claims that he would prefer satire from Dafydd's lips rather than praise from those of any other poet. It is clear that Gruffudd regarded Dafydd as a master of the *cywydd serch* or new love-poetry, yet none the less he placed him within the central tradition of Welsh poetry, as one who worthily perpetuated the tradition inherited from the *Cynfeirdd* or earliest poets. A parallel attitude is expressed by Iolo Goch and by

Madog Benfras in their *marwnadau* for Dafydd: for both he was *pensaer yr ieithoedd* (architect of words, literally 'languages'), and *pensaer gwingerdd* (architect of song), he was *athro pawb* (everyone's teacher), and by his death, according to Iolo, the *cywydd* will be reduced to a sorry state. Madog Benfras describes Dafydd as *digrif* (amusing), and as *tegan rhianedd* (the darling of girls), and prays that Mary and Jesus will forgive his levity; yet he too describes Dafydd as a worthy transmitter of the traditions of Aneirin and Taliesin. None of these poets offer any suggestion that they regarded Dafydd as the *inventor* of the *cywydd*; indeed, Iolo Goch appears to give pride of place to Llywelyn Goch ap Meurig Hen in this respect, describing him in another so-called 'elegy' as *primas cywydd Ofydd* (the primate of Ovid's *cywydd*), to be praised above all for his love-poetry: when a court-audience requests a song, no other *cywydd* but one by Llywelyn Goch will satisfy it, and in his verse no single word is misplaced; he is compared to the prophet David, who like Llywelyn, was a sinner in love who afterwards repented. The force and immediate application of all these compliments and innuendos would surely have been lost had not their subject been still alive to take note of them, and I think it is only natural to conclude that it was to the living Dafydd, or Llywelyn, that all these poems were addressed. This is no less obviously the case, I think, with the *cywyddau marwnad* addressed by Dafydd to Gruffudd Gryg, Madog Benfras, and Gruffudd ab Adda: the presumption is, indeed, that all such 'elegies' addressed during the early *cywydd* period by one poet to another are 'fictitious' elegies, addressed to men who were still living. The choice of the *cywydd* for compositions of this kind is an indication that they are not serious, but that they are to be regarded as friendly and admiring compliments to their subject, for almost invariably they contain touches of humour which betray their fundamental levity. They subscribe to certain recurrent conventions; one is the expression of regret that such-and-such a despised poet (a certain unknown 'Bleddyn' is alluded to in this way in Gruffudd's elegy for Dafydd) was not removed from the world instead of the subject of the elegy; another is a prayer for divine forgiveness for their subject for his frivolity in composing love-poetry. As in much medieval poetry, levity goes hand-in-hand with seriousness (in this case with genuine admiration and affection), as when Dafydd ap Gwilym in his 'elegy' for the poet-musician Gruffudd ab Adda follows up his marvellously sustained image of a nightingale singing enchantingly in an orchard, only to be struck wantonly by an arrow, with the abrupt assertion that the poet was killed with just such a 'discourteous' blow (*pond oedd wladeiddrwydd?*) as if one were striking off the head of a goose. Even Gruffudd Gryg's poem to the Yew-Tree above the grave of Dafydd ap Gwilym comes under suspicion for similar reasons, and on grounds of general probability: the poem echoes closely Dafydd's own *cywydd* to that other evergreen, the Holly; of both trees it is claimed that they will provide secure 'houses' for the poet, and both will share the additional advantage that their leaves will not be nibbled away by goats! And even Iolo Goch's comparison of Llywelyn Goch, in his eloquent tribute to him, with the prophet David who also sinned in love and subsequently repented, has on the whole a greater ring of authenticity if we are to believe that the poet was at the time still in the land of the living. These early *cywydd* poets were not as yet fully enfranchised from an inherited tradition, in that the *awdl* still retained for them the *aura* of its ancient prestige as the preferred medium alike for formal elegy and for the expression of genuine grief in bereavement, as I have already suggested in discussing Dafydd ap Gwilym's employment of the two media. The same probability that a *cywydd marwnad* enshrines a familiar personal tribute to a living friend is applicable to Dafydd ap Gwilym's address to Rhydderch ab Ieuan Llwyd; and very probably also, as Mr Dafydd Bowen has suggested, to Gruffudd Gryg's 'elegy' for Rhys ap Tudur of Penmynydd.

This convention of addressing elegies to the living, which appears so strange to present-day readers, seems to have been employed primarily for the purpose of making familiar, semi-humorous addresses by one poet to another. Outside this relatively well-defined category, there is frequently no possibility of distinguishing among the compositions of fourteenth-century poets between the 'fictitious' and the genuine *marwnad*. Already by 1356 we have Iolo Goch's *cywydd marwnad* to Sir Rhys ap Gruffudd, securely dated by the death of its subject in that year. This was followed after twelve years by the same poet's *cywydd marwnad* to Tudur Fychan of Penmynydd (1367), and later again by his elegy to Tudur's sons Ednyfed and Goronwy (1382), and by his dramatic and moving elegy to his friend and principal patron Ithel ap Robert, archdeacon of St Asaph—a poem which Mr Saunders Lewis acclaimed as one of the poetic masterpieces of the century. There can be no doubt but that all these are sincere and genuine elegies, each one a formal composition in honour of a man who wielded great power and authority, whether local or national. These are praise-poems which in their language, metaphors and concepts—in everything but in their metrical form—reproduce the traditions of the *canu mawl* of previous generations, employing the linguistic archaisms and all the familiar imagery of the traditional *awdlau*. Like Dafydd ap Gwilym, Iolo is believed to have been a man of good birth and standing who had taken minor religious orders. It is evident that he possessed deep learning and wide knowledge of biblical and classical sources, of divinity in translation (the *Elucidarium*), as well as of all branches of the native Welsh tradition as expressed in earlier poetry, in triads and romances, in saints' lives, in genealogy and in heraldry. There is also that 'subtle over-plus' of poetic vision which is characteristically his own: a remarkable power of evoking atmosphere and of conveying with intensity the sense of an impressive occasion; as in his portrayal of the immensely long funeral *cortège* which accompanied Ithel ap Robert to his burial, culminating in the church shaking like a ship at anchor in the March gale of rain and wind, or his description of the darkness which overcast all Anglesey upon the death of the sons of Tudur of Penmynydd.

No less strong an affiliation with the whole range of techniques of the Gwynedd court-poets who were his predecessors is apparent in Iolo Goch's many other *cywyddau mawl*: ironically enough, the earliest of these whose authenticity is without doubt may well be his remarkable *cywydd* in praise of Edward III (composed after 1347), in which after praising the king for his victories in France and Scotland, including Crécy (1346), Iolo takes it upon himself to impress upon the king his responsibilities, urging him to undertake a crusade to the Holy Land. It seems incongruous to meet here with all the age-old formulas: Edward is described as *anian Bedwyr* (of the nature of Bedwyr); he is the defender of Windsor, a lion, a boar, and a leopard. From every point of view this is a surprising poem: why was it composed at all? Mr Dafydd Bowen suggests that this may perhaps have been due to the instigation of Sir Rhys ap Gruffudd, a strong supporter of the king, to whom Iolo's *marwnad* attests his allegiance: one wonders, however, in what form, if at all, its import was ever communicated to the king. But here, in what may well be the earliest of all *cywyddau mawl*, is a poem of assured technical accomplishment and of unquestionably serious intention; the earliest extant example (to be followed later by Iolo's urgent advice to Sir Roger Mortimer on the occasion of his coming-of-age) of a succession of *cywyddau* in which poets ventured to offer weighty ideological, practical, or political advice to their patrons.

Iolo's gift for selecting the essentials of a scene and projecting them with an almost photographic immediacy is to be seen no less in certain of his praise-poems than in his elegies. It is most noticeable, however, in those of his *cywyddau* in which praise is offered to a patron by means of praising the splendour of his home; as in Iolo's minutely detailed description of Owain Glyndŵr's court at Sycharth, or his description of Cricieth castle when 'Sir Hywel of the Axe' was its constable. This is a poem-type which has an illustrious ancestry, leading as far back as the ninth-century 'Praise of Tenby' in the *Book of Taliesin*, and precedents for it in the older metres must presumably have been known to Iolo. Yet he gives to this type of poem a new orientation by presenting his description of Cricieth in the form of a dream, and in doing so he evokes in the plainest terms the closely similar description of the heroine's home at Caernarfon, seen in a dream, which occurs in the tale of *The Dream of Maxen*:

> I see in the first place, truly, a fair large fortress yonder by the sea; a splendid magnificent castle, with men at tables, a rampart, and a blue sea against a wall of comely stone. There are sea-waves about the womb of the dark and gloomy tower; music of flutes and pipes; a lively warrior and a man of note; sprightly maidens weaving pure and shining silk; proud men on the fortress's floor playing chess and backgammon on a dais. And a grey-haired man, a very savage Twrch Trwyth in battle, passing from his hand to mine a gold-chased goblet containing sweetly-tasting wine, with a fair tall black standard on the turret-top, bearing three identical white flowers with silver leaves—he was indeed a noble warrior.

The main cause for the transference in Gwynedd of the traditional techniques of court-poetry from *awdl* to *cywydd* must be sought in the rapid social changes which followed the conquest, but the obscurity which surrounds the successive stages in this change is thrown into relief by the fact that whereas Iolo Goch composed a *cywydd marwnad* to Tudur ap Goronwy of Penmynydd (d. 1367), his younger contemporary Gruffudd ap Maredudd was at the same time composing an elegy to him in the form of an *awdl*. The possibility can certainly be excluded that Iolo Goch's *cywyddau mawl* owe anything initially to the example of Dafydd ap Gwilym: indeed, the date assigned to the earliest of these, appearing as they do in a mature and assured form in the middle years of the century, is by itself sufficient to discredit it. The only possible influence which would need to be considered would be that from Dafydd ap Gwilym's four polished *cywyddau* to Ifor Hael, as to whose relative date in relation to Iolo's *cywyddau mawl* we can do no more than conjecture. And the Ifor Hael poems offer no sufficient explanation: the *cywydd* was for Dafydd the obvious medium for such poems of familiar personal address to a generous friend and patron; three of the four were composed, apparently, in response to particular incidents of a trivial nature: a journey planned or deferred, the gift of money in the fingers of a glove. Their whole manner and tone is entirely different from that of the genuine *cywydd mawl*: their originality consists in the way in which recognizable concepts from the new love-poetry have been blended with the inherited praise-formulas—the mutual dependence of poet and patron, praise of the patron's home, the poet's deserved reward compared with that given by Urien Rheged to Taliesin. It is, on the other hand, with the formal *awdl* which Dafydd addressed to Ifor that Iolo Goch's *cywyddau mawl* and *marwnad* deserve rather to be compared—with the essential difference that Iolo has transferred into the new medium all the traditional techniques known to him from the *awdlau* addressed to the Gwynedd princes. Nor does it appear that any other of the earliest group of *cywyddwyr* but Iolo Goch composed sincere and genuine *marwnadau* in the form of the *cywydd* (the only other questionable example being Gruffudd Gryg's supposed *cywydd marwnad* to Rhys ap Tudur—a 'fictitious' *marwnad*, in all probability, as has already been seen, and one whose penultimate lines link it with the Ifor Hael poems rather than with genuine elegy). We have no evidence that Iolo Goch had any predecessor in making the transference of serious praise-poetry from *awdl* to *cywydd:* as far as our existing knowledge will take us, the *cywydd mawl* originated with Iolo Goch in Gwynedd, just as the *cywydd serch* originated with Dafydd ap Gwilym in Dyfed. Both innovations were of equal magnitude, and were comparable in their far-reaching implications.

But already from the early years of the fourteenth century, and in a sense from a very much earlier date, love-poetry in *awdl* and *englyn* metres was being prefigured, and to some degree overtly expressed, by such poets as Gruffudd ap Dafydd ap Tudur, Goronwy Ddu, Casnodyn, and Hywel ab Einion Lygliw, as well as by a number of anonymous poets, of whose work we get a fleeting glimpse in the *exempla*, chosen to illustrate the various forms of *awdl* and *englyn*, which are to be found in the early texts of the bardic grammar. This was, indeed, an inevitable and natural development from the *rhieingerdd*, with its exalted ancestry going back to the earliest *Gogynfeirdd* in the twelfth century: it is nevertheless worth setting on record that elements of *canu serch* such as we associate with Dafydd ap Gwilym, in the form of notions borrowed from international love-poetry—love's sickness and sleeplessness, and the like—had penetrated the *awdl* and were very frequently celebrated in *englynion*, at a much earlier date than that at which serious *canu mawl* or praise-poetry had become acceptable in the form of the *cywydd*. Of Iolo Goch's two love-poems, one is the unique *cywydd* to a girl preserved in the *Red Book of Hergest*: Iolo here follows closely the traditional pattern of the *rhieingerdd*, but betrays the source of his inspiration (including, perhaps, that of the licence expressed in the last lines) by closely reproducing several lines from a poem to a girl by Hywel ab Owain Gwynedd. The poem is in almost all respects closer to the *rhieingerdd* tradition than it is to the *cywyddau serch* of Dafydd ap Gwilym. Yet Iolo's *cywydd marwnad* to Dafydd testifies to his recognition of his contemporary's high poetic status—*athro pawb oedd* (he was everyone's teacher)—thus magnanimously acknowledging in general terms his debt to Dafydd, though the nature and extent of this debt are by no means readily apparent. Parallel usages in vocabulary and in imagery are indeed more noticeable as between Iolo and Gruffudd Gryg on the one hand, and between Iolo and Llywelyn Goch ap Meurig Hen on the other; though in the instances which occur, there is no means of telling which poet it was who borrowed from the other.

It is to Llywelyn Goch ap Meurig Hen that Iolo Goch gives obvious priority, in his *marwnad* for him, as master of the *cywydd serch*, and he expressly names the woman with whose name that of Llywelyn has become indissolubly linked: it will, he says, be pleasing for the prophet David in Paradise to listen to *cerdd Lleucu Llwyd* (the poetry of Lleucu Llwyd); and Llywelyn, like David, will win forgiveness from God for the sinful love of which he has repented at the last. Llywelyn himself reiterates the name of Lleucu Llwyd more than once, as that of the supreme object of his song: in his *cywydd* to the Snow he expresses his gratitude to his two nephews, Hywel and Meurig, for their generosity in providing him, an infirm old man, with comfortable winter-quarters in his old age; his pleasant occupation, he says, will include reading with them the laws and historical texts of their country, and composing verse 'comparing Lleucu Llwyd to a beautiful rose in a fair garden, to bountiful Mary, or to the splendid sun'. The name of Lleucu Llwyd was no pseudonym to conceal the identity of an unnamed girl, but like Dafydd ap Gwilym's Morfudd, she was apparently a real woman, and—again as in the case of Dafydd and Morfudd—behind Llywelyn's allusions to her there appears to lie just such another story of a passionate and frustrated liaison with a married woman. The points of similarity between Llywelyn and Dafydd ap Gwilym go much further than this: both were by birth *uchelwyr* (Llywelyn belonged to the important family of Nannau, near Dolgellau) who did not depend upon their verse for their subsistence, and—significantly—both composed a group of *awdlau* in praise of patrons. Both, indeed, seem to have made a similar distinction between what they regarded as the proper function of *awdl* and *cywydd*, employing the *awdl* for serious, and in the main, formal praise-poetry and for devotional poetry, while the *cywydd* was used by both in the main for poetry of a more light and intimate nature. The tone of Llywelyn's address to his nephews is in many ways reminiscent of the tone of Dafydd ap Gwilym's *cywyddau* to Ifor Hael.

Yet there appears to be a virtually insurmountable difficulty in applying any such hard-and-fast distinction as to the themes accepted as proper to *awdl* and *cywydd* when considering what is undoubtedly Llywelyn Goch's most famous poem, his *cywydd marwnad* to Lleucu Llwyd. It is very difficult to doubt the sincerity of the passionate cry of grief which permeates this poem. Yet against all the internal suggestions, Dr Thomas Parry has preferred to regard the lament as belonging to the convention of 'fictitious' *marwnadau*, and as having been addressed to the poet's mistress while she was still living, and in the absence of positive evidence on either side it is difficult to reject this view out of hand. The poem is composed in the form of a direct address by the poet to the dead girl, in which he bids her rise up and answer his complaint of love:

> Pale girl in the oaken coffin, sad is my condition after you. Fair of form, Gwynedd's candle, though you be in the captivity of the grave, rise up, my soul, and give me answer, fair one. I am here at your grave—sun's beauty—a worn man grief-stricken for your loss, Llywelyn Goch who sounded the bell of your praise. I am a groaning poet, walking in affliction, the servant of cruel passion . . . But you, mute, lovely girl, would give me no answer from the deep pit, silent, solemn, and loveless. I will go from Gwynedd today—I care not where, lively girl with the moon's beauty—if you were alive, I would not go. I do not mind where it is that I may see you again, whether it be upon the Mount of Olives (i.e. at the day of Judgement) where love's bonds are cast aside, bright one, Lleucu with the wave's fairness. You have ensured that I will be there, fair bright-hued maiden, sleeping too long in a stone enclosure . . . Woe is me for the weight of earth and soil upon the mistress of beauty, woe that a coffin should guard you, a dwelling of stone between you and me, chancel of church and robe of rock, the weight of earth and a wooden garment. Woe is me for the fair girl of Pennal, it is a harsh dream that a roof covers your brow, a strong oaken lock (begetter of bitter grief), heavy door of oppressive bondage on the fair-browed one, the earth between me and her countenance, an enclosing wall with hard black lock, with a latch—farewell, Lleucu.

The exclamatory style, the torrential outpouring of grief and reproach to the dead girl for her silence, and for breaking troth with her lover by her death, is wholly in the style of the keen, or extemporary dirge, as this has been traditionally practised in Ireland and elsewhere. It gives to Llywelyn's *cywydd* an effect of vivid reality and spontaneity, which argues forcibly in its favour as a genuine expression of grief in bereavement. As W. J. Gruffydd pointed out some years ago, it is also strongly reminiscent of the form of a *sérénade*, in which the lover shivers outside his lady's window, and begs for admittance (Dafydd ap Gwilym's 'Under the Eaves' may be compared), and as such Llywelyn's lament formed the model for a number of subsequent *marwnadau bun* or *cywyddau* which were ostensibly composed in tribute to dead girls. A no less significant parallel to Llywelyn's elegy has been indicated by Dr Geraint Gruffydd: it is the parallel with Dafydd ap Gwilym's *awdl farwnad* to his uncle. In this *awdl* the poet similarly addresses the dead man directly, and reproaches him for his *mudandod* or silence and inability to answer. Dr Gruffydd suggests that Llywelyn Goch may actually have been influenced by his knowledge of this poem;

though this suggestion once more brings to the fore our ignorance as to their relative dates. Whether the points of resemblance between the two poems be fortuitous or not, Llywelyn's composition of a lament for a dead girl within the framework of a *sérénade* is a remarkable instance of the fresh adaptation of a poetic convention of foreign origin to a new and highly original purpose—and this once more invites a fruitful comparison with similar achievements by Dafydd ap Gwilym. A further question is, if the elegy is 'genuine', why should Llywelyn have composed it in the form of a *cywydd* and not of an *awdl*? Here one may compare not only Dafydd ap Gwilym's elegy to his uncle, but also his *awdl farwnad* to a woman—Angharad, the wife of his neighbour Ieuan Llwyd of Glyn Aeron—which shows verbal resemblances to Gruffudd ap Maredudd's *awdl farwnad* to Gwenhwyfar of Anglesey, and obviously shares with it the inheritance of a common tradition: a tradition in which one might well expect that Llywelyn Goch also would have composed. There are at once no clear answers and many answers to this question, in a century in which the new *cywydd* was gaining gradual acceptance, with Iolo Goch, as an alternative medium for serious elegy. If the *Marwnad Lleucu Llwyd* is 'genuine', it is unique in the fourteenth century in being a *cywydd marwnad* addressed to a woman; and that is perhaps the nearest that we can get to a reason for its form.

That the *marwnad* was but the final *cywydd* in a sequence of poems addressed to Lleucu Llwyd which have not come down, but which were above all responsible for Llywelyn's fame in his own day, is evident both from the poet's own allusions to them, and from Iolo Goch's comparison of Llywelyn's sinful love with the love-story of the prophet David. All this is corroborated by the words of Llywelyn's *awdl gyffes* or recantation (a poem which powerfully recalls the *marwysgafn* or death-bed poem of a forerunner, Meilyr Brydydd), in which the poet makes a line-by-line comparison between God's goodness to him and his own sins; these include his unlawful love for Lleucu and his expression of this in poems to her:

> I performed continual rape, incurring Thy rebuke; I neglected Heaven and men of faith; I performed *llateiaeth* (i.e. 'sent messages of love', probably); I dishonoured true religion; I made in writing (*ar draethawd*) a *cywydd* of false praise (*geuwawd gywydd*), compar-

> ing Lleucu of the snow's hue to the like of Mary; I performed hidden adultery. I confess to Thee, who knowest all things, the wrongs that I did, skilful in words . . . I broke the burden of my faith daily; I broke the Ten Commandments, the covenanted safeguard of religion, God's unbending Law for all lands . . . Because of Thy crown of thorns, because of Thy chastisement, because of Thy love, hear, Lord, my song. Because of Thy very certain death upon Thy bier, and Thy wise resurrection the third time, before my final day of death (grant me) Thy reconciliation.

If Llywelyn's lost poems to Lleucu included *englynion* as well as *cywyddau* (and no love-poetry other than *cywyddau* are anywhere ascribed to him), then it is possible, and has indeed been suggested by several scholars, that a stray stanza from one of them has been preserved in the early version of the bardic grammar, as an example of the measure known as *englyn lleddfbroest gadwynog*. The four lines may be translated:

> Neither the Sun, leaping through the sky, nor the moon has been more fairly coloured—bright and comely her shining form—nor more dazzling than Lleucu Llwyd.

The sun and moon imagery recalls the similar imagery in Llywelyn's *marwnad* (the name 'Lleucu' being derived from *Lucia*, meaning 'light'); yet since 'Lleucu' is among the most common of women's names attested in the fourteenth century, this identification can remain no more than a possibility—supported, as far as it goes, however—by the combination with the epithet 'Llwyd'. And Mr Saunders Lewis has pointed out the significance of the consequences which would follow, if indeed the *englyn* is the work of Llywelyn Goch ap Meurig Hen. This poet has been commonly regarded as a younger contemporary of Dafydd ap Gwilym. But this evidence would mean that he was already composing love-poetry in *englynion* at least a decade before the time at which we have any sure evidence that Dafydd ap Gwilym was composing *cywyddau*, since the 'archetype' from which each of the four early texts of the bardic grammar derive is now generally concluded to have been redacted early in the 1330s. Llywelyn Goch would then be a contemporary—perhaps even a slightly older contemporary—of Dafydd ap Gwilym, and his verses to Lleucu Llwyd would date from as early a period as that at which we have any knowledge of the earliest *cywyddau*.

This leads us back to the lines descriptive of a horse, which were quoted from the bardic grammar at the beginning of this chapter, and which purport to illustrate the measure *cywydd deuair hirion*. Among the early *cywyddwyr*, Iolo Goch is the only one to whom *cywyddau gofyn* or 'poems of asking' for horses are attributed. The two that have come down belong to Iolo's old age; they are in the form of a circumstantial, familiar, and humorous address to his patron the archdeacon Ithel ap Robert, recalling their youth together, and begging him for the gift from his stud of a decent sober horse suited to carrying an infirm old man—not one so weak that he would fall down under the burden, or one that jibs, or one that will not stand still while being shod, or a frisky young horse whose mane has not yet grown, who would start off on his own 'like a long-haired goat' leaving the poet behind or else clinging precariously to the saddle; if such a horse were to trip and cause him to bite his tongue, it is poetry which would suffer. One of the two *cywyddau* is in the form of a dialogue between the poet and the old horse who has died, and he thus addresses him:

> You were a fair, stout, straight-legged courser; it is sad you will never be so again. You were the best of runners, and it is sad and grievous after you to see the place where you were reared empty, and your manger without food. What can I do to obtain a large and gentle steed to carry me? It is wearisome for a feeble old man to have to walk without resting, lacking the gift of a horse—but whom I should ask in Is Conwy, I do not know.

The old horse is made to reply with the obvious answer, that the poet should go and ask Ithel ap Robert for a replacement, which he does with success: the only remaining difficulty being to obtain a mounting-block, since he is 'heavy and stooping like a hunchback', and then to avoid anything—like the noisy turning millwheel—which might startle or impede the new horse, as they ride on the familiar journey home. The whole tenor of these poems leaves the reader in no doubt as to Iolo Goch's particularly strong feeling for horses, and as to the striking wealth of his vocabulary for describing the *minutiae* of their behaviour (good or bad), and as to his knowledge of the various ailments which might befall them—knowledge which was widespread in his day, no doubt, but which is to us an almost obliterated technology. Mr Saunders Lewis has pointed out that in Iolo's description of the kind of horse which he would wish to have there is to be found the phrase *carn geugraff* (hollow-hoofed), which occurs also in the descriptive lines quoted from the Grammar. These lines also include the rare compound *amcaff* (greedy), of which the only other example attested from the fourteenth century is in a pejorative description of a dog, in a satire which is also by Iolo, preserved in the *Red Book of Hergest*. Mr Saunders Lewis therefore concludes that this, the earliest example of a *cywydd deuair hirion*, may quite possibly be a quotation from an early poem by Iolo Goch.

These suggestions as to the authorship of the two examples of *englyn* and *cywydd* in the earliest version of the bardic grammar have much to recommend them, and their acceptance would confirm the conclusion that both Llywelyn Goch and Iolo Goch were Dafydd ap Gwilym's close contemporaries in the second quarter of the fourteenth century, and that the early evolution of both *cywydd serch* and of the *cywydd mawl*—poems of love and poems of conventional praise in the new *cywydd* metre—are likely to have been closely contemporaneous developments, and are to be attributed to the activities of a group of poets rather than to any single innovator. And in so far as we can identify individually the pioneers of this development—and it may be that our lack of evidence is responsible for giving an inaccurate impression—the impelling force which instigated the evolution of the *cywydd* appears to have come from the poets of Gwynedd, whose 'security of tenure' was most quickly and catastrophically affected by the loss of patronage from their native princes which followed upon the break-up of the old society in the last decades of the thirteenth century.

BIBLIOGRAPHY

Editions

J. Gwenogvryn Evans, *The Poetry in the Red Book of Hergest* (Llanbedrog, 1911).

Helen Fulton, *Dafydd ap Gwilym: Apocrypha* (Llandysul, 1996).

D. R. Johnston, *Gwaith Iolo Goch* (Caerdydd, 1988).
Idem, *Iolo Goch: Poems* (Llandysul, 1993).
Idem, *Blodeugerdd Barddas o'r Bedwaredd Ganrif ar Ddeg* (Llandybïe, 1989).
Idem, *Canu Maswedd yr Oesoedd Canol / Medieval Welsh Erotic Poetry* (Cardiff, 1991).
Thomas Parry, *The Oxford Book of Welsh Verse* (Oxford, 1962).
G. J. Williams and E. D. Jones, *Gramadegau'r Penceirddiaid* (Caerdydd, 1934).
Ifor Williams and Thomas Roberts, *Cywyddau Dafydd ap Gwilym a'i Gyfoeswyr* (Bangor, 1914; second edition, Caerdydd, 1935).
Ifor Williams, Thomas Roberts and Henry Lewis, *Cywyddau Iolo Goch ac Eraill* (Bangor 1925; second edition, Caerdydd, 1937).

Critical Studies

D. J. Bowen, 'Dafydd ap Gwilym a Datblygiad y Cywydd', *Llên Cymru*, 8 (1964–5), 1–32.
Idem, 'Agweddau ar Ganu'r Bedwaredd Ganrif ar Ddeg a'r Bymthegfed', *Llên Cymru*, 9 (1966–7), 46–73.
Rachel Bromwich, 'Gwaith Einion Offeiriad a Barddoniaeth Dafydd ap Gwilym', in J. E. Caerwyn Williams (ed.), *Ysgrifau Beirniadol X* (Dinbych, 1977), 157–80.
W. J. Gruffydd, 'Y Farwnad Gymraeg', *Y Llenor*, xviii (1939), 34–45.
R. Geraint Gruffydd, 'Marwnad Lleucu Llwyd', in J. E. Caerwyn Williams (ed.), *Ysgrifau Beirniadol I* (Dinbych, 1965), 126–37.
David Johnston, 'Iolo Goch and the English: Welsh Poetry and Politics in the Fourteenth Century', *Cambridge Medieval Celtic Studies*, 12 (Winter 1986), 73–98.
Idem, *Iolo Goch* (Caernarfon, 1989).
Saunders Lewis, 'Y Cywyddwyr Cyntaf', *Llên Cymru*, 8 (1965), 191–6; reprinted in R. Geraint Gruffydd (ed.), *Meistri'r Canrifoedd* (Caerdydd, 1973), 56–63.
Idem, 'Kywydd Barnad Ithel ap Robert', in J. E. Caerwyn Williams (ed.), *Ysgrifau Beirniadol III* (Dinbych, 1967), 11–27; reprinted in *Meistri'r Canrifoedd*, 64–79.
Thomas Parry, 'Datblygiad y Cywydd', *Transactions of the Honourable Society of Cymmrodorion*, 1939, 209–31.
Eurys I. Rowlands, 'Y Traddodiad Moliant a'r Cywydd', *Llên Cymru*, 7 (1963), 217–43.
Idem, 'Iolo Goch', in J. Carney and D. Greene (eds), *Celtic Studies in Memory of Angus Matheson*, (London, 1968), 124–46.
Gilbert Ruddock, 'Amwysedd ac Eironi ym Marwnad Lleucu Llwyd', *Ysgrifau Beirniadol IX* (1976), 61–79.

Documentary

E. D. Jones, 'Cartre Gruffudd Gryg', *Journal of the National Library of Wales*, x (1957), 230–1.

A. N. Palmer, 'Records of the Bailiwick of Wrexham, 1339 and 1340', *Archaeologia Cambrensis*, v (1888), 258–62 (for Madog Benfras).

Idem, 'Notes on certain Powysian Poets', *Y Cymmrodor*, xxi (1908), 132.

Chapter 7

SIÔN CENT

G. E. RUDDOCK

The name of Siôn Cent is most especially associated in Welsh literature with religious verse of a kind common in European countries at the close of the Middle Ages. The poetry ascribed to him treats of the sinfulness of man, and of the deceiving and transitory nature of temporal things. It depicts with morbid intensity the horrors of the grave and the torments of hell, warning men and women of the urgent need to repent and change their ways before the fateful Day of Judgement (an event which was to the medieval mind an imminent reality).

Siôn Cent's *floruit* is usually given as 1400–30. There is, however, more than a little doubt who exactly the poet was, or even whether such a man ever existed. This problem is obviously of central importance with regard to the authenticity of those *cywyddau* ascribed to him in manuscript sources. We cannot be completely certain, for example, that Siôn Cent was the author of all eighteen poems included under that name in the 1937 edition of *Cywyddau Iolo Goch ac Eraill*, where the standard (but still far from completely satisfactory) text of his work is printed. An excellent example of this is the burden poem to his purse, whose general light-hearted spirit is quite foreign to the usual sombre religious tone of most of his other poems. An important aspect of the problem surrounding the identity and very existence of Siôn Cent is the fact that his name was frequently confused with the not dissimilar names of other people whose dates roughly coincided with that which is generally thought of as his own period.

The difficulty regarding the authenticity of poems commonly attributed to Siôn Cent is not unlike that which faced Dr Thomas Parry in the task of establishing the standard text of the work of Dafydd ap Gwilym (*fl.* 1340–70). The names of both poets became associated with a particular type of verse—Dafydd ap Gwilym's with a new kind of nature and love poetry in Welsh, Siôn Cent's with a particular *genre* of religious poetry. The result was that a great deal of material was spuriously attributed to both, each in his own field. In attempting to define the true corpus of Siôn Cent's work, his editors may be criticized for ascribing to him too much or too little, as Dr Parry was criticized by some scholars after the appearance of his monumental *Gwaith Dafydd ap Gwilym* in 1952. Such criticism is often valuable, but frequently amounts to little more than a matter of opinion.

However, this comparison between Siôn Cent and Dafydd ap Gwilym is far from exact. As regards the latter, there does exist a hard core of poems which may be attributed to him with a considerable degree of certainty. Although Dr Parry reduced the contents of the 1789 edition of Dafydd ap Gwilym's work by half, this still left some 150 poems for inclusion in the 1952 edition. It is less easy to feel confident as to what constitutes the essential core of Siôn Cent's compositions, and the problem remains a difficult one.

Certain evidence would appear to link Siôn Cent with some of the border counties of Wales and England, the most likely ones being those of Brecon and Hereford. For example, one *cywydd* commonly attributed to him is an eloquent eulogy to the people and land of Breconshire. Again, it is interesting, though inconclusive, that a painting of a solemn-faced man purporting to be Siôn Cent is to be seen on the stairway of Kentchurch Court, Herefordshire, *i.e.* in an area not so very far from Breconshire itself. If Siôn Cent was indeed the author of the *cywydd* to Breconshire, the poem may be regarded as evidence for his having been acquainted with the life of noble houses there, and becomes even more meaningful when considered in the light of his confession of frivolous living (which included, apparently, the singing of praise and love poetry) prior to his religious conversion. Note, for example, the following lines from his poem to the Seven Deadly Sins, where after comparing himself with the Biblical Saul, he continues:

I have borne without repenting
A terrible burden of sin . . .
Because of pride, my wont has been
Empty flattery and satire . . .
Gluttony and adultery
Were also enemies for me . . .
I shall try to give expression

To the life I led when young . . .
I praised without rule or grace
Fair countenance, and broke marriage.

Two important facts appear to constitute good evidence for the existence of a poet named Siôn Cent, and to give some idea at least of his period. Firstly, there has survived an *ymryson*, or bardic debate (incomplete though it be), between a Siôn Cent and the well-attested Rhys Goch Eryri (1385–1448). Secondly, in another *ymryson*, this time between Guto'r Glyn (*fl.* 1450–90) and Hywel Dafi (*fl.c.* 1450-80), the former refers unflatteringly to the latter as *Siôn y Cent ieuanc*, i.e. a young Siôn Cent. It would appear from this that a certain Siôn Cent had already earned himself a reputation for a particular kind of moralistic poetry by the second half of the fifteenth century. Bearing in mind that Siôn Cent has also been linked with Gwent, it may not be without significance that the *ymryson* between Guto'r Glyn and Hywel Dafi is connected with the receiving of patronage at Raglan.

Mr Saunders Lewis has suggested that Siôn Cent was a graduate of Oxford University, and that his work reflects the thought and philosophic approach of *scientia experimentalis* or, to use Stewart Easton's translation of the term, the 'science of experience'—a phrase particularly apt as a description of Siôn Cent's general attitude to life. (See further below, under *The Purpose of Poetry*.) He was, according to Mr Saunders Lewis, the poet of Christian pessimism, one able to lift his eyes above and beyond the sinfulness of this world and the putrefaction of the grave, and to see the blessed light and bliss of heaven, a region described by him as

Full, full, full, full of joyfulness,

a line in which the *cynghanedd sain* (a type of *cynghanedd* frequently used to great effect by the poet) echoes like the very bells of paradise.

In general, it seems reasonable to assume that there exists an essential core of genuine poems by a poet Siôn Cent, and that he flourished at the beginning of the fifteenth century. Notwithstanding the various tales and legends which grew up around his name, some of which describe him as a kind of magician or soothsayer, he is one of the comparatively few Welsh classical poets of importance from the early fifteenth century whose work has come down to us.

The particular kind of verse for which Siôn Cent is best known may fairly be termed death poetry: its basis is that all temporal things are transitory, that all people have to die. This is the one experience common to the whole of humanity, of every age and of every philosophy and religion. As Siôn Cent put it:

All men end by lying down.

Such words as these reflect the particularly morbid frame of mind current in much of Europe at the close of the Middle Ages. Death was never far from people's thoughts. There was much to remind them of its less pleasant aspects in their everyday lives. The years between the middle of the fourteenth and the fifteenth centuries were probably the most troubled and violent of the whole of the Middle Ages. This was the period of the Hundred Years War and of the Black Death, whilst in Wales itself the early years of the fifteenth century saw the upheaval of the abortive Glyndŵr rebellion. Medicine, of course, was by present-day standards primitive, and it was not uncommon for people to die from a relatively minor wound or ailment. Open charnel houses were a source of both horror and disease, and must have contributed to the special fear, reflected in the literature of the period, of growing old and infirm.

Death was also emphasized in the people's religion. The late Middle Ages were a time of much preaching by the Church against the sins of the period (which were, no doubt, linked to a degree of economic advance and an improvement in living standards) and of dire warnings concerning the approaching Day of Judgement. The Church's message was reinforced by dramatic and vivid pictorial representations of such themes as the Day of Judgement itself, or of the *danse macabre*, or Dance of Death (very few examples of which, however, have survived in Wales). It is nevertheless difficult to be certain to what degree there had been an emphasis on preaching in Wales prior to Siôn Cent, and to ascertain to what extent his own particular kind of verse had flourished here before, say, 1400. It may be argued that much of the populace had developed an imperviousness to threats of fire and brimstone, although they could scarcely have been unaware of them, any more than they could of their social surroundings. As regards Wales, however, it is not easy to ascertain just how many sermons in their own language the largely monoglot population could have heard. Not one sermon in Welsh from the period has survived in manuscript, although there are English examples in profusion. It is at the same time difficult to conceive of the Welsh as indifferent to sermons, and it is likely that a certain amount of material was lost,—possibly during the Glyndŵr rebellion. This absence of Welsh sermons may also be partly attributed to the Church's practice of sending non-Welsh-speaking priests into Wales. On the whole, it seems fair to assume that apart, perhaps, from certain religious festivals, the opportunities of hearing a sermon in Welsh were at this time comparatively few.

However, much of the contemporary Welsh classical religious poetry is full of what must have been current pulpit themes, and it was no doubt through such verse that many Welsh people heard the warnings of the Church. As Sir Ifor Williams said, in Siôn Cent's work is heard the voice of the preacher of the period. The poet himself, referring to the world's vanity, proclaimed:

> The world's a sermon, a cold thing.

It may well be that many themes and ideas reached some through the medium of English sermons and English poetry. Here, too, Continental influences were most likely to have had impact, and, as already suggested, Siôn Cent was essentially a European poet. He would doubtless have been very much aware of foreign influences impinging upon him, and in this respect a comparison with Dafydd ap Gwilym, who must have died just about twenty years previously, would not be inappropriate. The latter spent most of his time in what was probably a multilingual society, the Norman boroughs and taverns in Wales with which he was obviously so well acquainted being ideal places for him to imbibe various ideas and themes of Continental origin. Siôn Cent may well have had similar opportunities to come into contact with foreign literature and ideas. If it is accepted that he was a man of some learning, then he would no doubt have been in a position to appreciate and make use of such influences to an even greater extent. As noted below, it is possible to discern in his work the influence of both French and Latin literature, as well as links with English literature and with poetry of both a religious and an erotic character. In addition, the native Welsh poetic tradition, and the Scriptures themselves, must have exerted their own special influence on him and on other poets of a similar nature.

One theme common in death poetry was that of the dialogue between the living and the dead, with its variant forms of the discourse between body and soul, or (as in Shakespeare's *Hamlet*) between a man and a skull. The dialogue was, of course, a medieval literary form, and such themes occur in medieval Latin literature, where, for example, we meet the conversation with a skull. Whether the sources were oral or written, or both, Welsh literature too has several examples of the dialogue theme, certain of which date from periods considerably earlier than Siôn Cent. Regarding the link with Latin literature, it is interesting to note the existence, in Llanstephan MS. 34 (late sixteenth century), of what purports to be a prose rendering by the fourteenth-century poet Iolo Goch (*c.* 1320–98) of a Latin poem in the form of a debate between body and soul. It appears to be a fairly close translation, and, if genuine, seems to be good evidence that the Latin poems of the Goliardi, who traversed medieval Europe singing poetry in both solemn and light-hearted vein, were known in Wales at least at the time of Iolo Goch. Much of the content of this Latin poem is similar to themes found in Siôn Cent. Notwithstanding certain similarities noted in the past between the poetry of Siôn Cent and that of the *Cynfeirdd* (*c.* 600–1100) and *Gogynfeirdd (c.* 1100–1300), the correspondences are far from being always exact, and closer parallels (which nevertheless still vary in exactness) may be found in other native Welsh sources. In the *Black Book of Carmarthen (c.* 1200) there occurs an early example of the conversation or debate between body and soul. This is a didactic poem which includes references to the transitoriness of temporal things. Another didactic poem, also a dialogue between body and soul, occurs in the *Red Book of Talgarth* (Llanstephan MS. 27, dated *c.* 1400), the poem itself being possibly as early as the twelfth century (a fragment of it occurs in the *Black Book of Carmarthen*). It includes references to death and the grave. Yet another example of the body and soul debate is the poem attributed to the late medieval poet Y Bergam, which occurs in Peniarth MS. 50 (*c.* 1450). This poem dates from the twelfth or thirteenth century, and contains several references very similar to certain themes in the work of Siôn Cent. Here occurs the theme usually referred to by scholars under the Latin title *Ubi sunt*? (see below), and the body is described as being 'without house, without fire, without pleasant song, seeing no one'. The pomp and power and wealth of life have disappeared. Such is the fate of all, such is the lesson afforded to the living by the dead. This salutary lesson is, of course, the essential significance of all such dialogue poems, and much of death poetry as a whole.

Returning to the *cywydd* period itself, two interesting examples of dialogue death poems occur in the work of Llywelyn Goch ap Meurig Hen (*fl.* 1360–90). One *cywydd* of his takes the form of a conversation between the poet and a skull, whilst the other is his unique elegy to Lleucu Llwyd, set to a considerable degree within the framework of a particular kind of love-poem popular in the Middle Ages, and of Continental origin, namely the *sérénade*. In the sixteenth century, Wiliam Llŷn (*d.* 1580) combined death themes with elegy in his elegiac dialogue *cywyddau*. In the Lleucu Llwyd poem, Lleucu, the loved one, cannot, of course, answer the poet as he addresses her, and this adds dramatic poignancy. In Wiliam Llŷn's elegies, on the other hand, the departed is quite loquacious, thus affording the author an opportunity to underline certain death themes to good effect. The Lleucu poem, too, exhibits the influence of death themes. All this poetry in the *cywydd* period, ranging from Llywelyn Goch to Wiliam Llŷn, and also including poems by poets such as Ieuan ap Rhydderch (*fl.* 1430–70), Maredudd ap Rhys (*c.* 1440), and Ieuan Brydydd Hir (*fl.c.* 1450), may be regarded as belonging to the same *genre* of death poetry as the work of Siôn Cent. As is said in Llywelyn Goch's skull poem:

> Consider thy day, be not proud,

or in Ieuan ap Rhydderch's dialogue with the spirit:

> Great was my boast, yet death was my lot,

lines which exemplify the technique of salutary contrast, so important a feature of such verse. A chilling example from Siôn Cent is:

> Beneath the stone's nape, rather
> The fat grave worm than fine hair.

Although it is not certain that Siôn Cent ever composed a dialogue poem, nevertheless, as is inferred above, many of the themes linked with such poetry are manifest enough in his work.

Obvious here are the decay of the body in the grave, and the fate of the soul following the deeds of this life. Some of Siôn Cent's most famous lines are those referring to the body being 'tried', 'tested', or 'tasted' by, according to one poem, eight hundred worms, and, according to another, three hundred. Then there are the well-known lines in his great poem 'To the Emptiness and Vanity of the World':

> And his brave body in the oak chest,
> And his nose so sadly pale-white.

Unless the soul is well prepared, it does not know, after death, which way of two it shall follow—that which leads to Heaven, or the one to Hell:

> The soul then is not certain
> Which way of two it shall go.

According to religious dogma, the soul was obliged to pay for the sins of the body, and this too gains expression by the poet, who says of the soul:

> If it goes to Heaven, it must indeed
> Pay the fine for the wicked body.

Linked with this are a number of themes which centre around the idea of the transitory nature of temporal things. One of the best known is that of *Ubi sunt*? or 'Where are they now?' A technique employed here is the naming of famous people who were in their day great or powerful, but who have all succumbed to the call of death. They have all been obliterated. (A close variant of this theme is that which emphasizes that all grades of society are swept away by death, irrespective of social standing.) Physical beauty and strength are all lost in death's clutches, as are wisdom, learning, and political power:

> Where's all the world? Great the deception!
> Where's Adam, the first of men?
> Where's Rwling, king of Constantinople? . . .
> Alexander has perished,
> Hector, Arthur—it's very clear—
> Where's Guinevere, fair-faced and gossamer-like? . . .

Where's Tegfedd, once wonderful,
Darling of Owain Cyfeiliog?

As may be gathered from this example, the *Ubi sunt?* theme facilitates the development of a repetitive style, found frequently in the work of Siôn Cent, which seems particularly fitting in a poet who may be regarded as the preacher of his age.

Death is sometimes personified, conceived of as someone who visits all people and snatches them away. An important aspect of this is the *danse macabre*, much portrayed in various medieval art forms, where Death is depicted as taking his partner in the dance. The Dance of Death was a popular kind of folk game. Siôn Cent sometimes refers to *yr angau bach*, or 'the little death', using the adjective *bach*, as it is still frequently used, as a term of endearment. He also refers to *y bedd bach*, or 'the little grave'. There is a particular horror in the meiosis.

The *danse macabre*, with its closely associated ideas of death and the gaiety of dancing, would appear to represent the two opposed basic reactions to man's mortality. The one is clearly heard in the warning voice of a poet such as Siôn Cent, whilst the other may be summed up in the *Gaudeamus* refrain of much of the poetry of the Goliardi or *clerici vagantes* (wandering scholars). 'Let us enjoy ourselves while we may', they sang—What purpose is there in being sad? Life is too short for that. Such a theme may be traced over a considerable period of time, to at least as late as *c.* 1750, when a version of a *Gaudeamus* poem, including the *Ubi sunt*? theme, appeared in Germany. The two basic reactions to man's mortality are also reflected in Dafydd ap Gwilym's famous discourse with a Grey Friar, where the poet of love and nature defends his position against the moral onslaught of the Church, and chooses not to think of death yet awhile.

A theme also closely connected with that of the personification of death is that of life's wheel (*cf.* the idea of the wheel of fortune or fate). The wheel represents man's fate, to which he is bound. As the wheel turns, Death shoots at him. There is once again no escape. A possible reflection of this theme is seen in the phrase *rhwymyn rhod*, or 'wheel's captor'. In Siôn Cent's poem *Y Ffordd i'r Nef* (The Way to Heaven), after references to certain triads and some of the Oldest Animals (all of which are concerned with life-span or longevity), the poet says:

Each one of these, bound to a wheel,
Will perish without warning.

No one can oppose the onslaught of black death. The wheel is often linked in death poetry with the *Ubi sunt*? theme.

As the above-quoted reference to *rhwymyn rhod* suggests, some death themes are not always particularly well developed in the work of Siôn Cent, but appear, rather, as a brief yet meaningful glimpse of a wider canvas. Two other poems may be mentioned in this connection, namely *Nid Oes Iawn Gyfaill ond Un* (There is no True Friend but One) and *I Gyffelybu Dyn i Ddiwrnod* (To Liken Man to a Day), each of which holds both a thematic and a formal interest. The one true friend referred to in the former is Jesus Christ, the poem being a reflection of the Test of Friendship theme. This theme was further developed in the tale of Everyman (a character well known, for example, in medieval English drama). Such themes were popular as *exempla*, or illustratory moral tales, in medieval sermons. As has recently been suggested, there seems to be a quite close parallel between certain ideas in this poem by Siôn Cent and the friendship *exemplum* found in the early English versions of the *Gesta Romanorum*. Although this theme may well have reached Siôn Cent through the medium of English, he could, perhaps, just as well have had the opportunity of hearing of it in French or Latin. It was ultimately of Eastern origin, and appeared in a number of tales of similar pedigree which were Christianized by the medieval Church, which used such themes for its own purposes.

An undeniable parallel exists between the basic theme of the second of Siôn Cent's poems dealt with here and that of a fifteenth-century English religious poem, 'This World is but a Vanyte', or 'The Day of Life'. Here we have, not the well-known medieval theme of the three, four, six, or seven ages of man, but rather the comparing of man's life with the passing of a day. After the long, confident morning of youth, midday arrives, to be followed by the afternoon of later life, and before he realizes it, night has come upon the man, and death is very near. Siôn Cent depicts the progress to mature manhood as something essentially cruel, whilst in the English poem, an old man remembers the time when the world was at his feet, and weeps in bitter regret and distress. The thematic parallel between the Welsh and the English poems is striking indeed, and strongly supports the view that a direct relationship existed between the literatures of the two languages at the close of the Middle Ages.

Formally, the most noteworthy feature of *Nid Oes Iawn Gyfaill Ond Un* is that it is a burden poem, *i.e.* the *cywydd* is divided into sections, with the burden closing each section. In the standard printed text of Siôn Cent's work, there are five such poems. In four of these, the burden, or refrain, re-echoes and emphasizes the central, salutary moral, namely that this world is, like a painting, a deceiving (if clever) mixture of charm and colour, that worldly goods are useless to man if God is displeased, that there is no true friend but One, and that the author places his hope in that which is to come. The other burden poem is the *cywydd* to the Purse. Although its general tone is very unlike that of most of Siôn Cent's work, it could, perhaps, have been composed in the period before his religious conversion, although this seems improbable. The burden itself—'My purse, *gros merci* for this'—has an obviously French ring to it, and the purse theme has parallels in English literature (Chaucer, for example, has a burden poem of complaint to his empty purse).

Although the burden was, by the late Middle Ages, mainly a poetic ornament, its roots are probably to be found in such a practical context as the singing of a song during engagement in work of some kind (especially repetitive work), or in dancing. (Here, it is relevant to remember that the term *carol(e)* originally meant a dance.) The burden is found in Latin poetry, and has both religious and erotic literary connections. 'This World is but a Vanyte' is a burden poem, and a composition like this could have been influenced by the use of such a literary device in certain *genres* of medieval French love poetry (such as the *caroles* and *chansons d'amour*).

Whatever is said regarding Siôn Cent's contribution to the development of the *cywydd* metre, he certainly appears to have been the first to divide the *cywydd* into sections, and close each section with a burden. However, the pattern in this respect is not uniform, perhaps as the result of experiment, or, more likely, because the printed text is corrupt. In the printed text, the burden occurs at the end of each section in the same form in the 'Purse' and in *Gobeithiaw a ddaw ydd wyf* (I place my hope in that which is to come). This is true also of the friendship poem, except that the latter ends with two lines which follow the burden. In *Rhag Digio Duw* (Lest God be Angered) the exact form of the burden at the end of each section varies, although the central idea of God's anger is present each time. It is in the poem comparing this world to a painting that the greatest variation is found. Here, no burden occurs in lines sixteen and thirty. However, when it does occur, the burden's form is constant.

The length of the individual sections varies, but is on the whole fairly uniform, keeping usually to some eight to twelve lines. *Rhag Digio Duw* has one section of fourteen lines. *Hud a Lliw* . . . (the painting poem) begins and ends with a section of ten lines, and there are long sections in the body of the poem.

A further, if somewhat nebulous, link with Continental literature—and with erotic poetry most especially—may be discerned in the literary background of a poem such as *I Gyffelybu* . . . In France, from the twelfth century onwards, certain *genres* of love poetry were commonly set within a specific framework or situation, such as that in which the poet takes a walk in a wood or forest and meets with a maiden, engaging her in conversation. A like convention frequently occurs in the *pastourelle* or *pastorale*, where, for example, a nobleman meets a shepherdess. It is a modification of such situations that is seen in the English religious poem 'This World is but a Vanyte', where the poet meets an old man who tells him of his sorrow. (Regarding the link between England and France, it is important to recall that French was the language of status and esteem in England from Norman times until about the middle of the fourteenth century. Chaucer's friend, John Gower (1325–1402), wrote in English, French and Latin, whilst Chaucer himself (*c.* 1340–1400) has been considered by some to have been more French in spirit than English.) Although *I Gyffelybu* . . . was not composed within the framework of, say, a *pastourelle*, nevertheless the possible link, through a poem such as 'This World is but a Vanyte', is obvious.

The first complete printed translations into Welsh of the Bible and New Testament did not appear until the sixteenth century. However, the work of the *cywyddwyr* often provides an insight into the extent to which the Scriptures were known prior to that period, and that of Siôn Cent, together with Welsh poetry in similar vein from other periods, is no exception in this respect. Several of his themes reveal striking parallels with what are by now familiar biblical texts. A few examples will suffice to illustrate the point.

Much of Siôn Cent's attitude to life was clearly influenced by the doctrine of original sin. The explanation of man's mortality has to do with his first parents' transgression. In Genesis 3:3 it is stated: 'But of the fruit of the tree which is in the midst of the garden, God hath said, Ye shall not eat of it, neither shall ye touch it, lest ye die.' To quote Siôn Cent:

Utter vengeance, and plague,
For an apple did Eve cause.

In Genesis 3:19 we have: 'Dust thou art, and unto dust shalt thou return', and with these words may be compared the opening line of 'To the Emptiness and Vanity of the World', where the poet plays on *prudd (*sad) and *pridd* (earth or dust):

Woeful is the earthy body.

In lines 23–4 he proclaims:

From the earth naked he came, it's certain
That cold man will become dust.

Compare Job 1:21: 'Naked came I out of my mother's womb, and naked shall I return thither.' Here, man realizes his mortality and nakedness, this implying, of course, much more than mere physical nakedness. Following the original sin in the Garden man tries to hide his nakedness, but from now on his life is no longer ideal, neither is it reality. Life is, in fact, something that man receives but temporarily, to give him pain.

Siôn Cent more than once compares the world to a bird's nest which hangs precariously in the branches of a tree, liable at any time to be demolished by the wind. The grave he likens to a house or a bed, as in:

His bed will be low indeed,
With his forehead close to his house's rafters.

Or compare:

A hideous toad, dark the house,
If he looks, will be his bedfellow.

Such lines bring to mind words such as those of Job 17:13: 'If I wait, the grave is mine house: I have made my bed in the darkness.' In verse 14 occur the words: 'I have said to corruption, Thou art my father: to the worm, Thou art my mother, and my sister.' The reference to the worm here is particularly relevant when considering such lines as Siôn Cent's:

> And three hundred, they tell me,
> Worms are tasting him.

Although it is possible to trace themes similar to those of Siôn Cent in both native and foreign sources of earlier periods, it was in the fifteenth century that this particular kind of religious verse blossomed in Welsh literature, and a considerable body of such poetry is to be found in Welsh towards the middle of the century. Siôn Cent had brought a new emphasis and a new force to his subject-matter. No previous Welsh poet had ever sung quite like this, none had been so uncompromising or so mercilessly forthright. Death themes continued to influence Welsh classical poetry for a considerable time, and left their mark on the work of poets not generally thought of as either particularly morbid or religious —poets such as Guto'r Glyn (*fl.* 1450–90), Tudur Aled (*fl.* 1480–1525) and Wiliam Llŷn (d. 1580). However, the Welsh bardic tradition of praise continued to flourish unabated, although Siôn Cent had railed vehemently against it, and that most particularly in his *cywydd* to the Lying Muse which formed part of his debate with Rhys Goch Eryri.

The Purpose of Poetry

About the year 540—well before the composition of the poems attributed to Taliesin, on which was founded the Welsh bardic tradition of the Middle Ages—the cleric Gildas, in his *De Excidio et Conquestu Britanniae*, made a scathing attack on the poets of the court of Maelgwn Gwynedd (d. *c.* 547). In particular, he condemned the excessive and lascivious praise given by these poets to a wicked and oppressive monarch who had turned his back upon the Church. Thereafter, however, the tradition of panegyric remained virtually unchallenged for some 850 years, that is until the time of Siôn Cent and Rhys Goch Eryri.

The debate between the two arose naturally from a relatively peaceful exchange (the printed text of which includes some five *cywyddau*) between Rhys Goch and Llywelyn ab y Moel (*c.*1400–40). Rhys had composed an elegy to the poet Gruffudd Llwyd (*fl.c.*1380–1425) of Llywelyn's own native Powys, and Llywelyn, mistakenly feeling that this poem in some way defamed Powys, sang an elegiac *cywydd* in reply, thus opening the exchange, dated by Sir Ifor Williams to *c.* 1425–30. Both poets praise Gruffudd, although they give, as was noted by Mr Saunders Lewis, interestingly different pictures of him.

In their respective contributions to the debates, Rhys, Llywelyn, and Siôn Cent all reflect certain ideas regarding the origin of the Muse and the purpose of poetry. The two former, in accordance with their mentor Gruffudd Llwyd, acknowledged only one Muse, which was derived from the Holy Spirit, and considered that the essence of poetry was praise. They believed, to quote Mr Lewis, that 'the justification of their proud art was the beauty of the Christian portrayal of the ideal society'. This meant the offering of what was frequently excessive eulogy to men who were, in reality, far from perfect, not to say wicked or oppressive.

The question of the origin of the Muse and the purpose of poetry forms the very heart of the debate between Siôn Cent and Rhys Goch. Similar topics arose at later periods in debates between Guto'r Glyn and Hywel Dafi, and Edmwnd Prys (1544–1623) and Wiliam Cynwal (d. 1587). Siôn Cent's voice cuts like an axe through the eulogy and generalized ideals of the classical bardic tradition. He does, in fact, attack the very essence, the *raison d'être*, of that tradition, and although not all scholars would agree that an interpretation of this in philosophical terms is necessary, Mr Saunders Lewis's explanation, which regards Siôn Cent as a disciple of the *scientia experimentalis* propounded and taught at Oxford, still appears to be the most stimulating.

Siôn Cent seems to treat Rhys Goch Eryri as one who was out of touch with the latest philosophical ideas of his time, namely, according to Mr Lewis, the new teaching of *scientia experimentalis*. The Oxford tradition in this respect was formed by three men of genius, in particular Roger Bacon in the thirteenth century, Duns Scotus (who taught at Oxford during 1305–8), and, during the first half of the fourteenth century, William of Ockham. It was Roger Bacon who was chiefly responsible for giving the name *scientia experimentalis* to the new learning at the University, although it was most especially in William of Ockham's work (particularly in his commentary on Peter Lombard) that the meaning of the new scientific philosophy was revealed in full. One important aspect of it may be summed up thus: Neither general ideas nor abstractions have objective reality. Such was Siôn Cent's attitude towards the bardic tradition of praise. He attacked its Platonic basis, regarding the poets as heretics.

The poet maintains that there are two Muses—that which stems from Christ, and that of the Welsh bards:

> This is a Muse, weak its claim,
> From a furnace of hellish nature.

The true heavenly Muse rejects all flattery and excessive praise. The question whether hyperbolic panegyric was ethically acceptable was not unfamiliar in medieval European literature; what gave it a special significance in Wales was that it concerned the whole system of classical Welsh poetry.

The philosophy of *scientia experimentalis* could have been an important factor in Siôn Cent's religious conversion, and here it is relevant to note that, for him, the extreme (if conventional) praise sung by the Welsh bards was essentially a lie (*celwydd*). No matter how small an untruth might be, it contained sin. Gruffudd Llwyd maintained that it was not sinful to receive payment for praise, but Siôn Cent cites three authorities as contrary witnesses when dealing with falsehood. In spite of some textual difficulties, it appears, in his *cywydd* to the Lying Muse, that he actually refers to Peter Lombard (a twelfth-century Bishop of Paris), Alexander of Hales (*c.* 1175–1245), and Dietrich or Theodoric von Freiberg (1250–1310). All three may be regarded as opposed to the same kind of extreme realism as that attacked by Siôn Cent, and his reference to them, while not proving that he had actually studied their works himself, is nevertheless significant.

A knowledge on Siôn Cent's part of the work of such philosophers, as well as of the *scientia experimentalis* as such, could also have contributed an important element to the construction of his preaching poems, with their themes of judgement and death. However, the special nature of his religious verse cannot be entirely explained thus in terms of medieval philosophy, for, as has been shown above, this particular kind of poetry had its own definite and quite different roots.

Although the *cywydd* to the Lying Muse is stylistically different from the bulk of Siôn Cent's work—it is, for example, syntactically more complicated than most of his religious verse, whose style is, in general, as befitted the work of a preacher, relatively uncomplicated—it seems quite obvious nevertheless that the whole is united by common philosophical and religious bonds. Neither is this the only poem where the poet attacks the praise tradition—he does so by implication, for example, in 'Lest God be Angered'. Again, the *cywydd* to the Lying Muse is as much of a sermon as any one of his religious poems. It sets out to show the sinful foolishness of singing excessive praise to the corrupt and transitory objects of this world. Such poetry denies the facts, denies the truth. Siôn Cent seeks to show the Way to Heaven.

He has no doubts as to the true purpose and subject of poetry: it should depict man as he really is, not as an idealized type. It should proclaim the hurtful truth about him:

> A poet's estate is to study the world.

However, as man is the chief adornment of God's creation, satire (another feature of certain types of classical Welsh poetry) is not a suitable medium for his true portrayal, for this tends to degrade him too much (as well as being, perhaps, but a means, as it were, of scoring points against him, and taking unseemly pleasure in doing so).

Welsh has two words, *dychan* and *gogan*, both of which may be regarded as sometimes sharing such meanings as 'satire' or 'lampoon'. In his interpretation of Siôn Cent, however, Mr Saunders Lewis, mainly on the basis of a reference to *gogan* in the Lying Muse poem, draws a distinction between the two, saying that it was in *gogan* that the poet saw a suitable method of proclaiming the truth about man, as it represented the fruit of observation and experience.

Critics have drawn attention to Siôn Cent's frequent felicitous use of the *mot juste*, and, in the long run, the effectiveness of his *gogan* depends to an important degree on his use of words, as when he describes the eminent man being buried 'diligently' or 'busily' (*diwyd*) in the ground:

After wine, the dear friend's placed
Diligently in the ground.

It is the use of the word *diwyd*, following *annwyl gâr* ('dear friend' or 'dear relative'), that is especially effective here, and so typical of the poet's pithy style. The reference to wine may either convey the inevitable contrast with past glory, or, perhaps, a session of pre-burial drinking. In another poem, the body is described as being taken 'hurriedly' (*ar frys*) from the court or mansion to the church. Again, it is not the reference to the grave's putrefaction—such descriptions were common enough in medieval religious verse—but the use of *profi* (to taste, to test) that conveys the unpleasant truth in the couplet, already quoted:

And three hundred, they tell me,
Worms are tasting him.

The word *profi* in the original is suggestively ambiguous, and could perhaps be an echo of *scientia experimentalis* within the confines of the grave itself. The dry, almost casual, *sangiad* or parenthesis 'they tell me' adds a kind of grim humour to the already grizzly scene portrayed.

A great deal of Siôn Cent's work may be regarded as a reflection of *gogan* as interpreted by Mr Saunders Lewis. Perhaps the poet's most typical composition in this respect is his longest *cywydd*, 'To the Emptiness and Vanity of the World', described by Mr Lewis as a *cywydd* to a lord according to the new teaching of *scientia experimentalis*. The poem combines many of the most common death themes with a characteristically ruthless mode of expression which must have been awesomely effective in the transmission of the author's urgent and all-important message to his listeners.

BIBLIOGRAPHY

Texts

Henry Lewis, Thomas Roberts, Ifor Williams (eds.), *Cywyddau Iolo Goch ac Eraill* (Bangor, 1925; 2nd edn, Caerdydd, 1937).
Thomas Parry (ed.), *The Oxford Book of Welsh Verse* (Oxford, 1962).
Eurys I. Rowlands (ed.), *Poems of the Cywyddwyr* (Dublin, 1976).

Translations

Joseph P. Clancy, *Medieval Welsh Lyrics* (London, 1965).
Tony Conran, *Welsh Verse* (Bridgend, 1986).
Gwyn Williams, *Welsh Poems. Sixth Century to 1600* (London, 1973).

Critical Studies

W. Ambrose Bebb, *Machlud yr Oesoedd Canol* (Abertawe, 1951), esp. Chapter XVI.
Andrew Breeze, 'Llyfr durgrys', *Bulletin of the Board of Celtic Studies*, xxxiii (1986), 145.
Idem, 'Siôn Cent, the Oldest Animals, and the Day of Man's Life', *Bulletin of the Board of Celtic Studies*, xxxiv (1987), 70–6.
Idem, 'Llyfr Alysanna', *Bulletin of the Board of Celtic Studies*, xxxvii (1990), 108–11.
James M. Clark, *The Dance of Death in the Middle Ages and the Renaissance* (Glasgow, 1950).
Stewart C. Easton, *Roger Bacon and his Search for a Universal Science* (Oxford, 1952).
Anne Fremantle, *The Age of Belief* (New York, 1955).
R. Geraint Gruffydd, 'Marwnad Lleucu Llwyd gan Lywelyn Goch Amheurig Hen', in J. E. Caerwyn Williams (ed.), *Ysgrifau Beirniadol I* (Dinbych, 1965), 126–37.
S. J. H. Heritage (ed.), *The Early English Versions of the Gesta Romanorum* (Early English Text Society, London, 1879).
J. Huizinga, *The Waning of the Middle Ages* (Pelican, 1955), esp. Chapter XI.
Bobi Jones, 'Dau Besimist', in *I'r Arch* (Llandybïe, 1959), 70–97.
Idem, 'Ymryson ac Ymddiddan Corff ac Enaid', in J. E. Caerwyn Williams (ed.), *Ysgrifau Beirniadol V* (Dinbych, 1970), 44–61.
Henry Lewis, 'Dadl yr Enaid a'r Corff', *Bulletin of the Board of Celtic Studies*, iii, no. 2 (May 1926), 119–22.
Saunders Lewis, *Braslun o Hanes Llenyddiaeth Gymraeg* (Caerdydd, 1932), esp. Chapters IV and VI.

Idem, 'Sion Cent', in Gwynn ap Gwilym (ed.), *Meistri a'u Crefft* (Caerdydd, 1981), 148–60.

A. T. E. Matonis, 'Late Medieval Poetics and Some Welsh Bardic Debates', *Bulletin of the Board of Celtic Studies*, xxix, no.i (May 1982), 635–65. See also Ann Matonis, 'Barddoneg a Rhai Ymrysonau Barddol Cymraeg yr Oesoedd Canol Diweddar', in J. E. Caerwyn Williams (ed.), *Ysgrifau Beirniadol XII* (Dinbych, 1982), 157–200.

Dafydd Densil Morgan, 'Athroniaeth Siôn Cent', *Y Traethodydd* 138 (1983), 13–20.

Sean O'Tuama, 'Serch Cwrtais mewn Llenyddiaeth Wyddeleg', in John Rowlands (ed.), *Dafydd ap Gwilym a Chanu Serch yr Oesoedd Canol* (Caerdydd, 1975), 18–42.

Jean Rittmueller, 'The Religious Poetry of Siôn Cent', in *Proceedings of the Harvard Celtic Colloquium*, iii (1983), 107–47.

Nicholas Rogers, 'The So-called Portrait of Sion Cent', *Bulletin of the Board of Celtic Studies*, xxxi (1984), 103–4.

Gilbert E. Ruddock, 'Amwysedd ac Eironi ym Marwnad Lleucu Llwyd', in J. E. Caerwyn Williams (ed.), *Ysgrifau Beirniadol IX* (Dinbych, 1976), 61–79.

Glanmor Williams, *The Welsh Church from Conquest to Reformation* (Cardiff, 1962), esp. 112–13, 463–75.

Ifor Williams, 'Dafydd ap Gwilym a'r Glêr', in *Transactions of the Honourable Society of Cymmrodorion*, 1913–14, esp. 185–91.

Idem, 'Cywydd Cyfrinach Rhys Goch Eryri', *Bulletin of the Board of Celtic Studies*, i, no. 1 (October, 1921), 43–50.

Idem, 'Dwy Gân o Llyfr Coch Talgarth', *Bulletin of the Board of Celtic Studies*, ii, no. 2 (May 1924), 118–30.

J. E. Caerwyn Williams, 'Ymryson ac Ymddiddan y Corff ac Enaid', *National Library of Wales Journal*, iv, nos. 3 & 4 (Summer 1946), 184–8.

CHAPTER 8

DAFYDD NANMOR

D. MYRDDIN LLOYD

Dafydd Nanmor was prominent in a small group of poets composing towards the middle and in the latter half of the fifteenth century who were supreme in what has been described as the *grand siècle* of Welsh verse. There was among many a high standard of formal achievement and style as a consequence of a long period of metrical development reaching its completion, but there were a few masters, like Dafydd Nanmor, Dafydd ab Edmwnd, Guto'r Glyn, Gutun Owain, and a little later Tudur Aled, who in addition were men of individual genius. Not only could they say what was expected of them with polish, but although their work was largely governed by their social role as panegyrists, each had a vision and qualities of his own. For too long these classical poets had been regarded merely as models of formal excellence, for their mastery in the use of the language, but a new appreciation was heralded in 1925 by Saunders Lewis's essay on Dafydd Nanmor where the significance of what that poet had to say was emphasized.

There is a new directness in a Dafydd Nanmor poem. On the one hand there is simplification of diction, combined with stricter patterns than previously of alliteration and internal rhyme. This dual achievement meant great command over words, seen in a new simplicity, smoothness and dexterity. In *Gogynfeirdd* poetry the perfection of the individual line of verse was much sought, and in *cywyddau* prior to Dafydd Nanmor's day the sentence and the paragraph were what mainly mattered, but with him the couplet comes into its own, and he was also adept at building up a skilful sequence of couplets. His poems are not usually long (some 25 to 35 couplets), the unity of the whole poem is well achieved, he is master of the striking opening couplet leading direct to the central theme, and his best work is marked by lyrical warmth.

Let us consider one of his best *cywyddau*: the first of a series of poems to members of the Rhys family of Tywyn, on the Teifi estuary, his chief patrons. In the other poems one hears of various merits, but here unity is achieved by confining attention throughout to the excellence of Rhys's table, in quality and quantity. It is one sustained hyperbole, and without any preamble we are assured that 'Rhys, below Aeron (*i.e.* in southern Ceredigion) has the best table from Dover to Anglesey: the finest householders (he and his splendid fair one) from Adam to the present day'. This effusion can well repel or amuse us today, and indeed sometime before Dafydd Nanmor's day Welsh poets had been castigated, by Siôn Cent, for flattery and deception, and for fostering empty pride. The charge of deception was met by Guto'r Glyn, a contemporary of Dafydd Nanmor, who insisted that no one was deceived, that he meant no deception, and that the so-called flattery was nothing but pleasant or complimentary speech. It was, in other words, a well-understood convention, and once this is realized it can be appreciated for what was intended.

It was an effective means of presenting enthusiastically a picture of good living and generosity. Dafydd Nanmor was passionately concerned for the continuance of bardic learning and culture. The bards no longer enjoyed a protected status under the law, there were no Welsh princes or courts in the old sense, alien castles, boroughs and officials had been instituted and given power, so the bard was entirely dependent on the voluntary patronage of a not unlimited number of landed families and a few priests and abbots. Dafydd Nanmor was much concerned about a factor, often suspect and ignored in our 'democratic' age: leadership, and much of his verse is concerned with what it entailed and where it could be found. It must be admitted, too, that to a greater degree than many other poets he loved comfort and ease. Not for him the discomforts of travel and delight in wild things and the open country. The hard life he abhorred. This gives a very human quality to his enthusiastic praise of life in a well-stocked and protected country house.

Dafydd Nanmor is called after a village of that name, near Beddgelert in Snowdonia, where much of his early life seems to have been spent. He first arose to fame as a love-poet, much under the influence of Dafydd ap Gwilym, and some, though not all, of his extant *cywyddau* to ladies would appear to have been composed before his having to leave Gwynedd for south Wales. In fact he refers to the earlier Dafydd in a poem to a brooch of birch twigs shaped into a heart, given him by a girl in exchange for a *cywydd*: Dafydd ap Gwilym too had been thus rewarded. And in his elegy,

Hywel Rheinallt maintains that Dafydd Nanmor had gone home to heaven to his 'brother of the Teifi valley'. Like others before his day, and since, our poet seems to have got into trouble over a woman, a certain 'Gwen o'r Ddôl'. We do not know what was his offence but it must have been considered serious, for not only was he tried by jury, but he had to leave home and spend the remainder of his life in south Wales.

His descriptions of girls, although far more than merely conventional, do respect the conventions then prevalent not only in Wales but also in England, France and elsewhere. Great attention is paid to the girl's hair, which is golden, like flame, with the gloss of wax and the smoothness of silk; skin is white as foam, eyebrows are black, cheeks red and eyes azure blue, teeth are small, lips sweet as honey and the form slender and shapely. They, like those extolled by the *Gogynfeirdd* and by Dafydd ap Gwilym, are of cultivated quiet speech. The influence of ap Gwilym is nowhere stronger than in the mastery of the technique known as *dyfalu*. This term is difficult to translate in this context. It is an onrush of comparisons, a heaping up of metaphors and similes. Five of Dafydd Nanmor's poems are so constructed, two to the beloved's hair, two others being more extensive *descriptiones puellae*, and one where the object is a peacock.

The poet is suffering, struck by loose golden hair like a bush of silk, a pale moon of fine gold, a long golden bush under fine linen, broomlike, with sunlight weaving through it, *et alia, et alia*. Llio, the owner of the hair in another and more famous poem, stems from a leading north-Cardiganshire family where the muse was well honoured. The opening couplet is perhaps the best known of all Dafydd Nanmor's verses, 'Golden-haired Llio, silver hued, it (the hair) flashes like fine (gold) dust. It is plaited and like golden nobles' (a coin first struck by Edward III in 1339). No comb of wood is worthy of it, but one of skate bones. The poet compares it to the hair on the image of Mary in Menevia (St David's), or on Non (mother of Saint David) or flowing over the bosoms of mermaids. It is like a fine yellow cloak, like flame, golden wax, orange (not then a common fruit in Wales), honeysuckle; on the nape of Llio's neck it is like 'golden smoke' (a halo). The poem ends with an appeal to God that 'primrose-haired Llio shall not die'.

It is significant that the bird Dafydd Nanmor chose as a love-messenger is not any frequenter of the wild or open country, but a peacock, a bird of the lawn by the big house. How unlike Dafydd ap Gwilym! In a short opening passage it is incited to make mischief between Gwen o'r Ddôl and Eiddig (*Le Jaloux*), her husband, and the poem ends by begging it to bring her away from his home. But these are only trimmings to a magnificent series of comparisons. The bird's rich dress is a May-time cloak of feathers and flowers, magical, a thousand honeyed golden-coloured wafers, a beautifully woven cloak like many moons, like a bishop's robe, ornaments of gold, rainbow-like in variegated colours, a blue dragon of church glass.

There are two light-hearted love-poems, the already-mentioned one to the birch-twig heart-shaped brooch, and a 'confession' by the poet *à la* Dafydd ap Gwilym that he prefers to go for Gwen's sake to the fair than to mass, and that to impress her he dresses in the height of fashion with his hair bobbed like the bottom of a gown, and his shoes pointed like a bittern's beak. He would write compliments on her glove, would strive against the wind to the top of a hill (quite a feat for him!) and send her an eagle's load of letters.

'Grievous is reliance on this earth, life in this world is a brief semblance. I loved a lovely young woman, and she died.' Thus opens a fine poem in far more sombre mood. The pathetic fallacies it contains are among the finest in Welsh. 'Wretched on the hillsides are the cuckoo, the birches and trees, sad the song of the thrush and the grey nightingale. May should not bear leaves any more, the branches are all bare; for me the very sun is dead, and all generosity as nothing.'

Delightful and skilful as the love-poems may be, Dafydd Nanmor's stature as a major poet does not depend on these, but on the panegyrics to patrons and to the leading figures of the Lancastrian-Tudor nobility. These have far greater depth of reflection and insight into the very foundations of the Welsh civilization that meant so much to him. They may be divided into three groups. The first consists of poems to members of the Rhys of Tywyn family that befriended him for long years after his arrival as a fugitive in Ceredigion. The second is the verse to Edmund and Jasper, sons of Owain Tudor, and to Harry Tudor, before his accession to the throne as Henry VII. The third is a more miscellaneous group of poems to various patrons.

The Tywyn poems form an impressive unity that avoids being repetitive. Whereas the first, a *cywydd*, as already mentioned, through extremely hyperbolistic figures and descriptions concentrates on presenting with great feeling a rich impression of the feasting at Tywyn, the next two, to the same Rhys, are *awdlau*, and with a wider scope. In addition to his being a supreme master of the *cywydd*, Dafydd Nanmor made a notable contribution to the development of the *awdl* in his day, by introducing into what had been this more elevated form of verse the extreme simplicity, directness and brevity that mark his *cywyddau*. His *awdlau* are on the pattern, well established in his day, whereby they open with a series of *englynion*, effortlessly concatinated by the repetition of words and phrases, followed by the main body in specifically *awdl* metres. He is master of conveying deep feeling by means of ordinary words chosen with unerring skill. To Rhys's halls whereto people throng may there not come 'the *night* of want for ever and ever'. He adopts a figure, used previously by Gruffudd ap Maredudd ap Dafydd, which he is to employ several times and with powerful effect: he wishes for Rhys long life like an *oaktree* on his land. After glimpses of his wealth and trading (he buys from the great vineyards across the southern sea . . . eighteen shiploads of casks), an impression of the extent of his generosity is built up by a series of exaggerations: five thousand in his pay, a thousand clad in his clothes, a thousand poets, and 'like the snowflakes on Rhydodyn, numerous as leaves on ash twigs, and like the sowing of seed until every Mayday he sowed money and dealt it to us'.

The next *awdl* also opens with glimpses of great concourses gathering at Tywyn, where as in Rome 'he counted the whole world', and where three emperors could be amply supplied, but the poem is mainly a contrast between Rhys's gentleness and his anger. To the weak he was charitable, but he could well handle the alien townsfolk, rough and splendid in dealing with proud ones, 'the gravel from the seas trembled before him'. The French had known the force of his grip.

'Too taut snaps' says a Welsh proverb, and on one occasion, we know not why, Dafydd Nanmor had aroused the anger of his patron and friend, and had had to appeal in a *cywydd* for the restoration of the old happy relationship. He begins by reminding Rhys that on account of his songs to Gwen o'r Ddôl, the land of Gwynedd was closed against him, and that in his plight he had come south in disgrace and had found a protector. He feels he has not deserved a break of the relationship. Rhys's anger was not a pleasant New Year's gift, for where he showed offence, Ceredigion and the whole of the south would take his lead. Dafydd will be forced to a life of outlawry in the Berwyn forest, following wild deer on the slopes. He dreads the prospect, being one who loved his ease, and would sooner be in a sea where the bottom has never been seen. He appeals to Rhys's wife to plead for him, reminding her of several instances in Scripture and legend where the importuning of a woman had caused a man to be merciful.

A *cywydd* in praise of the household of Tywyn traces Rhys's ancestry back for several generations, with emphasis on the continuity (*olynol o hil Einion* —'successively from Einion's stock'). Here by the shore is the best of rearing— 'greyhound, goshawk, falconer, steed and ox, woman and man'. These men were salmon among herring. 'The eagle housed in the height of an oak is a terror to small birds.' Common folk are like thorn bushes but these are the strong oak trees. As the whole world turns to Rome so does Ceredigion to Tywyn. The fires of its kitchen are like great Etna, and if all the land were barren, bread and wine here would supply a kingdom.

The land of Tywyn, however, was not always immune from calamities, and a windstorm from over the sea once covered it with sand: 'Wind made the place of wheat and wine a barren seashore, except for gorse.' The poet appeals, in a *cywydd*, to Pedrog, the patron saint of the parish, to raise a counter-wind to blow the sand back into the sea. But a greater calamity was in store: the death of Rhys. In words of utter simplicity intricately woven into *cynghanedd* with consummate skill but with apparent ease, Dafydd Nanmor composed his finest elegy. The directness and anguish of the opening *englyn* have a piercing effect: 'Woe is me of my birth, and the hour I was born. God! What an end to my fate. If Rhys has gone from his bright and sheltered court, I also am about to go.' The reference to the comfort of Tywyn leads him on from his own woe to the greater loss, mitigated only by a passing reference to Rhys's two sons, the 'two young lions'. In recalling the feastings of yesterday, he mentions good wines by name, suggesting with what discrimination they had been chosen, but now there is lamentation. He cannot see clearly ahead through a flood of tears—a striking figure to convey the uncertainty of his future. Towards the end of a long series of complaints: woe . . . woe . . . woe . . . he bewails the coldness now of Rhys's hand, that formerly had closed to a fist of protection and opened to bestow gifts.

The two sons proved short-lived, and although Dafydd composed a noble elegy in *englyn* and *awdl* metres to Tomas, the finest poem of the whole sequence is a *cywydd* of advice to young Rhys, the grandson of his great patron, after the death of his father. The note is struck in the opening couplet: 'Rhys, you are the flower on the summer rose, Rhys's grandson, not of the lowest stock.' Before imbuing him with pride in his ancestry he reminds him of the obligations of high rank. 'To the country you are a heritage and a home to us, the right foot of the Tywyn land.' Then in striking figures comes the core of this social philosophy: 'Like an ashtree you grow from many patricians, and ear grows not on corn where there is no root; what grows from right seed grows from root to tip.' Rhys's stock is good from both sides: 'two streams in mid-valley will provide a strong current to the lake'. With this heritage, and with references to eagles, hawks, lions and stags, he urges the young heir to seek the heights, for 'a salmon takes the same course as his father upstream'.

In his poems to the Tudors, Dafydd Nanmor is working on a far larger canvas. It is no longer Tywyn and Ceredigion, not even Wales or even England alone, for Jasper and Edmund were the sons of Owain Tudor, and of Katherine of France, formerly the wife of Henry V and mother also of Henry VI. They were thus of European royal stock, a fact not lost on Dafydd Nanmor as we shall see. But to the poet their Welsh origins were no less illustrious. 'Two noblemen, from Troy and Greece, the root is good', thus begins a *cywydd* written between 1453 and 1456 to the two earls, sons of Owain Tudor. It is mentioned that as descendants of Rhodri they were of Welsh royal stock, but through Cadwaladr, of Trojan stock, they derived from rulers of the whole of Britain (according to the implicitly believed *Historia Regum Britanniae* of Geoffrey of Monmouth). Dafydd then refers to the stream of Continental royal blood through Katherine, after which in a manner much developed by the fifteenth-century Welsh poets, he describes in detail the Tudor crest. It was earlier than Mortimer's Cross, Owain Tudor was still very much alive, and the poet speculates that if he were to raise his banner, sixty thousand 'between here and Maelor' (in north-east Wales) would follow him. He makes clear what he has in mind by referring to an old prophecy that the dragon of Wales would destroy the white dragon of England. The spark of Llywelyn still kindles in Anglesey, and the Tudors were that spark and would 'keep warm Cadwaladr's hearth'.

The incitement is even more unambiguous and extravagant in the *awdl* to Jasper. Geoffrey of Monmouth had recounted that Arthur, after achieving power in Britain, had conquered far and wide in Europe, so why should not Jasper, of Trojan and French royal blood, do likewise? Welsh, English and European place-names are strung together in profusion. The metre (*rhupunt hir*) of the latter portion of the *awdl*, with its breathless accumulation of internal double rhymes, conveys the sense of onrush that the poet intends.

Edmund died in 1456 but soon was born his posthumous son, later to become Henry VII, and in Dafydd Nanmor's elegy in *cywydd* metre, to Edmund, Welsh hopes are held to remain high while Jasper and Henry live. 'The Welsh shall have as ruler a fine Welshman. Through God's help it will come some day.' The hopes and prognostications continue in a *cywydd* to the babe Harry ('If an earl's face is in the grave, an earl was born last year'), and in a later *awdl* to him, but obviously earlier than Bosworth. In the *cywydd* we read that the stem from the old tree will become a great ruling oak, a far-extending thick oak, its root in the Trojan sea, and its branches extending through the land of the *fleur-de-lis* and Germany. Like Alexander he will cross land and sea supported by two birds (a legend known in Wales as early as the *Book of Taliesin*). The euphoria reaches its height however in the *awdl*. A long string of hazards he will overcome is woven into a series of *englynion*, followed by the interlacing into an *awdl* metre of the names of scores of saints who will protect him. The climax is attained in foretelling his progress from earl to duke, to prince, to king and to emperor, ruler of the West, all of which he was to achieve except the last. Poems such as these, noisy rhetoric though they often were, prepared the way for Bosworth, and the strange confusion of ambitions and ideals they reveal deluded the Welsh into believing that the battle returned sovereignty to Wales and was a fulfilment of age-old prophecies.

The third group of panegyrics bring us back to the saner world of the Tywyn poems. They are addressed to various patrons, mostly from among the landed families of west Wales. Llandygwy is a few miles south of Tywyn, and Rhys ap Llywelyn, of that house, is addressed in an *awdl* and a *cywydd*. Not only is he commended for generosity ('Snow in a wood clings no longer encircling a branch, than money, old gold, stays in Rhys's purse') but we are told that he was thus hospitable 'for the sake of the *iaith*', which can mean the language or those that spoke it. We learn also some details of his devotional readings. The widening horizons of Welshmen are seen in references to Germany, Brittany, Cologne, Guienne and Guise as places that Rhys had known. In the *cywydd*, in particular, there is a fine exposition of the obligations of high status in society. Cheerfulness, absence of empty pride and superficiality, shrewdness without deceit, the scorning of bribery, good judgement, the wisdom of 'Solomon ap David', great love of God and the Church and the incumbent priest, not being habitually sad, but only so when encountered by evil: these qualities he finds in Rhys, whose *perchentyaeth* (householdership) is good.

It would be hard to find a more enticing description of sumptuous ease expressed with such mellifluous fluidity than in the *awdl* to Dafydd ap Thomas, priest in a lower Teifi parish, but a man of means and of landed stock. 'Chests full of white loaves from an abundance of wheat, and many courses with fine herbs, birds and fish.' We see the heavy loads from the kitchen; wines, bragget and mead like gushes from a fountain, the busy domestic staff, and, for a climax, the poet's bed 'worthy of a duke, plenteous its fine down, and above it a coloured tapestry with a picture of the sky and archangels'. But the obligations of such wealth were not forgotten for 'as God had generously given him riches, so he passed them on as gifts'. This conception of a sacramental quality about the civilized life as described by Dafydd Nanmor is a pervasive element in his outlook.

Golden-haired Llio was not the only member of the house of Gogerddan in northern Ceredigion to whom Dafydd sang. There is a *cywydd* by him to Dafydd Llwyd, whom he reminds, for some reason, of the fable by the 'man of Scythia' (Aesop) that arrows though easily broken one at a time cannot be snapped when kept together in a quiver. In this poem also the obligations of leadership are stressed. 'There is no false pride in my eagle. The proud man will be deserted by his men. He (the leader) has made all his servicemen and they have made him a man. A man can make men better, and men make a man better. A man makes men to follow him, and men make a man courageous.' There were certainly two sides to Dafydd's teaching on the role of patricians.

It is no wonder that he composed an *awdl* and a *cywydd* to the seasoned Lancastrian warrior, Dafydd ab Ifan ab Einion, who held

Harlech for seven years against the Yorkists. The more interesting is the *cywydd*, where we learn that it was while ab Ifan was warring in France that Dafydd Nanmor had to leave Gwynedd for good. He had been found guilty by a jury of twelve, on which there was no man from Edeirnion. Whatever the point of this remark, Dafydd praises Edeirnion for its strength and love of freedom, and it is interesting that when he had offended Rhys o'r Tywyn, it was to Berwyn, in the same region, he thought of going.

Lancastrian though he was, during the Yorkist ascendancy Dafydd did compose *awdlau* to two who had fought for the white rose. One is merely a metrical exercise exhibiting his skill in including all the twenty-four metres of the learned poets. It was addressed to Dafydd ap Thomas ap Dafydd, constable of Cardigan castle, and therefore one whom it was well that a protégé of the house of Tywyn should keep sweet. His ancestry is lauded, but little said of the cause he supported. The constable of Aberystwyth, Wiliam Fychan, was the other Yorkist. Again the praise is largely personal, particularly for prowess in battle: where his spear struck it was useless bringing ointment!

The *cywydd* to Rhys Morgan, abbot of Strata Florida, has features of its own. It is almost entirely a glowing description of the building and reveals a fascination, which was developing in Welsh poetry in the late fourteenth and in the fifteenth century in architecture, in the quality and appearance of building materials, and in ornament. The magnitude of the abbey impresses the poet, and on the other hand such detail as the carvings above the nave. He delights in the frost-like appearance of the lead, the molten glass-work on the doors, the oakwood, the stone arches, the kitchen, the bell-tower with its weather-cock, the enclosing wall and the panes of glass affording protection from the wind. He is awed by the great height above the altar. What a change from the time of the poets of the princes when praise was so largely confined to God, men and women. It is often maintained that the Welsh have ears but no eyes for man-made beauty, but that is certainly not true of the poets of the *grand siècle*.

Two *cywyddau* by Dafydd to God have survived, and also a series of *englynion* to the fifteen signs of the approach of Judgement Day, and *englynion* to the signs of the zodiac. They all display his usual formal dexterity, but otherwise they are somewhat commonplace. A *cywydd* to the names of God reveals some acquaintance with the three ancient languages, the poem to Doomsday ends not with the cataclasm but on a more serene note: the new heaven and new earth 'where no harm can come'. In a poem to God there are touches of poetic imagination as in describing Him as 'Emperor of myrrh and frankincense, sea and land'. There is one religious poem that reaches a higher level. The Black Death in the previous century, and devastating pestilences in Dafydd's day had left a frightful and haunting impression, and it was noted that the conjunction of Saturn with other planets had accompanied some of the worst of them. 'To God and the planet Saturn', a *cywydd* by Dafydd, twice his usual length, conveys powerfully the awe and fear and wonder excited by this coincidence. In a long series of questions, the poet struggles with the mystery, showing some mathematical knowledge of the planet's movements. In the end, however, he turns to the commonly held view that plagues, wars, and other misfortunes come because of God's anger at sins, particularly of the leaders in church and landed estates. Fervent prayer, fasting, strong faith in Christ, are the remedies, for the virtue of the good men of the world will prevail.

Dafydd Nanmor delighted in practising his verbal and metrical dexterity in such things as scraps of natural observation, weather lore and prognostications, riddles, the number of minutes in a year, tides, herbal remedies, the time spent by Adam in hell before being rescued by Christ, the divisions of Wales between the sons of Rhodri, and in *tours de force* such as the composing of verses consisting only of particles, or which could be read backwards or forwards, containing all the eight parts of speech, or only of pronouns or of nouns and adjectives, every syllable beginning with *d-*, or containing only one consonant.

Hywel Rheinallt in his elegy to Dafydd dwells on the dire loss to Welsh poetry in his death. One line in this poem sums up well what was really characteristic of this major poet: 'Gone is the great *myfyrdod*' (meditation or reflectiveness).

BIBLIOGRAPHY

Texts and Notes

Thomas Roberts and Ifor Williams (eds), *The Poetical Works of Dafydd Nanmor* (Cardiff, 1923). Text in Welsh. Introduction and notes in English.

Translations

J. P. Clancy, *Medieval Welsh Lyrics* (London, 1965).
Tony Conran, *Welsh Verse* (Bridgend, 1986).
Gwyn Williams, *The Burning Tree* (London, 1956).

Critical studies

Saunders Lewis, 'Dafydd Nanmor', *Y Llenor*, iv (1925), 135–48.
Bobi Jones, 'Beirdd yr Uchelwyr a'r Byd', in J. E. Caerwyn Williams (ed.), *Ysgrifau Beirniadol VIII* (Dinbych, 1974) 29–42.
Gilbert Ruddock, *Dafydd Nanmor* (Caernarfon, 1992).

CHAPTER 9

CYNGHANEDD, METRE, PROSODY

EURYS ROWLANDS

The classical Welsh metres of the late Middle Ages are syllabic, i.e. metre is determined by the number of syllables within the line. It has been said that 'most ears . . . discover that the count of syllables alone does not produce any pronounced rhythmic interest; syllabic metres in English generate a prosody more interesting to the eye than to the ear'. In Welsh, however, poetry in the syllabic metres was specifically aimed at pleasing the ear, for according to the mid-sixteenth-century *Pum Llyfr Cerddwriaeth* (Five Books of Poetics) poetry was not made but for sweetness to the ear, and from the ear to the heart. And of course, opinion in this matter does not depend on a statement in a bardic grammar, for if anything is generally recognized about medieval Welsh poetry it is the fact that it was especially designed to produce aural interest. The reason for this is that on the basis of syllabic metres was superimposed *cynghanedd*, a word meaning 'harmony' used as a technical term for the complex and intricate system of sound correspondences which became an integral part of Welsh prosody from the late thirteenth century onwards. The poetry of the fourteenth and fifteenth centuries that has been preserved to us, consisting of many hundreds of poems, and much of the poetry of the sixteenth century, has been written in *cynghanedd*, and is known as 'strict' poetry. In the sixteenth century however there emerged types of poetry without *cynghanedd* and this is known as 'free' poetry. To this day there is a distinction between the strict poetry composed according to the traditional rules of late medieval *cynghanedd* and free poetry which has no *cynghanedd* and is roughly comparable to English poetry although there has persisted a strong tendency to count syllables.

As one would expect, scansion into feet bears no relevance to the prosody of Welsh strict poetry, but it is not surprising to find that there is some connection between it and a strong-stress system of metrics, for *cynghanedd* was of course ultimately derived from a simpler system of internal rhyme and of alliteration similiar to that found in Old and Middle English strong-stress metres. It must be made clear that from the outset alliteration in Welsh, unlike English, was combined with syllabic metres; but alliteration, as well as internal rhyme, implies that in some way strong-stress is important metrically, for when words are alliterated or rhymed they are inevitably strongly stressed within the line.

Strong-stress metres have a fixed number of strongly stressed syllables and a varying number of unstressed syllables. Syllabic metres have a fixed number of syllables of which the number of those strongly stressed may vary though strong-stress is not normally regarded as an attribute of syllabic metres. By combining the features of syllabic metres with strongly stressed alliteration and internal rhyme Welsh strict poetry has evolved a unique prosodic system distinguished by a marriage between an iron rigidity of form and what can be a quite splendid variability of rhythm. The amazing quality of the rhythm is that it is the same time so pronounced and yet so variable.

In describing *cynghanedd* in English, writers have often quoted or composed lines in English to exemplify the system. This is quite misconceived, for *cynghanedd* is not only something quite foreign to English prosody, it is also a metrical embellishment which does not at all suit the English language, and sounds absolutely wrong in it, thus giving a completely false impression of the nature of *cynghanedd.* Welsh is phonetically a very very different language from English, and has three characteristics which make *cynghanedd* a most suitable medium for Welsh poetry: firstly, stress is regular in Welsh and occurs normally on the penultimate syllable (and never on a previous syllable) of polysyllabic words; secondly, consonants are all well-articulated and distinct; thirdly, vowel sounds are always pure and clear. As a result, whereas in English the effect is unnatural and unpleasant, the ordered chiming of consonants that occurs in *cynghanedd* is a very apt embellishment to the particular kind of beauty that characterizes the phonology of the Welsh language.

There are four main kinds of *cynghanedd. Cynghanedd lusg* ('dragging' *cynghanedd*) has internal rhyme only. *Cynghanedd groes* ('cross' *cynghanedd*) and *cynghanedd draws* ('across' *cynghanedd*) have consonantal correspondence only. *Cynghanedd sain* ('sound' *cynghanedd*) has both internal rhyme and consonantal correspondence. The special kind of consonantal correspondence that occurs in *cynghanedd* cannot be called 'alliteration', though it was evolved from primitive alliteration. Therefore, for the sake of brevity it will be called 'consonance' here. As the seven-syllable line was by far the most common in late medieval Welsh poetry, and still is, for that matter, in modern Welsh strict poetry, *cynghanedd* will be discussed here in relationship to the seven-syllable line, but of course, the basic principles of *cynghanedd* apply in the same way to lines of all lengths.

In *cynghanedd lusg* the line ends in a word of more than one syllable with the accent, regularly, on the last syllable but one. The end of a word elsewhere in the line rhymes with this accented penultimate syllable of the last word. The first rhyme may be accented or unaccented.

Ni thau y góg a'i chógor

Y ferch dáwel wallt-félen

The first rhyme may occur in any syllable in the line from the first to the fifth, though the rhyme must be unaccented if occurring in the fifth syllable so as to avoid having the two strong stresses in adjacent syllables:

Hi yw'r benna 'Nghaerllíon

Asgell archángel mélyn

As can be seen, the internal rhyme in *cynghanedd lusg* results in two words being strongly stressed with a caesura after the first strongly stressed word, and the other occurring at the end of the line:

Banhadlwyn | uwch yr wyneb

This is a general rule of *cynghanedd*, that the key-words in the correspondence or harmony are strongly stressed, or metrically emphasized, and are followed by a pause, one pause being a caesura and the other being the end of the line. Only the key-words, two in the case of *cynghanedd lusg, cynghanedd groes* and *cynghanedd draws*, and three in the case of *cynghanedd sain* which has two caesurae, are strongly stressed. It must be pointed out that all seven-syllable lines of *cynghanedd* have, except sometimes in *cynghanedd sain*, a system of secondary stresses, either one or two in the line, but this matter will not be discussed here though it can be stated that secondary stresses play an important part in the variability of rhythm in strict poetry.

In *cynghanedd groes* the correspondence between the key-words is a matter of consonance, and this is integrally connected with the accentuation of the two strongly stressed words: that is, if a consonant comes before the accent in one key-word it must occur before the accent similarly in the other key-word, and if it comes between the accented syllable and the following unaccented syllable in one key-word it must be repeated in the same position in the second key-word. Because of the nature of Welsh, a line may end in an accented syllable, or in an unaccented syllable with the previous syllable accented, and the position is exactly the same before the caesura. In *cynghanedd groes* the following possibilities are recognized:

(*a*) . . . ´ | . . . ´ e.g. . . . *Dúw* . . . *dýn*
cytbwys acennog ('balanced' with 'accented' last syllable)

(*b*) . . . ´ ˘ | . . . ´ ˘ e.g. . . . *tráwstĕr* . . . *trístŵch*
cytbwys diacen ('balanced' with 'unaccented' last syllable)

(*c*) . . . ´ / . . . ´ ˘ e.g. . . . *gwýllt* . . . *géllt*ŷ*dd*
anghytbwys diacen ('unbalanced' with 'unaccented' last syllable)

As is seen, the consonants at the end of the key-words do not correspond, but vary. The reason for this is obvious. If the consonants at the ends of the words corresponded, and if the vowels preceding them also corresponded, there would be full rhyme between the words, and in a line of *cynghanedd* it would be wrong to have the caesura rhyming with the end-rhyme which should only rhyme with the end of another line. Otherwise there was no restriction on the ends of the key-words having consonantal correspondence though it was not necessary for them to correspond and usually correspondence did not occur. In the later period not only was full rhyme between the caesura and the end of the line avoided but also *proest*, a semi-rhyme in which the end consonants tallied but in which the vocalic content of the syllable varied but belonged to the same general class, e.g. one short vowel corresponded to a different short vowel.

In *cynghanedd groes*, consonance encompasses not only the key-words but the whole of the line:

(a) Ewyllys Duw yw lles dyn
ll s d'- | ll s d'n

(b) Wedi trawster daw tristwch
d tr' sd˘r |d tr'sd˘ch

(c) Eryr gwyllt ar war gelltydd
r r g' lld | r r g' lld˘dd

In analysing the consonance of *cynghanedd groes* every consonant in the line must be accounted for. It will also be noticed that in analysing two of the lines above a difference occurs between the orthography and the consonantal analysis, i.e. *st* and *llt* are analysed as *sd* and *lld*. This is because *cynghanedd* analysis is not a mechanical matter for the eye, but for the ear. This means that several considerations must be borne in mind, for example two consonants coming together are regarded as one when analysing, e.g.—

Dy ddethol di oedd ddoethaf

d dd'th˘ l|d dd' th˘f

It should be remembered of course that *dd, ff, ll* are not doubled consonants but digraphs representing sounds totally different from the single letters.

Certain consonants, when coming together with other consonants, dissolve within the dominant consonantal sound, e.g. *-b* + *p-* > *p; -th* + *dd-* or *-dd* + *th-* > *th; -l* + *ll-* or *-ll* + *l-* > *ll; -f* + *ff-* or *-ff* + *f-* > *ff;*

Ym mhob pen y mae piniwn
m p' n| m p'n ˘ n

Praff fonedd pur a ffyniant
pr ff' n˘dd| p r ff' n˘ nt

Unvoicing of *b, d,* and *g* occurs when one of these consonants at the end of a word is followed at the beginning of the next word either by an *h*- (sometimes *rh*-) or by the identical consonant:

Llais y corn lluosog hir
ll s c′rn|ll s c′ r

Nid rhydd im anturio'i ddwyn
n tr dd′ m| nt r dd′ n

Y ddraig goch ddyry cychwyn
ddr c′ ch|dd r c′ ch ˘ n

In *cynghanedd groes* the whole of the line is treated as a unit, and in spite of the importance of the key-words it should not be assumed from what has been said that consonance requires a rigid correspondence of consonants before the accent in the key-word, as those consonants may occur in a previous word:

Ni chredir nychu'r ydwyf
n chr′d˘r|n ch r′ d ˘f

In this example, unlike *trawster / tristwch* (example *b* above), *chredir / ydywf* have not complete consonance, but the correspondence is complete when the line is taken as a whole.

A refinement of *cynghanedd groes* is *cynghanedd groes o gyswllt* ('cross' *cynghanedd* 'by linkage'). In this type of *cynghanedd*, consonant(s) before the caesura are linked with the consonant series after the caesura, and this often means that a consonant or consonants must be regarded as belonging to both sections of consonantal correspondence at the same time:

(a) Llawer yn well a rhai'n waeth
ll r n′ (ll | r. n′ th

Gwragedd a gwŷr i gudd gant
g r g dd (g′ r | g dd g′ nt

(b) Duw yn gwybod ein gobaith
d n g′ b ˘(d | n g′ b˘ th

(c) Serch a rois ar chwaer Esyllt
s rch r (s | r ch r′ s˘lld

Cynghanedd draws is similar to *cynghanedd groes* except that a consonant or consonants at the beginning of the second half-line are not included in the system of consonance:

(a) A braich hir fal wybr uwch haul
br ch ′r|f l) br ch′ l

Drud yr adwaenwn dy dro
dr′ d| r d n n d) dr′

(b) Fal gwennawl ar fol gwaneg
f l g′ n˘ l| r)f l g′ n˘g

(c) Pwy sydd mor gampus heddiw
p s′ dd|m r g m)p s′ dd˘

Cynghanedd sain has three key-words, the first and second linked by rhyme and the second and third by consonance. Rules of consonance in *cynghanedd sain* differ in two respects from those obtaining in *cynganeddion croes* and *traws*. Firstly the consonance does not have to be as complete, as will be seen from examples; secondly a fourth sub-classification according to accentuation is possible, i.e. *anghytbwys acennog* ('unbalanced' with 'accented' last syllable):

(d) . . .′˘ | . . . ′ *e.g. . . . mánwy̌dd . . . Mái*
or . . . *béuny̌dd . . . bén*

As is seen, the consonant before the accent must be answered in this type of *cynghanedd*, but whether the consonant after the accent is answered or not is a matter of choice, this being an indication of the greater looseness of consonance in *cynghanedd sain*. Here are some examples of the various sub-types of *cynghanedd sain*, and it will be noted that there is no rule about the accentuation of the rhyming key-words:

(*a*) A minnau ar y gau gynt
r) *g*´- | *g*´nt

Y bwa hwn gwn mai gwir´
g´ n|m) g´ r

Gwres mynych les Môn achlân
m n ch l´s|m n chl´n

(*b*) Gwae fi gwn boeni beunydd
g n)b´ n ˇ-|b´n ˇdd

(*c*) Truan mor wan yw'r einioes
m)r´ n| r´ nˇ s

Ni'th gêl pan ddêl poen ddolef
p n dd´l|p n dd´ lˇf

(*d*) Bronnydd a brig manwydd Mai
br m´n ˇdd|m—

Saith gywydd beunydd o'i ben
b´ nˇdd | b´n

The type of *cynghanedd sain* exemplified above has the more precise name of *cynghanedd sain lefn* ('smooth' *cynghanedd sain*). Types of *cynghanedd sain* which were rare, and which became increasingly so as the late medieval period progressed, were *cynghanedd sain gadwynog* ('chained' . . .) and *cynghanedd sain drosgl* ('clumsy' . . .).

An early form of incomplete *cynghanedd* is known as *cynghanedd bengoll* ('end-missing' *cynghanedd*) and in this form of *cynghanedd* the consonance did not reach the end of the line, e.g.—

Lle tew lletyau mwyeilch
ll t´- |ll t´-ˇ-(m lch

This form of *cynghanedd* soon became obsolete with the exception of its continued use as an integral part of the *englyn* metre.

The *englyn* is usually the name given to the metre more fully known as the *englyn unodl union* ('straight monorhyme' *englyn*), and *englyn* is in reality the generic name for a class of metres of which the *englyn unodl union* is but one, but by far the most important and most commonly used. This kind of *englyn* consists of two parts: firstly, a *paladr* (beam) which is a *toddaid byr* ('short' *toddaid*) of sixteen syllables divided into a first line of ten syllables with the end-rhyme coming after seven, eight, or rarely nine syllables, with the ten syllables being made up of a *gair cyrch* (link phrase) of three syllables, or two, or one, as the case may be, which links with the second line of six syllables to form a *cynghanedd bengoll*; secondly, an *esgyll* (wings) which is an unrhythmically rhyming couplet of two seven-syllable lines. By 'unrhythmical rhyme' is meant a rhyme in which one word ends in an accented syllable and the other in an unaccented syllable. Incidentally there is no rule about the accentuation of the end-rhymes in the *paladr*. The first line of the *englyn unodl union* up to the end-rhyme, and the two lines of the *esgyll*, all have full *cynghanedd*, but it is a rule that there must be a pause, not necessarily a caesura enforced by *cynghanedd*, after the fifth syllable of the first line, and the most frequent practice in the period was that this pause coincided with the caesura after the second rhyme of a *cynghanedd sain*. Here is an example of a typical fifteenth-century *englyn*:

> Gwae'r gwan dan oedran nid edrych, ni chwardd,
> ni cherdda led y rhych.
> Gwae ni wŷl yn gynilwych.
> Gwae ni chlyw organ a chlych.

In the above *englyn* the fifth syllable pause coincides with the caesura after the second rhyme 'oedr*an*' of the *cynghanedd sain*, and the end-rhyme -*ych* comes at the seventh syllable of the first line; and the *gair cyrch* plus the second line forms a *cynghanedd bengoll*:

> ni chwardd ni cherdda led y rhych
> n ch´ rdd|n ch´rdd˘-(l d r ch

The only other kind of *englyn* deserving mention is the *englyn proest*, usually consisting of four seven-syllable lines, each with *cynghanedd*, and with *proest* instead of end-rhyme, e.g.:

> Yfory i'w dŷ a'i dud,
> a heddiw y'm gwahoddid,

a thrennydd gwneuthur ynyd,
a thrannoeth saethu'r unnod.

In the fourteenth, fifteenth, and sixteenth centuries a series of *englynion*, each linked to the next by *cyrch-gymeriad* (*concatenatio*, 'catch-word'), usually formed the opening of an *awdl*. This latter term, which originally referred to a fairly lengthy monorhyme poem in special metres, is very often ridiculously and misleadingly translated as 'ode', a practice which serious students of Welsh literature should reject.

The end of the last *englyn* in the opening *englynion* series was linked by *cyrch-gymeriad* to the second part of the poem consisting of a long monorhyme section of perhaps about fifty lines in *awdl*-metre proper. The end of this section was then linked by *cyrch-gymeriad* to a concluding *englyn*, the end of which was linked by *cyrch-gymeriad* to the beginning of the opening *englyn* of the poem.

It must not be thought that what has been described formed a constant and inevitable metrical pattern, but it is a description of a typical *awdl* of the period, a norm from which it was possible to diverge in many ways; for instance, instead of there being one long section in *awdl*-metre proper there could be two sections linked by *cyrch-gymeriad* and with each section having its own separate monorhyme and different *awdl*-metre. As a general rule it can be taken that when rhyme was changed it was obligatory to link the differently rhymed stanzas by means of *cyrch-gymeriad*.

The term '*awdl*-metre proper' must be explained. According to Einion Offeiriad's bardic grammar of the first half of the fourteenth century there were twenty-four metres which the *prydydd* could use: eight *englyn* metres, four *cywydd* metres, and twelve *awdl* metres. By the time of Dafydd ab Edmwnd in the mid-fifteenth century another three *awdl* metres had been substituted for three of the *englyn* metres. There is no need to discuss here the *awdl* metres in detail, for some of them were hardly ever used, though attention can be drawn to a peculiar practice, of which there are a few instances, of composing 'exemplifying' *awdlau* in which examples of all metres were included. Einion Offeiriad, author of the first known bardic grammar, composed an *awdl* consisting of examples of the twelve *awdl*-metres recognized by him. In the second half of the fifteenth century Dafydd Nanmor composed an *awdl* consisting of examples of all twenty-four metres, a very strange departure as the *cywydd* metres were not to be used in *awdlau*.

Perhaps the most popular of the *awdl*-metres were the *cyhydedd naw ban* and the *toddaid*, and these two metres were traditionally used in conjunction. By our period this conjunction had been formalized into the use of a stanza called *gwawdodyn* consisting of two lines of *cyhydedd naw ban* plus a *toddaid*, or of a stanza of *gwawdodyn hir* consisting of four lines of *cyhydedd naw ban* plus a *toddaid. Cyhydedd naw ban* is simply a line of nine syllables with a caesura normally after the fifth syllable. A *toddaid* consists of two lines, the first being like the first line of an *englyn* divided into a seven-syllable part culminating in the end-rhyme plus a *gair cyrch* of three syllables (8:2 and 9:1 are possible variants). The second line of the *toddaid* has nine syllables, and the fifth syllable rhymes with the previous *gair cyrch*. Here is an example of a *gwawdodyn*:

> Siancyn gyff Watcyn â rhoi ni phaid.
> Siancyn bob blwyddyn yw'n nerth a'n plaid.
> Siancyn yw'n rhwymyn, a'n rhaid, a'n penrhaith,
> os penrhaith ein iaith ydoedd Groes Naid.

In an *awdl*, of course, all the *gwawdodyn* stanzas would have the same rhyme: for instance the above example has been drawn from an *awdl* by Lewis Glyn Cothi in which there are twelve *gwawdodyn* stanzas all with the rhyme *-aid*.

Closely related in origin to the *toddaid* was the *cyhydedd hir* which again is a double line of ten and nine syllables, but this time divided 5:5:5:4 and with the first three sections linked by secondary rhyme. In the period the practice was for each of the first two sections to form short independent lines of *cynghanedd*, whilst the last two formed one nine-syllable line for the purpose of *cynghanedd*. The end-rhyme, of course, comes at the end of the fourth section. Here is an example of a double line of *cyhydedd hir:*

> Ei daid Wyndawdwr a wnaid yn wawdwr,
> a'r gŵr yw'r brawdwr, a'r gwir brydydd.

In this particular example the secondary rhyme is a double-rhyme, but this is simply a chance further embellishment and not a rule, though it can be noted that there was a strong tendency in the fifteenth century to make some *awdl*-metres more and more complicated by introducing more complex systems of *cynghanedd* and double-rhymes.

Of the four *cywydd*-metres, we need only be concerned with the *cywydd deuair hirion* usually called simply the *cywydd*. This was originally a popular metre outside the court tradition to which the *englyn* and *awdl* metres belonged. After *cynghanedd* had been introduced into the *cywydd*, shortly before the middle of the fourteenth century, it became the most widely used vehicle for all aspects of the highest class of late medieval Welsh poetry. Unlike the *awdl* the pattern of the *cywydd* was not based on the monorhyme principle. It consisted of a series of independent couplets, each having two seven-syllable lines which rhymed unrhythmically. The *cywydd* couplet therefore coincided in form with the *esgyll* of the *englyn unodl union* already discussed. In the period with which we are concerned an average *cywydd* would have about sixty to eighty lines, but *cywyddau* might be as long as about a hundred and twenty lines or as short as about forty.

The three embellishments of a line of poetry were, according to the bardic grammar, *cymeriad* occurring at the beginning, *cynghanedd* in the middle, and *odl* (rhyme) at the end. *Cymeriad* should not be confused with *cyrch-gymeriad*, a modern term already used in this chapter to describe a feature of medieval *englynion* series and *awdlau* although there is no evidence for its use with this meaning before the nineteenth century, the term used in the medieval period being *cyngogion. Cymeriad,* however, is certainly a genuine medieval bardic term referring to an embellishment found at the beginning of lines of poetry, in particular the beginning of lines with the same consonant, or without a consonant. This was known as *cymeriad llythrennol* ('letter' *cymeriad*). When the 'letters' differed it was necessary to have *cymeriad synhwyrol* ('sense' *cymeriad*), i.e. to have the sense running on unbroken from one line to the next. *Cymeriad* occurred on a large scale in the *awdlau*, and, as for the *cywydd, cymeriad* was obligatory between the two lines of the couplet, and very frequently ran on over a series of couplets.

There is some doubt as to why the bardic grammar referred to *cynghanedd* as occurring in the 'middle' of a line of poetry. It could be that what was meant was that *cynghanedd* was 'within' the line though it formed the whole of its content; but it is also possible that the reference is more specific and is a relic from an older bardic tract composed at a time when *cynghanedd* had not fully evolved and was only a far less fully developed system of simpler consonance and internal rhyme which could be fairly described as occurring literally only in the middle of the line, as for example in these separate lines from Cynddelw's mid-twelfth-century *rhieingerdd* (woman-song) to Efa:

Cymraëg laesdeg o lys dyffrynt

Pell ydd wyf i'm nwyf oni thelir

Cadr amnaid gannaid ged a'th iolwyf.

The medieval Welsh bards were professionals who learnt their bardic craft by means of apprenticeship. It was a natural development therefore that metrical embellishments should become more and more refined as the manifestation of a developing yet closed bardic tradition. In this way *cynghanedd* evolved during the period of the court-poets so that before the end of the thirteenth century a typical *awdl* would have *cynghanedd* in every line, and each line of *cynghanedd* would be fairly fully developed, being either complete according to later standards or being *cynghanedd bengoll*, whilst in the typical *englyn*, with its shorter lines, the *cynghanedd* was usually complete.

After the Conquest of 1282–4 and the end of the court-poets, the bardic order continued to flourish (though not without crisis) in the new circumstances which followed the loss of the patronage of the Welsh royal courts. The fourteenth-century *awdl* became more and more formally ornamental: *cymeriad* was used inflexibly on a scale far greater than in the period of the court-poets; *cynghanedd* became more intricate but also less varied, the almost invariable tendency being to employ *cynghanedd sain*, sometimes a double *cynghanedd sain*, which was an innovation. By the second half of the fourteenth century, especially in the *awdlau* of Gruffudd ap Maredudd, even use of the extremely complicated double *cynghanedd sain* often seemed to be the rule rather than the exception: it occurs in every line of the following extract:

kyt vryt vrwydyr glwyf rwyf ruon dewred
kiwdawt ffawt ffynnyant varant vawred
kiriet ket kadyrblas gwanas gwned
kor dor yor eurwyrd kyrd kynnadled
kar dar dewrvryt gryt greidyawl dewred
koryf toryf lloryf lliaws o draws drossed

It will also have been noted that the first part of the double *cynghanedd sain* in two of the above lines, including the last, has the added complication of being triple-rhymed.

The prosodic features of the fourteenth-century *englyn* were rather different however. The lines were shorter, so the *cynghanedd* was never *pengoll* (end-missing) except, as required, in the second line. The double *cynghanedd sain* was not used, and also there was a greater variety of *cynghanedd* types employed, the *croes, traws* and *llusg* being commonly used.

By about 1340 *cynghanedd* had been introduced into the *cywydd*, and the usage followed was that of the *esgyll* of the *englyn*, so that the *cywyddau* of the fourteenth century read very differently from the contemporaneous *awdlau*. *Cynghanedd* in the *cywydd* was varied though it is true that even in this metre there was for a long time a very high proportion of lines of *cynghanedd sain*.

It can be said that *cynghanedd* had completely evolved by the time that it was introduced into the *cywydd*, yet a few changes did occur after that time. In the fourteenth-century *cywyddau* there still occurred very rarely an occasional example of a *cynghanedd bengoll*, but this incomplete *cynghanedd* was never found in the metre in the next century. *Cynghanedd sain gadwynog* and *cynghanedd sain drosgl* were used occasionally in the fourteenth century, but very rarely in the fifteenth, and the bards of the late fifteenth century and the beginning of the sixteenth hardly ever used these obsolete forms of *cynghanedd sain*. In the fourteenth century ordinary *cynghanedd sain* was used on a large scale but in the following century, and increasingly so as the period progressed, less use was made of this type of *cynghanedd*, and less use was also made, as time went on, of *cynghanedd lusg*, the simplest form of *cynghanedd*. What happened was that the bards increasingly mastered the more intricate forms of consonantal *cynghanedd* so that the *cynghanedd draws*, and especially the *cynghanedd groes* with its full consonance, came to be used more and more widely. So, the most intricate form of all of consonantal *cynghanedd*, the *cynghanedd groes o gyswllt*, never really occurring in the fourteenth century except accidentally, came to be used quite frequently by the mid-fifteenth century, and even more frequently by the early sixteenth century. The result of the changes in *cynghanedd* usage during the second half of the fifteenth century was that there was a considerable difference between the rhythmic qualities of a *cywydd* composed about 1450–75 and a *cywydd* composed about 1500–25. The mid-fifteenth-century *cywydd* greatly varied the type of *cynghanedd* used line by line, and, partly for this reason, the stress-patterns of the lines were diverse. In the early sixteenth century the *cywydd* was much more uniform in line-pattern, most lines being *cynghanedd groes* with the caesura halfway through, following the third or fourth syllable. This by no means led to monotony but did mean that the spectacular rhythmic variety of the previous generation of *cywyddau* was missing. Perhaps it is misleading to apply the term 'spectacular' to the quality of mid-fifteenth-century poetry in comparison with later poetry, for in the abstract it is the latter which seems to demand the epithet 'spectacular', for not only was the complex *cynghanedd groes* and the even more complex *cynghanedd groes o gyswllt* used extensively, indeed almost to the exclusion of other types of *cynghanedd*, but the very nature of consonance had become more intricate—in other words it became the practice to have more consonants corresponding in the *cynghanedd*. For these reasons the later *cywyddau* are much more staccato in tone than those of a generation earlier. The mid-fifteenth-century *cywyddau* are notable not only for the great diversity of the rhythmic patterns but also for an unexpectedly effortless concomitant smoothness of composition, which in turn is quite distinct from the more laboured construction of the *cywyddau* of the previous century. This is not simply a matter of prosody, however, but also intimately involves taking account of stylistic considerations affecting diction and syntax.

BIBLIOGRAPHY

D. J. Bowen, 'Cynganeddion Gruffudd Hiraethog', *Llên Cymru*, 6 (1960), 1–20.

T. D. Crawford, 'Cyfartaledd y Gynghanedd Sain yng Nghywyddau Dafydd ap Gwilym', in J. E. Caerwyn Williams (ed.), *Ysgrifau Beirniadol X* (Dinbych, 1982), 131–42.

J. Morris Jones, *Cerdd Dafod* (Rhydychen, 1925).

T. Parry, 'Pynciau Cynghanedd', *Bulletin of the Board of Celtic Studies*, x (1939), 1–5.

E. I. Rowlands, *Poems of the Cywyddwyr* (Dublin, 1976), Introduction pp. xx–xlix.

Idem, 'Dadansoddiad o Gynghanedd Lewys Mon', *Llên Cymru*, 4 (1956–7), 135–61.

Chapter 10

GUTO'R GLYN

J. E. CAERWYN WILLIAMS

With the year 1536, and the presentation to Parliament of the first of the two Acts which were to constitute the Union of England and Wales, there came to an end not only an era in the history of the Welsh nation but also a hundred years which have been rightly described as the most brilliant in the annals of its literature. Among the period's many poets of distinction Guto'r Glyn won for himself a reputation second to none among his contemporaries, and this reputation has been confirmed and upheld by both poets and critics in subsequent generations.

The name 'Guto' is a hypocoristic form of Gruffudd and we may assume that he was christened Gruffud *ap* or the son of (—), but unfortunately we do not know for certain what his father's name was. There is a group of *cywyddau*, nine in all, in Peniarth MS. 57 which appear to be attributed to Guto ap Siancyn, or *Anglice* Jenkin, although the name is not appended to two of them. Sir Ifor Williams was reluctant to ascribe poems bearing the name Guto ap Siancyn either individually or as a group to Guto'r Glyn, and one of his most distinguished students, Miss Enid Roberts, has already declared that for chronological reasons we must assume that Guto'r Glyn and Guto ap Siancyn were two different poets. On the other hand, the late J. Llywelyn Williams, who collected the poet's work for Sir Ifor's edition, had no hesitation in accepting Guto ap Siancyn as an alternative name for the poet, and his judgment was upheld by Thomas Roberts, an expert on fifteenth-century Welsh poetry, in a detailed study published in 1947. Until this problem has been solved, statements about Guto'r Glyn's life and work must of necessity be tentative. Whether he was christened as Gruffudd ap Siancyn or as Gruffudd y Glyn, as Miss Enid Roberts suggests, with the implication that he may have been related to the family whose representatives dwelt in Pengwern, Hendwr and Cryniarth at that time, must remain problematic, although we may safely assume that he was not born into the higher ranks of the nobility. In a *cywydd* addressed to

Dafydd, abbot of Valle Crucis (Glyn Egwestl), Guto tells us that three poets were trying to oust him in his old age from the monastery, and that, superior though they might be in birth, they were inferior in the poetic craft. Guto was at the time a crippled old man, suffering from rheumatism and blindness, but he obviously thought that he could still teach these presumptuous youngsters a trick or two! Although we do not have his lineage, as we have the ancestry of many of his fellow-poets, it so happens that, owing to a number of hints and allusions found in his work and that of others, we have a fairly vivid portrait of him in our mind's eye. A big man with large knees and large hands, he appears to have had a broad face with a prominent nose, and a shock of black hair, some of which was prematurely lost, leaving a bald pate. He tells us:

I have a patriarch's face
And a bald pate more than a horse's hoof.

In his youth he was extremely strong and excelled in stone-casting, one of the popular sports of the time. Even Gutun Owain thought that his skill in the game deserved mention when he came to compose an elegy on him. By nature warm-hearted, generous and loyal, he seems to have been able to evoke the same qualities in his patrons. Appreciative of fine fare, lively conversation and convivial company, not only was he humorous and witty himself but he could also elicit humour and wit in his companions. Nature, it seems, had endowed him not only with the artistic gifts of a bard but also with a personality and disposition calculated to make him enjoy to the full the social life which was inextricably bound to the bardic profession. It is not surprising that he could count among his patrons noblemen from almost every part of Wales.

If there is some uncertainty concerning his patronymic *ap Siancyn*, there is also some doubt concerning his byname (or surname) 'Y Glyn' (glen, vale), or rather its identification. He informs us in one poem that as a youth he had been a *blaeneuwr*, but, as was natural to an older man, he was now living in a town. As Guto speaks with affection of Oswestry, it is not unreasonable to assume that it was there that he eventually made his home. Indeed, there is evidence that he, like Tudur Aled, was made a burgess of the town, in recognition of his song in 'lawde and prese' of it and its inhabitants. But originally he had been a *blaeneuwr*, a dweller in the upland or mountain land as opposed to the lowland, and the most well-known and obvious *glyn* in the vicinity of Oswestry was, and is, Glyn Ceiriog. At that time Oswestry was the centre of a flourishing trade in wool and there would be continual traffic between it and the Welsh valleys, including Glyn Ceiriog, to the west. Not far from either place was the Cistercian monastery of Glyn Egwestl or Glyn y Groes (Pant y Groes Hen) where he was succoured in his old age. His association with this monastery must have extended over many years, and it is not surprising that the 'Glyn' in his name has also been identified with the vale in which the monastery is situated, Glyndyfrdwy: indeed, Miss Enid Roberts has reminded us that 'Y Glyn' to the poet's contemporaries was Glyndyfrdwy, and has suggested that the *blaeneuwr* was not Guto'r Glyn but Guto ap Siancyn. On the other hand, if Guto'r Glyn was the poet who addressed 'Syr Rhys' in poem CIX as *f'eglwyswr, fy nghurad* (my churchman, my parish clergyman), and as his confessor, and if 'Syr Rhys' was of 'Dre-wen' and in charge of Whittington, as 'Dre-wen' suggests, there is further corroboration that the Oswestry area was the poet's locality. A little farther away from Oswestry was another Cistercian monastery, Ystrad Marchell or Strata Marcella, with which he was associated. The Cistercians were famed for their sheep farming. Was it his experience with sheep in Glyn Ceiriog, or Glyndyfrdwy, that first took the poet to Oswestry, to Glyn Egwestl and to Ystrad Marchell? Did he take sheep from one or both of these monasteries to sell in Oswestry and further afield in English towns? That he was at one time a sheep farmer and a drover is certain. He has described in one *cywydd* how he went sheep droving for *Syr Bened* (Benedict), parish priest of Corwen, to Warwick, Coventry and Lichfield, how the journey had proved financially an utter loss, to the disbelief of his clerical employer, a disbelief encouraged, apparently, by Guto's rival in poetry and droving, Tudur Penllyn. He ends the *cywydd* with the resolve never to undertake such work again! Tudur Penllyn, whose *floruit* is given as *ca.* 1420–1485/90, reared sheep, sold wool and did some droving in addition to writing poetry. He answered Guto'r Glyn's complaint in a *cywydd* addressed to *Syr Bened* in which he warned the latter not to let himself be deceived a second time. Guto's rejoinder to Tudur Penllyn is spirited, if rather lame, but it appears that he and Syr Bened remained good friends, since he composed an elegy on him when he died.

The drover's trade probably called for more than mere experience with cattle: it demanded at least some knowledge of English and an elementary knowledge of figures, and this prompts the question where was Guto'r Glyn educated, and more especially, where was he trained as a bard. It was the custom for a would-be poet to be apprenticed to a *pencerdd* or master poet in order to have the training and the special qualification which were necessary to practise the trade. It was in accordance with this custom that Llywelyn ab y Moel had been trained by Rhys ap Dafydd ab Iorwerth.

Guto'r Glyn composed an elegy on Llywelyn ab y Moel and, although there is no evidence for it in the elegy, he must have been associated with him on occasions other than his death and burial. Llywelyn ab y Moel was a turbulent character of the kind that Guto must have found fascinating. He is best remembered for two *cywydd*-poems: one to Craig Lwyd Wood where he spent some time with a band of Welsh outlaws living on the proceeds of banditry and finding it a more lucrative living than *clera*, that is, than visiting patrons as a professional poet; the other, on the Battle of Gwaun Gaseg, tells how he and his companions resolved to waylay a band of Englishmen and not to let anything deflect them from their purpose, only to find themselves put to flight without any real fighting and with Llywelyn, as he himself confesses, conspicuously and rather unashamedly leading the rout. However, no one but a man confident of his reputation for bravery would deliberately set out to make himself a laughing-stock for running away to save his own skin; and to his fellow-poets, including Guto'r Glyn, Llywelyn was nothing if not a dare-devil. Llywelyn's home was at Llanwnnog, not very far from Ystrad Marchell, the monastery to which he retired to die. Guto'r Glyn was present at the end when the poet was given the last sacrament, and composed the elegy on him soon after he had been buried within the monastic precincts:

Yntau naf yn ein tŷ ni
A gladdwyd rhwng arglwyddi.

[And he, the peer, was buried among lords in our house.]

Thomas Roberts has shown that the poets often referred to their patrons' homes as their own, *ein tŷ ni*, and so, too much should not be read into the phrase, although Mr Saunders Lewis seems to have been influenced by it in writing his admittedly attractive account of how some monk in Ystrad Marchell was impressed by Guto's talents as a boy and took him into the monastery to be educated and even to be trained as a poet, and if not by Llywelyn ab y Moel, then by one of his admirers. The truth is probably less colourful. In a *cywydd* written when he was no longer a young man Guto mentions two men who had given him their patronage, and in naming them rather than any others among his numerous patrons he implies that their patronage had been considerably more substantial and decisive than that of the others: the first was the '*athro*' Dafydd Cyffin, parish priest of Llangedwyn to the east of Llanrhaeadr-ym-Mochnant, the second was 'Syr Bened', the parish priest of Corwen whom we have already mentioned, and now he is seeking the patronage of a third, Siôn Mechain, the parish priest of Llandrunio in Deuddwr. Have we in the mention of Dafydd Cyffin a clue to Guto's first teacher as well as his first patron? In Llangedwyn Dafydd Cyffin would have been well placed to meet and to notice a talented young boy who had no more ambition at the time than to be a sheep farmer and perhaps a cattle drover. Guto's *cywydd* XL and, probably, *cywydd* CXI are addressed to this Dafydd.

Sir Ifor Williams has argued with great plausibility that Llywelyn ab y Moel died in February, 1440. Mr Saunders Lewis would have us believe that Guto'r Glyn was then about twenty years old, and that he was just embarking on his career as a poet. J. Llywelyn Williams, on the other hand, thought that the poet had been born *c.* 1412 and that he had already made a name for himself as a poet by 1432. Miss Enid Roberts would attribute all the earlier poems to Guto ap Siancyn rather than Guto'r Glyn, for, in her opinion, the latter did not begin to compose poetry until 1455–60.

According to Mr Saunders Lewis, Guto'r Glyn left Ystrad Marchell after Llywelyn ab y Moel's death to undertake his first *taith clera*, i.e., his first tour of likely patrons' homes in south Wales as a professional poet. If his association with Ystrad Marchell had been as close as Mr Lewis assumes, it would be natural for him to make his way from there to Ystrad Fflur, where Abbot Rhys was presiding over the Cistercian monks. There are references to Rhys in some of the official records of the period: thus in the *Catalogue of Patent Rolls* for 1443 (p.151) we find that William Morys had been appointed to succeed Rhys as abbot and had held the office for two years. This would mean that Rhys had died *c.* 1440–1, apparently in prison, held there for debt. It would also suggest that Guto's acquaintance with Rhys did not begin after Llywelyn ab y Moel's death, for he addressed at least five poems to him. Of these, two are eulogies following the common pattern. In one Rhys is ill in England and the poet wishes him a speedy recovery. In the other the abbot has left Ystrad Fflur to visit Oxford, much to the distress of the monks and the poet. An elegy concludes with the poet's wish that God should repay the abbot with the same generosity as he has shown to others in his life:

> He paid out a million to a hundred thousand;
> Let God repay him (now), and he, Rhys, will not be poor.

If Mr Saunders Lewis's reconstruction of the poet's career is valid, Guto'r Glyn eventually found his way to the Cwrt Mawr, Euas, the home of Harri Ddu ap Gruffudd. In all, four poems, including an elegy, to Harri have been preserved. They show that the two men took to each other at once. Perhaps they were not unlike in appearance: they were both of dark complexion, and Guto goes as far as to say in one of his poems that only the dark-complexioned can be very brave. (He conveniently forgets that Mathau Goch, the most famous Welsh soldier of this period, was red-haired!) They vied with each other in sport. Harri, like Guto, was good at stone-casting. We catch a glimpse of the warmth of their friendship—the generous friendship of two men in the vigour of youth —in the fact that Harri enlisted Guto's aid to win for himself the affection of a certain lady called Gwladus Hael. Apparently, a poet, Ieuan Gethin, was also seeking the lady's favour. If Harri could write poetry at all, apparently he could not compete with his rival: hence his call to Guto to write a eulogy for the lady which included a panegyric on himself. On the other hand, Harri introduced Guto to a new life:

> My love, my counsellor,
> My book, my hand was he.

Harri was a courtier (*cwrtiwr*) and a soldier (*milwr*), and he introduced Guto to the duke of York from whom he received eighteen marks:

Dug fi at y Dug of Iorc,
Dan amod cael deunawmorc.

[He took me to the duke of York,
With the promise that I should get eighteen marks.]

Sir Ifor Williams was unable to decide whether these eighteen marks were given to Guto as a poet or as the price of his indenture as a soldier. Is the *dan amod* (lit. 'on condition') in favour of the latter interpretation? Mr Saunders Lewis does not even discuss the former possibility, and, as Guto was certainly a soldier at one period in his life, there is no reason to doubt that he was a soldier directly or indirectly indentured to the duke of York. Richard, duke of York, was first appointed lieutenant of the English forces in France in February, 1436. He was later appointed for a second period (1440–7) and left to take up his command in May, 1441. Among his vast possessions there were some in Monmouthshire, and it seems that he spent some time there in his castle of Usk. In the *Patent Rolls* for 1441 Robert Grendor of Clearwell, who was closely associated with Monmouthshire, is commissioned to raise troops in that region for service with the duke in France. Among the better-known people who joined the duke to serve on the Continent were Sir William ap Thomas of Raglan and his son, William Herbert, afterwards earl of Pembroke. If Harri ap Gruffudd and Guto'r Glyn were also with the duke's troops, then it may very well be, as Mr Saunders Lewis suggests, that Guto was indentured for service at the suggestion of Harri, and in the first instance to Sir William ap Thomas; for in his *cywydd* to the latter Guto refers to a payment which seems to have been an indenture payment:

There I received a payment
To wear your livery, Gwalchmai of Gwent:
There I received a great welcome,
And better by far was the respect I received.

(We are assuming that the duke of York to whom Guto'r Glyn refers was Richard. Miss Enid Roberts suggests that it was his son, Edward, later crowned king as Edward IV (1461), and makes the telling point that if, as Gutun Owain informs us, Guto'r Glyn became a member of Edward IV's 'guard', the poet must have been a young man in the early 60s. However, one would like to know whether, in those far-off days when birth certificates were not part of the machinery of government, a poet could be made a member of the guard as a mark of royal favour and in order to retain his undoubtedly valuable services as a propagandist.)

In France Guto'r Glyn heard more of the military exploits of his fellow-countrymen in the war which had already been in progress since 1337, and especially of the prowess of Sir Richard Gethin and Sir Mathau Goch (Matthew Gough). If Guto'r Glyn was initially indentured for a year, and if he returned to Wales at the end of that period, it may well be that it was during this year (? 1442) that he composed his *cywydd* to Sir Mathau. The poet refers to Sir Mathau's capture—it seems to have happened twice, once in a town, named as 'St Severine', in 1432, and a second time on the way to St Denis in 1434—as if he himself had been in Wales at the time:

> The poets were anxious and frightened
> When he was captured, there was continual weeping.

But the rest of the poem shows first-hand knowledge of the state of affairs in France—in Anjou and Maine—, of Sir Mathau's role and of the chief commanders of the French, La Hire and Poton de Xaintrailles:

> Gŵr antur ydyw'r mur mau,
> Gwŷr antur a gâr yntau.
>
> [An adventurous man is my protector,
> It is adventurous men whom he loves.]

The reference to *y mur mau* (my protector, lit. 'my wall'), and later on to *f'eryr* (my eagle), suggests that Guto regarded Sir Mathau not only as his 'patron' but also as his 'commander'. Things had already begun to go badly for the English in France, but Sir Mathau would soon put them right:

> Generous Mathau Goch's spear and body
> Will deliver the English from the grasp of the French.

When Guto'r Glyn returned to Wales he must have visited some of his friends and some of his old haunts. Mr Saunders Lewis suggests that he composed an elegy on Rhys, abbot of Ystrad Fflur, when he died in 1443, but as we have seen, Rhys had died in 1440 or 1441, and in that case perhaps before the poet had left for France. There is probably more substance in the suggestion that the poet had enjoyed military life so much that he was anxious to return to France and that on the way there he called on Tomas ap Watcyn Fychan of Llanddewi Rhydderch in Gwent and composed a *cywydd* which expresses extremely well his enthusiasm for the military life. He had heard a rumour that Tomas has enlisted to serve with the duke and asks:

> Is it true . . .
> That you have enlisted as one of the young troop,
> Fair of face, to serve with the duke in France?

The occasion was a feast and before the end of the *cywydd* the war against France has become a war of the banqueters against the wine, representing the Dauphin, with the latter an easy victor.

Guto'r Glyn returned to France to see the closing stages of the Hundred Years War. Mathau Goch was not to turn the tide against the French, but he and another Welshman, Sir John Eyton, were to figure prominently in the surrender of Anjou and Maine to the French, a surrender agreed upon by Henry VI as a condition of his marriage to Margaret of Anjou in 1445 but not actually executed until March 1448.

The truce that was extended from 15 March 1448 to 1 April 1450, was broken by the English, but their defeat in the battle of Formigny early in 1450 (April 15) dashed any hopes they might have had of saving Normandy. One by one the towns held by them fell to the French. Sir Mathau Goch's part in these events is fairly well documented. Not so the part played by Sir Richard Gethin. Both were at the battle of Verneuil (17 August 1424). Sir Richard was in charge of Maunte (Mantes) from at least 14 May 1432, until at least 12 November 1437. On 13 February 1438, he replaced Edmund Hulle as captain of Conches and bailli of Evreux but he himself was replaced in these posts in November of the same year. Mr Saunders Lewis informs me in a letter that in his reconstruction of events he was dependent on H. T. Evans, *Wales and the Wars of the Roses* (Cambridge, 1915) and on E. Carleton Williams, *My Lord of Bedford 1389–1435* (London, 1963) in which there is only one reference to Sir Richard Gethin: as captain of Maunte he lends money to pay the duke of Bedford's soldiers (p. 214). Up till now I have been unable to find any reference to Sir Richard's participation in the events of 1449–50 but the reference to him in 1438 and the fact that his fellow-Welshman, Sir Mathau Goch, lived to see those events, goes some way to support the suggestion that he took part in the general retreat of the English forces from France.

Guto'r Glyn composed two *cywydd*-poems to Sir Richard: in the first, Sir Richard is reported to have been captured by the French; in the second, the report has been proved false. J. Llywelyn Williams believed that the *cywyddau* were composed while Sir Richard was in Normandy in 1432–4; Saunders Lewis thinks they were composed in 1449. In favour of Mr Lewis's dating is the *Sitz im Leben* demanded by the *cywyddau* themselves—they do not reflect the mood of victory which must have possessed Gethin and his fellow-soldiers in 1432–4, but rather the mood of defeat which must have pervaded the defeated English army as it prepared to leave Normandy irrevocably—as well as some references such as that to leaving Rouen. On the other hand, the French led by La Hire and Poton nearly took Rouen *c.* 1437. Whichever date we accept for the *cywyddau* to Gethin, it is reasonable to assume that it was as a reward for them that Guto'r Glyn received from him a 'golden' cloak.

Before the end of 1450, if we are to believe Mr Saunders Lewis, the poet was back in Wales. On his way home he called on Sir William ap Thomas in Raglan Castle and while invoking his protection and patronage for the future he reminded him of the time he had indentured with him. Since then both of them have advanced in the world:

> Higher art thou, flower of the party,
> Above the men with a golden cloak.

Obviously the poet was proud of his 'golden' cloak which was of the kind usually worn by lords to distinguish them from the lower orders—indeed, Parliament before very long was to make it illegal for any one else to wear such apparel—but just at this time many a lord had fallen on the field of battle and many a golden cloak had been taken as part of the spoils of war. If Guto'r Glyn had received this cloak many years previously, there would be no point in referring to it in the *cywydd* to Sir William ap Thomas, and this, I suppose, is one reason why Mr Saunders Lewis believes that it was a recent gift even in 1450. However, according to the editorial notes on the *cywydd*, William had been knighted in 1426, and the last official reference to him is in 1450.

Unfortunately, the cloak is a matter of more than academic interest. On one of his journeys Guto'r Glyn called on a fellow-poet, Ieuan ap Hywel Swrdwal, who was living on the estuary of the Dyfi, not far from Machynlleth, and showed him the cloak, challenging or charging him at the same time to compose a *cywydd* to its donor, Sir Richard Gethin. Ieuan's *cywydd* has survived, and one of its most significant couplets is:

> Enquiring of one or two,
> Who is the lord who owns it?—(*i.e.* the cloak)

This *cywydd* may have been composed *c.* 1450, soon after Guto's return from France, as Mr Saunders Lewis suggests, although we should remind ourselves that J. Llywelyn Williams assumed that it was composed *c.* 1432 when Sir Richard was still making a name for himself in Normandy. Ieuan's reference to Guto as *Clo ar awen clêr ieuainc* (A crown on the muse of young bards) seems to suggest that he regarded Guto as a young, rather than an old, poet at the time.

Llywelyn ap Gutun composed a satire on Guto in which he suggests that Guto has been drowned and is roaming around Malltraeth as a ghost. It is one of the wittiest satires in the language:

> Boddi wnaeth ar draeth heb drai,
> Mae'n y nef am na nofiai!
>
> [He was drowned on a beach without ebb,
> He is in heaven because he did not swim!]

Guto's reply falls below the standard of the satire, but he taunts its author with the gibe that he desires to see himself, Guto, dead in order to secure possession of his cloak and sword:

> Mewn môr y myn im orwedd,
> Mae'n chwannog i'm clog a'm cledd.
>
> [It is in the sea that he wishes me to lie,
> He covets my cloak and my sword.]

As Llywelyn ap Gutun refers to Guto'r Glyn as an old man in his question *Pwy fydd capten yr henfeirdd?* (Who will be the captain of the old poets?), it would appear that Guto'r Glyn was wearing the cloak in his old age.

As one of his admirers and one of his former soldiers, Guto must have heard with genuine sorrow of Mathau Goch's death on 5 July 1450, on London Bridge in the attack on John Cade's followers, and it is significant that when Siôn Dafi was sentenced to have his hand struck off 'for striking a man before the Judges at Westminster Hall' in 1462 and had a silver hand made to replace it, Guto composed a *cywydd* eulogizing the new hand. According to Mr Saunders Lewis, the *cywydd* provides evidence that Guto had been with Siôn Dafi and with Humphrey Stafford's army at the battle of Towton, Yorkshire (1461). Perhaps there is more evidence in support of the assertion that Guto'r Glyn had fought with King Edward's soldiers in Gutun Owain's couplet:

> He wore the collar of the guard,
> Its splendour, and the mark of King Edward.

Edward was proclaimed king in March 1461, and this suggests that Guto'r Glyn served him after that date. Whether Guto was at the battle of Towton or not, he does not seem to have taken any further part in the so-called 'Wars of the Roses'. But this does not mean that he did not retain his interest in military events. Thus when William Herbert, the eldest son of his former patron, Sir William ap Thomas of Raglan, attacked Harlech Castle in 1468, Guto addressed to him a *cywydd* in which he begged him not to act as a harsh foreign conqueror and to have regard for the unity and the well-being of the nation:

> Dwg Forgannwg a Gwynedd,
> Gwna'n un o Gonwy i Nedd.
> O digia Lloegr a'i dugiaid,
> Cymru a dry yn dy raid.
>
> [Bring together Morgannwg and Gwynedd,
> Unite the land between Conwy and Nedd.
> If England and its dukes take offence,
> Wales will turn (to thee) in thy need.]

Again, in a *cywydd* on the occasion of a feast which William Herbert gave before setting out on the fateful journey which was to end in the battle of Banbury (1469), Guto expresses his misgivings and warns William not to trust the English: he says that he fears what England and its corrupt men, all ready for treachery, will do to his favourite. The battle resulted in the death of William and his brother Richard and this was generally attributed by the Welsh to the treachery of Lord Devonshire. Indeed, in his elegy to William, which is remarkable among other things for the use made in it of the imagery of a folk dance and summer games, Guto repeats the charge of treachery:

> Traitors were the men who turned the tide of fortune
> At Banbury against the Earl of Pembroke,

and describes the battle of Banbury in so much detail and with such chronological accuracy that it has been suggested that he must have had eyewitness accounts of it. The victory in the battle of Barnet (April, 1471), on the other hand, was regarded as just retribution for the treachery at the previous battle. Thus Guto begins his *cywydd* to Sir Roger Kinaston with the statement that Pembroke's death in 'August' at Banbury was avenged at Easter in 1471. Obviously, as he grew older, Guto also grew wiser in the affairs of men, and if in the flush of youth he had enjoyed his days as a soldier in the English army fighting an English war, with advancing years and deeper reflection he came to understand that neither his interests nor those of his fellow-Welshmen had been advanced by military exploits on the fair fields of France. A couplet in his one truly religious poem seems to suggest this:

> Moli bûm ymylau byd,
> Malu sôn melys ennyd.
>
> [I praised the fringes of the world,
> Grinding out noises for a sweet (pleasant) interlude.]

This does not mean that Guto became a convinced nationalist in his old age. Far from it. In his *cywydd* to Edward IV Guto reminds the king of the Welsh blood running in his veins, though he must have realized that there was very little of it in the sovereign, and that it was a poor foundation on which to base any claim, and he counsels him, as he had counselled William Herbert on a previous occasion, to use his power to the advantage rather than the detriment of his kinsfolk.

The only reference to Bosworth I have noticed in Guto'r Glyn's work occurs in his eulogy to Sir Rhys of Abermarlais, and it is not explicit:

> Concweriodd y King Harri
> Y maes, drwy nerth ein meistr ni.
>
> [King Henry won the day
> Through our master's strength.]

But that he lived to hear of the battle of Bosworth there can be no doubt. Among his latest poems there are six to Dafydd, abbot of Glyn Egwestl. Dafydd was consecrated bishop of St Asaph in 1500, but according to Browne Willis he 'obtained a Licence of Consecration March 1, 1492'. Although Guto refers to him as worthy of consecration as a bishop,

> Yn esgob iawn ei wisgaw,

he does not refer to him as a bishop, and it is safe to assume that Guto did not live to see his patron made bishop. This means that he did not survive the fifteenth century. When he sang for the abbot, he himself was an old man, crippled and blind, and he had outlived most, if not all, of his contemporaries. He could well ask:

> Mae'r henwyr? Ai meirw'r rheini?
> Hynaf oll heno wyf i.
>
> [Where are the old men? Have those died?
> Oldest of all I am tonight.]

As he had grown older, his bardic peregrinations had become shorter. Whereas formerly he had visited Môn and Gwynedd in the north and Gwent in the south, now he is content to wander around Iâl. But as long as he has the patronage of Abbot Dafydd, Siôn Trefor Hen and Siôn Edward of Chirk (Y Waun) he will not complain.

As we have seen, Guto served as a soldier and liked soldiers and their life. But he seems to have been equally at home in the company of clergymen and churchmen, for he composed poems for Abbot Rhys of Ystrad Fflur; Wiliam, parish priest of Merthyr Tudful; the abbot of Shrewsbury; Bened, parish priest of Corwen; Hywel ap Dai of St Asaph; Richard Cyffin, dean of Bangor; Dafydd Cyffin, parish priest of Llangedwyn and dean of Bangor (if they were not two different persons); Siôn Mechain of Llandrunio; Siôn, abbot of Glyn Egwestl; and Dafydd ab Owain, abbot of Ystrad Marchell. Hywel Dafi remonstrates with him for his predilection for clergymen and his love of life in a monastery, but Guto is unrepentant. *Âb ydwyf i abadau*, he replies (I play the ape to abbots), and if he were to take the tonsure, he knows what he would be called as he tells Abbot Dafydd of Glyn Egwestl:

Gwn f'enw, pe'm gwnâi'n fynach,
'Gwas Duw o Lyn Egwestl iach'.

[I know my name, were he to make me a monk,
'The servant of God from flourishing Glyn Egwestl'.]

It was Abbot Dafydd who succoured him in his old age, and it was to him and his abbey that the poet came to end his days, presumably as a corrodiary:

At the end there I will come,
To the graceful citadel of the graves,
Among its roots I will lie.

It would have given him great satisfaction to know that the abbot gave him a sumptuous funeral feast, as Gutun Owain tell us:

Many were the feasts provided
For good Lord Dafydd's poet here,
And the feast at his funeral
Was as lavish as that of Merwydd;
White bread, roast meat, and the honey of an
early bee-swarm,
And wine was given for the good of his soul.

Yet in spite of his familiarity with monks and churchmen, Guto does not give the impression that he was a religious man, and he certainly does not qualify as a religious poet. We know of only one 'religious' song, composed at the instigation of his patron, Abbot Dafydd, who charged him to praise God rather than men. The song, *Ystyriaeth Bywyd* (The Consideration of Life), was probably a *marwysgafn*, a death-bed poem, but although the poet admits cause for repentance there is no great depth of feeling and it is significant that in the course of the poem Guto has recourse to a commonplace which is found in Middle English verse, as Mr D. J. Bowen has shown, and probably in the verse of other languages, since it occurs in Latin:

Sunt tria vere que faciunt me dolere:
Est primum durum quia nosco me moriturum;
Atque sequens plango magis quia nescio quando;
Inde magis flebo quia nescio quo remanebo.

Tri amod trwm a wyddwn,
Tri chledd a'm trawai â chlwyf,
Trwm ddolur tra meddyliwyf.
Marw fyddaf i'm arfeddyd,
Ni wn ba awr yn y byd.
Ac ni wn a gynanaf
Heb oludd im, i ble'dd af.

[Three heavy conditions I knew,
Three swords dealt me an injury,
Grievous pain whilst I consider.
I shall die as I purpose,
I know not what hour in the world.
And I know not whether I shall utter
Without hindrance to me, whither I go]

Guto'r Glyn's lack of interest in religious poetry is matched by his lack of interest in love-poetry, although this does not mean that he disliked women; *merch a garai* (he used to love a maiden), Gutun Owain tells us. His songs to the opposite sex, apart from his one poem to Gwladus Hael on behalf of Harri Ddu ap Gruffudd, are addressed to married ladies who could excel in the part of hostess. Characteristic of these is his eulogy to Siân, the wife of Sir Siôn Bwrch. He had gone to their home suffering from severe pain in his knee, but it had been quickly dispelled by Siân's hospitality, her fire and her food and wine.

In an interesting anecdote we are told that the abbot of Basingwerk once asked Tudur Aled a series of questions, such as which poet was supreme in composing an *awdl*, etc. To the question who was the best poet at composing a *cywydd mab* Tudur Aled replied 'Guto'r Glyn', and it is significant that Gutun Owain expressly refers to Guto'r Glyn's *mawl gwŷr* (the praise of men), and that even in his satire on the poet, Llywelyn ap Gutun has to refer to him as *gwalch cywyddau gwŷr* (the falcon of praise-*cywyddau*). Guto'r Glyn himself says: *Gweithydd fûm ar gywydd gŵr* (I have been a craftsman of the praise-*cywydd*). The *cywydd mab* or *cywydd gŵr* (lit. '*cywydd* of a man') was in the direct line of descent from the heroic songs of Taliesin and Aneirin, and was prized as such, and although Guto sang on the one hand to many clerics and on the other to many soldiers, he was faithful to the tradition that dictated that *cerdd dafod* was primarily the singing of praise and the singing of man's praise at that, and it may very well be that he considered it a virtue on his part that he had composed praise-poetry to a great number of noblemen. He was certainly in favour of cultivating as many patrons as possible and of getting other poets to do so. Significantly, he wrote a *cywydd* to persuade Hywel ap Dafydd to move out of Raglan Castle, not with great effect to judge from Hywel's reply.

The years 1436–1536, as we have said, were brilliant years in the annals of Welsh literature, and it is possible that they were brilliant not only because they produced so many gifted poets but also because they provided these poets with so many worthy patrons, for there can be no doubt that this period saw a resurgence in the vitality and in the vigour of the nobility. In Wales as in England noblemen asserted themselves with increased force. This seems to reflect their increased consciousness that they were the ruling political *élite*, that they were the 'great' men, the 'best' in the realm. Among them there is found incessant strife and almost unbounded ambition. Perhaps the best key to the comprehension of this strife and ambition is a proper understanding of the family and its role, for the family's prominence, extension and aggrandisement come as close to being universal motives for the wide variety of aristocratic activity as any other single force. There was added emphasis on possessions, on lineage, on blood ties, and on the desire to maintain the family identity across the generations. The poets, as the traditional experts on genealogy, discovered that their services were in greater demand. They also found that there was an increase in the emoluments of their craft, for the noblemen of the day were out to impress each other and the lower orders, and one way of doing so was to be lavish in hospitality and to give great feasts. Marriages and funerals were traditionally the occasions *par excellence* for such feasts and public hospitality, and attendance at such occasions was regarded as the mark of goodwill towards the family, just as absence was interpreted as the sign of hostility. The presence of the poets at these feasts was solicited. The propaganda value of their poems was keenly appreciated. Their ability to confer some measure of immortality was not to be disregarded by any head of family with some claim to ambition, especially the ambition to perpetuate his good name and that of his family. And the poets were not only propagandists but also prophets or vaticinators, *brudwyr*. It is no mere accident that this age witnessed a resurgence in the *canu brud*. Indeed, if we knew more about them and about the esteem in which they were held by the public, we might be surprised to find that poets still retained a good deal of the mantic aura of their predecessors in the Dark Ages. When Hywel of Moelyrch injured his knee, Guto'r Glyn composed a *cywydd* to help him to recover, for

> Many a man has been healed by a *cywydd*—
> Golden-handed art thou.

When Edward ap Hywel of Maenor decided to build a house, Guto'r Glyn brought his contribution in the form of a *cywydd*:

> I have fashioned the song of a place like paradise,
> I fashion a song to advance the building.

If a *cywydd* can exercise such a beneficent effect on an inanimate object such as a house or on a living organ such as a knee, what are the limits of its effects on spiritual things? Who can estimate the effect of praise on a man's character, his well-being or prosperity? Who can estimate the effect of an elegy?

We have already mentioned Guto'r Glyn's elegy to Rhys, abbot of Ystrad Fflur. In it we find the lines:

> O rhennir yn yr hoywnef
> I Rys o aur a roes ef,
> Mawr o dâl am aur o'i dŷ
> A gaiff Rys o goffr Iesu.

[If in bright heaven all the gold that he has given
Will be distributed to Rhys,
Great will be the repayment which he will get from Jesus's
    treasure-chest
For the gold he handed out in his house.]

It is tempting to regard these lines as a conceit, but the idea behind them is grounded in the deep-rooted belief that a man should give as much as he can, because the measure of his giving is also the measure of his receiving. Throughout the Middle Ages, in popular thought if not in theology, meanness or avarice was the capital sin and generosity the capital virtue, and there can be no doubt that Guto and Rhys shared this belief. In early society a gift was considered to impose an obligation on the recipient as well as to confer a benefit upon him, and many a piece of land, many a building, was donated to God with the expectation that He would not be able to refuse to repay the gift in one way or another.

To compose a *cywydd* to a patron was to donate a gift to him, and a very valuable one at that. Guto concludes his elegy on Gwerful the daughter of Madog of Bro Tanad with the lines:

The grave where she resides
Has been filled with generosity.
If generosity is repaid,
Let her generosity be repaid to this one.

But the poet has already told us:

There is a long drawn cry on account of her burial,
And her *cywyddau* will (never) be buried.

Whether the *cywyddau* were of her composition or of someone else's is irrelevant to the point which is being made—they themselves are deathless. And the point is extremely important. One is reminded of the words of an Irish poet, Andrew Mac Curtin (*fl.* 1718–43), which in translation read: 'Although rich men of herd, merchants, or people who put out money to grow, think that great is the blindness and want of sense to compose a *duan*, or poem, . . . nevertheless, it is by me understood that they are very greatly deceived, because their herds and their heavy riches shall go by like a summer fog, but the scientific work' (i.e. a well-made poem) 'shall be there to be seen for ever'.

It is probable that the origin of the request-*cywydd* must be sought in the idea that the request-*cywydd* itself was a gift which merited a return gift. We know from the history of Ireland that a poet's request, however unreasonable, could not lightly be refused. Whatever the origin of the request-*cywyddau* may have been, there are a number of them among Guto's poems. Thus there is a request for the gift of a foal, a headguard, a coat of arms, etc., etc. Corresponding to the request-*cywydd* there was the thanks-*cywydd*, and Guto has also a number of these, two expressing gratitude for the gift of a purse, one for a steed, one for a rosary and another for a buckler or shield.

All these *cywyddau* are an indication of the kind of relationship which existed between the poets and their patrons, a relationship which may have become closer in this period than it had been for a considerable time. Such a development could be expected, because by the fifteenth century, if not by the fourteenth, the majority of noblemen (including their wives and children), were literate in England. Whether they were literate to the same extent in Wales, and whether they were equally literate in Welsh and English, are questions which remain to be answered, but there is evidence that some at least of them were bilingually literate, and there is still more evidence that poets and patrons began to enjoy common cultural interests. Dafydd, the abbot of Glyn Egwestl, made through Guto'r Glyn a request to Trahaearn ab Ieuan of Penrhos Bwrdios near Caerleon for a copy of the *Greal*. And there is a charming picture of a two-way educational process between poet and patron in Guto's *cywydd* to Rhys ap Siancyn of Glyn Nedd:

> I will also be given instruction
> Concerning the three ages of this world,
> Prophecy as it was shaped
> And the chronicle of few words,
> The legends of saints who sinned not,
> And the genealogy of Owain Gwynedd of yore.
> Thou and thy minstrel, Rhys, will number the kings,
> Rulers over the land of our kingdom.

As the average level of literacy and of education rose, the general and special knowledge expected of the poets increased, but the standard attained by them was by no means uniform, and in this respect as in others Guto'r Glyn stands above most of his contemporaries. Even a cursory glance through the index of names attached to his work is sufficient to show that he had a sound knowledge of the popular literature which circulated throughout Europe in his time. It is not impossible, of course, that he owed much of this knowledge to his travels as a soldier, and if, as has been suggested, he was made an official poet of some kind to Mathau Goch or to the Welsh forces serving in France, he must have come to know the services which other 'official poets', the *jongleurs*, offered their clients. No doubt, Guto was influenced by his audience. Mr Saunders Lewis suggests that the number of curses in one *cywydd* reflects the taste of the audience. It may be also that Guto was forced in composing *cywyddau* for soldiers like Mathau Goch and Richard Gethin to adopt a simpler style using less archaisms and more neologisms than would be used in a more complex style. Indeed, one is struck by the number of 'English' words found in his poetry. Some of these are technical legal terms: *prifei sêl* (privy seal), *comyn plas* (common pleas), *patent, rhentolion, sifil, endeintio, deintur* (indenture), *comisiwn, rhysyfwr* (receiver). The use of some of these words was dictated, no doubt, by his subject-matter, just as his use of military terms was unavoidable in dealing with the exploits of Mathau Goch. A striking example is the use of *main gwns* for 'cannon balls'. But whatever the explanation, these borrowed words show that Guto'r Glyn was prepared to employ the Welsh language creatively and was determined not to allow himself to be fettered by convention.

In Welsh as in Irish literature, the 'backward look' predominates over the 'forward look'. In other words, tradition tends to outweigh innovation. In only a few poets do tradition and innovation achieve a perfect balance. Dafydd ap Gwilym was a great innovator but his immediate successors, although they imitated him, did not emulate him in his practice of innovation, with the result that the fourteenth-century *cywyddwyr* who followed him display a certain uniformity in their poetic techniques, e.g. in their use of the *cynganeddion* and of the *cywydd* metre. Like Dafydd ap Gwilym they use to a considerable extent the *cynganeddion* which contain internal rhyme as compared with those which use only consonantal correspondences. In the same way when they saw that the single line had ceased to be the natural unit, once the *cywydd* metre had superseded the *awdl*-metres, they began to use the two lines of the *cywydd* couplet as their unit and even experimented with the unit which contained several couplets. In either case it was not easy to adapt sentences to the couplet structure of the *cywydd* and the poets had recourse to *sangiadau* (parentheses) and *torymadroddi* (intercalation). Towards the end of the fourteenth century it looked as if there was to be a struggle for supremacy between the sentence and the couplet, i.e. between the *cywydd* in which the sentence would overrun several couplets and the *cywydd* in which the sentence would be confined to the couplet. In the event it was the latter, the sentence-couplet, which won the day. Its merits were too obvious to ignore, and indeed it resulted in *cywyddau* which gleamed with couplets of gemlike concision. But this type of *cywydd* was not without its drawbacks. Even in the hands of the skilful it sometimes became monotonous and lacked the feel of movement.

However, a poet's skill in *cynghanedd* could help him to overcome the limits imposed by the couplet structure of the *cywydd* metre, and in the hands of virtuosi like Lewis Glyn Cothi and Guto'r Glyn in the fifteenth century, a mastery over the medium was achieved which makes some of the fourteenth-century *cywyddwyr* appear at times amateurish.

Cynghanedd, as Sir John Morris-Jones once said, is not suitable to express thoughts already formed: in it ideas and the feelings behind them seem to form themselves in the music. This describes precisely Guto'r Glyn's art. As one reads a *cywydd* of his, one is struck by the effortless ease with which he brings forth his consonantal *cynganeddion*, gracefully avoiding the Scylla of extreme ingenuity on the one hand and the Charybdis of hard-won correctness on the other. Their conversational quality has often been noticed. Take, for example, the beginning of the *cywydd* to Mathau Goch:

Pan sonier i'n amser ni
Am undyn yn Normandi,
Mathau Goch, fab maeth y gwin,
Biau'r gair yn bwrw gwerin.
Eryr yw ar wŷr ieuainc,
Arthur ffriw wrth aerau Ffrainc,
Enaid y capteiniaid da
A blaenor y bobl yna.

[Whenever there is mention in our time
Of any one in Normandy,

It is of Mathau Goch, that wine-reared (or well nurtured)
man
And his overthrowing of the populace.
He is an eagle (soaring) over young men
With Arthur's countenance facing the French battles,
The soul of the good captains,
And the leader of the men there.]

Here there is such a happy union of sense and metre achieved so effortlessly that one is lost in amazement at the resultant perfect harmony. Guto'r Glyn's mastery over *cynghanedd* is such that, although the thought must have been formed simultaneously with it, the impression which is left on the reader is that the thought is throughout in control.

Mr Eurys Rowlands has drawn attention to the fact that our poet uses less the technique of piling descriptive epithet on descriptive epithet than the technique of developing the implications of a single idea or image. Earlier poets use the device called *dyfalu* extensively: it is not unlike the kenning and essentially it is the art of describing one thing in terms of several other things which it resembles in some particulars. A notable example of its use is Dafydd ap Gwilym's *cywydd* to the Wind. Guto'r Glyn employs the technique when it serves his purpose, but the technique which is distinctly his is that of seizing upon an idea or image and exploring it to its farthest limits. Thus he speaks of his relationship with Hywel ab Ifan Fychan as a marriage and proceeds to develop the implications of the image in thirty-two lines, mostly, of course, in terms of its indissolubility:

Ar dy barth erioed y bûm,
A nithio cerdd a wneuthum.
Mwythau ni ad im weithian
Fyned o'th gwrt, fendith gwan.
Rhodd priodas urddas oedd,
Rhwymyn Duw rhôm ein deuoedd.

[I have always been on thy premises
And at the task of purifying (distilling) song.
Now (thy) indulgence does not allow me
To depart from thy court, thou blessing of the weak.
It was the boon derived from a stately marriage,
A bond (made) by God between us.]

The reasons why Guto'r Glyn was accounted a great poet by his contemporaries are as manifest today as they ever were, and there can be no doubt that his name will always be linked with the names of the giants of the *canu caeth* or strict-metre tradition in Welsh poetry.

ACKNOWLEDGEMENTS

I should like to thank Miss Anne E. Curry (of Teesside Polytechnic), Miss Enid Roberts, Mrs Llinos Beverley Smith, Mr D. J. Bowen, and Professor R. R. Davies for their kindness in answering my questions to them while I was preparing this chapter.

BIBLIOGRAPHY

Text

J. LlywelynWilliams and Ifor Williams, *Gwaith Guto'r Glyn* (Caerdydd, 1939; revised, 1961).

Historical Background

H. T. Evans, *Wales and the Wars of the Roses* (Cambridge, 1915; reprinted Stroud, 1995).

Critical Studies

D. J. Bowen, 'Nodiadau ar Waith y Cywyddwyr', *Llên Cymru*, 10 (1968–9), 121.

Idem, 'Guto'r Glyn a Glyn-y-Groes', in J. E. Caerwyn Williams (ed.), *Ysgrifau Beirniadol XX* (Dinbych, 1995), 149– 83.

W. J. Gruffydd, 'Marwnadau i Ddynion Byw', *Y Beirniad*, i (1911), 34–8.

Idem, *Llenyddiaeth Cymru o 1450 hyd 1600* (Lerpwl, 1922), 26–31.

Bobi Jones, *Guto'r Glyn a'i Gyfnod* (Llyfrau'r Dryw, 1963).

Idem, 'Pwnc Mawr Beirniadaeth Lenyddol Gymraeg', in J. E. Caerwyn Williams (ed.), *Ysgrifau Beirniadol II* (Dinbych, 1966), 257–76, esp. 269–70.

T. Gwynn Jones, 'Guto'r Glyn and Oswestry', *Montgomeryshire Collections*, xl (1922), 141–5.

Idem, *Llenyddiaeth y Cymry. Cyf. 1. Hyd Ymdrech y Tuduriaid* (Dinbych, 1915), 80–4.

Cynfael Lake, 'Goblygiadau Clera a Golwg ar Ganu Guto'r Glyn', in J. E. Caerwyn Williams (ed.), *Ysgrifau Beirniadol XX* (Dinbych, 1995), 125–48.

Saunders Lewis, 'Gyrfa Filwrol Guto'r Glyn', in J. E. Caerwyn Williams (ed.), *Ysgrifau Beirniadol IX* (Dinbych, 1976), 80–99.

J. E. Lloyd, 'Gwaith Guto'r Glyn', *Bulletin of the Board of Celtic Studies*, x (1939), 126–7.

Thomas Parry, *A History of Welsh Literature*, translated by H. Idris Bell (Oxford, 1962).

Enid Roberts, 'Cywydd Marwnad Llywelyn ap y Moel', *Bulletin of the Board of Celtic Studies*, xvii (1956–8), 182–3.

Idem, *Y Beirdd a'r Noddwyr ym Maelor*. Darlith Eisteddfod Genedlaethol Cymru Wrecsam a'r Cylch, 1977, 14–19.

Thomas Roberts, 'Guto'r Glyn', *Y Llenor*, xxvi (1947), 34–40.

Eurys Rolant, 'Rhamant Hanes y Beirdd', in J. E. Caerwyn Williams (ed.), *Ysgrifau Beirniadol III* (Dinbych, 1967), 33–5.

Idem, 'Arddull y Cywydd', ibid., *II* (1966), 36–57.

D. Roy Saer, 'Delweddaeth y Ddawns Werin a'r Chwaraeon Haf ym Marwnad Guto'r Glyn i Wiliam Herbert', *Transactions of the Honourable Society of Cymmrodorion,* 1969, 265–83.

J. Llywelyn Williams, 'Guto ap Siancyn, neu Guto'r Glyn', *Y Llenor*, x (1931), 152–60.

CHAPTER 11

LEWIS GLYN COTHI

E. D. JONES

Nineteenth-century writers record a tradition that Lewis Glyn Cothi lived at a place called Pwlltinbyd in Cwm Cothi. Others maintain that the correct name of this tenement, which no longer exists, was Pwllcynbyd. There was, however, a more important place, a hamlet known as Pwllcynbyd, a name which survives as that of a substantial farm in the parish of Llanybydder. This Pwllcynbyd formed part of the forest of Glyn Cothi in the parishes of Llanfihangel-rhos-y-corn and Llanybydder, in the commotes of Mabudrud and Mabelfyw in Cantref Mawr, the last possessions of the princes of Dinefwr to fall to the English Crown. It fell on the collapse of the rising of Rhys ap Maredudd, 1287–90. Edward I carved out of Cantref Mawr the forest of Glyn Cothi and its associated forest of Penneint in the parish of Caeo, placing the whole territory under the jurisdiction of a chief forester independent of the civil administration. According to tradition, nine men settled in this combined forest. One of the nine, said to have been a thief, settled in Pwllcynbyd in the southern part of Llanybydder. The settlement flourished, a royal mill was established there and remained on the royal rentroll till recent times. By 1584, there were fifteen tenements in the hamlet, with fifty-three residents, eight of them freeholders of the Crown. One writer seeks to confirm the association of Lewis Glyn Cothi with Pwlltinbyd by reference to the burial in Llanfihangel-rhos-y-corn in 1771 of one Elizabeth Lewis, with the suggestion that the name had survived till then in the family. In fact, this record points to the Glyn Cothi Pwllcynbyd which adjoined the parish of Rhos-y-corn, and not to the Caeo tenement similarly named. In the late eighteenth century, Tomos Glyn Cothi, also born within the confines of the forest, took his bardic name from it. It is therefore more reasonable to place Lewis Glyn Cothi in the parish of Llanybydder rather than in that of Caeo. Unfortunately, he has left us no record of his family. In a *cywydd* to Rhys ap Dafydd of Blaen Tren, in the forest, he has an idyllic description of the wooded environment of his youth. The forest, he describes, abounded with fruit, acorns, swarms of bees 'in the brushwood of Bydder', roebucks, harts 'by tens', stages below Pencader, woods with falcons, copses full of blackbirds, herons' nests in summer, and haunts of squirrels in winter. This was Glyn Cothi in his day with none of the conifers of today. He is generally known as Lewis Glyn Cothi, but he also called himself Lewis, or Lewys, y Glynn. His baptismal name was Llewelyn or Llywelyn, of which Lewis was but a hypocoristic form.

Lewis Glyn Cothi stands out amongst his contemporaries in the bardic fraternity as the only one whose poems are textually securely attested. Out of the two hundred and fifty or so of *awdlau* and *cywyddau* attributed to him, all but twenty or so survive in texts of unimpeachable authenticity. A writer of about 1600 states that Lewis never wrote on paper, but on parchment. Luckily, some of these parchments still exist and are supplemented by a paper manuscript containing copies of seventy-seven of his poems not in the parchment manuscripts, but even this exhibits the orthographical and other characteristics of the parchments. It belongs to the early years of the sixteenth century when many of his patrons were still alive.

He is a classic example of the fifteenth-century *pencerdd*. By this time, the functions of the *pencerdd* and *bardd teulu* had long been merged, and the bards by the force of circumstances had become established itinerants. Lewis was one of the most ubiquitous of these itinerants. He was fully aware of the traditions, lore and social responsibilities of his profession. He used both the older and more formal medium of the *awdl*, and the more recent and more intimate *cywydd* metre, which had become so popular in the fourteenth century. The original arrangements of his parchment collections, though disturbed by the vicissitudes of time and neglect, reflect the basic principles of bardism. One of his collections undoubtedly opened with his ode to the Trinity, in accordance with the rule laid down in Welsh laws. The *awdl* still commanded a higher status than the *cywydd*, so his other volume of collected poems begins with odes, introduced by *awdlau* to the two leading Herberts, Lord Herbert of Raglan, and his brother, Sir Richard. The *awdlau* consisted of intricate metrical forms, at which the *penceirddiaid* through long training were most proficient. Lewis occasionally experimented with methods of expressing the intricacies of the *awdl* metres visually in his calligraphy. On account of the status of the *awdl* it was a higher compliment to a patron than a *cywydd* though the latter would be much more intelligible. The *cywydd* probably derives from the functions of the *bardd teulu*, who was required to sing to the queen in her chamber, but was taken over by the *penceirddiaid* when the different functions were fused together. As more than half his poems are *cywyddau* it would seem that he preferred this metre. The bards were divided into three grades, and though the *pencerdd* was allowed to exercise the functions of the *bardd teulu* he was not to demean himself by using the versification of the *clerwr* who was a kind of itinerant minstrel. The *pencerdd* was forbidden to resort to satire which was the antithesis of eulogy. It seems from some references in Lewis Glyn Cothi's poems that a *pencerdd* could send a *datgeiniad* (a singer or a declaimer of poetry) to convey his *cywyddau* to a patron, though one of his clerical friends warned the possessor of a collection containing his poems to keep it from *datgeiniaid* as 'it contains many good things'. The *penceirddiaid* in the fifteenth century were skilled in genealogy and heraldry. Pedigrees are woven into their poems and, less often, heraldic charges. Lewis Glyn Cothi is the first *pencerdd* known to have embellished his work with the heraldic shields of patrons, but if we had the holographs of the works of others of his period or earlier, Iolo Goch, for instance, their occurrence in Lewis's works might not be such an innovation.

The geographical distribution of his surviving poems indicates the wide range of his bardic peregrinations. The following figures for poems that can be localized are set out for our present territorial divisions (as used 1974–95):

Dyfed	75	Powys	74
West Glamorgan	10	Gwent	10
Gwynedd	9	South Glamorgan	3
The English border	19		

The high figure for Powys is largely due to the great number of poems to patrons in the commotes of Elfael, Maelienydd, Gwerthrynion, Ewyas, and Maesyfed or Radnor. Together, these poems exceed the total for Cantref Mawr, his *patria*. The *penceirddiaid* of that 'great century' of Welsh poetry were much at home in what are now Anglicized areas of Wales and indeed beyond Offa's Dyke.

We shall never know who taught Lewis Glyn Cothi the rudiments of his craft. He was patronized by Griffith ap Nicholas and his family, nine poems to them surviving, but there is no acknowledgement of a disciple's debt, even in the majestic ode to the father who was interested enough in bardism to sponsor an eisteddfod in Dinefwr or Carmarthen around 1450. There is a suggestion in his *awdl* to Morgan ab Owen, prior of Carmarthen, that he received some education at the priory:

> To the holy White-hill, to a second Cynog
> I, as a youth, was servant,
> And his song, his butler, and his cook,
> And his humble servant, and his officer.
>
> My office for my lord was to direct from my lips
> The muse to the prior of Carmarthen;
> Never was seen a possessor of Latin
> So wise, and so free of his wine.

The abbey at Talley was nearer to his birthplace, but there is no evidence that he derived any advantage from its proximity. As far as we know, he had no associations with Strata Florida. The abbeys which figure in his poems are Whitland, Deuma or Llantarnam, and towards the end of his life, Margam. Whitland to him was the Florence of Dyfed and its abbot the keeper of the cadence of Oxford. No man except the king of France had such a countenance; there was no lord of Wales of better governance. John ap Roger Vaughan of Deuma deserved an *awdl* and a *cywydd.* He was a true father of religion, a swan of six hundred tenants—'greater is the wave from his mead than a sea under a boat'. John and his men had built a house after the design of Virgil. It was a copy of Troy. In an elegy to William, abbot of Margam, who died in 1487, Margam is said to be like Durham, a hospice for all Wales, its Rome, and 'William is my pope'. A number of poems reflect his happy relationship with ecclesiastics from Robert Tully, bishop of St David's, to the vicar who, like a knight of God, made the chancel of Darowen church his castle.

Lewis Glyn Cothi's cultural contacts were by no means confined to clerics. His poems testify to the high level of culture in the homes of the laymen of the period. He could discuss poetry with them, and they could appreciate the literary and historical allusions which abound in his poems. As a youthful bard to Llewelyn ap Gwilym of Bryn Hafod in Cetheiniog Lewis would have him called Emrys and himself a slim Myrddin. Llewelyn would call him Elijah and he would call Llewelyn Matthias. Llewelyn would call Lewis Adda Fras the elder and he would be called Melwas. Ieuan ap Llewelyn of Nantmelan was equally well versed in the bardic tradition to appreciate the compliment of being called Ifor Hael, Lewis being Dafydd ap Gwilym, or Rhydderch ab Ieuan Llwyd with Lewis as Iolo Goch. Lewis was then young and would sing *Armes Brydyn* for Ieuan. The relationship between Lewis and William ap Siôn of Llanegwad was that of teacher and pupil; as Iolo Goch had been to Rhydderch Lewis was William's Iolo. 'My office to my mesne lord,' he said, 'is to explain poetry, reading another art better, reading history still better, Genesis which abides through science, the island's pedigrees, its chronicle, recalling the old songs, and love-songs from old tradition.' This was indeed a liberal curriculum. Hopkin ap John of Gower would order wine and buy it like a king, play the harp and tune it like an amiantine bell, sing a *pennill* (verse) to a tune, cause wine to be brought in, 'asking us in addition to a poem of greeting, the pedigrees of May and a love *cywydd*'. The two brothers, Llewelyn and Henry ap Gwilym of the Vale of Tywi, 'made me drink their wine every hour long ago, and by St James, recite the stories of Brutus of Troy, the old poetry, the names of heroes, and the parents of the ancients'. Good living and culture went together at Harpton in New Radnor, where Lewis was a *cywyddwr* to Dafydd ap Rhys, his host there. There was fine fare in the form of fish and poultry, pastries, good old liquor, sweet food on eight tables, vegetables from shops, a sewer for every herb, dishes on course, white sugar, intoxicating mead, and other delicacies. But, if drink allowed it, the poet's task was to read the books, to put an end to rumour and, together with his host, argue sense. If verses were not understood, Dafydd, by Gwion's *cywydd*, would explain them thoroughly. Dafydd Goch of Gwerthrynion, brave as Lancelot and strong as Arthur, was a keen huntsman, but when he came in from the chase he would call his bard to have his reward and enjoy Weobley ale and venison. Phelpod ap Rhys of Brilley knew all the legends and had the best Welsh; he knew the chronicle of the island's heroes. There was no one like him apart from Gildas. Seven ancients knew the seven arts of the old world. Phelpod knew a little of each one of them. This poem is an elegy which contrasts Phelpod's two habits:

> Scarlet, like Tewdwr's father,
> And ermine he used to wear,

but now

> A narrow robe of blue-black cloth
> And an outer robe of green earth.

Now his feet were in one hose, and his hands in one glove, but 'his soul was in the grace of One and Three'. Rhydderch ap Rhys of Cetheiniog knew more good than any man in India. He knew the chronicle of every corner of the island and every word of the Bible. He was, withal, a good husbandman with his nine gardens around a white-washed hall.

Lewis Glyn Cothi refers to his very early visits to Ewyas, when he went there 'on a blue north wind'. John ap Howel invited him as his father had done before him. The father's gold and John's gift of purchased clothing were the first he ever received in Ewyas. In spite of his undisguised Lancastrian sympathies the border Yorkists welcomed his visits. Patron and poet understood the basic principle of bardism. The poet was professionally bound to praise his patron for his loyalty to his overlord and the patron accepted eulogy without questioning the poet's political affiliations. There was innocent leg-pulling, as when Meredydd ap Dafydd of Llinwent would invite him he would cast a question about 'tall Jasper', teasing the bard, but still giving him gold and bidding him fetch a horse. So would Morgan ap Howel of Llanbister mock him. 'Morgan,' he writes, 'I am not without thy satire. By Christ, by the relic, I will not forget thee, not one of the decalogue will be forgotten.'

The troubles of the period, however, did not pass him by. His first datable poem is an elegiac *cywydd* on the treacherous execution of Sir Griffith Vaughan of Guilsfield in Powys Castle in 1447. A touch of vaticination, which breaks out occasionally in his work, appears in this powerful elegy. He prophesied remonstrance and chastisement on Mochno bog, Rhuddlan predicted his family's vengeance. It was meet that there should be warriors in Cyminod because of this. 'There will be trouble on account of Sir Griffith. For him we are undergoing penance.' This is not the work of an apprentice, so that we can assume that he had composed a good deal before 1447 when the clouds of civil strife were gathering.

Wales was deeply involved in the struggle. The Principality and the extensive lands of the Duchy of Lancaster in Wales meant close links with the Crown. The local officials, many of whom were Lewis's patrons, were naturally supporters of the reigning monarch. The lordship of Pembroke was held by Jasper Tudor, Henry the VI's half-brother and loyal adherent. The Marcher lordships were divided, but, through the Mortimer interest, were mainly Yorkist and the lordship of Glamorgan was held by the earl of Warwick, a strong supporter of the duke of York and of his son Edward IV. Lewis Glyn Cothi's poems are set against this background. In the early fifties, when efforts were made to strengthen the Lancastrian following in Wales, Edmund Tudor, earl of Richmond, Jasper's elder brother, came down to Pembroke. During his short stay (for he died there in November 1456, two months before the birth of his son, Henry) he enlisted the support of the powerful Griffith ap Nicholas. The presence of the son of Owen Tudor in Wales had kindled Welsh patriotic fire, and in his elegy on the death of Edmund, 'brother of King Henry, nephew of the Dauphin and son of Owen', Lewis bitterly complained that 'poetry woven into prophecy had been but mist'. Jasper stepped into the breach, and throughout the rest of his life the unhappy Henry VI could rely on his half-brother's support. Jasper took his infant nephew under his wing and lived to style himself 'brother and uncle of kings'. To this period, around 1456, belong Lewis Glyn Cothi's *cywydd* to William Herbert and his *awdl* to Griffith ap Nicholas. Two of his odes to Jasper Tudor belong to the early months of 1461. Lewis was then an outlaw 'on account of the Earl of Pembroke'. He had obviously been involved in the campaign which led up to the defeat of the Lancastrians at Mortimer's Cross on 2 February. The tradition that he was an officer in Jasper's army can not be substantiated. It is more likely that he was in the company of the sons of Griffith ap Nicholas. Jasper had crossed to Brittany, but the bard expects and predicts his return as the hawk of Queen Catherine. He places him third in precedence in the realm, coming next after Henry VI and Prince Edward. He predicts that young Henry of Richmond would follow his uncle to Llifon. These two odes contain vaticinatory elements, the second particularly full of allusions to beasts and birds of the menagerie of vaticination, some of which can be identified by reference to the heraldic cognizances of participants in the struggle. The bard concludes that Jasper, like Brân ap Dyfnwal, would win half of France and Lombardy. There is no suggestion that young Henry would succeed to the Crown.

A *cywydd* to Meredydd ap Meredydd of Trefeglwys on the eastern slopes of Pumlumon reveals the bard's hiding-place when he was 'an outlaw on account of the Earl of Pembroke'. He describes his lair in a hollow oak, where Owen Glyndŵr's men used to be, how he spent his days in Pennant Bacho, hiding in the heather of Cwmbuga, but making for Meredydd's house for his supper and his bed. In a *cywydd* of a later period he recalls how Owen ap Griffith ap Nicholas shared his outlawry in Gwynedd. Pumlumon lies on the borders of Ceredigion and Powys, and could hardly be placed in Gwynedd, so that it is possible that this *cywydd* relates to an earlier outlawry. Owen had been in trouble in 1442–3 when the Privy Council ordered his arrest and that of a militant monk who was holding *cymhorthau* (assemblies for aid), declaiming Welsh chronicles and traditions, and stirring people to rebellion. H. T. Evans made the suggestion that the monk might have been Lewis Glyn Cothi.

For Welshmen, the most significant result of the Yorkist victory at Mortimer's Cross and the accession of Edward IV was the meteoric rise to a position of authority of William Herbert of Raglan and his elevation to the peerage as Lord Herbert in 1461. Lewis Glyn Cothi celebrates the event in a majestic *awdl* in which Edward and Herbert are linked together, the former also regarded as a Welshman by virtue of his descent from Gwladys Ddu, daughter of Llewelyn Fawr:

Edward the conqueror, in place of Edwin,
Is Julius Caesar over the English host;
Herbert is brave on a wheeling charger
Measuring Wales in his commission.

Edward is Charlemagne, by St Martin's grave!
Herbert is Roland to the generous;
Edward is Arthur, as is fitting,
Herbert is Gwalchmai with the broken spear.

Lord Herbert is vividly portrayed as he charged in battle:

> He came by like Julius Caesar
> With the spear of Gwalchmai ap Gwyar,
> And his shield, his spirited steed from Gwent,
> His arm and his javelin made a cold scatter on Trent;
>
> And his face afire on a wild steed,
> And his grand mien like an ocean of glowing coals,
> And his spear from his breast like an oak on a sallet,
> And his halberd flashes of lightning or a glowing fire.

In a companion *awdl* to his brother, Sir Richard Herbert, the arms of three lions rampant and the badge of a sheaf of arrows are described, and Edward IV and Sir Richard are urged to join in a crusade. Lord Herbert, on capturing Harlech Castle in 1468, was created earl of Pembroke, the earldom being in abeyance since the attainder of Jasper Tudor in 1461. No poem by Lewis Glyn Cothi to mark this further elevation has survived. The new earl's tenure was brief. A rising engineered by the earl of Warwick from resentment of the power wielded by the king's friends involved the Herberts in a short campaign which ended in disaster near Banbury in July 1469. The Herberts were executed by Warwick's command, and this, with the loss of the flower of the Welsh March in the battle made Banbury an emotive word in the poetry of the period. Lewis Glyn Cothi has several poems on the subject. In one of them, an elegy on the death of Thomas ap Roger Vaughan of Hergest, a half-brother of the Herberts, all being sons of Gwladys daughter of Dafydd Gam, he reflects the confusion of battle-cries at Hedgecote—'some "Herbert", some "Our Edward", "Earl of Warwick", others "Harry"'. He refers to the grief of his widow, Ellen Gethin, and to the three sons who were bent on revenge: 'they will avenge their father upon England before their eyes are closed'. In another *cywydd* he describes the fine alabaster tomb which is still to be seen in Kington church. A vaticinatory poem to Dafydd ap John of Gower urges him to avenge his family upon the tribe of Banbury, and in an *awdl* to Watkin Vaughan, son of Thomas ap Roger, Lewis charges him to spare not Banbury, nor its crows, nor its magpies.

Edward IV had to seek refuge in Burgundy and Henry VI was restored to his kingdom. Edward returned in March 1471, and in

April the earl of Warwick was slain when trying to escape from the battle of Barnet. According to Welsh tradition he was slain by William Vaughan of Rhydhelig. For the Welsh, Barnet avenged the treachery of Banbury. Lancastrian hopes were crushed at the battle of Tewkesbury and Edward IV reigned without interruption until his death in 1483. Lewis Glyn Cothi commends Llewelyn ap Rhys of New Radnor for his part in the restoration of King Edward, by performing 'paschal work' at Barnet on Easter Sunday, and for his valour at Tewkesbury. For the remainder of Edward's reign Lewis was able to enjoy in peace his peregrinations from house to house.

His longest poem is his *awdl* to the Trinity already mentioned. It is an abecedarian sequence of six score *englynion*, six to each letter in an alphabet of twenty, every line, except one, beginning with the same letter, often with the same word. In the following examples he uses his baptismal name:

> For the sake of the nine spheres of heaven,
> For the sake of the ten trees of life,
> For the sake of all that Thou did'st create from Thy throne,
> From grievous injury receive Llewelyn to Thy feast.
>
> Lily of the gentle earth is he, a jewel for all,
> Lily of the world and its circumference,
> Lily of heaven is he to us.
> Lily, preserve Llewelyn!

His other religious poems include a *cywydd* on the Crucifixion and Resurrection which introduces the legend of the four kinds of timber in the Cross, two *cywyddau* and an *awdl-gywydd* to St David, versifying his *vita* and appealing to him to bring peace to Elfael. Lewis loved Elfael and its thirteen saints and had great faith in the efficacy of their intercession. Another poem, unfortunately incomplete, names a large number of saints in whom the hope of the country lay—'our land and houses have for ever become glebelands of churches, every district and valley has become a sanctuary. There is hardly a slope, hardly a strip of ground, without confession and procession.' He has *cywyddau* also to St Llawddog, St Nicholas, and the apostles Simon and Jude. He asks Llawddog to bring prosperity to his parish, his men, his children, every harrow and yoke, all the ploughs, every furrow, every hill and ridge and all grain. The grace of St Nicholas would spare the bard from rejection on the Day of Judgement.

Invocations of saints proliferate throughout his work. Pilgrimages are also noted. Dafydd ap John of Gower had gone to Rome to fetch parchment pardons for many, and in an *awdl* Lewis relates how he, his poet, and Dafydd's wife had made an oblation to God for his safe return over the Alps and along the banks of the Rhine. Griffith ap Rhys of Branas in Edeirnion had gone to Santiago and in a *cywydd* Lewis describes the ship which was to bring him home. Another *cywydd* describes the ship which brought Elliw of Glyn Aeron from Santiago to Pembroke, where she was to take another to bring her back to Cardiganshire. There is no reference to pilgrimages to shrines in England, though Lewis knew of some of them. Judging from references to friars and mendicants in an elegy to Einion ab Ieuan of Abernant, in his native district, he shared his dislike of the practice of carrying images and relics of saints about the country. 'Einion,' he says, 'would not have Welsh saints dragged from their houses.'

An *awdl* to Eva, daughter of Llewelyn ap Meredydd of Rhaeadr, and a *cywydd* to Howel Prainche of Cowbridge, thanking them for rosaries, lead to the *genre* of poems of solicitation and thanks (*cywyddau gofyn a diolch*). In these, the poetic device of description (*dyfalu*) is developed into a fine art. The object sought or acknowledged is described in great detail. The request could be personal to the poet or on behalf of another. Most of Lewis's *cywyddau gofyn* are his own personal requests. Three of them refer to an incident in Chester which has attracted much attention from writers on Lewis Glyn Cothi. If we are to take these references literally, the poet was robbed of all his possessions in the city. In one of the poems he begs a coverlet from Elin, daughter of Llewelyn of Llwydiarth in Anglesey, because Chester had robbed him of his house, his splendid coverlet, and his bed. 'They left me more naked than a salmon swimming in a brook' is his description of his plight. The next is more sinister. It is a *cywydd* soliciting, from Dafydd ap Gutun of Oswestry, a sword which he would whet on the heads of every villain in Chester. The third is an ode to Annes, wife of the mayor of Caerleon, soliciting a piece of arras. This contains a similar complaint against the citizens of Chester—'a deceitful stunted bush robbed me . . . of my grandeur, of my entire dwelling, and of my tapestries'. Annes had a piece of arras depicting the Herbert arms, lions rampant, a leopard, Edward's lion, and crescents. The play on the two place-names Caerlleon Gawr and Caerllion casts doubts upon the actuality of the episode. The traditional explanation derives from notes on an *awdl* to Rheinallt ap Griffith ap Bleddyn attributed in comparatively late manuscripts, and of doubtful authenticity, like the *cywydd* to the Englishmen of Flint. There are two main streams in this tradition. According to one it happened after the battle of Mortimer's Cross, when Lewis is said to have prophesied that Henry of Richmond would become king. There is no evidence to support this account. The other version accounts for the action of the citizens of Chester by saying that the bard had married a widow of the city without permission. Some texts inevitably add that the widow was wealthy. If there is a basis of fact underlying the story, the rational explanation would be that there had been a re-enforcement of the Lancastrian penal code against Welshmen. Another request for a bed and furnishings from two ladies in St Harmon's (one being a daughter of Owen Glyndŵr) makes no reference to Chester. In this, Lewis refers to his little son 'who loved to stretch himself on a white bed'. He calls him his *disyn* (literally, a 'little dice') the word he uses in that poignant elegy which he composed after the child's death at the age of five.

Among other objects solicited are two cows from two ladies in Elfael, a green mantle from Elis Holh of Gladestry, and a bow and arrow from Dafydd Llwyd of Abertanat. Dafydd had already given him a bow, but a thief had taken it. Dafydd had another bow 'such as no one can draw to his face'. Lewis boldly declares: 'I will draw it, by John, behind my ear . . . It will make me proud to shoot a roebuck with a white arrow . . . and, drinking osey, to show the gift bow to everyone . . . I shall send a *datgeiniad* with a poem for thy red bow, Dafydd.' Lewis may well have been a skilled archer, at any rate he uses the metaphor of shooting a *cywydd*. But the most curious of his *cywyddau gofyn* is the one asking William Vaughan, constable of Aberystwyth Castle, to shave his beard for him as he had grown to be like the holy Anthony or John of Beverley or a stag in a ravine. He attributes his hairy face to a pilgrimage—'I came a penitent . . . to Peter and Paul. I walked to seek them from Anglesey to far-away Rome, through the valley of the Rhine, the wide lands of Burgundy, Italy, Lombardy, Brabant, Alman . . . Swabia and Flanders . . . I was a sane brother, with a wild intent, of Myrddin Wyllt with his feast in the Caledonian forest and his grey beard on his chest.' He made several requests for horses,—one 'obedient to the rein' from Rhys Aubrey and Gwilym ap Morgan.

He thanked Dafydd ap Meredydd Fychan for a three-year-old colt. He begged of 'Syr' Huw Iolo and Howel ab Ieuan of Elfael for harness for a horse which he expected to receive from the earl of Pembroke. From Ieuan ap Meredydd of Builth he requested a plain saddle easy to mount or dismount, a sign of old age, for when he asked Ieuan to lend him a stool so that he could reach the stirrups 'Ieuan, in his wine, gives his bard Myrddin's chair'. In another poem, combining lavish praise of Elfael with a request for a horse, he recalls the time when in his youth he had been merry there, but now, to have more of Elfael's gold he needed a horse 'tame as a sheep' and a plain saddle, bald as his own head. 'I am as bald as a friar' is his confession. The need for a horse is fully explained in a *cywydd* to John ap Phillip of Cilsant. The common rhymesters all had their rouncies or hackneys, beating him to the weddings and picking up their two groats, leaving him, arriving later on foot, without a penny. Rhys the Piper had told him that John would give him a horse. It would have to be tame, neither too young nor too old. Then he would be first at weddings, and the guests would readily give him six shillings. It may be a reflection of the lawlessness of the time that Howel Prainche, 'the truthful Welshman', gave him a poniard. In a *cywydd* thanking him, he recalls the rosary which he had earlier received and the white wine. The poniard was no ordinary dagger. Its hilt was of gold, with a lion on one side and a leopard on the other,—a gift worthy of the wealthy merchant of Cowbridge. All the requests, however, were not personal. He asks Jenkin ap Thomas for a cuirass or brigander on behalf of Griffith Basset, John ap Dafydd of Carnwyllon for a buckler on behalf of Griffith Llwyd ap Meredydd, and Roger Kynaston for a suit of armour for Edward ap Dafydd of Erbistock. In these *cywyddau gofyn* on behalf of third parties, the practice of praising the recipient and tracing his pedigree, which later became an additional feature of this *genre*, had not begun. In Lewis's *cywyddau gofyn* only the would-be donor's pedigree is given.

Associated with requests for material objects are poems to wish the healing of wounds or the restoration of health. Dafydd Llwyd, the poet and *brudiwr* (vaticinator) of Mathafarn in Powys had fallen from his horse, dislocating his shoulder. Lewis wished that he could fetch from Avalon one of the physicians who had restored Arthur from his wounds, or that he could use the vernicle so that he himself could cure Dafydd within the hour. Dafydd ap John of Kilvey had been wounded by a rabble from the gutters of Cardiff. Lewis had his remedies, he would summon five bards, who out of their learning could heal his wounds. They were Dafydd Nanmor, Huw Dafi, William Tew, Ieuan Deulwyn, one Einion and Lewis himself, who would offer two *cywyddau* to Ciwg. Wax should be sent to Non at Llangyfelach, and to Samlet. Dafydd the physician would help with his herbs. He would not be inferior to Hippocrates. The Son's ointment from Mary's hand would lubricate Dafydd's thigh bone. Doctors, saints and bards co-operated in this work of healing. Incidentally, Lewis mentions two other contemporary bards in other connections—Hywel Swrdwal, who preceded his Newtown patron to heaven, and Llywelyn Goch y Dant, who had enjoyed an ocean of drink at Kilvey. Bedo Coch of Rhaeadr had been wounded in the face in a battle—the true mark of bravery. Griffith ab Ieuan, the surgeon, better than Ptolemy or Hippocrates, had printed an indenture in the form of the letter S between his teeth and his cheek, and had soldered an enamel cross on his forehead. Lewis wanted to gild the scar with an ointment made by angels out of myrrh and frankincense. A *cywydd*, with its opening lines missing, conveys the bard's desire to see his sight restored to a certain Rhys, possibly of Caeo. His wife had been to the holy rood in Struet, Brecon, but if he could have the aid of St Colman and ointments from St George and St James, Rhys by the month of May would be able to see the deer, and by summer would be able to count the heads of wheat. John ap Dafydd ap Griffith of Kidwelly, had taken a more modern approach by summoning a specialist from England. Lewis could not disguise his bitterness in the elegy which he composed upon John's death. 'On St John's day, I heard, yes, that John had put his trust in an Englishman. A physician with bean physic from England came here,—an Irishman, or a dog of a Jew, or a dog of an Englishman partial to broth—with his powder, his steel fleams like a flame of fire, and his urinal, God be judge, he would kill young and old.' Lewis himself was taken ill at Garth in Myfennydd, but was well nursed by Tanglwyst and Ieuan ap Lewis, her husband. She made him pray to the Gracious Son and called a priest. After three confessions, Christ broke the fever and the bard's soul gave a leap in the arms of 'Syr' John William. Ieuan gave him wine and Tanglwyst gave him nurture and old delicacies, canel from France, pepper in all kinds of food, saffron, mace, garden grains, tree orange, sugar-candy, ginger, cinnamon, almonds, cummin, balsamum, custard and pomegranate. Such was life in fifteenth-century Wales.

The wine which Lewis Glyn Cothi drank at Garth in Ceredigion had come by sea. In another *cywydd* he mentions wine from Brittany. Dafydd Llwyd and Lleucu, his wife, had a remarkable cellar at Castell Hywel, judging by the impressive list given in Lewis's *awdl* to them—romnay, malmsey, osey, Rochelle wine, French wine, Burgundy wine, Poitou wine, Bordeaux wine, Rhenish wine, Gascon wine, vernage-wine, hard camplete, caprike, claret, doucet (probably a sweet custard rather than wine) and muscadel. In a *cywydd* to Thomas Philip of Picton, Lewis states that they imported wines by the hundred tuns to Picton from Bayonne, fresh wines of Mantes, wines of Normandy, Bordeaux, Rochelle, Speier, Spain, and Brittany and two kinds of muscadel. When Rhys ap Meredydd, of Tywyn near Cardigan, died the question in Lewis's elegy was 'will wine reach the mouth of the Rhine from ten islands now that Rhys is not alive. No duke or king from Asia equalled him for wine.' Rhys ap Llewelyn of Llanllawddog and Gwenllïan, his wife, would not allow him in his decrepit old age to drink in the tavern, they had ready for him a vineyard of liquor, and would speed the bread and the most tender boar's brawn that he had ever tasted.

From the evidence of his surviving poems, it is clear that Lewis Glyn Cothi confined his circuit to west Wales during the last years of his life. The later poems show that he lived to see Henry VII on the throne, Jasper Tudor elevated to the dukedom of Bedford, Sir Rhys ap Thomas knighted, and Prince Arthur born. This brings us to 1486. In a *cywydd* to John, Sir Rhys's brother, Lewis refers to the strife which began in the time of Henry VI, continued under Edward IV, increased under Richard III, and was now threatening 'tall Harry'. 'The intention of the English . . . was to crush the ravens and strike the king', but 'the intention of the horses and the brother of the knight (i.e. Sir Rhys) was to crush their skins and hang them.' This is probably a reference to the campaign against Lambert Simnel in the summer of 1487.

A rumour reached the vicar of Llanfihangel Iorath that Lewis had died on a visit to Glamorgan, possibly at Margam. The vicar immediately sang a mass to illuminate his soul's path to heaven, and a requiem to preserve him from major sin. The rumour proved to be unfounded, and the vicar '*Syr*' William ap Rhys was rewarded with the grateful bard's *cywydd*. The date of his institution to Llanfihangel is not known, but as he was not an ordained priest until 31 May 1488, the poem must be later than that. Lewis composed an elegy on the death of '*Syr*' Dafydd ap Gwilym, vicar of Llanarthne. His successor was collated to that living on 29 July 1488 on Dafydd's resignation. In the elegy it is said that the retired vicar died on the approach of 'the feast', and that they were without St David's Day. There was a chapelry dedicated to St David in Llanarthne, and it would appear that Dafydd died towards the end of February, which would date the elegy at the earliest in 1489. This was probably the poet's last work, so that his *floruit* is 1447–89. According to tradition he was buried at Abergwili.

This very general survey of his poems is meant to illustrate the range of his interests and his importance in the literary life of the fifteenth century. He may not have been the best Welsh poet of the century, and some of his verse is somewhat prosaic. On the other hand, he could at times rise to a high level of inspiration and expression. A selection of a few *cywydd* couplets would show him at his best, though the very nature of *cynghanedd* poetry makes it impossible to convey the charm of the original in translation. The vital element of *cynghanedd* can not be conveyed. The intimate marriage of *cynghanedd* and meaning is dissolved in translation. The following examples illustrate his gift for epigrammatic expression:

Breuach na bar o ewyn
Yn ei stad yw einioes dyn.

[Brittler than a bar of foam/ In his estate is man's life.]

Iesu, ai hud yw'r oes hon
A adeilodd hudolion?
Dail a ddigwydd bob blwyddyn,
Dis a'i dwyll ydyw oes dyn.

[Jesus, is this life an illusion / woven by jugglers? / Leaves fall every year, / Man's life is a die and its deception.]

Rhyfedd diwedd blodeuyn,
A rhyfedd yw diwedd dyn.

[Strange is the end of a flower, / and strange is the end of man.]

Nid marw y tad f'ai dradoeth
A fo byw dewr ei fab doeth.

[The father who was very wise is not dead / whose brave wise son is alive.]

Gwell fydd hen dderwen yn ddâr
No dwy ieuainc mewn daear.

[Better an old oak tree as timber / Than two young ones in the soil.]

Y dyn a gaffo enw da
A gaiff gan bawb ei goffa.

[The man who gets a good name / Will be remembered by everybody.]

A fo gwan genfigennwr
Hir yn was a hwyr yn ŵr.

[He who is a foolish jealous [person] / Will be long a servant and late a master.]

Ni châi Duw arian anhael,
Nid rhaid ond amnaid ar hael.

[God would not get a miser's money, / A nod on the generous is enough.]

Ni chyrchaf ddŵr dros afon
Er bod rhyd i'r byd ar hon.

[I shall not fetch water over a river / Though it has a ford for all.]

A dawo a wrandewir,
O dewi gwers y daw gwir.

[He who is silent will be heard, / From being silent awhile truth will come.]

As a concise, vivid, description of a river in flood it would be difficult to beat

Is y tai, dengys Tywi
Maint yw lled ei mantell hi.

[Below the houses, Tywi shows / how great is the width of her mantle.]

BIBLIOGRAPHY

Editions

Walter Davies and John Jones, *The Poetical Works of Lewis Glyn Cothi, a celebrated bard who flourished in the reigns of Henry VI, Edward IV, Richard III and Henry VII* (Oxford, 1837).
Dafydd Johnston, *Gwaith Lewys Glyn Cothi* (Caerdydd, 1995).
E. D. Jones, *Gwaith Lewis Glyn Cothi. Y Gyfrol gyntaf. Testun Llawysgrif Peniarth 109* (Caerdydd ac Aberystwyth, 1953).

Translations

Joseph P. Clancy, *Medieval Welsh Lyrics* (New York, 1965).
Gwyn Williams, *An Introduction to Welsh Poetry from the beginning to the sixteenth century* (London, 1953).
Idem, *The Burning Tree. Poems from the first thousand years of Welsh verse* (London, 1956).
Tony Conran, *Welsh Verse* (Bridgend, 1986).

Critical Studies

Dafydd Johnston, 'Lewys Glyn Cothi, Bardd y Gwragedd', *Taliesin*, 74 (Haf 1991), 68–77.
E. D. Jones, 'A Welsh *pencerdd's* manuscripts', *Celtica*, v (1959), 17–27.
Idem, *Gwaith Lewis Glyn Cothi, 1837–39*. The G. J. Williams Memorial Lecture (Cardiff, 1973).

Chapter 12

GUTUN OWAIN

J. E. CAERWYN WILLIAMS

Gutun Owain, or, to give him his full name, Gruffudd ap Huw ab Owain, was a poet and a nobleman who lived in the parish of Dudlust in the lordship of Oswestry although he also owned land in the neighbouring parish of Llanfarthin and was buried, so it is said, in its church. The fact that he was a landowning nobleman is not irrelevant to his career as a poet, for although, as we have seen in our study of the work of Guto'r Glyn, there were factors in the social and economic history of Wales in the fifteenth century which were favourable to the poets, their profession and its practice, these became less pronounced with the passage of time and soon there was ushered in a period when the poets begin to complain that they lack patrons, that their work is unappreciated and unrewarded. In Wales as in England the nobility had to suffer the consequences of the Wars of the Roses, and in Wales the very success of the Tudors had dire results: the poets who had hailed it with such fervour found that it attracted some of the Welsh nobility to the court in London and encouraged others to turn their backs on the native culture and to leave its main upholders, the poets themselves, neglected and despised.

Another fact of considerable significance is that Gutun Owain served his apprenticeship as a poet with Dafydd ab Edmwnd, another poet-nobleman, who was born in the parish of Hanmer in Bromfield (Maelor Saesneg) and owned a great deal of land there but spent most of his life in his mother's homeland in Tre Wefra in Tegeingl. Dafydd ab Edmwnd was the winner of a silver chair at the Carmarthen *eisteddfod* or session of the bards convened before Gruffudd ap Nicolas *c.* 1450, according to Mr D. J. Bowen (*Barn*, Awst 1974), and he was regarded as one of the foremost authorities of his day on matters of metre and language. Although he lived during the Wars of the Roses, significantly he does not refer to the upheavals of the time, and this fact and the nature and quality of his work, apart from his achievements in the *eisteddfod* in Carmarthen, confirm our impression of him as a scholar-poet who cultivated his art more for his personal pleasure than for public approval or reward. It is probably true, as Sir John Morris-Jones has suggested, that the purpose of the Carmarthen assembly was to tighten up the rules of prosody, etc., but the enthusiasm which Dafydd betrayed in devising two new metres, his *cadwynfyr* and *gorchest y beirdd*, both of extreme difficulty, and in adding to the requirements of other metres, such as the *rhupunt hir* and the *rhupunt byr* and the *tawddgyrch cadwynog*, as well as the ingenuity which he displayed in his own work, leaves no room to doubt that the scholar in him vied with, and at times threatened to overcome, the poet. This is also true to a considerable extent of his pupil, Gutun Owain. Indeed it might be said of Welsh poets in general down to the seventeenth century, as it has been said of Irish poets of the same period, that they were more academic than those of other countries, and that they never ceased to be 'sons of learning'. Gutun Owain, there can be no doubt, was one of the poets who set great store by learning.

Tradition tells us that he accompanied his master, Dafydd ab Edmwnd, to the *eisteddfod* in Carmarthen *c.* 1450. The occasion doubtless introduced him to other bards and to more of their lore, but it is difficult to imagine that he learnt there much more than he had learnt at home from his master, especially as both of them were living in a part of the country where the native learning was probably cultivated to a greater extent than anywhere else during this period.

Poets were traditionally expected to be experts in their own language, as it was the second of the three fields of learning or of 'memory' (*tri chof*) of which they were the recognized masters. The other two were the history of the nation and the genealogies of the nobility. A treatise compiled in the beginning of the seventeenth century, perhaps by that indefatigable scribe, John Jones of Gellilyfdy, has this to say of the second *cof*:

> And the second of the sayd thre *cof* is the languaige of the Bruttons for which thee Bards ought to giue accompt for every word and sillable therein when they are demaunded thereof and to preserue the auncient tonge & not to intermix ytt wyth any forrayne tonge or to bring any forrayne word amongest yt to the preiudice of there own words wheareby they might eyther be forgotten or extyrped.

As the late Professor G. J. Williams repeatedly emphasized, this is one of the most important statements to be borne in mind in any study of the Welsh language or of the language of the bards, for it explains why the literary language was preserved almost unchanged until the dissolution of the bardic order towards the end of the sixteenth century. As has been shown, the bards had a grammar with which the names of Dafydd Ddu Hiraddug and Einion Offeiriad are associated: it is interesting in several ways, and not least in that it shows us their preoccupation with linguistic matters. Of course, the very existence of a written grammar was the result of innovation, for in earlier times all instruction, including instruction in grammar, must have been oral. But literacy increased among the bards as it did among their patrons, the nobility, and gradually some of them became expert in the art of writing as well as in the art of memory, and whereas the earliest manuscripts with few exceptions were the products of monastic *scriptoria*, during the later Middle Ages the bards took a hand in the production of manuscripts and in their preservation: indeed they incurred the wrath of some of the earlier Renaissance humanists because, so it was alleged, they wanted to keep these manuscripts hidden from the public. However, there are more than enough examples to prove that the bards had no objection to sharing most of their knowledge with their patrons, and Professor G. J. Williams is undoubtedly right in suggesting that they objected only to the publication of that part of their lore specifically called *Cyfrinach Beirdd Ynys Prydain* (The Secret of the Bards of the Island of Britain), and they did so for the obvious reason that they formed a professional guild and naturally did not want the knowledge, on which their profession depended, to be published in books for all and sundry to read and learn. That is why they ran foul of some of the humanists. They had a practitioner's interest in restricting access to *Cyfrinach Beirdd Ynys Prydain*: the humanists thought of it as something of universal interest, as interesting to the courtier, the soldier, the doctor and the lawyer as to the bard.

Gutun Owain was introduced to the knowledge which underlies *Cyfrinach Beirdd Ynys Prydain* by the *pencerdd* or master-poet Dafydd ab Edmwnd, and he himself became a master-poet, but tradition has made him the historian of the abbeys of Basingwerk and Strata Florida. There is no evidence of any connection between him and the latter, but there is tangible evidence of his association with the former in the so-called *Black Book of Basingwerk* (NLW MS. 7006D), which is partly in his hand. Gutun Owain is thus connected with the two institutions which preserved the medieval manuscripts for later generations, the monastic and the bardic institutions, and as Gutun Owain played a significant part in the manuscript tradition it is necessary to bear this fact in mind, and in considering his manuscripts it is equally necessary to remember that the three branches of learning or of memory for which they assumed special responsibility were these:

> The one of the sayd three *Cof* is the History of the notable Acts of the kings & princes of this land of Bruttaen and Cambria; And the second of the sayd thre *cof* is the languaige of the Bruttons . . . And the Thyrd *Cof* was, to keepe the genealogies or Descents of the Nobi[li]tie, there Division of lands and there Armes.

There has been considerable discussion with regard to the manuscripts which should be ascribed to Gutun Owain's pen or quill, and with regard to their dating, but as a result there appears to be agreement that the following eight manuscripts are wholly or partly written by him, that they were all written after 1470, and that most of them were written between 1475 and 1495:

Llanstephan MS. 28.
Jesus College MS. 6.
Peniarth MS. 131, 71–138.
Peniarth MS. 27, pt. iii.
Mostyn MS. 88.
NLW MS. 7006 D (*Llyfr Du Basing*), 89–308.
Peniarth MS. 27, pt. i.
Peniarth MS. 186.

Llanstephan MS. 28 deserves notice because it contains (pp. 10–16) a section on *kelfyddyd kerdd davod a dysc kerddwriaeth* (the art of poetry and the discipline of minstrelsy), and (pp. 33–68) a section entitled *Llyma gyvrinach beirdd ynys brydain yr hwn a elwir y dwned ynghymraec* (Here is the secret lore of the bards of the Island of Britain, also called (lit. 'which is called') the book of grammar in Welsh). Both sections are in the hand of Gutun Owain, and the colophon at the end of the *kyvrinach: Oed yr arglwydd pann wnaethbwyd y llyfr hwnn oedd bymthenghymlynedd a deugain a ffedwar kant a Mil. Phylib ap Madoc ap jeuaf ap Jerwerth biav y llyvr hwn.*

Guttvn ywain a ysgrivennodd hwnnyma (the age of the Lord when this book was made was 1455. Phylip ap Madoc . . . owns this book) was in all probability in Gutun Owain's exemplar. These parts of the so-called 'bardic grammar' are not original to Gutun Owain, but in the first section he has drawn from his own *awdlau* examples of the following metres: *gwawdodyn byr, tawddgyrch cadwynog* and *byr-a-thoddaid*, and the example of the last is from his *awdl* to Siôn ap Rhisiart, abbot of Glyn Egwestl, so that there is evidence and reason to believe that Gutun was more than a mere transcriber. The metres are apparently given according to the arrangement made of them at Carmarthen by Dafydd ab Edmwnd and it is from his work that examples of these have been taken: *cywydd llosgyrnog, awdl-gywydd, proest cyfnewidiog, gwawdodyn hir, hir-a-thoddiad* and *cadwynfyr*. In Hafod MS. 24, pp. 649–711, there is another section of the bardic grammar in the hand of John Jones of Gellilyfdy. It is taken, so we are told, from a *llyfr dwned* which had been written by Gutun Owain, *prydydd a disgibl i Dd. ap Edmwnt*, and in it the examples of *gorchest beirdd* and *tawddgyrch cadwynog* are taken from Dafydd ab Edmwnd's work, while the examples of *gwawdodyn byr, byr-a-thoddaid* and *cyhydedd hir* are from Gutun Owain's. Whatever part we assign to Gutun Owain in the formation of the bardic grammar in its final shape or form, it is certain that he and especially his teacher, Dafydd ab Edmwnd, exercised considerable influence on it,—indeed, it had been suggested that the *dwned* proper, i.e. the section dealing with Latin grammar, was extended by Dafydd ab Edmwnd in 1455—and there can be no doubt either that Gutun Owain's version formed the basis of Simwnt Fychan's, and thus the basis of all sixteenth-century versions. In this way he discharged honourably his task of preserving one of the three branches of bardic learning, one of the three *cof*.

What of the other two?

Jesus College MS. 6 contains *Ystorya Dared, Brut y Brenhinedd* and 'a sort of paraphrase of *Brut y Tywysogion* &c.', according to its cataloguer, Gwenogvryn Evans, and the whole 'forms a sort of continuous *History of the world from Adam to A.D. 1471*'. There is no need, then, to examine further Gutun Owain's manuscripts to find evidence that he discharged his bardic obligation with regard to our second, but the treatise's first, *cof*, 'the History of the notable Acts of the kings & princes of this land of Bruttaen and Cambria'. And in this respect also he was no passive tradition-bearer, but one who was prepared to widen the perspectives of his fellow-poets, for in Jesus College MS. 6 he has given us the oldest extant copy of the *Llyfr Arfau* (Book of Arms), a Welsh version of the De Bado *Tractatus de Armis*, a heraldic treatise.

As for the third *cof*, the genealogies or descents of the nobility, Peniarth MS. 131, pp. 71–138, is in the hand of Gutun Owain and forms part of an extremely important collection of pedigrees. This, apparently, is the sole survivor of several pedigree collections compiled by him, and the many references to his work in this field by later genealogists show that he was the source of their information for the pedigrees of Gwynedd, Powys and the Marches, just as, indeed, he was one of the chief authorities of the commission appointed to trace the lineage of Henry VII.

Presenting the genealogy of Dafydd ab Ieuan ab Iorwerth, abbot of Glyn Egwestl, Gutun Owain styles him *esgob* (bishop), and as the abbot became bishop in 1500, this can be taken to prove that the poet lived to see the beginning of the sixteenth century, but we do not know how many years he survived into that century. As Bishop Dafydd died in 1503 and as there is no elegy to him by the poet, perhaps we may conclude that the bishop outlived his panegyrist.

Some indication of the limits of Gutun Owain's *floruit* may be derived from his elegies to persons whose obits are known. Among these are the elegies to Dafydd ap Gruffudd of Berffordd in 1476, Elisau ap Gruffudd ab Einion in 1489, Thomas Salbri in 1490, Siôn Trefor Hen in 1493–4, Siôn Edward of Y Waun (Chirk) in 1498. Bachellery, the editor of the poet's work, has succeeded in dating the elegies of the following: Eutun ap Siamys, 1477; Annes Trefor, 1483; Alis, daughter of Huw Lewys of Môn (Anglesey), 1485; and Robert Trefor of Hob (Hope, Flintshire), 1487. The earliest *cywydd* which can be dated with some certainty is the one to Rheinallt ap Gruffudd of Y Tŵr near Yr Wyddgrug (Mold), No. XVI in Bachellery's edition, in 1464–5. Gutun Owain must have composed other songs between 1462 and 1475 and his *floruit* can confidently be given as *c*. 1460–*c*. 1500–3.

Bachellery classifies Gutun Owain's poems thus:

I. Seven Love-Poems (I–VII).
II. Ten Request Poems (VIII–XVII).
III. Fifteen Eulogies and Elegies addressed to abbots (XVIII–XXXII).

IV. Twenty-eight Eulogies and Elegies addressed to laymen (XXXIII–LXI).
V. Two Elegies on poets (LXII–LXIII).
VI. Three Satires (LXIV–LXVI).

Of these sixty-six compositions, fifty-four are *cywyddau*, one (XXXI) is an *awdl-gywydd*, eight (II, XVIII, XIX, XX, XXV, XXVI, XXVII, XXXIII) are *awdlau*, and three (LXIV–LXVI) are *englynion*-series. There seems to be very little justification for differentiating between categories III and IV, as abbots were regarded in much the same way as the lay nobility. In other words, very little distinction was drawn between temporal and spiritual lords. Whereas it was inevitable that this should be so in the Dark Ages and even in the early Middle Ages, it may be somewhat surprising to find this lack of differentiation in the period preceding the Reformation in the sixteenth century. And yet it is not altogether unexpected.

In Britain as in Europe in the fifteenth century the spiritual and theological assurance of the earlier Middle Ages had been lost. It is probably wrong to describe it as a period of disbelief, but it was certainly not a period characterized by a very positive faith. Men no longer felt that God was as accessible to them as He had been to their forefathers, and this sense of God's inaccessibility led in one direction to philosophical scepticism and in another to a disbelief in the ancient apparatus of priestly and sacramental mediation. Although Gutun Owain wrote many poems to abbots and clerics, he does not seem to show much spiritual awareness, and he cannot by any means be called a religious poet.

On the other hand the general rise in the level of literacy among clergy and nobility alike led to curiosity and in some quarters to an intellectual awakening which foreshadows the Renaissance. The late Middle Ages have been described as a period of flight from intellect on the one hand and as a period of increased intellectual curiosity on the other. The higher realms of speculation are avoided but the lower realms of practical curiosity are explored.

In Wales poets such as Dafydd ab Edmwnd and Gutun Owain are conservative rather than innovatory. Their period compared with that of Dafydd ap Gwilym and his contemporaries is one of a return to the older standards. Even their innovations in metrics are in the spirit of the traditionalists rather than of the innovationists.

One is more conscious of the need to warn the reader that he has to adapt himself to the medieval concept of poetry before approaching the poetry of Dafydd ab Edmwnd and Gutun Owain than before approaching the poetry of Dafydd ap Gwilym. Thus it is even more important in our reading of Dafydd ab Edmwnd than in our reading of Dafydd ap Gwilym to realize that medieval Welsh poetry was written primarily for the ear rather than for the eye, that it was meant to be more a joy to the reader's aesthetic appreciation than a means to his intellectual illumination.

There is more than a little justification for the dictum that the Middle Ages were the period of artistry rather than the period of art, that their poets wrote poems and not poetry; in other words they were craftsmen interested in the production of finely written, artistically finished poems, rather than romantic artists pouring out their visions and emotions in a stream of poetry arbitrarily divided into units.

Fully to appreciate the work of a poet like Gutun Owain one has to adjust oneself in two ways: first, mentally and emotionally to the social preoccupations of his age, and second, artistically to his preoccupations as a craftsman fulfilling his functions in a tightly integrated society.

To illustrate the first adjustment. One scholar has summarily dismissed Gutun Owain's eulogies and elegies with the curt remark that the poet is primarily interested in the food provided by his patrons. Saunders Lewis was aware of this preoccupation with food when, more generously than his fellow-critic, he described the age as the age of the connoisseur in food and drink.

As I have had reason to remark in discussing Guto'r Glyn, the fifteenth century saw the nobility displaying remarkable vitality and vigour in self-aggrandisement. They felt that they had to compete with each other and that their success had to be made visible to their contemporaries. One way of making their prosperity visible was to give great feasts on such typically family occasions as weddings and funerals and on such public occasions as festivals and holidays. As A. R. Myers has said: 'No more than a bank could a magnate afford to look shabby and poverty-stricken: on the contrary, in this lethally competitive society, he must impress men by his ostentation and attract them by his hospitality. It is not uncharitable to see other motives besides unlimited generosity in the princely bounty of "Warwick the Kingmaker" or in the gargantuan feast of his brother George Neville at his installation as Archbishop of York in 1467.' A nobleman who gave a banquet on a large scale did so to attract public attention, and a poet, who was to some extent at least what we would now call a publicity officer, would fail in his duty to his patron and to his society, if he did not give adequate attention to such a banquet.

Of course, to be able to give banquets of this kind, a nobleman had to be prosperous, and prosperity was the result of what Mr Saunders Lewis in his famous essay on Dafydd Nanmor called *perchentyaeth*, i.e., the husbandry and management of estate and home. It is not a coincidence that Gutun Owain, who in his eulogies and elegies gives so much prominence to the feasts his patrons provided, should use the words *perchen tŷ* several times.

With regard to the second adjustment, the artistic adjustment, in order to appreciate the eulogies and elegies of Gutun Owain, one should be able to hear them with a mind not unlike his, i.e., a mind in which hundreds of well-wrought lines were stored up in the memory, and thus one would be able to bring to their appreciation and criticism a faculty for comparison which would compel concentration of attention on the artistry of construction rather than on irrelevant considerations. In this way one's preoccupation would be, for example, to compare this poet's opening couplet with that poet's, and to evaluate the *cywydd*'s concluding lines with the concluding lines of scores of other *cywyddau*. For example, to ask whether Gutun Owain can compete with Guto'r Glyn's opening couplet in his elegy to Llywelyn ab y Moel,

> Mae arch yn Ystrad Marchell
> Ym mynwent cwfent a'i cell;
>
> [There is a coffin in Strata Marcella,
> in the cemetery of the congregation and its cell;]

or with Tudur Aled's opening couplet in his elegy to Rhobert ap Siôn o Degeingl,

> Y gŵr marw, e gâr morwyn,
> Ddaear dy fedd er dy fwyn . . .
>
> [Thou dead man, a maiden loves
> the (very) earth of thy grave for thy sake . . .]

or his opening couplet to his elegy on Dafydd ab Edmwnd,

> Llaw Dduw a fu'n lladd awen,
> Lladd enaid holl ddwned hen.
>
> [God's hand has been slaying the Muse,
> smiting all old grammatical learning lifeless.]

Again, do his concluding couplets bear comparison with Tudur Aled's or with Guto'r Glyn's, e.g. the latter's concluding lines to his elegy to Llywelyn ab y Moel?

> Ei gorff ef aeth i grefydd,
> Ancr i Fair yn y côr fydd.
> Yr enaid i oreunef,
> A chywydd newydd i nef.
> Fy Nuw a fu'n ei wahodd
> Yr ŵyl, a nef yw ei rodd.
>
> [His body has betaken itself to religion (a religious order),
> he will be an anchorite for Mary in the (heavenly) choir.
> His soul has betaken itself to transcendent heaven,
> And a new *cywydd* to heaven.
> It is my God who has invited him
> for the feast-day and who has granted him heaven.]

I do not believe that Gutun Owain is as good a poet as either Tudur Aled or Guto'r Glyn, but it is not so much in technique as in intellectual vigour that he fails. Thus in the course of his elegy to Siôn ap Madog he says:

> If God transfers
> Siôn's nature to the soil in which he is buried,
> then that soil will be very fruitful.
> His hand will come from the earth
> to give wine to those whom he loves.

This may qualify as a conceit but I doubt whether contemporary poets were impressed by it. And this brings us to the difficulty under which Gutun Owain and his generation of poets laboured. Constrained by their own conservatism as well as by that of their poetic tradition, they had no choice but to work over themes which had been the stock-in-trade of scores of poets before them in a system of metres which could be restrictive on all but the best poetic talents. Their dilemma is essentially that of all poets in a classical poetic tradition—to introduce a note of individuality and originality into productions the themes and media of which were dictated by a tradition many centuries old.

Gutun Owain can describe a feast with the best. Here, for example, is his description of the banquet provided by Siôn, abbot of Glyn Egwestl:

> Abbot John's Shrovetide, his wines and his food,
> would transform the world into heaven.
> His lineage was of the lords
> who deserved (merited the power) to give feasts.
>
> The feast given by John, (that) lord of (good) sense,
> provides the best food which is obtainable.
> The kaprike wine of Caer does not come to an end
> in Iâl, any more than the cold water spring.

He can describe his host's intellectual interests as well as he describes his banquets; indeed, as one would expect, he appreciates these interests probably more than any of his contemporaries. In his elegy to him, he praises Robert Trefor o'r Hob for his interest in words, and refers to his delight in poetry, history and story:

> From his abode, the root of every word
> And its development, he knew.
> A musician was he, historian of our nation,
> Of our language and of our kings.

Compare his eulogy to Elisau ap Gruffudd ab Einion:

> Relying on the world law he penetrated
> to the root of every knowledge.
> He did not leave—it was not his will to leave—
> any word of the Bible unknown (to himself).
> He has at his finger tips the science of heraldry
> and the chronicle of the island's (kingdom's) genealogies.

It is in his elegies that Gutun Owain is most disappointing to the modern reader. They follow the same pattern: first, the pedigree of the dead man is given; then come three or four lines in which his wife is named and her loss is mentioned; and finally the sons are named and the hope is expressed that they will be as generous to the poet as their father was. Of course, there had to be adjustments to the pattern when the dead man was a cleric. Professor W. J. Gruffydd with more than a little justification called Gutun Owain the 'coldest elegy-writer' in the Welsh language, and although the word is not used in its literal sense, one is struck by the frequency with which the poet himself uses the word *oer* (cold).

Gutun Owain wrote only a few love-poems and they have been somewhat harshly criticized. Thus W. J. Gruffydd dismissed them as 'formal and rather cold'. As I have already implied, it is always a temptation and invariably a mistake to apply the standards of modern poetry to medieval poetry, and not least to medieval love-poetry. Modern poetry is mostly romantic in temper; medieval poetry is classical and anti-romantic even in its treatment of love. As a most distinguished student of their poetry has had to conclude, even the Troubadours were unaware of the 'cosmic implications of love as they are expressed by more modern poets'; instead of all-embracing lyrical emotions, he found 'a system of conventions'.

To appreciate Gutun Owain's love-poems, one must regard them not as expressions of genuine feelings but as exercises in wit on well-established themes. Even when emotions were present, and sometimes they were inevitably present, although their presence was not necessary to justify the poem, the medieval poet did not think that he was absolved from the duty of being witty. To us the presence of wit seems at times to indicate lack of feeling. We have no sympathy with the poet who wished to reveal his beloved's name covertly but not overtly and said:

> Si vertas caput bachi primamque sibille
> Invenies pro quo duco suspiria mille.

That is: reverse the first syllable of this poem to produce *is*. Similarly, reverse the first syllable of *bachus* to produce *ab*. Now add the ending *-illa* and there appears the name Isabilla.

Gutun Owain's love-poems, it is true, are not original in thought or sentiment, but they show considerable virtuosity in ringing the changes of expression:

Thou maiden with the rubicund hue of the blackberry,
most delicate with (thy) gentle frown,
on thee I have bestowed the (same kind of) love (as)
Tristan bestowed on Iseult.
I have the same cry as Maxen,
the same indignation as Guy of Warwick.

It will be noticed how Gutun Owain sports his knowledge of legendary loves and lovers.

One love-poem is a dialogue between the poet in the role of a lover and the unsympathetic recipient of his devotion. He begins:

Y lloer hael â lliw'r heli
Oll ydd wyd yn fy llad i.

[Thou generous moon with the (white) hue of the
brine(-wave),
Completely doest thou slay me.]

She replies:

Taw, fab dielw, â'th gelwydd!
Tydi i'm siomi y sydd . . .
Nid af na lliw nos na dydd
I'th briodi fyth, brydydd.

[Thou good-for-nothing youth, cease from thy lies!
Thou art (bent on) deceiving me . . .
Never, night or day, will I go
to marry thee, bard!]

It is a poem which deserves to be quoted at length and to be compared with some of the characteristic Elizabethan love-songs and of the Irish *dánta grádha*.

Apart from his love-poems the *cywyddau* in which Gutun Owain displays his art to best advantage are the request-*cywyddau*, the *cywyddau gofyn*. These, like the elegies, have a fairly static pattern. They open with a eulogy of the person to whom the request is made. They then proceed to describe the person who is to receive the gift. Needless to say, usually the would-be donor and recipient are friends. They conclude with a description of the gift. Among Gutun Owain's requests, three are for horses, one for hunting dogs (beagles), one for a falcon, one for a woodknife, two for bucklers, one for a spear and arrest, and one for a sword. It will be seen that they are all connected with outdoor life.

In the *cywydd* making the request for hunting dogs to Hywel ap Rhys of Rhug on behalf of his nephew Dafydd ab Ieuan, Gutun Owain speaks of the dogs as artists and of their hunting as an art, and more specifically as the poetic art:

> Llunio'r gerdd yn llwyni'r gog,
> A llunio angau llwynog.
> Da gwyddant, ar gleinant glyn,
> Riwlio mydr ar ôl madyn;
> Medran' fesur y ganon,
> Musig ar ewig a rôn',
> Carol ar ôl yr elain,
> Cywydd ar yr hydd yw'r rhain,
> Clerwyr cysonlef nefol . . .

> [. . . fashioning the song in the cuckoo's bushes
> and executing a fox's death.
> Well do they know on the clay bed of the glen
> how to master (to rule) the metre after the reynard;
> they are able to use the tune of the rule-book;
> they make music on the track of the hind,
> a carol on the track of the fawn,
> a *cywydd* on the track of the stag,
> heavenly bards with a melodious voice.]

This is a good example of the art of *dyfalu*, basically the art of describing an object by means of numerous comparisons with other objects. In Gutun Owain's description of the beagles the comparisons are all drawn from one field rather than from many. This shows ingenuity but results in a certain nebulousness, as concrete objects are described in less concrete terms. More satisfactory is Gutun Owain's *dyfalu*-description of a steed. W. J. Gruffydd compared it with Tudur Aled's description of a steed and concluded that both poets were following a set pattern. Whether they did this because they were pupils of the same master, Dafydd ab Edmwnd, or whether there was a pattern common to all poets, is not certain. This is Gutun Owain's description:

> Erchi'dd wyf, arch ddiofal,
> Gorwydd i arglwydd o Iâl:

Tew anifail teneufwng
A dry yn flaidd pan dro yn flwng,
Ewyn gwyn yn y genau,
A'r ffriw yn gam a'r ffroen yn gau,
Llygaid bualiaid i'w ben,
Lliw gwydr a blew llygoden,
Y min fal y damunwn
Y sydd ar fynwes ei ŵn;
Wrth yr awen, arth rywych,
Yr â'r war fal aerwy'r ych;
Os buan yr ymwanwr
Ehedai gae o hyd gŵr;
Ei neidiau ef a nodir,
Ei wryd yw erw o dir.

[I make a request, a carefree request,
for a steed from a lord from Yale:
for a lusty animal with sparse mane
which will turn into a wolf when he becomes angry,
white foam in his (*lit.* the) mouth,
his visage aslant and his nostrils hollow,
eyes like those of a wild ox in his head,
a sheen glassy and hair like a mouse's,
lips, as I would have them,
close to his breast-cover;
obedient to the rein, like a very fine bear,
goes the upper part of the neck as though it were the
collar of an ox;
if the darting one is in swift movement,
he could clear a hedge as tall as a man;
his leaps are commented upon,
his stretch is an acre of land.]

Supported as he is on all sides by a strong literary tradition, Gutun Owain never writes without a strong feeling for style, and although he lacks the originality and creative energy of the great *cynganedd-wyr*, his technical skill is such that he is never mediocre.

BIBLIOGRAPHY

Text

E. Bachellery, *L'Oeuvre poétique de Gutun Owain* (Paris: Librairie ancienne Honoré Champion, 1950–1, 2 vols.).

Critical Studies

D. J. Bowen, 'Dafydd ab Edmwnt ac Eisteddfod Caerfyrddin', *Barn*, Rhif 142, Awst 1974, 441–8.

W. J. Gruffydd, *Llenyddiaeth Cymru o 1450 hyd 1600* (Liverpool, Hugh Evans, 1922) 60–3.

E. J. Jones, *Medieval Heraldry* (Cardiff, 1943).

Saunders Lewis, *Gramadegau'r Penceirddiaid* (Darlith Goffa G. J. Williams, 1966).

J. Morris-Jones, *Cerdd Dafod: sef Celfyddyd Barddoniaeth Gymraeg* (Oxford, Clarendon, 1925).

Thomas Parry, 'The Welsh Metrical Treatise attributed to Einion Offeiriad', *Proceedings of the British Academy*, xlvii (1961), 177–95.

Enid Roberts, *Y Beirdd a'r Noddwyr ym Maelor* (Darlith Eisteddfod Genedlaethol Cymru, Wrecsam a'r Cylch, 1977, 12–14).

Thomas Roberts, 'Llawysgrifau Gutun Owain, a Thymor ei Oes', *Bulletin of the Board of Celtic Studies*, xv (1952–4), 99–102.

J. Beverley Smith, 'Einion Offeiriad', ibid., xx (1962–4), 339–47.

G. J. Williams, 'Gramadeg Gutun Owain', ibid., iv (1927–9), 207–21.

Idem, 'Tri chof Ynys Brydain', *Llên Cymru*, 3 (1954–5), 234–9.

Idem, 'Traddodiad Llenyddol Dyffryn Clwyd a'r Cyffiniau', *Transactions of the Denbighshire Historical Society*, i (1952), 20–32.

Idem, 'Eisteddfod Caerfyrddin', *Y Llenor*, v (1926), 94–102.

Idem, in Aneirin Lewis (ed.), *Agweddau ar Hanes Dysg Gymraeg,* (Caerdydd, 1969).

G. J. Williams and E. J. Jones, *Gramadegau'r Penceirddiaid* (Caerdydd, 1934).

Chapter 13

PROPHETIC POETRY

R. WALLIS EVANS

The vast amount of prophetic material found in Welsh is largely in poetic form and thus in the main Welsh tradition. It falls, broadly, into four periods:

(1) pre-thirteenth century verse attributed to Myrddin and Taliesin.

(2) verse written between 1200 and 1400 mainly by people like Adda Fras, Goronwy Ddu and Rhys Fardd.

(3) verse written between 1400 and 1500 and attributed to Heinyn Fardd and others.

(4) poetry of the pre-Tudor and Tudor periods written mainly in the *cywydd* metre and known as *y cywyddau brud.*

The various elements contained in early Welsh prophetic poetry are very mixed and they developed in much the same way as they did on the Continent. These were early kinds of divination which gradually assumed more distinguishable forms like prognostications about the weather and the stars, religious prophecies and finally political prophecies. Much of this material still remains as part of Welsh folk-lore. The poet-prophet was an essential figure in the Irish literary tradition as was the prophetic poet in the Hebrew.

Most of the prophetic poetry in Welsh, however, is mainly political and arose naturally from the endless conflict between Welsh and English and later between Welsh and Norman. As time passed it assumed a special significance and took the form of prophesying the return of a hero—a Cynan, a Cadwaladr, an Owain and eventually an Arthur to free the Welsh from bondage and take vengeance upon the English. Finally, the prophecies settled around Henry Tudor and were considered to have been fulfilled on Bosworth Field when he became Henry VII, the first Tudor king.

In 1136 and 1148, two works were published each attributed to Geoffrey of Monmouth (1090?–1155)—the *Historia Regum Britanniae*, and the *Vita Merlini* which echoes an earlier Welsh poem *Armes Prydain* to which reference is made below. Each contains the prophecies of Merlin. Taylor in *The Political Prophecy in England* suggests that the prophecies of Merlin had already appeared in a book called *Libellus Merlini* also by Geoffrey, now lost, but referred to in the work of Ordericus Vitalis. This book popularized the prophecy, and one may gather from Geoffrey's introductory remarks that he had set about publishing the prophecies in the same volume as the *Historia*.

There are two distinct versions of the Brut in Welsh, one containing the prophecies of Merlin and the other the story of *Lludd and Llefelys*. They are discussed in some detail together with the versions of Geoffrey's *Historia* in the late Professor Henry Lewis's invaluable introduction to *Brut Dingestow* (The Dingestow Brut).

Geoffrey claims that he obtained much of his material from a very ancient book written in Welsh shown to him by Walter, archdeacon of Oxford. Gerald the Welshman states that he, too, saw such a book after much diligent search, while John of Cornwall declares that it was from Welsh sources that he obtained his own prophecy. It is now generally agreed that Geoffrey collected his prophecies from a vast amount of Welsh material he found to hand and heard from people up and down the country. Had Geoffrey written the prophecies himself, one would have expected in them some kind of order and pattern, but this is not so. They are piled one upon another with constant repetition. We can, thus, safely agree with Miss Margaret Enid Griffiths that 'the type of prophecy found for the first time in Geoffrey's *Historia* was not . . . invented by him, but was a *genre* of Welsh origin which had come into existence long before the twelfth century'. And this, of course, is perfectly true as Sir Ifor Williams points out in his introduction to his edition of *Armes Prydain*.

Unfortunately, no Welsh prophecies appear in writing before the twelfth century, though, of course, there existed a long oral tradition extending well back into the sixth century. We have to rely, therefore, upon references in Latin works for our knowledge of earlier periods. The ninth-century *Historia Brittonum* tells the story of how King Vortigern (*Gwrtheyrn* in Welsh) tried to build a fortress in Snowdon at the behest of his wise men, and of how the foundations vanished each night as they were built. Faced with the problem the wise men concluded that only the blood of a fatherless boy could break the spell and allow the work to proceed. After a long search, such a boy was found, who, having understood the purpose of the search, explained that beneath the foundations was a lake and in the lake two cauldrons each containing a dragon, one white and the other red. The white dragon symbolized the English race, and the red the Welsh, and after great conflict the red dragon would win the day and put the white dragon to flight. Having made this prophecy, the boy revealed that his name was Ambrosius (*Emrys*). This is the first reference in prophetic literature to the final victory of the Welsh over the English.

Geoffrey clearly took over the *Historia Brittonum* story lock, stock and barrel, and associated it with Caerfyrddin. He called the boy Merlin (in Welsh *Myrddin*) and got over the difficulty by explaining that Emrys was his second name. It should be remembered that there already existed in Welsh tradition another Myrddin, a 'historical' character of the sixth century, namely Myrddin ap Morfryn. Geoffrey simply brought the two together. In spite of all this, however, the poets of the *cywyddau brud* still recognized *two* Myrddins:

A'r llew melyn a bryn brad,
Y *ddau Fyrddin* a ddyfad.

[And the yellow lion will bring treachery, the two Myrddins said.]

Apart from the translations into Welsh, Geoffrey is important because we have in his work a special kind of prophecy not met with before. Its characteristic is its reference to people by the names of animals and birds. In this it differs from the Sibyllic prophecy which refers to people by the initial letters of their names. Both types occur in Welsh in the earlier prophecies and in the *cywyddau brud* sometimes within the same prophecy, but the Galfridian type predominates by far.

There are few references, on the whole, in existing early Welsh prophecies to people by the names of animals. Names like *arth* (bear), *llew* (lion) or *blaidd* (wolf) occur, and recur in names like *Arthur, Llewelyn* and *Bleddyn*, but they could well have been a major characteristic of the vast amount of prophetic material which has not survived. Geoffrey certainly saw their value for the purposes of political prophecy and they became the hall-mark of his work. He popularized the prophecy, gave it a literary form and emphasized its importance as a medium of political propaganda.

He also laid stress on Welsh antiquity and traced the nation's roots back to Brutus and the fall of Troy. 'This Latin learning', state the Chadwicks in their volume *The Growth of Literature*, 'had . . . a history of its own, a genealogy . . . partly classical, partly Hebrew. Thus, when British antiquarians, probably in the seventh or eighth century, began to trace the origin of their nation to Brutus and the early Kings of the Latins, they were merely continuing and adapting to their own case, work which had been carried on, long before, by Roman antiquarians themselves when they traced their origin back to Aeneas and the Trojans.'

The earliest recorded Welsh prophecies appear in the *Black Book of Carmarthen* (*Llyfr Du Caerfyrddin*) towards the end of the twelfth century and the *Book of Taliesin* (*Llyfr Taliesin*), dated *c.* 1275. They are fairly long poems which refer to events extending from the eighth to the thirteenth century and attributed to poets of standing like Myrddin and Taliesin, probably to invest them with the necessary authority. It is clear, however, that they deal with events that took place much later and were put together long after the period of Myrddin and Taliesin. There were, of course, two Taliesins—one the poet of Urien Rheged of the sixth century, and the other the poet of Elphin in the folk *Tale of Taliesin*. The two are discussed in some detail in Sir Ifor Williams's invaluable introduction to *Canu Taliesin*. One characteristic of the poems is that they prophesy the return of a traditional Owain to free the Welsh from the hands of the English:

> A mi ddisgoganaf gad Coed Llwyfain,
> a gelorawr rhuddion rhag rhuthr Owain.
>
> [And I prophesy the battle of Coed Llwyfain
> and red biers following Owain's attack.]

'In Arthur', we are further told by Miss M. E. Griffiths, 'the Cymry had a stalwart defender against the Saxons, and again under Cadwallawn for a short time their hopes were raised, so that it was natural for them to long for the return of Arthur and Cadwaladr, the son of Cadwallawn, their last king, to lead them in their long and arduous struggle. Each leader of promise was hailed as a Cadwaladr, an Owain or an Arthur, returned again to triumph over the English, and predictive poems centred around him for a time till he too fell into oblivion, beaten by overwhelming odds.'

The earliest prophecy in Welsh is *Armes Prydain* which goes back to about 930 and pre-Norman times. The poet relates not the past but the future to give heart to a nation facing a period of oppression and tribulation. He recalls the glorious past and takes pride in heroes of former days and prophesies vengeance upon the enemy and complete victory for the Welsh. As in other early prophecies the leaders of the victorious armies will be Cynan and Cadwaladr. Reference is made to *y llyfrawr*—the *librarius*, a term formerly used for a writer or keeper of books, but which had now come to mean a 'soothsayer' who prophesied events to come and demanded payment for this. Such people existed as early as the tenth century and according to *Armes Prydain* were to be avoided.

Some of the early prophecies often became part of older poems like *Yr Afallennau* and *Yr Hoianau*, in which references are made to genuine historical characters like Rhydderch Hael and Gwenddolau, who lived in the sixth century. They also refer to the sufferings of Myrddin and his madness in *Coed Celyddon*. They reveal nothing of Geoffrey's influence and most of them were written before his time. They belong to a native Celtic tradition which emerged quite naturally from the political problems of the nation. To quote Miss Griffiths again, 'these Welsh poems attributed to Myrddin represent different stages in the adaptation of older poems for vaticinatory purposes. The *Afallennau* and *Hoianau* represent the earliest stage we have, then comes the *Cyfoesi*, and lastly the *Bedwenni* and *Gwasgargerdd*, which have lost practically all connection with the older material.' It is worth noting, in passing, the references to *Yr Afallennau* (The Apple-Trees) and *Y Bedwenni* (The Birch-Trees), as this custom of addressing trees and birds became customary in political prophecy and continued well into the *cywydd brud*. There exists a *cywydd* addressed to *Y Fedwen* (The Birch-Tree) which replies in prophecy.

From 1200 onwards there is a wealth of prophetic poetry. Prophecies are now attributed to Adda Fras, Goronwy Ddu, Y Bergam and Rhys Fardd as well as to Myrddin and Taliesin and reference is made to each of them as sources of prophecy in the later *cywyddau brud*. Adda Fras and Goronwy Ddu were natives of Anglesey, Y

Bergam came from Maelor, and Rhys Fardd or Y Bardd Bach, as he is sometimes called, was a southerner from Ystum Llwynarth or Oystermouth near Swansea.

Of the four, Rhys Fardd is by far the most important. He has left a substantial body of work in recognizable literary form which must have been memorized considerably as parts of it are scattered throughout the manuscripts and were used for later purposes. The patterns of his prophecies imitate that of the short prophecy, which begins:

> Mi a dystiaf yn gyntaf i'r haf hirfelyn.
>
> [I will first bear witness to the long yellow summer.]

This was added to in later times and became known as *Proffwydoliaeth yr Haf Hirfelyn*.

The prophecy to the trout which begins

> Y brithyllod yng ngenau y rhyd py ryw fyd ysydd yn dyfod?
> byd brith pen gwenith a gwenwyn ar dafod
>
> [O trout at the mouth of the ford, what manner of world
> is to come?
> A world in which the wheat tops will be speckled and
> poison on tongue]

continues the pattern of *Yr Afallennau* and *Y Bedwenni* and persists unbroken into the period of the *cywyddau brud*. Here the trout are addressed and reply in prophecy. There is a similar *cywydd brud* to *Y Gleisiad* (The Young Salmon).

There are references in this period to historical characters like Owain ap Thomas ap Rhodri (Owain Lawgoch), murdered in 1378, and Owain Glyndŵr (*c*. 1354–1416) as possible saviours, real live people, not dead heroes of the past, and this is particularly characteristic of the *cywyddau brud*:

> A chyfodi arth o'r Sycharth o Eryri llechfa.
>
> [A bear from Sycharth (the house of Owain Glyndŵr) shall arise from a hiding place in Eryri.]

A Sais heb gyweithas
A baedd Glyndyfrdwy yn rhannu'r deyrnas.

[The Saxon without friends
and the Boar of Glyndyfrdwy sharing the kingdom.]

By 1400 the influence of Geoffrey begins to make itself felt. The signs and omens and the animal names are borrowed in profusion and it is clear that there is considerable acquaintance with the English prophecies. Poems are now attributed to Heinyn Fardd, Y Bardd Glas and Y Bardd Ysgolan all of whom are referred to in the *cywyddau brud*. The most important prophecy of this period is *Proffwydoliaeth yr Haf Hirfelyn* of which mention has already been made. A marked characteristic of the period is the large number of prophecies relating to specific dates like 1494 and 1500. They reveal the influence of many of the English prophecies and the same prophecy is often given for more than one date.

The influence of Geoffrey's *Historia* is revealed in the references to Brutus and Rhonwen, Hengist's daughter, and to *hil Rhonwen*, Rhonwen's race, namely the English. Mention is made of the return of *esgyrn yr hen frenin* (the old King's bones), the bones of *Cadwaladr Fendigaid* (The Blessed Cadwaladr), from Rome to Britain. The names of animals are used much more frequently to denote people (though they are not always easy to identify, but this, perhaps, is in the nature of political prophecy), names like *hydd* (stag), *tarw* (bull), *gwadd* (mole), *ci* (dog), *asen* (ass), *carw gwyn* (white stag), *bwch* (goat) which are repeated, some of them a little more specifically, in the *cywyddau brud*.

Around this period the nature of the prophecy subtly began to change. There is still the hope and longing for a deliverer—an Arthur or an Owain to free the nation from its bondage, but there is slightly greater emphasis on fulfilling the prophecies. There is talk of *brudiau'r Deheudir* (the Bruts of south Wales) and of *Ysgol y brud a'r gwybodau am a ddelai* (the Schools of the *brud* and the knowledge of what is to come). There are a number of major translations from English and Latin prophecies like *Proffwydoliaeth y Fflwrdelis* and *Proffwydoliaeth y Lili* and there appears to be a major build-up of prophetic material from which the poets of the *cywyddau brud* could draw.

We now come to the *cywyddau brud* themselves—the pre-Tudor and Tudor prophecies which circulate around the Wars of the Roses and find their fulfilment in the victory at Bosworth Field in August 1485. Nearly all the poets of the period bring some measure of prophecy into their poetry and all seem to be politically conscious in some degree or other.

A major factor was the development of the *cywydd* metre by Iolo Goch (*c.* 1320–98) as a major political instrument, thus inevitably including in his work some element of prophecy, and what a wealth of prophecy existed for those poets who sought it! He set the fashion and the *cywydd brud* developed swiftly until it found its full expression in the poems of Dafydd Llwyd ap Llywelyn ap Gruffydd of Mathafarn (*c.* 1420–1500) who pulled out all the stops and had the *cywydd brud* ranging over all the *cywydd* genres from the eulogy through the love-poem to pure prophecy.

Before discussing the political implications of the *cywyddau* it would be well to continue with the nature of the prophecy itself. There can be no doubt that the prophecies were collected, sought and read. Lists of omens exist in the manuscripts and the battles to be fought are enumerated; as one poet says:

> Wrth y brud a astudiais
> I'r Saeson trychion mae trais.
>
> [According to the *brud* I studied
> violence will come to the broken Saxons.]

Some poets claim a special understanding of the *brud* beyond the ken of the English:

> Mae dull, mi a'i deellais,
> Ar hyn, er nas edwyn Sais.
>
> [This has a pattern. I have understood it
> though the Saxon knows it not.]

The animal name was meant to conceal and not to be too specific:

> Anfoddus yw, ni feiddiaf
> Enwi neb, hynny a wnaf.
>
> [It is not becoming; I dare not
> name anyone; this I shall do.]

The old omens and signs are used in profusion as are the names of birds and animals, while reference is made over and over again to earlier writers of prophecies like Addas Fras, Y Bergam, Y Bardd Glas o'r Gadair, Y Bardd Bach o Ystum Llwynarth, Heinyn Fardd as well as Myrddin and Taliesin. Sometimes authors of English or Latin prophecies are named like John of Bridlington, the author of a well-known Latin prophecy and an authority on prophecy:

Ac Adda Fras, gwiwdda frud,
A Briltwn, gwelwn eu golud,

[And Adda Fras of favourable prophecy
and Bridlington, we recognize their value]

or Thomas of Erceldoune, author of a whole cycle of prophecies:

A Thaliesin, dewin da,
A Thomas o'n hiaith yma.

[And Taliesin the good diviner,
and Thomas of our genealogy.]

Some of the poets of the *cywyddau brud* are themselves referred to by their contemporaries as authorities on prophecy. Such a one is Robin Ddu, a man of Môn (*fl.c.* 1450):

A Robin, y dewin da,
A Thaliesin Tholosia.

[And Robin, the wise diviner,
and Taliesin Tholosia.]

The sources of the omens and signs are pretty well established. They come from Geoffrey's *Historia*, from the English prophecies, the Continental prophecies and the wealth of material that exists in Welsh both in the verses of the authors already referred to and in the anonymous prophecies collected from time to time and preserved in the manuscripts.

The animal and bird names, however, present a problem as they can be highly confusing and many names can refer to the same person. Their use in one or two of the *cywyddau brud* is here examined to discover their particular connotation.

Towards the end of August 1485, shortly after the battle of Bosworth Field, Dafydd Llwyd ap Llywelyn ap Gruffydd addressed a poem in the *cywydd* metre to Henry VII congratulating him on his victory. It goes like this:

Mae'r goron ym mrig eryr,
Os gwir lladd y wadd a'i wŷr.
Cwncwerio mae King Harri,
Coron aur sydd i'n câr ni.
Llyna'r byd yn llawenach,
Llwyddo o'r beirdd lladd R bach,
Llythyren aflawen lwyd
Fforchog, yn Lloegr ni pharchwyd.
Ni allai'r R yn lle'r I
Na rhywlio Lloegr na'i rholi.
Nid âi, er reportiai'r part,
I'r adwy yr âi Edwart.

[The crown is on the eagle's head, if it be true that the mole and his men have been killed. King Harri is conquering, our kinsman has a golden crown. Lo! the world is happier now that the bards have succeeded in killing little R, an unhappy, grey letter, forked, and not respected in England. R could neither rule nor control England in E's place. He could not, so report has it, fill the breach that Edward filled.]

'Little R' is of course a term of contempt and the 'I' in line 9 stands for the sound of the English 'E' as the *cynghanedd* in the following couplet confirms:

Dioer yw I, oergri ergryd,
Ag H yn unair i gyd.

A close examination of the twelve lines quoted above reveals that *eryr* (eagle) and *King Harri* refer to Harri Tudur, while *y wadd* (the mole), *R bach* (little R) and *R* refer to Richard III, and *I* (the English letter E) and *Edwart* stand for Edward IV. It is clear, therefore, that more than one name or letter can stand for the same person, and that some animal names like *eryr* denote the hero, while others like *y wadd* denote the enemy whoever they may be. This is a very useful device which avoids complicity whichever side a poet happens to favour.

A detailed analysis of the *cywyddau brud*, the poems specifically contained in numerous collections and presumably regarded by their collectors as such, shows that the animal names tend to fall into two categories—those that describe the hero, the deliverer, the *mab darogan* (the son of the prophecy) or *daroganwr* (the man about whom it is prophesied), and those that describe the enemy. They are noted briefly below. The list (which includes a few non-animal descriptions) is truly formidable and constitutes a veritable menagerie as one can see:

Names describing the Hero

Aderyn (Bird)
Aderyn llwyd (Grey bird)
Alarch (Swan)
Arth (Bear)
Asen (Ass)

Baedd (Boar)
Baedd glas (Blue boar)
Banw (Young pig)
Barcutan (Kite)
Bastart (Bastard)
Blaidd (Wolf)
Brân (Raven) *Sir Rhys ap Thomas*
Buwch gethin (Dun cow)
Bwch (Buck)
Bwch danas (Buck deer)
Bwla (Bull)

Cadnaw (Fox)
Cadwaladr
Carw (Stag)
Carw degcainc (Ten-branch stag)
Carw o Wynedd (Stag from Gwynedd)
Cath (Cat)
Cath fraith (Speckled cat)
Ceiliog (Cock)
Cnyw (Foal)
Creyr (Heron)
Cyw (Young animal)
Cyw bach cyfrinachol (Little secretive animal)
Cyw eurwalch (The young golden hawk)
Cyw'r eryr (The young of the eagle)

Daroganwr
Draenog (Hedgehog)
Dragwn (Dragon)
Draig (Dragon)
Draig goch (Red dragon) *The Welsh Nation*

Edn (Bird)
Eidion (Bullock)
Eilon (Hart)
Elain (Fawn)
Eryr (Eagle)
Eryr du (Black eagle)
Eryr llwyd (Grey eagle)
Eryr o liw euraid (The eagle of golden colour)

Gafr (Goat)
Gwalch (Hawk)
Gwalch gwyn (White hawk)
Gwenci (Weasel)
Gwennol (Swallow) *Owain Tudur*
Gwiber (Viper)
Gŵr marw (A man from the dead)
Gŵr o gudd (A man from hiding)
Gŵr o Gaer Droea (A man from Troy)

Hebog o Ddeheubarth (A hawk from the South)
Hydd (Stag)

Lili (Lily) *France*
Llew (Lion)
Llew coch (Red lion)
Llew gwyn (White lion)
Llew melyn (Yellow lion)
Lloer (Moon)
Llwdn (Young animal)
Llwynog (Fox)

Mab darogan (Son of prophecy)
Mab hirfelyn (Tall fair son)
Mab y dyn (Son of man)
March gwyn (White stallion)
Milgi (Greyhound)

Mwyalchen (Blackbird)
Neidr fraith (Spotted snake)

Oen (Lamb)
Owain

Piod (Magpie)
Pysgod (Fish)

Rhosyn (Rose)

Sant (Saint) *Henry VI*
Sarff (Serpent)

Tarw (Bull)
Tarw du (Black bull)

Ych (Ox) *Jasper Tudor*

The list of animal names denoting the enemy is considerably smaller:

Arth (Bear) *Warwick*

Baedd (Boar)
Baedd gwyn (White boar)
Bwbach (Bogey)
Bwch (Goat)

Cath (Cat)
Ci (Dog)
Cigfran (Crow)
Cranc (Crab)
Cŵn (Dogs)

Dragwn (Dragon)

Ffawlcwn (Falcon)
Ffwlbart (Polecat)

Gafr (Goat)
Gwadd (Mole)
Gwrab (Ape)
Gŵydd (Goose)

Lindys (Caterpillar)

Llewes (Lioness)
Llewpart (Leopard)
Llwynoges goch (Red vixen)

Moch (Pigs)

Neidr (Snake)

Porchell (A little pig)

Talpa (Latin for 'mole')
Tremyniad (Goblin, phantom)
Twrch daear (Mole)
Tylluan (Owl)
Tyrchod (Moles)

The lists are by no means exhaustive. Some names like *baedd* (boar) and *arth* (bear) occur on both lists. *Baedd gwyn* came to refer to Richard III whose emblem was the White Boar, while *arth* usually at a later stage implied treachery and referred to Warwick, whose banner was a Bear with a Ragged Staff. *Gwadd, neidr, talpa, tremyniad* usually refer to Richard III, *cŵn, moch* and *tyrchod* to the men of England.

On the hero's list *brân* usually refers to Sir Rhys ap Thomas who bore a raven on his crest, *y sant* invariably refers to Henry VI, *gwennol* to Owain Tudur or the Tudor family, *lili* to Francc and *ych* to Jasper Tudor.

An integral part of the prophecy, of course, were the signs and omens, the strange things that were to happen before the deliverer arrived:

> Yr oedd i mi arwyddion
> I wyliaw Manaw a Môn.
>
> [I had signs to watch the Isle of Man and Môn.]

These were taken from the mass of material to hand, but, sometimes, specific prophecies are mentioned like *Y Broffwydoliaeth Fawr* (The Great Prophecy):

> Dilid y *Broffwydoliaeth*
> *Fawr* y bûm, ofer o beth.
>
> [I followed the Great Prophecy, but in vain.]

Three of the *cywyddau brud* are earlier prophecies in *cywydd* form. Iolo Goch's *cywydd* to Edward III follows very closely the English 'Prophecy of the Six Kings to follow King John'. The *cywydd brud* beginning

> Y mae brwydwyr am Brydain,

attributed to Dafydd Llwyd ap Llywelyn ap Gruffydd, is none other than *Proffwydoliaeth y Wennol* in *cywydd* form, while the *cywydd* wrongly attributed to Iolo Goch, which opens with the line

> Brawd llid urddas llwyd urddol,

is *Proffwydoliaeth y Fflwrdelis* translated into the *cywydd* metre.

The omens include references to many battles like *Cad Cwminod, Cad Ieithon, Cad Afon, Cad Cors Fochno* (Cors Fochno, Cardiganshire) and *Cad Môn*, and there are lists of these battles in Welsh manuscripts. A man will arise from the dead, Thames will be set on fire, the monetary system will collapse, there will be moaning by a maiden, ships will come from the Isle of Man, Cadwaladr's bones will be brought back from Rome, the planets will conjoin, the Saxons will grow weak—and so the omens pile up—hundreds of them and their sources can be easily recognized by anyone conversant with the earlier Welsh prophecies and versions of the *Historia*. The poets of the *cywyddau brud* note their coming and look forward to the fulfilment of the prophecies.

The *brud* pervaded all the *cywydd* forms—four are addressed to *Y Llyfr Brud* (The Book of Prophecy), one to *Y Ceiliog* (The Cock), one to *Y Dylluan* (The Owl), one to *Yr Eirin* (The Cherries), one to *Y Fedwen* (The Birch), one to *Y Garnedd* (The Cairn), three to *Y Gigfran* (The Crow), two to *Y Gleisiad* (The Young Salmon), one to *Y Gog* (The Cuckoo), one to *Y Bi* (The Magpie), one to *Y Tŵr* (The Tower), one to *Yr Wyddfa* (Snowdon) and one to *Yr Wylan* (The Seagull). All these are generally in the form of question and answer after the fashion of some of the earlier prophecies. The questioner, usually the poet, is admonished not to be so impatient. Let him wait until certain omens appear and the prophecy will then be fulfilled. They are all almost pure prophecy.

There are two *cywyddau serch* (love-poems) and three *cywyddau ymofyn ac ateb* in which two of the poets, Gruffudd ap Llywelyn Fychan and Dafydd Llwyd ap Llywelyn ap Gruffydd, question each other about the *brud*. There are two *cywyddau ymryson* in which Owain Twna and Dafydd Llwyd ap Llywelyn ap Gruffydd cross swords with each other. Two are *cywyddau gofyn* in which the poets seek a buckler and a breastplate respectively. There are three *cywyddau diolch* which give thanks for a sword, a staff and a cloak.

The collections of *cywyddau brud* also contain five elegies, *marwnadau*, two to Owain Tudur o Fôn and one each to Henry VI, Henry VII and Thomas ap Gruffydd ap Nicholas, Sir Rhys ap Thomas's father. There are, furthermore, over sixty *cywyddau brud*, which are, to all intents and purposes, pure prophecy. Such a poem is the one which begins

Afon Demes demhestlir

and is attributed to Syr Dafydd Offeiriad. Finally, there are ten poems addressed to specific persons like Dafydd ab Ieuan ab Einion, Owain Tudur, Harri (Iarll Ritsmwnt), Richard III and Henry VII, Edward IV, Rhosier Fychan and Jasper Tudor. The *cywyddau brud* thus cover the whole range of uses made of the *cywydd* metre and contain an immense volume of prophecy. Edward IV, himself, was once looked upon as a *mab darogan*—the possible deliverer. In addressing Jasper Tudor one of the poets exhorts him to join forces with the raven, namely Sir Rhys ap Thomas, and this is just what happened:

Cymer di, gŵyr Cymry d'ach,
Y frân yn dy gyfrinach.

[Welshmen know thy stock; take the raven into thy confidence.]

The poems in the collections are attributed to a large number of poets— Dafydd Llywd ap Llywelyn ap Gruffydd of Mathafarn, Robin Ddu o Fôn, Llywelyn ab Owain, Sir Dafydd Offeiriad, Dafydd Gorlech, Edward ap Rhys, Maredudd ap Rhys, Y Guto o Bywys, Sir Huw Pennant, Owain Twna, Gwilym Tew, Gruffydd ap Dafydd Fychan and scores of others. The most prolific writer by far, however, was Dafydd Llwyd ap Llywelyn ap Gruffydd of Mathafarn.

And now for the political background. In 1430 Owain Tudur of Penmynydd, Môn, secretly married Catherine, widow of Henry V. There were three sons and a daughter of the marriage and two of the sons, Edmund, later earl of Richmond, and Jasper, later earl of Pembroke, played an important part in the events that led to the battle of Bosworth Field in 1485. Henry Tudor, later Henry VII, was Edmund's son, while Jasper assiduously supported Henry's cause and with the help of Sir Rhys ap Thomas finally gained Henry the Crown. Edmund Tudor had married Margaret Beaufort, a descendant of John of Gaunt, and was, of course, by his father's marriage to Catherine, half-brother to Henry VI.

Henry VI was born on 6 December, 1421. He was the only son of Henry V and succeeded to the throne of England and France on 31 August 1422, when he was scarcely a year old. The later period of his reign was marked by the rivalry between the Yorkists under Richard, duke of York, and the Beauforts, the descendants of John of Gaunt, duke of Lancaster, aided by the queen, Margaret of Anjou.

York was recognized as protector during the king's temporary madness and was thus in power. In 1460, however, Henry was taken prisoner and it was agreed that he should retain the Crown, but that his successor should be Edward, duke of York. Henry managed to escape, but in 1465, was recaptured and imprisoned in the tower. In 1470, Warwick revolted and again set Henry on the throne. In 1471 Edward crushed the Lancastrians at Barnet and Tewkesbury and Henry VI was put to death. Following the defeat Henry Tudor escaped to France, but returned in 1485 landing in Wales and defeating Richard III at the battle of Bosworth Field.

In 1460 Edward IV, the eldest son of Richard, duke of York, had become leader of the Yorkists. He defeated the Lancastrians at Mortimer's Cross and was crowned king in London in 1461. When Warwick joined his foes, his position became precarious and he left for the Netherlands whence he returned in 1471 to win the battles of Barnet and Tewkesbury.

In 1483, Richard III, Edward IV's youngest brother, usurped the throne, setting aside his nephew Edward V and was crowned king on 6 July of that year. Edward V and his brother were imprisoned in the tower where both were murdered.

Such, broadly, were the events surrounding the Wars of the Roses, the period covered more or less by the *cywyddau brud.* To the poets there was no dynastic question. To them the unity of Wales was of primary importance, and as far as Wales itself was concerned there could be no more happy union than that of the Tudors and the Herberts, both of whom claimed descent from Ednyfed Fychan. When Herbert stood in solitary pre-eminence they appealed to him as fervently as they had appealed to Jasper to achieve unity in Wales. Wales should not be made the cockpit of contending English factions, but should seek to unite in an endeavour to rid the country of the baneful rule of English officials. In the whole range of fifteenth-century Welsh literature, there is no more fervent longing for leadership, unity and patriotism than that of Guto'r Glyn in a poem written immediately following the fall of Harlech Castle:

Na fwrw dreth ar Fôn draw,
Ni ellir ei chynulliaw.
Na'd trwy Wynedd blant Rhonwen
Na phlant Hors yn y Fflint hen . . .
Cymer o wŷr Cymru 'rawron
Bob cwnstabl o Fenstabl i Fon.

Dwg Forgannwg a Gwynedd
Gwna'n un o Gonwy i Nedd.
O digia Lloegr a'i dugiaid
Cymry a dry yn dy raid.

[Tax not Anglesey yonder: it cannot be collected. Let not the children of Rhonwen (= the English) rule in Gwynedd nor the children of Hors (= the English) in ancient Flint. Appoint from the men of Wales this hour every constable from Barnstable to Anglesey. Make Glamorgan and Gwynedd from Conwy to Neath a united whole. If England and her dukes resent it, Welshmen will rally to thy need.]

Owain Tudur had already been executed following the battle of Mortimer's Cross in February 1461. Later Herbert fell foul of the English and was executed at Northampton on 28 July following the defeat at Banbury on 26 July 1469, and the hopes of Wales began to centre around Harri Tudur, grandson of Owain Tudur and son of Edmund Tudur, earl of Richmond. The ranks began to close. The poets, who sometimes appeared to favour the Yorkists, sometimes the Lancastrians, were basically realists. Poets as different in their outlook as Guto'r Glyn and Dafydd Llwyd of Mathafarn were one in their fervour in furthering the cause of the Welsh nation.

In the sixties of the fifteenth century William Herbert appeared to be the man who could lead Wales along a responsible national path, and it was thus he appeared to Guto'r Glyn. Dafydd Llwyd of Mathafarn was also attracted by the realistic policies of Herbert, and saw in him a means whereby Harri Tudur could fulfil the prophecies and win the Crown. This ebb and flow leading to final realization and the fulfilment of the prophecies in Harri Tudur make fascinating reading. They certainly prepared the way and the nation for the victory at Bosworth. They throw important light on a fateful period in the history of Britain when prophecy literally overwhelmed politics, poetry and the minds and thoughts of the Welsh people.

The pattern began with the political *cywydd* of Iolo Goch and reached its perfection in the almost pure prophetic *cywyddau* of Dafydd Llwyd ap Llywelyn ap Gruffydd. The sweep of the *cywydd* metre can be heard as the prophecies fulfilled themselves on the road to Bosworth:

Mae'r hydd ar y môr heddiw,
Mae'r tarw a fu farw yn fyw

[The stag has put to sea this day, the bull that was dead is alive!]

and in the lines already quoted celebrating the final victory:

Mae'r goron ym mrig eryr,
Os gwir lladd y wadd a'i wŷr.
Cwncwerio mae King Harri,
Coron aur sydd i'n câr ni.

BIBLIOGRAPHY

Texts and Editions

Henry Lewis,'Rhai Cywyddau Brud', *Bulletin of the Board of Celtic Studies*, i (1921–3), 240–55; 'Cywyddau Brud', ibid., 296–309.
W. Leslie Richards, *Gwaith Dafydd Llwyd o Fathafarn* (Caerdydd, 1964).
Erwain H. Rheinallt, *Gwaith Dafydd Gorlech* (Aberystwyth, 1997).

Critical Studies

Basil Clarke, *Life of Merlin* (Cardiff, 1973).
H. T. Evans, *Wales and the Wars of the Roses* (Cambridge, 1915; reprinted Stroud, 1995).
R. Wallis Evans, 'Canu Darogan: Testunau Amrywiol', *Bulletin of the Board of Celtic Studies*, xxxvi (1989), 84–96.
Idem, 'Beirdd a luniodd un Cywydd Brud yn unig', *Llên Cymru*, 18 (1995), 363–4.
M. E. Griffiths, *Early Vaticination in Welsh with English Parallels* (Cardiff, 1937).
A. Griscom, *The Historia Regum Britanniae of Geoffrey of Monmouth* (New York – London, 1929).
A. O. H. Jarman, *The Legend of Merlin* (Cardiff, 1976).
W. Garmon Jones, 'Welsh Nationalism and Henry Tudor', *Transactions of the Honourable Society of Cymmrodorion*, 1917–18, 1–59.
W. Leslie Richards, 'Cywyddau Brud Dafydd Llwyd ap Llywelyn ap Gruffudd o Fathafarn', *Llên Cymru*, 2 (1952–3), 244–54.
Enid Roberts, *Dafydd Llwyd o Fathafarn* (Caernarfon, 1981).
Eurys I. Rowlands, 'Dilid y Broffwydoliaeth', *Trivium*, ii (1967), 37–46.

R. Taylor, *The Political Prophecy in England* (New York, 1911).

Glanmor Williams, 'Proffwydoliaeth, Prydyddiaeth a Pholitics yn yr Oesoedd Canol', *Taliesin*, xvi (1968), 31–9.

Idem, 'Prophecy, Poetry and Politics in Medieval and Tudor Wales', chapter III in *Religion, Language and Nationality in Wales* (Cardiff, 1979), 71–86.

G. A. Williams, 'The Bardic Road to Bosworth: A Welsh View of Henry Tudor', *Transactions of the Honourable Society of Cymmrodorion*, 1986, 7–31.

Chapter 14

THE CONTINUING TRADITION

EURYS ROWLANDS

At the Carmarthen *eisteddfod*, held about 1451, all the prizes—for poetry, reciting, and string music—went to men from Tegeingl in north Wales. At the bardic competitive gathering at Aberteifi (Cardigan) in 1176 the poetry prizes had gone to the men of Gwynedd. Of the poets whose works are still extant, many of the most prominent bards of the subsequent period, usually regarded as the fourteenth, fifteenth, and early sixteenth centuries, came from north Wales, and when an *eisteddfod* was held in 1523 to regulate and regularize the bardic order it was held at Caerwys in the same county as the home of Dafydd ab Edmwnd who had won the prize for poetry at Carmarthen about 1451.

It might appear to many that medieval Welsh poets were too obsessed with the formal aspects of poetry. Dafydd ab Edmwnd was certainly a bard who in some ways carried this tendency to the extreme limit. Most of his *cywyddau* were love-poems, very skilled formally and using traditional themes with great virtuosity. But Dafydd ab Edmwnd's preoccupation with form was really seen in his use of *awdl*-metres, for at the Carmarthen *eisteddfod* he had brought about a reform of the traditional system of *awdl*-metres and had introduced a few new metres as well as some new rules for rhyming which could be described as being absurdly complicated. In fairness to Dafydd ab Edmwnd, it is likely that these metres were really to be used as tests of bardic skill rather than as metres to be used much for the practical purpose of composing everyday poetry. Here is an example of Dafydd ab Edmwnd's *cadwynfyr* in which the *cynghanedd* is extremely complicated, and in which not only the ends but also the middles of the half-lines rhyme:

I'ch llys iach llawn, wiw Rys yr awn,
A gwŷs a gawn, agos ged;
A'th fudd, wyth fael, o gudd i'w gael,
Aur rhudd, ŵr hael, rhwydd y rhed.

In the Welsh bardic tradition of *cywydd*-poetry there were several poets who seem to have composed love-poetry mainly. Of these the first and greatest was Dafydd ap Gwilym in the mid-fourteenth century. There had been love-poetry before his time, in the *awdl*-metres of the court-poets, and we do not know how much popular love-poetry of the period has been lost, though it is reasonable to assume that such popular poetry did exist. However, Dafydd ap Gwilym must have wrought a revolutionary change in the tradition of Welsh love-poetry. He inspired a school of followers, and though none of them had his genius, much of the *cywydd* love-poetry of the late medieval period, after Dafydd ap Gwilym's time, is interesting, varied, and attractive in technique. Many bards composed a proportion of love-poems amongst their works, but some, like Dafydd ap Gwilym before them, seemed to be mainly concerned with love-poetry. Of such bards there is no doubt but that Dafydd ab Edmwnd of all the followers of Dafydd ap Gwilym was the chief exponent of such poetry.

There were many ways in which Dafydd ab Edmwnd continued traditions established by Dafydd ap Gwilym. Just as his great predecessor had composed a poem to the hair of his sweetheart Morfudd, Dafydd ab Edmwnd sang a number of poems on the subject of his loved one's hair. Dafydd ap Gwilym said of Morfudd,

> God set—I am a good witness —
> two plaits to entice two parishes:
> from the blessings of love, they are gold,
> fair coils on a woman's crown,
> gold torques, and the beloved produce
> of the alight fruit of a modest crown-load . . .
> a bush of wax . . .
> Proudly does the unscowling slender maid bear
> a sheaf of broom . . .
> as a round hairstyle, as a meet coronet . . .

Dafydd ab Edmwnd is in the same descriptive tradition, but he is more obviously colourful and more strikingly fanciful in his kenning: he is far less restrained:

> That which surrounds
> the maiden whom I love
> is that which surrounds the bush of light,

with the tip of silk like a star
of the sky with gold posts from her head;
dragon fire shining through a door,
three ropes like the Pleiades:
it kindles in one bush
from the top of a hairstyle in one bonfire.

Clearly there has been an evolution in the tradition of describing the appurtenances of the loved one. Dafydd ap Gwilym, though imaginative, was basically natural, but Dafydd ab Edmwnd, following in his footsteps, was at the same time both more consciously artistic and more conventionally artificial. This is what was gained and lost through pursuing the practice of an evolving yet restricted poetic tradition, consequences familiar to students of all medieval art.

Dafydd ab Edmwnd also followed Dafydd ap Gwilym in composing songs describing his sweetheart's kiss. Like the master too, Dafydd ab Edmwnd sang serenades. But it was not only in subject-matter that Dafydd ab Edmwnd emulated Dafydd ap Gwilym, for both poets employed on occasion similar technical devices. Both sang one or two *cywyddau* in which each line began with the same consonant, and also *cywyddau* in which each couplet ended with the same word.

Like Dafydd ap Gwilym too Dafydd ab Edmwnd sang of natural phenomena, but the spirit of the two bards was very different. Whereas Dafydd ap Gwilym sang of nature and incidentally of love, Dafydd ab Edmwnd sang of love and incidentally of nature. To Dafydd ab Edmwnd nature simply furnished a scenic background to love-poetry, and even this intrinsically unimportant use of natural descriptions occurred comparatively rarely in his poetry. Even so Dafydd ab Edmwnd made greater use of such descriptions than did his contemporaries who only make occasional passing references to nature.

By the middle of the fifteenth century love-poetry was in many ways different in spirit from the poetry of Dafydd ap Gwilym. Although varied in actual content, it nevertheless gave generally the impression of being conventional, though it must be realized that this fact does not necessarily constitute an artistic fault.

It is true of course that the inspiration of Dafydd ap Gwilym lay at the root of all the love-poetry of the following period, but other poets were directly influenced to a lesser degree than Dafydd ab

Edmwnd. Of course there were some very obvious direct influences. For instance Dafydd ap Gwilym composed a *cywydd* to the Rattle which described, firstly, the state of lovers' bliss which was, secondly, disturbed by a loud noise, and this was followed, thirdly, by a satirization of the noise. Two poems were sung in the mid-fifteenth century which followed exactly the same pattern, the *cywydd* to the Owl by Robin Leia and the *cywydd* to the Thunderclap by Maredudd ap Rhys.

A south Walian contemporary of Dafydd ab Edmwnd was Ieuan Deulwyn from Cydweli, and he also sang quite a number of love-*cywyddau*. In one of these poems he refers, as Dafydd ap Gwilym had done before him, to the birch-tree as a court of love. The opening couplet of this poem is

> There is a birch-tree at the end of a wooded slope,
> green-boughed, with its beautiful hair long.

This metaphor of 'hair' as applied to a verdant tree has a long ancestry. The *Pervigilium Veneris* has the following line:

> et nemus comam resolvit de maritis imbribus,

and Dafydd ap Gwilym on more than one occasion refers to the 'hair' of the birch, a tree for which the application of the metaphor was particularly apt. So did Gruffudd ab Adda, a contemporary of Dafydd's in his poem to the birch-tree felled to be a maypole at Llanidloes; and the metaphor continued to be used by such bards as Ieuan Deulwyn and his contemporaries and followers. Also, the metaphor was inverted, and a girl's hair was often likened to a birch.

In this particular poem by Ieuan Deulwyn occurs the couplet:

> And the paternoster of love—pleasant is the sound—
> from the rosaries of the fresh birches.

The kind of image, derived from religion, was extremely common in the love-poetry of the period. Dafydd ap Gwilym had composed an extended description of the cock-thrush as a priest officiating at mass, but religious metaphors were not developed in this way by fifteenth and early sixteenth-century bards: they simply made frequent passing references to religion in their love-poetry. In this poem to the birch by Ieuan Deulwyn there is no mention of religion except in the above couplet, and also in this unrelated passage:

> There is given under the pavilion of summer
> a lesson next St Jacob's eve:
> there are there in the famous May
> green altars and the cuckoo's place.

'The religion of the forest and the cuckoo' was an integral part of the background of the love-poetry of the period, but no attempt was made to develop fully the literary implications of this.

There were many themes and motifs used conventionally in love-poetry. One fairly common feature was the description of feminine beauty, and, just as Iolo Goch in the fourteenth century had followed the prescribed rhetorical pattern of describing the individual items in order from the head to the feet, so did the poets of the second half of the fifteenth century, though a variation sometimes followed, especially by Robin Ddu, an Anglesey bard, was to invert the order.

As the description of the beauty of women naturally was such a prominent feature of love-poetry, and as the nullity of human beauty was so frequently delineated in sermon-poetry, it is rather surprising that these two themes were hardly ever brought into connection; but this was perhaps done once by Robin Ddu, the link being provided by the theme of the treachery or fickleness of women:

> An image which is gilded (of a silver forehead,
> of pure bright beautiful countenance)
> perhaps (it is fairer than a man)
> it is rotten inside.

A more definite example of the theme of the vanity of beauty is provided by Bedo Brwynllys, quite a prolific love-poet of the period, who is on the whole rather exceptional, being notable for the relative prosiness of his verse:

> Young leaves until the feast of St John
> will last tightly on a fair tree;
> after that—trees of old nest—
> they will become more and more sere and withered.
> In the same way, though she does not acknowledge it,
> does God measure a woman's time.

Sermon-poetry was of course an important *genre* in the period, especially the poetry concerned with the imminence and pervasiveness of death; and the way in which this theme was dealt with by Welsh bards reflected a common western European tradition. There had been references to the vanity of earthly qualities and to the nullity and the decomposition in death in earlier Welsh poetry but it was not really till the poetry of Siôn Cent in the early fifteenth century that this attitude found full artistic expression in Welsh, as far as we can judge, though of course it must be granted that Siôn Cent was an extremely shadowy figure who may never have existed at all. It is difficult to know how many of the compositions attributed to Siôn Cent do actually belong to the early fifteenth century, but perhaps it may be taken that those sermon-poems which are definitely of the second half of the fifteenth century, and the first quarter of the sixteenth, do represent a continuing *cywydd* tradition going back at least to the early fifteenth century, and possibly further, for there is a *cywydd* to the Skull which may be the work of the fourteenth-century Llywelyn Goch Amheurig Hen.

A fine sermon-poem is that which compares Man to a Day by Maredudd ap Rhys, a mid fifteenth-century bard from Ruabon near Wrexham. It reminds us of such Middle English religious poems as 'The Mirror of the Periods of a Man's Life' (Furnivall, *Hymns to the Virgin* . . ., p. 58) and especially 'This World is but a Vanyte' (op. cit., p. 83). Maredudd's poem starts off thus:

> Yesterday comes as a simile:
> it was a day with an end to it.
> Morningtide, a fine bold exemplum,
> midday after that,
> the afternoon went to expound
> that the life of the day would be a long night.

A couple of the best of sermon-poems were composed by Ieuan Brydydd Hir from the commote of Ardudwy, another mid fifteenth-century bard. One of these *cywyddau* is an excellent example of the well-known motif of a conversation between the living and the dead. The scene is set in a church and the living is disturbed by the manifestation of the dead. This version of the motif then gives the Welsh versified form of the traditional questions '*Quis es tu? Quem video?*'. The dead then explains who he is and describes his state, taking care to point the moral by pronouncing at the appropriate times the traditional statements 'I was as you are' and 'You will be as I am'.

The other sermon-poem by Ieuan Brydydd Hir is a fine, if morbid, *cywydd* to old age. It starts off:

> Woe to him who puts—memory of a cold man—
> his faith in the world, a shallow traitor.
> He who is wise and rich
> and freely healthy, in fine condition now,
> I venture to acknowledge it to everyone
> that his continuation will be very short.

This poem contains the only known reference in Welsh literature to the well-known medieval European legend of the three living and the three dead:

> I am a gift of an exemplum
> to the world, a vain thing:
> I am of the same appearance in my disease,
> as sad in my pain,
> as one of the three tamed kings
> who blackened in the earth.

There is a well-known poem attributed to Siôn Cent which makes extensive use of the *Ubi sunt*? motif. The best poem in this tradition was composed in the early sixteenth century by the Anglesey priest 'Sir' Dafydd Trefor. It starts thus:

> Is it not unwise that we do not understand
> the long life and this world?
> Man has only a short time to give well,
> and how briefly does he last.
> Why are they not seen from afar,
> the goodmen that were in Wales formerly?
> Where is Solomon—he was not unwise
> in learning; and where is the Wise Sibyl?
> Where is the forehead and the hair of Absalom
> of fair countenance? Bring him to our presence!
> Where is Samson, the heart of powerful men,
> and where is Arthur's nephew?

The culmination of medieval thinking about death was the Dance of Death, and there are several references in Welsh poetry, especially in sermon-poetry and in elegies, to the Dance. Yet there is no poem about or of the Dance of Death in Welsh. There is however one very powerful *cywydd* of the mid-fifteenth century, composed by the Glamorgan bard Llywelyn ap Hywel ab Ieuan ap Gronwy, which is a song about Death personified. The bard says:

> Bravely and wrathfully on a foot that silences,
> without a word Death comes.

He describes how vain it is to flee, for Death's approach is inexorable:

> What guarantee can a king give
> to a foolish man who gives goods as a fine?
> Edward could not give a pardon
> for the body, marked out by this one, to live.
> In spite of land, when one is doomed to die,
> in spite of goods one cannot flee.
> One must await the hour
> when the body and the soul are separated.

Religious poetry of a more devotional character had an apparently longer and more definite history in Welsh than sermon-poetry. In addition to a more popular religious poetry there was a prominent place for religious poetry in the royal courts of medieval Wales where it was the custom to sing a song to God before the 'king' was praised. Also some poems to saints were composed in the same poetic tradition. In the late medieval period perhaps the pessimistic sermon-poetry already described overtook the more straightforward devotional poetry in popularity. Nevertheless there were many devotional poems sung, and many of these were in connection with images, such as of saints, but more especially the rood. Of the rood-poems the best known is that to the rood of Brecon by Huw Cae Llwyd of the mid-fifteenth century. The poem starts with a description of the rood:

> The Man put His span/virtue
> on the cross for the sake of the five ages of man.
> It is a good place where He was placed
> above us with His arms outstretched
> above the green land of Hodni—fine church—
> with His privilege extending to heaven above,

where He is above the nape of the rock—
the cross of God bearing Christ in fairness.

Then there is a description of the Passion:

He suffered—was it not good of Him?—
the striking of keen steel through the palm of the hand.
Through His breast and through His tunic there was
a blind man with a spear piercing Him.
Through His hair were driven three by three
spines to deeply hurt Him.

There follows an expression of personal feeling:

I was trying to watch every wound
on God of heaven.
One whole part I did not find
without finding His blood and without a wound.

The poem ends with this piece:

Two drops from the Passion,
this one's tears saved me from my disease.
True God the Father, rather than anyone,
listen to me, for the sake of my innocence.
To praise Him divinely I make
a *cywydd* to the Son.—Invite me:
on a feast-day I shall go to the holy perfect feast
without death, without end.

Many other poems were sung to roods and to Mary in connection with specific images of her. Often poems of hagiographic interest were composed to saints, such as the poems to Tydecho, the patron saint of Mallwyd, by Dafydd Llwyd o Fathafarn, and to St Bride by Iorwerth Fynglwyd who had been born at St Bride's Major in Glamorgan. Generally speaking, poems to images reflected the importance of pilgrimage in the period, and some poems were connected with pilgrimage to distant lands, such as the poem by Huw Cae Llwyd to the relics at Rome which he saw during the jubilee year of 1475. Some poems were not so much about the aims of pilgrimage as about pilgrimage as such. The fourteenth-century bard Gruffudd Gryg had composed a poem to the Moon, based on his experience as a pilgrim voyaging from Santiago de Compostella. Robin Ddu, an Anglesey bard of the mid-fifteenth century, composed a poem to the Ship in which he was going on pilgrimage, the time being again a jubilee year—1450. This poem made extensive use of the poetic device of *dyfalu*, a term fairly close in meaning to 'kenning'. So, the poem mainly consists of fanciful descriptions of the ship. Here are extracts:

> The ship under the long mantle,
> fair-light, comely, which is feared,
> you plough the sea,—
> you are the plough of the saints across it.
> Weary, my darling, is your voyage,
> the weary dwelling-house of the tip of waves,
> the handsome court of cord ropes and a sail,
> a chest with the form of a dear castle.
> You are a quiet girl, if I rule / possess you,
> under a wizard from Gwynedd.
>
> . . . a pavilion of oak and canvas,
> a slender white-mantled falcon,
> a parlour like a tower on a wave's belly,
> the wooden-chest of pilgrims.

Another very different poem which yet contains a fanciful description of a ship is by Deio ab Ieuan Du. Of this ship it is said, amongst other kennings:

> This one is an almary of the briny
> formed for enemies.

The *cywydd* is a poem to Siencyn Amhredudd ap Rhys Du of Tywyn near Cardigan who had been taken prisoner at sea by a French ship; and there is in the poem an interesting reference to the tale of Madog ab Owain Gwynedd (the legendary discoverer of America) who had been lost at sea. This poem is mentioned here as indicating how comparable *dyfaliadau* could be found in poems of very different content.

In the fifteenth and early sixteenth centuries the fullest use of the device of *dyfalu* was made in request-poetry, and although we cannot trace the practice further back, in extant poetry, than the second half of the fourteenth century, we can be reasonably sure that the use of *dyfalu* in request-poetry goes much further back, and is probably to be connected with the characteristics of such riddle-poetry as *Canu y Gwynt* (The Song to the Wind) in the *Book of Taliesin.*

The typical request-poem of the end of the medieval period had a fairly set pattern consisting of, firstly, praise of the *uchelwr* from whom the gift was requested, secondly, a brief stating of the identity of the person requesting the gift, thirdly, a long series of descriptions of the gift, and finally a brief promise of gratitude or reciprocation.

Apart from the works of bards who have been allotted special chapters in this book, between the *eisteddfodau* of Carmarthen (*c.* 1451) and Caerwys (1523), at least eighty extant request-poems were composed, and in these poems seeking individual gifts about thirty different items are represented. The gift by far most frequently solicited was a horse, there being thirteen examples of this. Of these poems four were sung to Dafydd ap Owain (later bishop of St Asaph) when he was abbot of the Cistercian abbey of Maenan (Aberconwy). Three of the poems were, as was most usual, composed by bards on behalf of a commissioner, these poems being by Owain ap Llywelyn ab y Moel, Dafydd ap Maredudd ap Tudur, and Lewys Môn. The other poem, on his own behalf, as sometimes occurred, was by Gruffudd ap Llywelyn Fychan soliciting a 'hackney'. Neither the poem by Dafydd ap Maredudd ap Tudur nor that by Gruffudd ap Llywelyn Fychan contain much *dyfalu,* but that by Lewys Môn has an appreciable amount of fanciful description, though perhaps it is not *dyfalu* in the sense of 'kenning'. Here is an example:

> Its voracious mouth over the lips of stickiness
> chastised foamingly.
> There were two eyes in the animal's pate,
> two cauldrons coming from his nape;
> and leaping, with its hind hoof
> it made gunpowder with its horseshoe:
> the front foot—it is necessary not to become tired—
> is in the hand of holy St Lo;
> and from its nostrils, when a yoke excites,
> the breath of bellows is bred.

The next most popular item solicited, there being seven examples, was a team of oxen; six oxen being requested by Huw Cae Llwyd, Dafydd ab Edmwnd, Owain ap Llywelyn ab y Moel, Hywel Dafi and Ieuan Deulwyn; whilst on other occasions Hywel Dafi and Ieuan Deulwyn requested teams of eight. These poems were different from the ordinary request-poem in that the gift was each time solicited from a group rather than from a single individual. The poem by Owain ap Llywelyn ab y Moel contains a very imaginative description of the oxen ploughing:

Soldiers of animals,
I shall have oxen taller than a man,
and give them the task now
of marling a field, the great barrels.
The tame ones within a furrow will not want
there to be one butt of land not unturfed wavingly.
They were the uprooters of earth
fashioning the land like tight clothes,
shelving in wide posts
the ribs of the field like stonemasons.
In traces the bears are placed,
fair ships, to skin land.

There are poems to request other animals, five for a bull, a ram, a stag, a terrier, three for a greyhound, three for a pair of greyhounds, three for a pair of other hunting dogs, and even a poem by Huw Cae Llwyd requesting the gift of an ape. Hywel Dafi requested hives of bees; and there are several poems soliciting birds, hunting or fishing birds naturally for there are three poems requesting a goshawk, two a falcon, and one a heron. There is also a poem asking for swans in which Deio ab Ieuan Du has this couplet:

It supports a breast like a forester's daughter,
a high rein; and grazes in water.

Several poems solicit gifts of weapons or military accoutrements: one poem asks for a sword, four others for a bow. Of these poems the best is by Iorwerth Fynglwyd, who describes the bow thus:

I bear for my blow-striking
the saint's bow to cast an arrow:
it is a fear to the two towns the golden implements
that are made for its back,

maidens for us to divide,
the daughters of a fine hard bow.
Let the powerful daughters
learn from their father a stern whistle:
his shape is bent and straight,
youthful and very old-manish:
youthfully he does not know shouting,
and when bent he makes a cry.
My gift was imprisoned and bound:
it was a long hemp that imprisoned him.
A weapon with its beak on my knuckle,
it is a rainbow which injures many:
if its belly is yellow
I find its back to be white.

There are three poems soliciting a buckler, and one asking for a sword and a buckler. Tomas Derllysg refers to the manufacturing:

Expert is the workmanship of its making,
good chiselling on steel foam.

There are also four poems requesting various kinds of coats of arms, including a cuirass and a brigandine. Another poem solicits a saddle.

Some poems request items of clothing: there are poems asking for a tunic and for a jacket of tawny. But the item of clothing usually solicited was a mantle, as evidenced by poems by Dafydd Epynt, Ieuan Deulwyn, Bedo Brwynllys, and Hywel Swrdwal, whilst Dafydd ab Edmwnd has a *cywydd* to thank for the gift of a mantle. In each case, as in Guto'r Glyn's poem on the same subject, the mantle described was a red Irish one. Amongst his descriptions of the mantle Ieuan Deulwyn compared it to 'a covering for a bed', and this brings to mind that another request-poem, by the Glamorgan bard Gwilym Tew, was for a featherbed.

Several poems were composed requesting musical instruments: Gruffudd ap Dafydd ap Hywel in the early sixteenth century wrote a poem asking for a crowd and another asking for a pair of pipes, whilst there are four request-poems for a harp. The priest 'Sir' Dafydd Trefor went further. On his own behalf he asked Sir Wiliam Gruffudd, chamberlain of north Wales, for a harp and a concubine.

Other miscellaneous items requested were millstones (in three poems), a pair of stocks, a rosary (two poems), the *Book of the Grail*, and spectacles.

Reference has already been made to one thanking-poem, representing a *genre* fairly similar in content to request-poems and going back to Dafydd ap Gwilym's *cywydd* thanking Ifor the Generous for the gift of his gloves; but such poems are scarce. The best known is a poem by Deio ab Ieuan Du thanking for the gift of a red bull, whilst perhaps the most interesting is a poem by Dafydd Epynt thanking his fellow-bard Dafydd ap Hywel for his gift of a horse to him when he as an old man was travelling afoot.

Extensive descriptive passages were found not only in request-poetry and thanking-poems, and sometimes in love-poetry, but also on occasion the practice characterized certain aspects of praise-poetry. This was especially so in poems in which the patrons' houses were described. The first poem known of this kind was Iolo Goch's famous song to Owain Glyndŵr's court at Sycharth in the second half of the fourteenth century. The tradition of singing such poems continued. Of the works of the bards with which we are concerned here, perhaps the best of these poems were that composed by Lewys Môn in the early sixteenth century to the court of Wiliam Edwart at Plasnewydd, Chirk, and especially that sung by Gwilym ab Ieuan Hen half a century earlier to the court of Gruffudd ap Siancyn at Llwydiarth in Powys. In the opening line of the following quotation Gwilym ab Ieuan Hen uses again a famous phrase used by his predecessor when describing the court of Owain Glyndŵr, sacred to the memory of all true Welshmen:

> Placed without latch or lock
> were oaks as one cloak:
> their single tunic is varnish,
> the veronica of Vyrnwy-side.

A very common feature of praise-poetry was to include a description of the feasting at the patron's court. Usually such descriptions were fairly short, and often quite abstract. Sometimes, however, the descriptions were very specific. Dafydd Llwyd o Fathafarn lists the wines served in the court of Walter Devereux, Lord Ferrers:

> . . . the wine of Gascony,
> Osey, Rumney, Rhine-bank,
> and Claret, it does not feel cold weather;
> and broaching the wine of distant Poitou

is what they can do there, a hundred tuns;
and bringing Bastard wine, like a wave's tumult,
to land, there was a fine store;
Malmsey, I have no drink before it,
Raspis from the land of Spain;
one praises the sweet wine
of Muscadel . . .

Dafydd Llwyd has also a detailed description of a feast at Penrhyn, the court of Sir Wiliam Gruffudd. Although such lengthy specific descriptions of feasts were rare, it is interesting to find that two bards, Tudur Penllyn in his old age and Lewys Môn in his youth, both refer in some detail to the feasting at the court of Huw Lewys at Prysaddfed in Anglesey. Once again, however, it was Gwilym ab Ieuan Hen who composed the outstanding poem to feasting. It does not contain a description of a feast, but is a long peroration eulogizing the generous festivity prevailing at the court of Faenor, Aberriw, near Welshpool. Here is an extract:

To Anthony there are two hundred
free houses—he is a good man.
All the hospices of St John,
they too are an advantage to the weak.
Where Roland was, a hundred men run—
a free court, there licence is had:
for all I know, in heaven
is the emperor of Roncesvalles:
there are here, close to me,
houses [i.e. a court] of an equivalent expenditure . . .

From the time of Taliesin in the sixth century Welsh poets had praised the feasting and carousing and gift-giving at their patrons' courts. This tradition had received a new impetus and a new direction in the poems sung by Dafydd ap Gwilym to Ifor the Generous. Perhaps the most interesting picture of courtly enjoyment in the second half of the fifteenth century was drawn by Dafydd Llwyd o Fathafarn in his poem to William Herbert, earl of Pembroke, at his renowned court of Raglan in Gwent:

The court of Raglan . . .
a hundred chambers containing victuals,
a hundred towers, a hundred parlours, a hundred gates,

a hundred chimneys for men of honour,
a hundred bonfires of long-cut fuel . . .
I turn to go in where the island-kingdom comes,
through a hundred lofts. I stay in the court.
From the vast great new hall
to the cellar which is the width of the building;
from the cellar to the mass,
and to the table near its top;
to the high lead [roof] to see
the round circle of the earth of Christendom.
Some to the dance above the dungeon,
earls with cards, others with dogs;
some to carousal . . .
some to the parks, some to the wine gardens . . .

As is seen, Dafydd Llwyd approved of card-playing as an entertainment. Huw ap Dafydd took a rather different attitude to gambling. This was his advice to Rhys ap Siôn from near Ruthin:

Your face did not have calumny,
do not let a card change your good reputation.
From playing dice there did not go
to the top of the island-kingdom a single chieftain.
Woe to such play as there was
for the tunic of the Son Jesus.
It is the worst business of the hands
for a man to put gold on a trump:
put your money on lands,—
hold your share, it is genuine.

Hywel Swrdwal, who is reputed to have been bailiff of Newtown, Powys, towards the middle of the fifteenth century, also referred to the playing of indoor games. He did so figuratively in an elegy to Jenkin Turberville from Glamorgan:

At what kind of play is the Son of Mary
upon an unsatirized family?
If tables, let His grace be besought —
He has interned our realm;
or if chess, for ever and ever
it was check-mate to the four countries.

In elegies, inevitably, reference was always made to the loss resulting from the death of the subject. Very often this was expressed fairly directly and not so figuratively as by Hywel Swrdwal, but Hywel Cilan also referred to the loss of a patron with an effective metaphor:

> It is a great gap to unwall
> a tower at the crest of the land and the neighbourhood.

Both eulogies and elegies very frequently refer to their subject as a defender of his people, and, naturally, the epithet 'tower' was an apt metaphor for expressing this. It also conveyed an impression of height and might, and these characteristics were often praised as being worthy attributes of members of a warrior class in a warlike and turbulent society. Lewys Môn, for example, referred to the height of Sir Richard Herbert of Montgomery, one of the many Welshmen knighted after the Battle of the Spurs in 1513, and a son of a father renowned for his tallness:

> Ride horses and men, O Urien,
> the ox and the great bugbear are on high:
> the tallest man is at the crest of the hill,
> and he measures the length of a month of summer:
> you are set higher than a verdant oak;
> you are seen yonder through eight walls.
> Where were pillars gilded?—
> In the Atlantic Ocean for your length.

If Sir Richard Herbert reminded Lewys Môn of the Pillars of Hercules, Ieuan Deulwyn in a quite exceptional *cywydd* of praise showed how shortness could also bring to mind a picture of a praiseworthy man. This is what he said of Hywel ab Ieuan Coch from Llansanffraid in the Wye Valley:

> He was always brave: to the host would go
> a little one of high face.
> It is not the big which is good now:
> Ifor the Generous was not big.
> That is the size and shape of my lord:
> in the taverns of the size of Ifor.

The bards of the period under review were very aware of patronage as a long-continued tradition, of which the patronage of Dafydd ap Gwilym by Ifor the Generous was a shining example.

Very many praise-poems of the period contain references to the generous relationship between the patron and bards in general or the particular bardic author of the poem, and to the loyalty felt by the bard to a particular patron or his family. Owain ap Llywelyn ab y Moel, towards the end of the fifteenth century, gave expression to the special relationship between himself and the family of Brompton in Chirbury:

> Our one bard would go in old age
> to the top of the table to which he used to go in youth . . .
> I run to the same place
> like rough waters in the middle of a declivity.
> I am a mill at the head of a river—
> (I praise Huw) there is profit for this one.

Even at a time when so very many centres of patronage existed all over Wales, some courts stood out as special bardic sanctuaries for generations, notably the courts of the powerful families of Gruffudd at Penrhyn in Gwynedd and of Herbert at Raglan in Gwent. It would seem as if these exalted native officials of a foreign power wished to continue the traditions of the formerly independent royal courts of Wales.

Throughout the fifteenth and sixteenth centuries bards sang to the successive heads of the Gruffudd family at Penrhyn. In the mid-fifteenth century Robin Ddu is reputed to have held a special position at Penrhyn but only two, or perhaps three, of his poems in praise of Wiliam Gruffudd Fychan have survived, but more poems of a later bard, Lewys Môn, are extant, one poem being to Wiliam Fychan's son Sir Wiliam Gruffudd and seven to his grandson also called Sir Wiliam Gruffudd. These songs by Lewys Môn are particularly powerful praise-poems and reflect adequately the formidable position held by the family of Gruffudd in north Wales, as is shown by this quotation which refers to the difficulty the last Wiliam Gruffudd had in succeeding to his father's estate:

> Master Wiliam, give ointment over here,
> it mends where you will it.
> Send judgement for the sake of the man who rules,
> and do rightly by Gwynedd.
> Watch the sun and the brightening of the weather
> before turning yonder the wind of tempestuous weather.
> Through you warmth has transcended:

the backbone of the whole of Gwynedd was feeble before.
They, your father's men, were beleaguered:
call again the falcons to you.
If some men have gone astray
entice them into unity under your sign.
Keeping vigil at your court on the feast-day of Tygái
you made a book for a hundred in livery.

Lewys Môn also has a very fine elegy to Sir Wiliam Gruffudd's first wife, Siân Stradling. This is not surprising, for of all the bards of the period, Lewys Môn was undoubtedly the master at the composition of elegies, the most artistically remarkable of these being perhaps his elegy to Sir John Grey, earl of Powys, who died in 1494.

A group of poems connected with Penrhyn brings us to consideration of a further aspect of bardic poetry in relationship to patrons and their courts, namely satire and contention. It should be remembered that both satire and bardic contention had a long history in Celtic communities. In ancient Gaul and early Ireland the poets satirized as well as praised, and it is clear from thirteenth- and fourteenth-century poetry that it must have been so throughout the history of Welsh poetry too; whilst it is well-known that disputation was an integral practice of bardism in medieval Wales. In the early sixteenth century, Ifan Delynior sang a *cywydd* to Sir Wiliam Gruffudd, which consisted of elements of satire as well as praise. In particular, Sir Wiliam was accused of being too much of a womanizer:

If a girl in the boughs of May sees
your eye, she would faint . . .
The feet make many a turn
from the white lodge to the star of love,
yonder to the garden if you get the concubine.

'Sir' Dafydd Trefor composed a *cywydd* in defence of Sir Wiliam and satirizing Ifan Delynior who then wrote a *cywydd* of reconciliation which, however, did not prevent contention upon the issue continuing between him and another bard, Ifan Amhadog.

There was a contention arising from a rather similar issue between Lewys Môn and Llywelyn ap Gutun who had initiated the dispute by accusing the dean of Bangor of offering money to a girl whom

Llywelyn ap Gutun himself fancied. Llywelyn ap Gutun, who, like the later Ifan Delynior, was primarily a harpist, was notorious for his bardic contentions, for he disputed with Guto'r Glyn and Dafydd Llwyd o Fathafarn as well as Lewys Môn.

Contention on several occasions arose from rivalry for a patron's favours. The best-known example of this is that between Hywel Dafi and Guto'r Glyn over patronage at the Herbert court of Raglan. Iorwerth Fynglwyd, half a century later, was engaged in more than one contention over patronage, and it is interesting to see that one of them was with his own bardic teacher Rhisiart ap Rhys. It seems that Iorwerth, as a young man, wished to take over Rhisiart's favoured position at John Stradling's mansion at Merthyr Mawr in the Vale of Glamorgan. He accused Rhisiart of deserting Merthyr Mawr for the court of the great Sir Rhys ap Tomas, yet wanting to retain his privileges at Merthyr Mawr. Iorwerth compared Rhisiart to the dog in Aesop's fable.

As has been mentioned Ifan Delynior sought reconciliation with Sir Wiliam Gruffudd following his satirical poem to him. Contention at patrons' courts often led to this, and in any case reconciliation-poems were in general manifestly connected with bardic patronage. There was a very long Welsh tradition of reconciliation-poetry, and the *genre* flourished during the period under review, culminating in a fine poem by Iorwerth Fynglwyd to Mathïas Cradog, sheriff of Glamorgan, and a poem containing an unprecedented display of bardic erudition by Lewys Môn to John Puleston, one time chamberlain of north Wales.

During the second half of the fifteenth century there appeared a new type of reconciliation-poem, though one suspects that there must have been many such poems sung previously that did not survive. These were poems to reconcile and pacify different factions. Perhaps the precursor to such songs was the poem by Hywel Foel ap Griffri ap Pwyll Wyddel protesting about the imprisonment by Llywelyn the Last of his brother Owain Goch. Whatever may be the truth about continuing a tradition or not, there is no doubt but that this type also of reconciliation produced some exceptionally good poems, there being again a tendency by the bards in such poems to indulge to an even greater degree than usually in learned allusions, as is shown for instance in Deio ab Ieuan Du's poem to pacify the quarrelling relatives Rhys from Tywyn in Cardiganshire and Gruffudd Fychan from Corsygedol in Merionethshire. In this poem sixteen lines are devoted to citing relevant parallels from Geoffrey's *Historia*.

In one poem Hywel Dafi tried to bring about peace in a quarrel between the men of Glamorgan and the men of Brecknock. In a poem of personal reconciliation Lewys Môn attempted to appease the men of Caereinion in Powys:

> If peace is suitable for me,
> I shall go bowed to seek grace,
> I shall go in a hurry to a blue-white court,
> under God's protection to Neuadd Wen.
> It is easier for Heiliarth to assoil me
> from every evil than for the Pope.

Considering this poem to the men of Caereinion brings to mind that some praise-poems, from the time of Dafydd ap Gwilym's poem to Rhosyr (Newborough) in Anglesey, were to towns and their burghers. Like some other bards, one Dafydd ap Hywel sang the praises of Oswestry, whilst Wiliam Egwad sang an *awdl* in praise of the land of Uwchaeron and the town of Aberystwyth, in which this quotation occurs:

> Let there be as far as heaven and its roof
> on the town of Padarn the protection of Peter and Non.
> The protection of Non on its breast against the treachery
> of enemies and the look of an evil eye.

Nevertheless, the vast majority of hundreds of praise-poems were eulogies or elegies to individual patrons, usually fairly straightforward and conventional, though when analysed in detail found to be, within their limitations, surprisingly varied and imaginative. Some bards, seemingly, did not wander very far afield in search of patronage; for example that good poet of the early sixteenth century, Iorwerth Fynglwyd, kept almost entirely within the bounds of his native Glamorgan and the neighbouring south-eastern land of Gwent. But many bards kept to the traditional practice of wandering afar.

Taliesin in the sixth century, after having patronage in Powys, went to Rheged in the old North (in the south-west of Scotland). In the twelfth century Cynddelw Brydydd Mawr sang at the royal court of his native Powys, but also at the royal courts of north

Wales and west Wales. In the fourteenth century Iolo Goch composed a poem in the form of an Altercation between the Body and the Soul, in which he described his journey from noble court to noble court all over Wales. He was emulated in the second half of the fifteenth century by Deio ab Ieuan Du who described his journey through the eleven commotes of Cardiganshire:

I'll measure the whole shire,
I'll go from Teifi to Dyfi . . .
there they are on the string,
the pedigrees of all these commotes . . .

A brief indication of the way in which the bards wandered abroad can be given by considering how Rhys Degannwy, who came from the bank of the Conway estuary on the northern coast of Wales, sang the praise of a patron at the town of Cydweli on the southern coast, whilst on the other hand we have two request-poems by Ieuan Deulwyn, who was from Cydweli, addressed to members of the Prysaddfed family in the farthest north-western corner of Anglesey.

The time between the *eisteddfodau* held at Carmarthen and Caerwys was a period of great bardic activity, and fortunately much of the poetry composed has been kept to us, though undoubtedly much has also been lost. Yet we know that bards from all over the country practised their art and were generously received all over the face of Wales, at centres of patronage from Anglesey to Gwent, from Flintshire to Pembrokeshire, from Aberystwyth to Oswestry.

BIBLIOGRAPHY

Text, with critical apparatus in English

E. I. Rowlands, *Poems of the Cywyddwyr* (Dublin, 1976).

Texts, with critical apparatus in Welsh

D. J. Bowen, *Barddoniaeth yr Uchelwyr* (Caerdydd, 1957).
M. P. Bryant-Quinn, '"Enaid y gwir oleuni": y Grog yn Aberhonddu', *Dwned*, 2 (1996), 51–93.
P. J. Donovan, *Cywyddau Serch y Tri Bedo* (Caerdydd, 1982).
L. Harries, *Gwaith Huw Cae Llwyd ac Eraill* (Caerdydd, 1953).

H. Ll. Jones ac E. I. Rowlands, *Gwaith Iorwerth Fynglwyd* (Caerdydd, 1975).
Islwyn Jones, *Gwaith Hywel Cilan* (Caerdydd, 1963).
J. C. Morrice, *Gwaith Barddonol Howel Swrdwal a'i fab Ieuan* (Bangor, 1908).
W. L. Richards, *Gwaith Dafydd Llwyd o Fathafarn* (Caerdydd, 1964).
T. Roberts, *Gwaith Dafydd ab Edmwnd* (Bangor, 1914).
T. Roberts, *Gwaith Tudur Penllyn ac Ieuan ap Tudur Penllyn* (Caerdydd, 1958).
Eurys Rolant, *Gwaith Owain ap Llywelyn ab y Moel* (Caerdydd, 1984).
E. I. Rowlands, *Gwaith Lewys Môn* (Caerdydd, 1975).
Idem, *Gwaith Rhys Brydydd a Rhisiart ap Rhys* (Caerdydd, 1976).
Idem, 'Moliant Dafydd Llwyd o'r Drefnewydd a'i Ddisgynyddion', *Llên Cymru*, 5 (1958–9), 174–84.
Ifor Williams, *Casgliad o Waith Ieuan Deulwyn* (Bangor, 1909).

Texts, without critical apparatus

D. J. Bowen; E. I. Rowlands, 'Ymryson rhwng Hywel Dafi a Beirdd Tir Iarll', *Llên Cymru*, 3 (1954–5), 107–14.
D. J. Bowen, 'Two "Cwrs Clera" poems', *National Library of Wales Journal*, vii (1951–2), 174–6.
I. George, 'The Poems of Syr Dafydd Trefor', *Anglesey Antiquarian Society and Field Club Transactions*, 1935, 90–104.
H. Lewis, 'Cywyddau Ymryson Ifan Dylynior, Syr Dafydd Trefor a Ieuan ap Madog', *Bulletin of the Board of Celtic Studies*, xvii (1956–8), 161–75.
Idem, 'Ymrysonau Dafydd Llwyd a Llywelyn ap Gutun', *Bulletin of the Board of Celtic Studies*, iv (1927–9), 310–25.

Critical Studies

W. Davies, 'Hywel Rheinallt', *Llên Cymru*, 9 (1966–7), 200–8.
I. George, 'A Survey of the Poems of Syr Dafydd Trefor', *Anglesey Antiquarian Society and Field Club Transactions*, 1936, 33–48.
E. D. Jones, 'Some Fifteenth Century Welsh Poetry Relating to Montgomeryshire', *Montgomeryshire Collections*, lii (1951–2), 3–21; liii (1953–4), 3–17; liv (1955–6), 48–64.
E. I. Rowlands, 'Lewys Mon', *Llên Cymru*, 4 (1956–7), 26–38.
Idem, 'Owain ap Llywelyn ab y Moel', in J. E. Caerwyn Williams (ed.), *Ysgrifau Beirniadol IX* (Dinbych, 1976), 100–13.
Idem, 'Un o gerddi Hywel Swrdwal', in J. E. Caerwyn Williams (ed.), *Ysgrifau Beirniadol VI* (Dinbych, 1971), 87–97.
Idem, 'Canu Serch 1450–1525', *Bulletin of the Board of Celtic Studies*, xxxi (1984), 30–47.
G. Ruddock, 'Rhai Agweddau ar Gywyddau Serch y Bymthegfed Ganrif', in J. Rowlands (ed.), *Dafydd ap Gwilym a Chanu Serch yr Oesoedd Canol* (Caerdydd, 1975), 95–116.

Chapter 15

TUDUR ALED

EURYS ROWLANDS

Tudur Aled was one of the two bards regarded as some sort of special counsellors in arranging the first of the two *eisteddfodau* held at Caerwys in Flintshire in the sixteenth century. This *eisteddfod* of 1523 was a historically important attempt to reform the bardic order in Wales and to provide new controls over the practice of bardism. At the time when the *eisteddfod* was being arranged there is no doubt but that Tudur Aled was the primary figure among the bards, and his postion was confirmed at the *eisteddfod* where he won the chair and his status as bardic master was ratified.

Within four years Tudur Aled was dead, and very shortly after this his two most prominent contemporaries, Lewys Môn of Anglesey and Iorwerth Fynglwyd of Glamorgan also died. Another quite prominent poet who died about the same time was 'Sir' Dafydd Trefor, an Anglesey priest.

It would seem that in the poetry of the most important bards who flourished in the first quarter of the sixteenth century, and amongst whom Tudur Aled was the acknowledged master, the tradition of late medieval Welsh praise-poetry reached its apogee, for in their work the sheer technique of 'strict' poetry was superb and polished and at the most brilliant stage of its development, whilst after their time it is generally and correctly recognized that the bardic tradition entered into a state of manifest decline. So the Caerwys *eisteddfod* of 1523 and the death in 1527 of Tudur Aled and his chief contemporaries are events which mark the end of an era in the history of Welsh culture, a change shortly to be emphasized in the political field by the Act of Union of 1536.

No doubt much of the poetry of the bards of the *uchelwyr* has been lost, and possibly that is why we have not a great many elegies composed to the memory of dead bards. Nevertheless it is likely that bardic mourning on the death of Tudur Aled reached an unprecedented scale, and no fewer than nine elegies to him are extant. These elegies were, naturally, eloquent in praise of Tudur Aled's greatness as a poet and learned bard. Lewys Daron says,

His song will always reach
into a pinnacle for our living.

The elegies also give some information about Tudur's death. It seems that he was visiting the court of Sir Rhys ap Tomas at Dinefwr far from his native Gwynedd and that he assumed the habit of a friar before dying at the nearby friary of Cwrt-y-brodyr, Carmarthen.

Tudur Aled had been born at Llansannan, in the western part of the modern county of Denbighshire, probably about 1465–70 (but see Cledwyn Fychan's article cited in the Bibliography). It is known that like most bards he was descended from *uchelwyr*, although his pedigree is only very imperfectly known. According to his own testimony in his elegy to Dafydd ab Edmwnd, that master bard of the mid-fifteenth century was an uncle of his and had been his bardic teacher. Tudur Aled also states that he first graduated as a bard, whatever that may mean, at the hall of Ieuan ap Dafydd ab Ithel Fychan located fairly closely to the home of Dafydd ab Edmwnd at Gwepra in Tegeingl (modern Flintshire).

There is a tradition about a conversation between Tudur Aled and Tomas, abbot of Basingwerk Abbey. Tudur stated that the best poet at composing an *awdl* was Dafydd ab Edmwnd, the best at a praise-*cywydd* Guto'r Glyn, and the best at a love-*cywydd* Dafydd ap Gwilym; yet he himself, claimed Tudur Aled, had composed poems in each of those fields which had not been excelled by the masters. Could this claim be vindicated? It is certainly true that the three poems cited by Tudur Aled in substantiation of his claim are very fine poems indeed, and it is also true that as a bardic craftsman Tudur Aled was unequalled. One hesitates to accept that, in general, Tudur Aled's muse was in any way comparable to that of Dafydd ap Gwilym or Guto'r Glyn, whatever about Dafydd ab Edmwnd, yet he was an excellent poet, and the kind of poet whose works would be particularly appreciated by fellow-bards, which may perhaps explain the large number of elegies to him.

Not only was Tudur Aled regarded by his contemporaries as a pre-eminent poet because of his remarkable mastery over *cynghanedd* and the richness of his use of traditional imagery, but also because he was in every way a fine representative of the bard in the traditional role of praise-poet and had, moreover, subtly adapted praise-poetry to meet the circumstances of a changing world.

Tudur Aled, of course, used the accepted metres of strict poetry and did so conventionally. Of the poems extant, by far the greatest number are *cywyddau:* eleven poems are *awdlau*, all of them praise-poems, eulogies and elegies; and there are about a hundred and twenty-five *cywyddau*, about eighty-five of which are praise-poems.

Almost all of Tudur Aled's extant praise-poetry was composed to the *uchelwyr* of north Wales, and of the poems over three times more are to patrons in the eastern half than to those in the western half. This seems to suggest that Tudur Aled, although he did visit south Wales, probably more than once, almost certainly did not spend his life as an itinerant minstrel wandering over the face of the country. Almost all of his patrons lived within a radius of about twenty-five miles from his birthplace at Llansannan: a great many lived within about twelve miles either from Llansannan or from Oswestry where it is possible that Tudur Aled set up a second home, or at least where there is evidence that he spent a good deal of his time.

Tudur Aled sang four praise-poems to Sir Rhys ap Tomas and one to his son Sir Gruffudd ap Rhys. Sir Rhys was the renowned supporter of Henry VII and was a great patron of the bards. He had several courts in west Wales (as the south-western portion of Wales was known to the English—*Deheubarth* to the Welsh) and it is difficult to know which was visited by Tudur Aled, whether it was Caeryw (Carew in Pembrokeshire) or Dinefwr or Abermarlais (in Carmarthenshire). It seems however that it was when visiting Sir Rhys that Tudur Aled withdrew to the friary at Carmarthen where he died. He also sang one *cywydd* to the archdeacon of Carmarthen. Otherwise there is no evidence at all of any poems composed by Tudur to south Wales patrons when visiting Sir Rhys, yet it seems inconceivable that he would not have sung any praise-poems to other patrons in the course of his journey or journeys to the court of Sir Rhys ap Tomas.

Judging by what has been kept to us it was very rarely too that Tudur Aled visited southern Powys (the modern Montgomeryshire), but he went frequently to Gwynedd west-of-Conway, singing to a number of patrons in Anglesey, Merioneth, and Arfon, as well as composing several poems to that well-known cleric, the chaplain of Cardinal Wolsey, Robert ap Rhys whose ancestral home was in the upper Conway Valley. Yet Tudur Aled apparently sang comparatively few poems to the foremost patrons of poetry in north Wales, namely the Gruffudd family of Penrhyn, Bangor. This family had a more or less hereditary hold on the important office of chamberlain of north Wales and there are many poems by many bards sung in their praise for generations. There are only three praise-poems extant to members of this family by Tudur Aled as well as one request-poem, whereas we have ten composed by Lewys Môn, his friend and contemporary.

It was in the north-east that most of Tudur Aled's patrons were found, in the regions of Gwynedd east-of-Conway and northern Powys, which together make up the modern counties of Denbighshire and Flintshire; and also in Edeirnion (the easternmost part of Merionethshire, now included with the two shires in the county of Clwyd as formed in 1973). Although many of these patrons were located near Oswestry, Tudur Aled's foremost patrons were members of the powerfully ramified Salesbury family whose centre and chief court was at Lleweni close to Tudur's birthplace at Llansannan, and no fewer than ten poems composed to the Salesburys are extant.

It is clear that the Salesburys were special patrons of Tudur Aled, and in a poem to Sir Thomas Salesbury the bard referred to this, comparing his lot with that of other bards to whom special patronage, renowned in the history of Welsh bardism, had been granted. As a poem to Sir Thomas's heir, Roger, shows, generosity remained a noted feature of the family tradition and was praised by Tudur Aled. It is true of course that this virtue is regularly eulogized in poems to patrons, but such a sustained praise of generosity is unusual:

> The heir of Lleweni, with the face of an earl,
> with the heart of Nudd [the Generous] above everyone . . .
> What would make bards alive
> if one were without you today?
> We live on the one who shares,
> may it be long that you have money.
> Your ready hand makes gifts:
> may God repay you that this [hand] is so generous.
> God did not give, under a healthy sky,
> goods in the right hand of a more generous man.
> With your fist—and it was but one day—
> you made an end to a hundred pounds.
> In spite of how much you give, gold runs,—
> and the pure water runs to the hollow.
> Although some doubt it,
> in spite of this, it is God who shares goods.
> The share of Nudd—and this is known—

did not become more scarce nor last long:
your share, in the right fist,
it does not last long nor become scarce.
Take through glory your part:
let others keep money.
May your produce go to a hundred men
according to your father's precedent . . .

Not only did Tudur Aled compose many poems to *uchelwyr* living close to Oswestry, he also sang a poem of praise to the town of Oswestry and its burghers:

The grace of the fortress, and its men, is certain,
and the word of God, and of strangers.
There is an able-minded constable here,
a receiver—may they stand long,—
tables, gifts to bards, red gold;
the bailiffs of this place are a plate of gold:
a fort, a gifted mayor rules it,
two sergeants of a choice throne.
Far-reaching is men's mention to the harpstring—
everybody—of the worshipfulness of every merchant.
Craftsmen, labourers, may the hand of Mary
and Cedwyn and Non keep them in harmony.

Tudur Aled also refers to religion in Oswestry:

Churchmen calling on Jesus
and the great organ making song.
Will anyone alive, in a great church, hear
better oratory on eight altars?

Indeed, the Church had an important place in Tudur Aled's poetry for about twenty of his extant poems are to clerical patrons, several of whom were abbots. A feature of this poetry is the way in which the material and the spiritual qualities and circumstances of the churchmen are interrelated, for example, after mentioning the death of the previous abbot, Tudur Aled says of Sieffre Cyffin, abbot of Maenan (Aberconwy):

That his brother was abbot
brought Maenan back up.
Foods are carried in, corn and honey are had,

the stones of a hundred quarries are garnered:
beer, wine, mead, white bread, more,
the wheat-grain malt of Aberconwy.
There is a soul in Maenan
who makes the body from wine and the white bread.

There is one elegy to a cleric but otherwise all of Tudur Aled's twenty-eight elegies are to laymen. Like the eulogies, the elegies are mainly conventional in general content but have a great rhetorical power which is of course enhanced by the vigour of the *cynghanedd.* In the elegies naturally the two main themes are the loss incurred as a result of the death of the subject and the grief of the bard and others because of the loss. In spite of being conventional there is nevertheless a variety of ways in which these themes are developed. For example, this is how the bard describes the loss of Rhys ap Llywelyn, sheriff of Anglesey:

The hunt has become extremely lethargic
so that today neither stag nor fish flees.
Birds go to your freedom,
an uncle to the bards has gone from the world,
without gold to them, without gifts,
without warmth any more, without Rhys in Anglesey.
Our money is in heaven,
our complete gift is in the soil of Cybi.

The death of Tudur Llwyd of Bodidris in Yale is lamented with stark references to his funeral and is combined with an expression of the bard's personal grief:

On his steed my support went
in the host yesterday a lion of a man;
and the second day, and the country behind him,
on four mortal men.
I fell, I fainted to the ground
when I saw the front of his bier.
I called greatly in my grief upon him,
I cry through the rock and the oak and the gravel.
If he heard me, even if his wall were locked,
the grave of Tudur would open.

A noteworthy feature of the elegies is the striking opening couplet of most of them. The elegy to Dafydd ab Edmwnd, Tudur's bardic teacher, opens:

The hand of God slew the muse,
slew the soul of old grammar wholly.

The elegy to Rhys ap Llywelyn, sheriff of Anglesey, begins:

When did Britain fall?
When Rhys went, the chief of these people.

Thomas Salesbury's elegy has this opening couplet:

I know lament for one man.
Greater is the lament than if a hundred men died.

It is, indeed, a notable characteristic of Tudur Aled's poetry that the couplets of his *cywyddau* are usually expressed with a conciseness and verve which sometimes becomes epigrammatic, as in this couplet:

Steel will not hold where you venture,
no gap where you are will be without a wall.

Yet, even more than most poets, Tudur Aled's work loses much in translation as he depended so heavily on the sound effects consequent upon his supreme mastery of *cynghanedd.* More often than not, when reading Tudur Aled, it is the clash and balance of the elaborate consonantal pattern rather than the content of the lines that excites the reader. On the whole this effect was achieved with surprisingly little syntactical contortion. The ideas expressed are usually straightforward and concise, making use only of imagery so traditional as to have become stereotyped. In translation the different syntactical patterns of another language spoil the rhetorically satisfying poise and proportion of the phraseology, and, of course, a different phonology utterly destroys the almost unbelievably complex harmony of the *cynghanedd.* Tudur Aled was not an imaginative poet but a supreme craftsman, and his craft was specifically and uncompromisingly Welsh.

Tudur Aled's craft was the composition of praise-poetry according to traditional standards which had continued to evolve up to his time, and which he himself developed even further. One aspect of the bardic craft was the use of metaphors, which had become to a large extent stereotyped, when describing patrons. The concentrated use of these epithets could lead to a mixing of metaphors, as for example in the *cywydd* to the five sons of Siôn Salbri who had just died:

> Even if a pleasant tree be broken
> five trees came from the one trunk,
> the paradise-apples of Siôn like five stars
> are five spears in Britain, five brothers . . .
> Strong-armed Thomas, a keenly injuring bar,
> would break a spear with ease, he of the broken shield.
> A door of tiles over an avenger,
> steel being the dress of an oak-man,
> a kindly-fair ten-tined stag.
> Foulke will keep us, a steadfast falcon,
> the staff of St George—he will make a skirmish a trodden
> ruin . . .

Just as Tudur Aled used a greater concentration of consonants than his predecessors in forming his lines of *cynghanedd*, so did he treat the traditional metaphorical epithets. It is a very marked feature of his verse that he built on the tradition of previous generations of bards, and greater intensified the formal elements found within traditional praise-poetry. He was acutely aware of his place in this tradition, and in yet another poem to a member of the Salesbury family he showed the importance he placed on the relationship between a patron and praise-poets, making clear that he regarded his own position at Lleweni as being in the succession of the patronage granted to Dafydd Nanmor in the middle of the fifteenth century, and a century before that to Dafydd ap Gwilym and Iolo Goch, the great founders of the *cywydd* tradition:

> Fair is the extent of your taxes
> from the length and breadth of this country.
> There were eight smokes of fire in your court,
> it was from the heat of the powder of Cheap,
> dogs, falcons, men garnering wine,
> venison is fetched to your kitchen.
> Minstrelsy is heard as being thine,
> the string music of chief musicians also.
> A man of song makes for nobility,—
> I retreat to your grace.
> I put my trust in that which I respect
> for freedom in paradise,
> like Nanmor . . .

who went at rent to Tywyn.
Dafydd, the free steward of Ifor the Generous,
Iolo came to Ithael's country.
With you completely, if I may have
you as master, I shall spend my life.

In the above quotation it is also seen that one of the chief qualities praised in a patron was that he had feasts prepared in which the bards participated; and it is not surprising, in view of the relationship between bard and patron, that the praise of generosity is a constantly recurring theme in the poetry of Tudur Aled as of other bards from the sixth century onwards. When Rhys ap Llywelyn, sheriff of Anglesey, died in 1503, Tudur Aled mourned at length the loss of his generosity:

He did not put gold to usury,
he put it to better use so that it lasted.
There is not talk about retaining through trickery
but about what he gave.
In his purse gold was not left for an hour
to become rusty.
He was liberal to the bards.
If there was trouble in the world, it was a good
world in Anglesey.
The land is cold from seeing his funeral:
warm was his welcome on a feast-day.

Descriptions of feasts are common in the poems of Tudur Aled, and one of the most striking lines referring to a patron's generosity at table is this:

You draw all the blood of a tun of wine.

Of course qualities other than generosity in the hall were eulogized when patrons were praised, but when a wife was the subject of encomium it was inevitable that particular stress should be laid on her position as a preparer and dispenser of festive liberality. A particularly good example of this is found in the poem to Rhys ap Maredudd who had been Henry Tudor's standard-bearer at Bosworth. Half the poem is devoted to his wife Lowri, of whom it is said:

Lowri gave much on feast-days,
Lowri has been good to minstrels for two ages . . .
She is named in song by a hundred.
She has fame which they [i.e. others] do not deserve.
Her fame—and she has been so generous—
could not be bought by a skimpy hand.
Her hand gave dinner to the weak ones,
Nudd of the Silver Hand had less fame.
It is God's hand, at our destination,
that makes possible the gilding of Lowri's hand.
Under the sun there is expenditure by her:
there are eight wines which are delicacies.
To the great dinner of Gwynedd
is the name of the spice of the Kingdom of the Sepulchre.
Cinnamon, saffron and incense,
venison broth, raisins, currants,
cloves, mace, as we heard,
canel, orange, did Lowri give . . .

In spite of the way in which he so frequently laid stress on generosity, especially at table, Tudur Aled, when he referred specifically to the two virtues, which he attributed to Richard Hanmer and his wife, said this:

It is the two virtues that we share out [in song]—
she is chaste and he brave.

Yet inevitably Tudur Aled returns to the familiar theme in the next line, and says:

My lion is generous, and so is she.

But the mention of bravery, and the epithet 'lion', bring us to another favourite theme in the praise-poetry of Tudur Aled as of his contemporaries and predecessors. Often there are references to weapons, —sword, spear, bow, arrow, staff. Sir Thomas Salesbury was compared to Arthur:

They wondered at the drawing of a sword
formerly through the strength of one man from the stone.
Let a stone in your country hold,—
you are a man to draw it again.

There is a very fine extended description of the drawing of the bow in another poem to a member of the Salesbury family:

> Yew nor healthy wood was not encompassed
> within the knuckle of a livelier man.
> Nothing was aimed, by means of a limb,
> other than the force in your flesh.
> You tie the wood with the hemp,—
> until your birth it was never drawn.
> Yew like a wheel is aimed
> and drawn in this a long aspen [arrow].
> Draw the arrow at a stag's life,—
> the yew became splintered wood.
> Your stout bow from the growth of a tree
> by means of the two notches it becomes a loop;
> you arched its two tips towards you,
> a loud knot as if a bell were rung.

As has been seen the epithet 'lion' could be applied to a brave man, and this was frequently done in the *cywyddau*, often when expressing an opposition between bravery and gentleness or mercy, as in this description of yet another member of the Salesbury family:

> The smile is pleasant, unless you be angered:
> a lion's bristling when your wrath is at its harshest.
> A lion in the presence of England and its king,
> you are a gentle lamb when you give wine.

Another prominent feature of Tudur Aled's poems, as was generally the case, was the praising of lineage. In his poem to Rheinallt Conwy, Tudur Aled gave epigrammatic expression to what he was certainly convinced was an important universal truth:

> Manifestly every man shows
> from what degree his root is.

When singing the praises of Pirs Conwy, archdeacon of St Asaph, a relative of Rheinallt, Tudur Aled showed that he did not think a pedigree had to be purely Welsh, not surprisingly considering the lineage of many of his patrons:

> The name of Conwy is in the canon,

> your mother's side has a finer pedigree.
> An archdeacon from knightly blood,
> a pedigree does not grow finer than your blood:
> the stag of Stanley bearing grey-old Christ,
> you are from the seed of the earls of Hooton.

Yet when praising the stock of Maredudd ab Ieuan ap Rhobert who was descended from the Welsh princes, Tudur Aled gave vent to a very different attitude:

> If every alien pedigree were recorded
> I know that there would be gaps in the pedigrees of the proud.
> The nobility of the two Venedotias was thine.
> Your parties are the flowers of the shire.
> I sang to the nobility of Venedotia,
> the flowers of the shire without the half-blood of an
> Englishman.

These differing attitudes do not necessarily represent a dichotomy, or a hypocritical or cynical attitude. When praising a patron it was natural enough, when appropriate, to praise the connection with a high-born English family, and just as natural, even more natural, to praise when relevant a pure descent from Welsh princes. One should not look for absolute consistency of opinion in praise-poetry. The same conclusion must be drawn when considering the ambivalence of Tudur Aled's attitude towards the holding of offices by his patrons.

It was quite natural that Tudur Aled should look forward to the promoting by Henry Tudor of such a patron as the abbot of Valle Crucis, to whom Tudur Aled sang thus:

> Although a hat to this crown be delayed
> as a result of the disputation given
> there was belief in true promising,
> what Harry has done will not be broken.

When praising another cleric, Tudur Aled said:

> There are eighteen offices under you.

In praising Sir Wiliam Gruffudd of Penrhyn who was chamberlain of north Wales he said:

In spite of the offices which others hold
the country will only follow one man.
Taxes on land now
are ten times better than a weak official.
He does not go to his office oppressively:
he does not demand anything but what is just.

Generally speaking, Tudur Aled tended to deprecate the holding of offices. To Rheinallt Conwy he said:

It is better to have satisfaction and ability to live
than to hold the office of a man who is today.

And to Maredudd ab Ieuan ap Rhobert, the descendant of the princes of Wales, he said:

Evanescent offices are wrong.
Go, without office, over the shire.

T. Gwynn Jones emphasized that Tudur Aled's sympathies were with the old pre-Tudor Welsh society, whilst Saunders Lewis to the contrary insisted that he was bard of the brash, pushing, eager-for-advancement squirearchy of Tudor Wales. There is undoubtedly a measure of truth in both views, but it is likely that Tudur Aled's deeper feelings were of sympathy with and understanding of the old society.

He was deeply worried by rifts in family unity and in the social entity as a result of individual greed and ambitions. This was seen for example in his frequent advice to patrons to be merciful or to control anger, as in his poem to Sir Roger Salesbury:

Hear justice lest the unwise be believed,
damp up your wrath, listen to the wise.

But by far the best example of Tudur Aled's reaction to a quarrelsome society is seen in his famous *cywydd* to reconcile Hwmffre ap Hywel of Ynysymaengwyn and his relatives. Here are extracts from the poem:

Holy God, why did men become vexed
through the mischief of slanderers?
Blood was hateful, which, through a weak cause

brought fighting to Camlan . . .
Today is an age of office-holding
like this to cause us to hate each other . . .

No one is believed, truly,
except one with two faces . . .

If there was anger between the flowers of the rose,
consider whether the cause was good . . .

It is better to hold back the black word
which is harmful than to let it go:
to stop an arrow—this is impossible
once it has left the string.

Such comparisons as that found in the last couplet quoted arose naturally from the background of the life of the period. Inevitably this was the case with all of Tudur Aled's imagery. As has been said, much of this consisted of the use of stereotyped epithets, but sometimes use was made of imagery no less representative of the period, but not so common in Welsh praise-poetry. In the elegy to Rhys ap Llywelyn, sheriff of Anglesey, Tudur has the following lines:

Land—it is easy to oppress it today:
a town without a wall, except while he was alive;
A broken ship—dropping men—
without a captain. Where will Anglesey go now?
If appearance were good, Venedotia completely
is paternosters of a rosary with the string lost.

A familiar medieval belief is evidenced in this couplet:

You are pure sky, which causes light,
water, fire, and earth.

The popularity of football inspired this next couplet:

To the live land did you take the ball
as far as religion and war are concerned.

The same image supplies an unexpected secondary meaning to the last couplet of a quotation from a request-poem addressed to four related patrons:

Rhobert . . .
you are Marcus . . .
like a lion . . .
Rhys . . .
you are Matthew, foster-son of love.
Dafydd, you are as happy
as Saint Luke who is in the image of an ox . . .
Rhys . . .
you are Johannes . . .
an eagle . . .
May there be between you, you four angels,
the four corners of the world, and the ball.

Although the passage is unusual, Tudur Aled was following a traceable tradition. About half a century earlier Deio ab Ieuan Du composed a poem to a patron called *Ieuan* which is of course a name derived from the Latin *Johannes*. The poem begins with the line:

The eagle with the gilded dress . . .

and later is said:

We see four angels
supporting the top of this world:
Johannes—Jesus on his own—
is in the fourth quarter.
Johannes—the bosom of mead—
is your name, were there wings.

The word 'top' is translated from the Welsh *tâl* 'forehead', but a homonym is *tâl* 'payment', and it is possible to take this meaning in an apocalyptic image, and in reference to Jesus.

Guto'r Glyn referred briefly to the same belief whilst Lewys Glyn Cothi, like Tudur after him, made extended and even more complicated use of the imagery.

A century earlier still, about the middle of the fourteenth century, Gruffudd ap Maredudd had written:

Let God be my leader, you four live ones:
the labour of evangelists
is to support—as is praised—
the world and heaven—it is not in vain.

The imagery is obviously inspired by iconography, such as is found for example on the tapestry of the Apocalypse at Angers in France. Perhaps the continuous, extended description, unusual in Tudur Aled's work, was acceptable to him only because the complete image consisted of a series of separate images linked together. The incongruous secondary meaning contained in the last couplet is typical enough of the muse of Tudur Aled as well as of his contemporaries. They seemed to think, sometimes in a quite involved way, by means of the concrete pictures with which their praise-poetry abounded.

BIBLIOGRAPHY

Text

T. Gwynn Jones, *Gwaith Tudur Aled* (Caerdydd, 1926).

Critical Studies

D. J. Bowen, 'Graddau Barddol Tudur Aled', *Llên Cymru*, 18 (1994), 90–103.

Cledwyn Fychan, 'Tudur Aled: ailystyried ei gynefin', *National Library of Wales Journal*, 23 (1983–4), 45–74.

Saunders Lewis, 'Tudur Aled', chapter XII in R. Geraint Gruffydd (ed.), *Meistri'r Canrifoedd* (Caerdydd, 1973), 98–115.

J. Morris-Jones, 'Tudur Aled', *Transactions of the Honourable Society of Cymmrodorion*, 1908–9, 21–52.

CHAPTER 16

THE PROSE OF THE *CYWYDD* PERIOD

MORFYDD E. OWEN

By the time that Dafydd ap Gwilym had sung his first *cywydd* the great bulk of the medieval Welsh prose which is usually considered to represent the classic tradition had been composed. By 1300 there had evolved a tradition of standard prose which manifested itself in story, in chronicle and in law. Such a tradition usually flourishes, as has been amply demonstrated by writers on English prose, when political and social circumstances are favourable. In England, at the end of the Anglo-Saxon period, prose flourished in the writings of Wulfstan and Aelfric. Later, the linguistic and political changes that followed the Norman Conquest seem to have caused prose-writing, apart from the composition of certain religious texts like the *Ancrene Wisse*, to have ceased for three or four centuries. In Wales, under the princes, a tradition of native rule and a fixed social and legal organization nourished the propagation of law texts. Storytellers, who probably travelled from court to court, safeguarded a standard language and idiom which was intelligible alike in the courts of Aberffraw and Dinefwr. The Edwardian Conquest of 1282, it has been maintained, had a cataclysmic effect on the poetic tradition, and it also, I believe, had traumatic repercussions on the history of Welsh prose.

During the period of native rule, the poetry of the official bards was native in outlook, eulogistic or elegiac in nature and aimed very largely at exalting the position of the native ruling class. Very little of it, if any, could be considered as light entertainment. After 1282, although the element of eulogy remained, poetry of the trained poets from the time of Dafydd ap Gwilym onwards also became the medium for presenting humorous entertainment in the form of anecdote and *fabliaux*. Much of the emphasis of the content and tenor of poetry shifted. In the earlier period, classical prose represented the literature of entertainment; by the later period the great creative impetus manifested in the *Mabinogi* seems to have spent itself and, apart from the great bulk of translation, most of the prose written and preserved was technical or historical.

In the first volume of this series, chapters treated the material of story, and of functional prose, most, but not all, of which was written before 1350. The purpose of this chapter is to examine the continuity of the prose tradition during the period of the *cywydd*, namely the fourteenth, fifteenth and sixteenth centuries. The very definition of the period is difficult, since in the middle of the sixteenth century a group of Welsh humanists introduced into Welsh new ideals and a Ciceronian style of writing which changed completely the nature and syntax of Welsh prose. The period after 1546, the date of the first Welsh printed book, is generally regarded as that of the Welsh Renaissance. Nevertheless, at a time when a humanist like Gruffudd Robert was aiming at writing Ciceronian periods, others like Robert Gwyn and lesser mortals were continuing to write and to translate in an idiom which was in direct line with the prose of the Middle Ages. This medieval prose continued to be written until the seventeenth century, and continued to be copied in Glamorgan.

The time is not really ripe to write a synthesis of the history of the prose of the period of the *cywydd*, since many texts and manuscripts remain unworked fields and exciting discoveries are continually being made. For instance, Graham Thomas has recently identified in a fifteenth-century manuscript a Welsh translation of the 'Bestiary of Love' of Richard de Fournival, *Llythyr Ofydd.* Gerallt Harries has recently published a discussion of the Welsh text of *The Kalender of Shepherdes.* I can in this chapter only indicate what seem within the limits of our present knowledge and the general state of research to be the general trends and characteristics of the period. One of its most striking features is that it exhibits greater fusion between the literary traditions of Wales and England, shown in translation from English and also in common literary trends. Another marked feature is that certain traditional technical prose forms like legal texts, grammars and medical compilations continued to be propagated. Perhaps the most important feature of the period, however, is the increase in the production and copying of manuscripts, for if the first creative period of medieval prose had spent itself by 1350, it is the fourteenth, fifteenth and sixteenth centuries that ensured the preservation of early Welsh prose and to a limited extent preserved the tradition of the composition of prose in Welsh. In this chapter, I propose to treat of the continuity of the prose tradition of medieval Wales by looking at certain manuscript collections, by considering the kind of prose which seemed to have been actively produced, and by trying to deduce what developments came about in prose-writing and style. For the student of Welsh manuscripts, one of the most exciting features of the period is the fact that it is increasingly possible to identify the scribes, patrons and provenance, if not of works of literature, certainly of the books which contained them. These scribes and patrons reflect in their story a particular political chapter in the history of Wales. Their books to a certain extent reflect the literary fashions of the age. Patrons to whom Dafydd ap Gwilym sang were Ieuan Llwyd and his wife, Angharad, of Glyn Aeron. Their son Rhydderch held the office of *bedellus* or *rhaglaw* of Mabwynion in 1387; he was dead by 1398/99. Tradition maintains that the earliest of complete collections of Welsh stories, the *White Book of Rhydderch* (Peniarth MSS 4 & 5), was owned by this man. The *White Book*, as it survives, is incomplete; it contains ten of the eleven native tales, religious texts and some early poetry. Before the end of the fourteenth century an addition was made to the text of *Culhwch and Olwen* in the *White Book* by one of the men who copied the other great codex of native prose, the *Red Book of Hergest*. The *Red Book* is the largest of an extensive group of manuscripts written by the same scribe. One of them, Philadelphia MS. 86800, contains a colophon attributing its writing to Hywel Fychan ap Hywel Goch:

> This book, Hywel Fychan, son of Hywel Goch of Builth, wrote completely (save that his failing memory caused him to omit a word or a letter), and that on the instruction and by the command of his master, namely Hopcyn, son of Thomas son of Einion. These men beseech everyone of those who may read this book to pray to God on their behalf for forgiveness for their sins; and that unfailing, unending, true joy be permitted to them in the company of the Father, the Son and the Holy Ghost. Amen.
>
> And in their opinion, the most despicable of the above princes who ruled were Gwrtheyrn and Medrod. Because of their treachery and deception, the most excellent princes were destroyed. For this, their descendants have suffered after them from thence up until today. These men suffer pain and need and exile in the land of their birth.

Recent palaeographical work connecting the *Red Book* with this manuscript which has a named scribe and patron, would seem to confirm that Hopcyn ap Tomos is one of the most important known patrons of literature of the later medieval period. Surprisingly little information can be gleaned about him from historical sources. A number of eulogies were composed to him by the poets—the *Red Book* itself contains five. These eulogies praise him as possessing the traditional virtues of a Welsh nobleman, famed for his generosity and his bravery; he is praised also for his learning and his wisdom, and reference is made to his splendid library. 'Learned in books, gifted, brilliant', he possessed copies of the *Elucidarium*, the '*Annals*', the *Grail* and the law books. Some eight manuscripts apart from the *Red Book* were written by the scribes of the *Red Book* and it is a tantalizing problem whether all these were in fact copied for Hopcyn ap Tomos and formed part of his library in the *calchlys* in Ynystawe; law manuscripts, like Peniarth 32 and Jesus 51; the historical collections of Peniarth 19 and Philadelphia 86800; the religious texts of Llanstephan 27 and Peniarth 190; the medical texts of Rawlinson B 467; and a copy of the *Holy Grail* itself in Peniarth 11. If all these were in the possession of Hopcyn, it would be fair to say that he had indeed 'wealth to hand in his court', namely a library which preserved all the wealth of literature of the early Welsh Middle Ages. The greatest of his surviving books is without doubt the *Red Book*, which contains a selection of nearly every kind of medieval literature, excepting legal tracts, the earliest poetry and religious prose. A breakdown of the contents of the *Red Book* reveals the following categories of content:

1. The great trilogy of medieval Welsh historical writing which comprised the *Ystoria Dared, Brut y Brenhinedd* and *Brut y Tywysogion*.
2. A miscellany of wisdom and prophetic texts mostly in translation.
3. A series of medical, scientific, historical and gnomic texts.
4. A bardic grammar.
5. The corpus of native Welsh prose, the eleven tales of the Mabinogion whose other major complete source is the *White Book of Rhydderch*.
6. One of the two great collections of *Gogynfeirdd* and late *Hengerdd* poetry, notably poems of the Myrddin and Llywarch Hen Cycles.

Categories 1–4 typify the prose *genres* found in the manuscripts in the century after Hopcyn. Most of the texts derive from the period before him. Hopcyn ap Tomos would seem to have been the cultured gentleman *par excellence* of the end of the fourteenth century, yet tantalizingly little is known about him. In 1403, Owain Glyndŵr sent for Hopcyn to come to Carmarthen to consult him as a seer. He is referred to as *Master of the Brut*, and on the grounds of his familiarity with history and prophecy his advice was asked on the outcome of Owain's campaigns. What we know about his manuscripts reflects to a certain extent the culture and knowledge which was available to an enlightened Welsh nobleman. It suggests too that noblemen by 1400 were acquiring libraries of considerable size and import. Nothing is so far known of Hywel Fychan, the copyist. There is nothing in the colophon quoted above to suggest that he was in holy orders of any kind. He did, however, have access to a considerable number of texts and helpers. The evidence of these manuscripts suggests influential lay patronage of a lay scribe and his associates.

From the middle of the fifteenth century onwards, the copying of manuscripts seems to have become particularly associated with poets. A series of manuscripts of different kinds were written by Lewis Glyn Cothi and Peniarth 51, a manuscript containing texts on palmistry, prophetic material, poetry and triads, is in the autograph of the Glamorganshire bard, Gwilym Tew. A good example of a poet who was a competent copyist and perhaps writer of prose, whose works deserve more attention than they have hitherto received, was Gruffudd ap Huw ab Owain, more commonly known as Gutun Owain. Gutun was a nobleman from Dudlust in the lordship of Oswestry. He was a pupil of Dafydd ab Edmwnd and accompanied that poet to the Carmarthen Eisteddfod. His poetry shows the wealth of traditional learning that he had inherited. He was an accomplished genealogist and one of the authorities of the commission appointed to trace the descent of Henry VII. Some eight manuscripts survive in Gutun Owain's hand, suggesting both the extent of his own learning and the kinds of prose circulating in Wales in the late fifteenth century. One of his manuscripts, Peniarth 131, consists entirely of genealogies—he was famed as a herald bard. Peniarth 186 and 27 (i) consist of calendars and computing tables. Peniarth 27 (iii) consists of religious texts, most of them at least a century and a half or two centuries old, and vaticinatory material. One manuscript partially copied by him, the *Black Book of Basing*, connected with Basingwerk Abbey as was Gutun himself, is one of the chief sources of historical texts found in Wales containing the classic trilogy of *Ystoria Dared*, a *Brut Tysilio* version of *Brut y Brenhinedd*, and *Brut y Saeson*. Llanstephan 28, the most varied and extensive of his manuscripts, contains an odd mixture of material: a new redaction of the bardic grammar, a couple of saints' lives, genealogies of the saints, the *Fifteeen Signs before Doomsday*, a number of Arthurian texts like the *Twenty-four Knights of Arthur's Court*, religious texts and traditional and other historical learning. Another of his manuscripts, Mostyn 88, contains a collection of medical texts and drawings of some interest and importance. A cursory survey of these manuscripts shows that by the third quarter of the fifteenth century, a Welsh poet of noble blood had access to a considerable body of prose, most of it technical, antiquarian or historical in nature. His connection with the *Black Book of Basing* suggests that he was a frequent visitor to monastic libraries, as do his poems.

Two manuscripts were copied some quarter of a century after the death of Gutun Owain by a priest from the same area of Wales, Sir Thomas ab Ieuan ap Deicws. Sir Thomas, who was ordained by the Pope at Rome on Easter Day, 1500, and became one of the Pope's scribes or notaries, returned to Wales in the early years of the sixteenth century (he fathered a daughter born in 1507). The first of Sir Thomas's manuscripts, Peniarth 127, consists of an extensive collection of genealogies, a copy of *Emmanuel's Compot* and treatise on arms called the *Dosbarth Arfau*. The second manuscript, BM Addl 12,193, consists of a complex historical text. Sir Thomas probably died sometime after 1520.

Shortly after Sir Thomas ab Ieuan ap Deicws died a soldier from the same part of Wales, Elis Gruffydd, was one of the guards of the Tudor king in Calais. Elis was one of those Welshmen who took part in the exodus of Welshmen to Tudor London. He had been a member of the household of Sir Robert Wingfield. Four manuscripts survive which belonged to him. One testifies to his interest in Welsh literature and contains a miscellaneous collection of Welsh poetry, genealogies, saints' lives, vaticination and a version of the *Seven Sages of Rome*. A second contains four medical or pseudo-medical texts: (i) an English version of the *Compot of Ptolemy*; (ii) a herbal; (iii) a translation of the *Castle of Health* of the humanist Thomas Elyot; and (iv) a translation of the *Regiment of Life* by Thomas Phayer. This manuscript, Cwrt Mawr 1, was copied by Elis in 1548 and is a translation of texts which were circulating in contemporary London, written by English humanists. Two manuscripts remain in Elis's hand containing a history of the world down to the year 1522.

These manuscripts and their writers typify some of the trends which may be discerned in this period. In the first place, they suggest the existence of a continuous series of non-monastic scribes and patrons involved in the production of manuscripts. This activity presupposes a lay educated class, which, as has recently been pointed out by Eurys Rowlands, is amply indicated by references in the *cywydd* poetry:

> And my office with my mesne lord was to interpret the muse for him, to read another art better, to read history better and better, history which remains as a result of science, the genealogies of the island-kingdom and its chronicle and the old poetry in this memory, and the love poetry of the old lore (*Poems of the Cywyddwyr*, xvii).

The scribe of the *White Book of Rhydderch* is unknown. The otherwise unidentified Hywel Fychan would seem to have been a lay copyist in the employ of Hopcyn ap Tomos. Gutun Owain was a fairly well-to-do poet. Sir Thomas ab Ieuan ap Deicws was a secular priest who had been to Rome and Elis Gruffydd a professional soldier in the service of Sir Robert Wingfield. This last trio all came from the north-east corner of Wales, and much identical material is found in their manuscripts suggesting that they were drawing on a fairly localized font of texts. This area became particularly important in the period of the sixteenth-century Welsh Renaissance and the careers of the three mirror certain aspects of Welsh life during their period. The years following 1282 were an era of transition and insecurity. Despite certain abortive attempts to renew Welsh rule, an English machinery of government became daily more evident. Welsh nobles and scions of the old native royal lines became important in the English government of the period. Men like Ieuan Llwyd and his family and Llywelyn ap Gwilym, the uncle of Dafydd ap Gwilym, were servants of the English Crown, *dosbarthwyr* or specialists in Welsh law, patrons of literature and of the poets. By the end of the fourteenth century nationalist sentiments began to manifest themselves, culminating in the revolt of Owain Glyndŵr. Hopcyn ap Tomos, as a master of native prophecy, was called upon to give predictions as to the outcome of that campaign 'in times of pain, need and exile'. Yet despite the racial hatred that followed Glyndŵr's rebellion, and which amply manifested itself in the poetry of that period, the Welsh during the Wars of the Roses became paradoxically more and more caught up in English affairs. Poets, in the ancient Welsh tradition, looked for a deliverer to rescue them from their political troubles and manifested that hope in the *canu brud*. In the end, these hopes were pinned on the person of Henry Tudor and the link with England was finally forged ideologically, as well as practically, when Henry won the battle of Bosworth in 1485, and hardened when his son promulgated the Act of Union in 1536. More and more Welshmen sought their fortunes in England and in the parts of France which were in English possession. Elis Gruffydd was one of these. It is the strengthening of the link with England, politically, religiously and culturally, that eventually brought about the limited cultural and religious movement referred to as the Welsh Renaissance. Elis Gruffydd was on the fringe of that Renaissance, translating humanist works yet still in touch with the native medieval traditions and preserving them.

What are the themes of the prose of these centuries of uncertainty, of 'sympathy and antipathy', in the words of Glyn Roberts, towards England? Compared with that of the centuries which immediately preceded them the tradition is an impoverished one. The above somewhat cursory survey of manuscript collections pinpoints the chief *genres* which were being copied—history, prophecy, science, medicine, genealogy and law, that is, functional texts or texts which are characteristic of the period. There is a paucity of original story prose.

All the manuscript collections hitherto mentioned contain some sort of historical writing, all of which is indebted to a greater or lesser extent to the works of Geoffrey of Monmouth. It might be fair to say that whereas before 1282 the most important factor in the shaping of the prose tradition was the promulgation of law texts, later the chief single influence was the work of Geoffrey. This is significant, for whereas it was the functional prose of everyday living that in the days of independent Wales formulated the dialogue of the *Mabinogi*, it was the idealism of a dreamer and inventor, basing his work on tradition and imagination, that determined the prose themes of a period of subjugation and uncertainty either directly or through foreign works which ultimately derived from the *Historia*.

The works of Geoffrey of Monmouth are indirectly Wales's greatest contribution to world literature, in that they gave to the world for the first time the Arthurian legend in its full flowering, the tradition of Merlin and his prophecies and a boldly conceived concept of British history connecting these islands with the classical past and with the fall of Troy in a way which was to influence historians for six centuries. The literary products of the end of the Middle Ages in Wales reflect very clearly these themes in prophetic and historical writings and in Arthurian texts which are based ultimately on Geoffrey's works.

Two of Geoffrey's three works had a far-reaching influence in Wales, namely the *Prophetiae Merlini* and the *Historia Regum Britanniae*. The *Historia* aimed at recording the history of Britain from the fall of Troy to the loss of overlordship to the Saxons in the seventh century. The Britons had their finest flowering during the period of Arthur. The *Historia* seems to have been 'published' first in 1136. It was soon translated into Welsh under the title *Brut y Brenhinedd*—there are in all six separate translations. Five copies survive from the thirteenth century, twelve from the fourteenth and four from the fifteenth. The early copies are close translations of the Latin original. Some of the later versions are new translations, much freer in their nature. The increasing interest in and influence of the *Brut* is shown by the fact that three completely new versions were formulated in the fourteenth century. Another version, often referred to as the *Red Book* version, probably compiled early in the fourteenth century, is a composite text, combining two earlier manuscript versions of the *Brut* and adding to them a text of the *Prophecies of Myrddin*. The version found in Peniarth 21 is another translation following Geoffrey's book fairly closely but incorporating the Welsh text *Lludd a Llefelys*. The Cotton Cleopatra version of the fourteenth century is yet another new translation where the process of adaptation of other material into the body of the *Historia* is much more obvious; this version is shorter than the Latin text since the translator has cut out speeches and descriptions of battles. There are, however, many additions which make it more narrative than the other translations. These additions come from a number of sources, the *Dream of Maxen,* Wace's *Brut* and various historical Latin texts. Another abridged version belonging to the fifteenth century is the so-called *Brut Tysilio*, which later centuries considered to represent the original *liber vetustissimus* on which Geoffrey's work was supposedly based.

In all the translations of the *Historia* there is an obvious attempt to equate the characters and episodes of Geoffrey's work with what is known of the same characters from the independent native Welsh tradition of the triads and the tales. It is evident from references to the characters of the *Brut* which occur in the poetry that it is through the medium of the Welsh translations that the poets became acquainted with Geoffrey's work. The attempt to equate the text with the traditions of 'Ynys Prydain' is manifested in several different ways. Traditional Welsh epithets were added to the names of famous heroes like Gwrtheyrn (Vortigern) Gwrthenau, Brochfael Ysgithrog, Gwerthefyr Fendigaid. There are echoes in the texts of the triads and of facts not known from Latin sources. In fact, all the versions to a greater or lesser degree illustrate the fusion that came about between the native bardic tradition and that of Geoffrey. The preservation of the historical traditions of the nation had always been part of the function of the poets. Just as material from the triads and from other traditional sources was grafted on to versions of the *Brut*, conversely the subject-matter of the *Brut* became fused with the native tradition and, in Rachel Bromwich's words, is 'the first of the great additions made from literary and external sources which received the *imprimatur* of the *Ynys Prydain* formula, and became accepted as belonging to the canonical body of bardic lore'. The Arthurian characters of the *Brut* during the period of the *cywydd* became an increasingly obvious element in the poetry and replaced traditional heroes in the later redactions of *Trioedd Ynys Prydain*.

During the fourteenth and fifteenth centuries certain mnemonic texts usually associated with bardic learning appear, following the traditional patterns of numerical rhetoric which seem to have been associated with native learning in Wales from the Dark Ages. These patterns involve a use of numerical symbolism combined with rhythmic and alliterative sentences. The mnemonic texts of the late Middle Ages are indebted to the wealth of Arthuriana which appeared to be flooding the Welsh literary market. Gutun Owain's manuscript, Llanstephan 28, included among its contents a list called: *Y Pedwar Brenin ar Hugain a farnwyd yn gadarnaf* (The Twenty-four Kings judged to be most strong). The text was probably no earlier than the mid-fifteenth century. Its purpose seems to have been to give a brief résumé of the most important kings mentioned in *Brut y Brenhinedd*, their achievements and the cities which they are said to have founded. The author seems to add information which had come to his knowledge from sources not found in the *Brut*. Some of this additional matter can be traced in chronicles and other writings later than the *Brut* and its translations. There is also information evidently drawn from Welsh tradition which appears especially in the section on Maxen Wledig. The text illustrates how *Brut y Brenhinedd* material was adapted and added to in the vernacular. Another Arthurian text which appears in the autograph of Gutun Owain is that entitled *Pedwar Marchog ar Hugain Llys Arthur* (The Twenty-four Knights of Arthur's Court). A triadic text, it lists the knights of Arthur's Court. I quote an example:

> Three Knights of Battle were in Arthur's Court: Cadwr Earl of Cornwall and Lanslod Lak, and Ywain son of Urien Rheged. The peculiarities of those were that they did not flee for fear of spear or sword or arrow; and Arthur was never shamed in battle on the day that he saw their faces in the field. And therefore were they called Knights of Battle.

According to Rachel Bromwich, of the twenty-four names in this list, two-thirds belong exclusively to the native Welsh narrative tradition or else were known in this tradition before they were utilized by the redactors of the *Brut* to render names in Geoffrey's *Historia*; the other third consists of adaptations of names derived from the *Historia Regum, Y Saint Greal*, and the thirteenth-century French Vulgate cycle of Arthurian prose romances.

Another numerical text which belongs to the period of the *cywyddwyr* of the fifteenth and sixteenth centuries is the *Tri Thlws ar Ddeg Ynys Prydain* (The Thirteen Treasures of the Island of Britain). The oldest version of this text belongs to Peniarth MS.51, written by Gwilym Tew. It consists of a bare listing of the treasures; later redactions amplify the detail. The list possibly goes back to a group of stories which connected not only Arthur but a number of other early heroes with otherworld visits. This item of the list taken from a copy in Peniarth MS. 77 refers to the *Romance of Owain*:

> The stone and ring of happy Luned which she gave in order to extricate Owain son of Urien who was between the gate and the portcullis struggling with the Black Knight of the Fountain. This ring had a stone in it, and if the stone were concealed, the one who concealed it would not be seen.

The earliest Arthurian story texts in Welsh to show Geoffrey's influence are probably the three Welsh Romances treated in Volume I. There is evidence that other less noteworthy Arthurian tales survive from the *cywydd* period which are indebted in a greater or lesser degree to the *Historia*. Mention was made in the first volume of the two stories of the thirteenth-century French Arthurian prose cycle, *La Queste del Saint Graal* and *Perlesvaus*, which were translated into Welsh as *Ystoryaeu Seint Greal*. Other parts of the Vulgate cycle were known in Wales, perhaps in translations into the vernacular. NLW Manuscript 1-A contains a fourteenth-century text of the *Birth of Arthur*. This text derives from the Merlin cycle but it is obvious from the proper names that the redactor was familiar with native legends connected with Merlin and also with Welsh redactions of *Brut y Brenhinedd*. There are other hints in the poetry of the fifteenth century that the poets were familiar with the Merlin cycle: for instance they recognized that Cai was Arthur's foster-brother, a tradition which must ultimately derive from some form of the prose *Merlin*, though the Welsh poets tacked the tradition on to a Welsh onomastic tale localized at Caer Gai in Merioneth; and as we shall see later, Elis Gruffydd's version of the Merlin legend is heavily indebted to the Vulgate text. Another branch of the Vulgate cycle, the *Lancelot*, was used by the redactor of some versions of the *Trioedd Ynys Prydain*. Rachel Bromwich has pointed out that this range of allusion to French romance is an indication of a movement in the fourteenth and fifteenth centuries towards greater awareness of the contemporary literary fashions of France and England; for the same Vulgate texts were popularized in England during the last quarter of the fifteenth century in the *Morte d'Arthur* of Sir Thomas Malory.

Apart from fragments of the great Arthurian Romance cycles, certain stories apocryphal to the *Historia* were also translated into Welsh. An example of this is *Ystori'r Llong Foel* (The Story of the Rudderless Boat). In the *Historia* Geoffrey tells how Brutus, the founder of the British nation, left Greece and wandered the seas with his followers until he landed at last in the Island of Britain which was at that time called Albion. The only inhabitants of the Island were a group of giants who were conquered and killed by Brutus and his men. After the publication of the *Historia*, and in the years when the book was studied as the chief source of British history, chroniclers and historians tried to trace the history back as far as possible by explaining the lineage of the first inhabitants of the island and the origin of the name Albion. The story in the different French, Latin and English versions varies in detail, but they all contain an account of the daughters of a certain king all of whom tried to kill their husbands: these daughters were punished by being sent into exile and turned away in a rudderless sail-less boat. The youngest daughter loved her husband too much to kill him and she was saved from her sisters' fate. The other daughters wandered the seas and landed through fate in the Island of Britain which was uninhabited. The island was called Albion after the eldest girl. Sometime after they settled, an *incubus* (or a devil in the shape of a man) visited the girls who gave birth to a race of giants. These were the giants with whom Brutus had to fight. The story is doubtless based on the classical story about Danaus, king of Argos. There were two main versions of this tale, both of which were translated into Welsh. In Welsh sources the first version always occurs with the text of the *Description of the Island of Britain*, at the commencement of the *Historia*, the second as an independent story. A variant text of the second version based on the English work of John Rastell, *The Pastyme of People. The cronycles of dyvers readings and most specially of the realms of England*, is found in Elis Gruffydd's writings. The story does not seem to have reached Wales before the fifteenth century and was not a direct result of the earliest spate of native interest in the *Brut*.

All these texts are in a sense fabulous amplifications of the basic stock of the *Brut*. The *Brut*, however, was an important factor in the historiography of the age in other ways. From the early fourteenth century, the texts of *Brut y Brenhinedd* (*vide* Volume I) are invariably coupled in the manuscripts with texts of *Brut y Tywysogion* and the *Ystoria Dared. Brut y Tywysogion* purported to be a chronological continuation of *Brut y Brenhinedd*, although in fact it represents a quite different historical *genre* and is based on monastic annals belonging to the period of Welsh independence. After 1282 other minor chronicles purport to carry on Geoffrey's narrative. One of these, the *Brut Brenhinedd y Saeson*, giving the history of the kings of England until 1382, is based on an English source. Another chronicle, *Teyrnasedd y Saeson*, found in Jesus MS. 141, is also derived from English material and extends to the fifteenth century. These records which belong to the fourteenth century are bare and brief and sometimes the references in them to Wales are limited. They are to an extent an expression of the searching for roots which is part of the Welsh and English contemporary climate of thought. Other manuscripts contain short chronicles directly relevant to Welsh life and history, in the tradition of the monastic annals.

An example of this trend is the so-called *Chronicle of Owain Glyndŵr*. Another short text which occurs in many manuscripts is *O Oes Gwrtheyrn Gwrthenau*.

The end of the Middle Ages was a period of increasing interest in general narrative histories. In England, works like the *Chronicles of London* and the *English Brute* were manifestations of this. The same interest perhaps inspired the syntheses found in the histories of Sir Thomas ab Ieuan ap Deicws and Elis Gruffydd. Both these writers attempted to write a history of the world; both of them had spent time outside Wales. How much either or both of them were influenced by Renaissance ideas is a moot point. Sir Thomas took as the basis of his work the *Fascisculus Temporum* of Werner Rolewinck. Werner was a Westphalian born at Laer near Hörstmar. Educated at Cologne University he took Carthusian Orders in 1447. He wrote in all some ten historical works and some forty religious treatises. The *Fascisculus Temporum* is the best known of his works. It was first printed in 1474, although it had been available before that date. The *Fascisculus* remained a standard historical work for some sixty years after its first printing. Sir Thomas prefixed to his history a colophon associated with the short text known as *Disgrifiad Ynys Prydain*, which is perhaps to be associated with other geographical-historical texts of a native kind like *Enwau Ynys Prydain*. The colophon and *Disgrifiad Ynys Prydain* derive ultimately from Ranulf Higden's *Polychronicon*. Other elements found in the history are sections from a Welsh chronicle and large sections of Genesis taken from *Y Bibl Ynghymraeg* and set out according to the pattern of the *Fascisculus Temporum*; the genealogy of Brutus is based on the work of Geoffrey of Monmouth together with sentences added here and there by Sir Thomas out of the Vulgate and also from his own thought and comment. An example of this is his homiletic note written when he records the birth of Christ:

> The most noteworthy time of all times and the chief for Christians is the birth of Christ of Mary the Virgin, the daugher of Joachim, according to human lineage and of the Father from Heaven by the grades and virtues of the Holy Spirit, according to Divine right. And thus, he is true God and true man and the only son of God, Creator and Redeemer of the World.

Elis Gruffydd's chronicle is more complex. Beginning with the Garden of Eden, Elis attempts to record the history of the world down to the year 1552. He used a great variety of sources which he had acquired in London, Wales and Calais: Higden's *Polychronicon*, Robert Fabian's *Chronicle*, Jean Froissart's work, the *English Brute*, the works of Geoffrey of Monmouth, of Guido de Cologne and of Robert Gauguin; and for Welsh history a text of *Brut y Tywysogion*. He also referred to some anonymous works using terms like 'English authors', 'Welsh authors' and 'French chronicles'. For the modern reader, the sections of the work which are most readable and exciting are those where Elis describes the events of his own day or his own personal experiences. He began the chronicle in 1530 with these words:

> After I settled down in Calais, I began to record world events with particular reference to the realm of England, the king still persisting in his love for Anne Boleyn who was very angry with the Cardinal of England.

In the service of Sir Robert Wingfield, he saw many of the crowned heads of his day. He witnessed the landing of Charles V at Dover; he went to the field of the Cloth of Gold and describes the day-to-day events of the meeting between Henry VIII and Francis I of France. Many of his descriptions are concerned with events of his own life. He described the drought in London in 1539 which was so great that salt water came up the Thames. Parts of these sections dealing with contemporary life are written in a dramatic and lively style which ensures for Elis an important place among the prose-writers of this period. He went to Calais with the guard in 1529 and describes the stormy and hazardous crossing. His boat set sail on a bad day, 'with a sky full of black clouds and winds which blew stormily out of the west'. The ship took anchor but was blown adrift with the force of the storm. All was chaotic; Elis lost all his best clothes given to him by his noble patrons; everyone took to praying to their patron saints,—'at that time my faith was as weak as that of any other man so that I promised to go by foot with a penny for Saint Dwynwen as soon as God and the saints would give me leave to place a foot on the soil of England'.

The chronicle continues until the year 1552, by which time Elis would seem to be an old man. Its last sentence charges some compatriot to bear the work home to a relative of Elis in Wales:

> May thou come safely from the possession of Elis Gruffydd, the soldier of Calais, into the hand of Thomas son of Thomas son of Siôn son of Gruffydd Fychan, to Pant y Llongdy in Gwespyr in the parish of Llan Asaph in Flintshire in Tegeingl.

Fortunately this thesaurus of Welsh prose did not get lost in a storm and survived as a witness to the prose-writing of that period! Apart from its function as a chronicle and a record of contemporary events, Elis Gruffydd has preserved a number of stories and traditions which suggest that the art of story-telling had not completely died out. At the end of the sixteenth century, a document belonging to the Council of the Marches refers to the continued oral practice of the art:

> Upon the Sondaies and hollidaies the multitude of all sortes of men woomen and childerne of everie parishe doe use to meete in sondrie places either one some hill or one the side of some mountaine where their harpers and crowthers singe them songs of the doeings of their auncestors, namelie, of theire warrs againste the kings of this realme and the English nacion, and then doe they ripp upp theire petigres at lenght howe eche of them is discended from those theire ould princs. Here alsoe do they spende theire time in hearinge some part of the lives of Thalaassyn ('Taliesin'), Marlin ('Myrddin'), Beno ('Beuno'), Pybbye ('Cybi'), Jermon ('Garmon'), and suche other the intended prophetts and saincts of that cuntrie.

Attention was drawn to most of the major story texts of the whole of the Middle Ages by Brynley Roberts in Volume I. Some of these texts like the translations of the *Saint Greal* and the story of *Amlyn ac Amig* belong to the *cywydd* period. Notable as a translation which had a recurrent popularity was *Chwedlau Saith Ddoethion Rhufain*. The earliest version of this text is found in the *Red Book of Hergest* and is thought to be the work of Llywelyn Offeiriad. It represents a Welsh reworking of the *Seven Sages of Rome* theme; the collection is a series of stories relating how the Sages of Rome endeavoured to save the emperor's son from his jealous stepmother. It is remarkable because of the way in which the redactor uses the style and idiom of classic Welsh *cyfarwyddyd* and because he has added two new stories to the original stock. This *Red Book* redaction of the *Seven Sages* is not the only one found in Welsh. Another belonging to a slightly later period and in different language was produced probably in south Wales, possibly in Glamorgan from an English version, and preserved and copied in the writings of Glamorgan scribes like Llywelyn Siôn. This later redaction testifies to the continued interest which the *Seven Sages* seemed to hold for the Welsh *littérateur*. An example of a development of one of the stories in the collection is seen in the story of *Alexander and Lodwig* found in one of the manuscripts of Llywelyn Siôn, who was the most important of the late sixteenth-century Glamorgan scribes. The story is set within the framework of the prophecy that the parents shall bow down before their son. This motif is found among the original nucleus of the *Seven Sages of Rome* and is referred to as the *Vaticinium* motif. In *Alexander and Lodwig* this theme is combined with the motif of the faithful friends most familiar in Welsh from the text of *Amlyn ac Amig*. Although this combination of themes is found in versions of the *Vaticinium* in other languages it is not certain from which particular version the Welsh text derives. The language of the text and the English loan words suggest that the source might be an English version. In the manuscript of Llywelyn Siôn the story precedes a copy of the later redaction of the *Seven Sages of Rome*. This text, it was suggested by G. J. Williams many years ago, was one of a number translated by a school of scribes at work in the sixteenth century in Glamorgan. The prose found in these texts follows the pattern of the Middle Ages rather than that of the Renaissance humanists. More recent scholarship suggests that the works themselves do not necessarily derive from Glamorgan; most, however, probably belong to south Wales.

These texts consist of both religious works and secular narrative. *Dives a Phawper*, a religious work, is the translation of an English book by Henry Parker which was published in 1493. *Darn o'r Ffestifal* (Hafod MS. 22) is a translation of a collection of homilies written by John Mirk, prior of the monastery of Lilleshall in Shropshire and published by Caxton in 1483. The text, according to Professor Henry Lewis, showed characteristics of the dialect of Dyfed and Professor Geraint Gruffydd has argued that the translated sections of the New Testament found in the same manuscript, together with the Welsh translations of the litany and of the *Order of Communion* of Thomas Cranmer, were all the work of a man who belonged to the bishopric of Saint David's, and probably the products of a Protestant drive in that bishopric between 1536 and 1552. Another text which possibly emanated from the same source was the *Gesta Romanorum*, a collection of moralizing anecdotes for the use of preachers, composed in Latin at the beginning of the fourteenth century. These stories were translated into English at an early date and perhaps from the English found their way into Welsh. A story text coupled by Professor G. J. Williams with these other compilations was *Y Marchog Crwydrad*, a translation of William Goodyeare's English version of the French *Voyage de Chevalier Errant*. A story based on the medieval *Chevalier Errant* theme and written in the form of an allegory, and reminiscent of *Pilgrim's Progress*, it seeks to demonstrate the human weakness for pursuing empty and vainglorious paths. The heading of the first section reads:

> The wandering knight shows his foolish intention and senseless adventure in desiring and thinking to find happiness in this life.

The *Marchog Crwydrad* is written like the other texts in a prose which is in direct lineage of the prose of the Middle Ages:

> A minnau yn bwriadu myned i'm taith, mi a ddeallais fod yn rhaid im gael cyngor, drwy wybod mai pob peth ag a wneler heb gyngor da, ni ddaw i ddiwedd da. Y peth yn ddeallus a ddechreuir, yn ddawnus y diweddir.
>
> [And as I was about to set out on my journey, I understood that I must take advice, knowing that everything which might be done without good advice would not come to a good end. That which is initiated intelligently ends well.]

The last of the sixteenth-century works which Professor G. J. Williams thought might have originated in Glamorgan was the recusant *Drych Cristianogawl*. It has by now been proved that it is the work of a north Walian, Robert Gwyn, but this work again is written in a style far removed from the Ciceronianism of the other humanists of the sixteenth century. The importance of all these compilations of the sixteenth century is that they show that whereas one section of the Welsh literate class at that time was abandoning the parataxis of medieval prose for the syntaxis of classical models, another section was continuing to follow the pattern set down in previous centuries within the confines of the Welsh tradition. They also attest to the constant influx of material into Welsh from the other side of Offa's Dyke.

The texts discussed in this last section were all translations, some of them works of length and importance like *Y Marchog Crwydrad* and *Saith Ddoethion Rhufain*. Story texts of less importance but of equal interest also survive attesting to a continued, if impoverished, tradition of story-telling, on a native level. Some of these are preserved in compilations like Elis Gruffydd's chronicle. Others are preserved in late copies but internal evidence suggests their existence at a much earlier date. Two texts recorded by Elis which preserve folk-tale themes are the story of *Maelgwn Gwynedd's Wife and Ring* and the story of *Llywelyn ab Iorwerth and Cynwrig Goch of Trefriw*. The latter is also found in one of Gutun Owain's manuscripts. It is sometimes difficult to be sure whether Elis acquired his stories from an oral or a written source: he himself speaks of written texts. The story relating to Maelgwn Gwynedd contains a version of the folk-tale motif knows as *Polycrates's Ring*. The theme is found in other Celtic sources such as the *Life of Saint Kentigern* and the Irish story, *Tain Bó Fraich*. In this Welsh version, the wife of Maelgwn Gwynedd loses a precious ring (which she owned jointly with King Maelgwn) in the sea while walking on the rocks above Degannwy. This loss causes such grief that she sent a message to Saint Asaph who told the story to the angry king. The ring was eventually found in the belly of a salmon, the king was appeased and all forgiven.

Two versions of the story of *Llywelyn ab Iorwerth and Cynwrig Goch of Trefriw* have survived, one in Elis Gruffydd's chronicle, the other in Gutun Owain's manuscript. The story tells how Llywelyn ab Iorwerth met a Strange Red Man who went with him to London and how he was helped by this man to outwit the English in a contest of conjury at the king's court. The story is connected with Trefriw and one version pays particular attention to St Mary of Trefriw. It seems likely that the story was current in north-east Wales and that Gutun Owain and Elis Gruffydd alike were drawing on a particular local tradition, a font of material connected with that locality. A later scribe who drew on the same font was John Jones, Gellilyfdy. A unique text copied by John Jones is *Ystoria Ysgan ab Asgo, Arglwydd Bodeugan*. John Jones copied the text in 1608, but the language would suggest that it came from an earlier exemplar. The story tells how Ysgan ab Asgo, lord of Bodeugan in Isaled, seeing people dying about him decided to flee from death. After wandering, he reached a fortress where he was joyfully received but warned by the inhabitants not to visit a neighbouring hill. One day he disregarded the warning, went to the hill, and saw there countless souls in agony. When he returned to the fortress he told what he had seen and was ordered to return home to Bodeugan. In his own country he found that everything had changed. On inquiry, the inhabitants told him that ages before there had been a lord called Ysgan ab Asgo. He then went away and returned to the fortress where he had found such joy and happiness. He still lives there in paradise with Elias and Enoch. The themes of the story, the otherworld visit, the Rip van Winkle motif and the flight from death are interesting. The last motif is not found in other sources. The style of the story is reminiscent of the pattern of medieval tales. It begins by setting the scene: 'Ysgan ab Asgo was Lord of Bodeugan in Isaled.' The dialogue is punctuated with typical medieval oaths and tags:

> Ac ymaith y kerddodd ef ar ddiwenfa oni weles gastell tec ar berfedd y llynn mwyia a'r a welsai ef erioed; ac ysgraff a welai ef wrth did ynglann y llynn; a'i varch a rwymodd wrth brenn ac i'r ysgraff yr aeth; a thy ar kastell y rhwyfodd. A'r nifer bychan oedd yn y kastell a'i derbynniassant ef yn barchvs, a gofyn iddo i hynt. 'Dioer,' heb ef, 'ffo yr wyf rhag angav.' 'Llyma,' heb wyntav, 'le da i ti, pan ni byddwn veirw oni el y llynn yn hysbydd oll.' 'Pa dravl ysydd ar y llynn?' 'Nid oes dim,' heb wyntav, 'oddierth a ddykom i gyweirio bwyd'. 'A dderfydd ef o'r diwedd gan hynny?' heb ef. 'Derfydd,' heb wynt. 'Gan hynny,' heb ef, 'ni thrigaf i yma ddim a vo hwy.'

> [And then he went on his wanderings until he saw a fair castle in the midst of the largest lake that he had ever seen; and he saw a boat tied up on the shore of the lake; and he bound his horse to a tree and went to the boat, and rowed to the castle. And the small number who were in the castle received him respectfully and asked him his journey. 'God knows,' he said, 'I am fleeing from death.' 'Here,' they said, 'is a good place for you whence we shall not die, save that the lake be used up.' 'What calls are there on the lake?' 'There are none,' they said, 'save what we may take from it to prepare food.' 'Will it be exhausted in the end from that?' he said. 'It will,' they said. 'For that reason,' he said, 'I shall not remain here a moment longer.']

These minor texts attest to the continued tradition of story-telling albeit on a folk-tale level. Other stories preserved in later manuscripts indicate that the tradition was perhaps stronger than contemporary sources would suggest. In the year 1600, Siôn Dafydd Rhys, the Welsh humanist, copied a series of tales about giants. In

1585, a scribe, possibly David Thomas from Parc y Prat, copied into BM Egerton MS. 2586, a series of stories from Dyfed. Some stories with an obviously medieval origin are referred to at an even later date. *Trioedd Ynys Prydein* lists the hero March fab Meirchion, the King Mark of the Tristan legend, and the heroine Tegau Eurfron. No stories about them have survived from a Welsh medieval source. In the nineteenth century, Sir John Rhŷs recorded in the Llŷn peninsula the orally transmitted tale of March, a king who, like Midas, had horse's ears. Gwallter Mechain in the eighteenth century recorded the story of Tegau Eurfron and Tristfardd, the poet of Urien Rheged. The story, as he recorded it, is concerned with the theme of testing the chastity of the women of Arthur's court with (1) a mantle that only a faithful wife can wear, (2) a drinking horn from which only the husband of a faithful wife may drink, and (3) a boar's head that no cuckold's knife may cut. Some of these motifs are found in Arthurian romances like the *Lanzelet* of Ulrich von Zatzikhoven and also in a lowland Scottish ballad, *The Boy and the Mantle*. Late texts like these only serve as a reminder of the enormous wealth of earlier story, which must have been lost.

The quotation from the document belonging to the Council of the Marches mentioned the heroes of two Welsh sagas which had a continuous history in Wales throughout the Middle Ages: Taliesin and Myrddin. Their legends were both discussed in Volume 1. The fourteenth-century *Book of Taliesin* contains poems which derive perhaps from the ninth century depicting the poet Taliesin as a visitor to the court of Maelgwn Gwynedd. These poems suggest that Taliesin was the central figure in a series of stories of a semi-mythological nature involving various mythological characters like Gwydion fab Dôn. Some of the poems contain transformation passages similar to those found in very early Irish sources, such as the poems attributed to Amairgen in the *Lebor Gabála*. These mythological traditions about Taliesin were long current in Wales. A saga existed which was a mixture of prose and verse. None of the prose sections of this saga have survived from a period earlier than that of Elis Gruffydd. His chronicle contains a rather garbled version of the prose story which, he says, was well known (*sathredig*) throughout Wales. The story tells how the boy Gwion Bach received the magic drops of poetic inspiration from Ceridwen's cauldron. After a series of transformations he was reborn eventually as the boy Taliesin who was fostered by the son of Gwyddno

Garanhir, known as Elffin, and later was successful in a poetic contest against the bards of Maelgwn Gwynedd at Degannwy. Through the popularity of this saga, Taliesin had become regarded as the mantic poet *par excellence* of Welsh tradition. His name was at an early date coupled with that of the prophet poet *par excellence*, Myrddin.

Myrddin is regarded by some as a historical person of the sixth century, by others as a solely legendary figure whose name was originally Llallogan. As early as the tenth century his name is cited in *Armes Prydain* as that of a great political prophet. A group of slightly later poems allude to a story about Myrddin's life, according to which Myrddin was a north-British warrior who fought at the battle of Arfderydd in Cumberland where his lord, Gwenddolau, was slain. Myrddin became insane as the result of the battle and spent many years as a wild man in the forest of Celyddon where he lived in terror of King Rhydderch. One of the poems in the *Red Book of Hergest*, the *Cyfoesi*, is in the form of a dialogue between Myrddin and a certain Gwenddydd who is generally represented as his sister.

Native traditions about Myrddin were taken up by Geoffrey of Monmouth who transformed his name to *Merlin* and devoted two works to him; the *Prophetiae Merlini* and the *Vita Merlini*. Geoffrey in the *Prophetiae* confused traditions about the wonder-boy Ambrosius associated with Vortigern and traditions about Myrddin so much that Giraldus Cambrensis subsequently distinguished two Merlins: Merlin Silvester, the Myrddin Wyllt of Welsh tradition, and Merlin Ambrosius, the Merlin of the *Prophetiae*. The ramifications of the Merlin legend in later European literature are many. When Elis Gruffydd devoted a long section of his chronicle to give the first Welsh prose synthesis of the Myrddin traditions, he drew his material from a variety of sources, both native and European: from texts deriving from Geoffrey of Monmouth, from the French Romances and from native oral sources. To these he added a great deal of the prophetic material which was circulating in Britain and episodes from the story of Taliesin whom he regarded as Myrddin in another form. One of the most interesting parts of this compilation is the tale of Myrddin Wyllt localized in the Conway Valley which derives ultimately from an oral source. According to this story Myrddin, a wild man of the woods, is visited by his sister, Gwenddydd, who tells him of her five dreams which he then proceeds to interpret. The dreams consist of vague vaticinations which are difficult to date, though it has been suggested that the social criticism voiced in them is not unlike that of William Langland's *Piers Plowman* deriving from the second half of the fourteenth century:

> Gwenddydd and my dearest sister, do not marvel too much at thy vision, for no harm will come to thee from it. And be it known to thee that the field thou sawest represents this island. And the small cairns represent the husbandmen of the kingdom and its labourers of each and every grade who live lawfully and win their livelihood by the labour of their bodies and put their trust in God alone. And the big cairns represent the chiefs of the kingdom of each and every grade. And the peoples whom thou sawest gathering the stones from the small cairns and casting them into the big ones represent the servants of noblemen who are and always will be ready to keep their servants to take the wealth of the labourers and the husbandmen without ceasing for ever, sometimes under pretence of the offices of the law, sometimes by force, sometimes by stealth.

Geoffrey of Monmouth's *Prophetiae Merlini* was a milestone in the history of political prophecy in Britain and in Europe and no survey of the prose of the *cywydd* period in Welsh could be complete without some reference to this *genre*. Geoffrey's version of the story of Merlin as found in the *Prophetiae*, which he later modified in the *Vita Merlini*, is based on the tale found in the *Historia Brittonum* of the wonder-boy whose blood was needed to secure the foundations of Vortigern's citadel in Snowdonia. According to Geoffrey, the wonder-boy's name is Merlin. After finding two dragons Merlin proceeds to explain their symbolism and then utters a series of prophecies. In true Celtic fashion, the first of these consists of a listing of events already past, like the conquests of Arthur: a listing used to give credence to predictions about the future (a device seen in the vision of the kings in Shakespeare's *Macbeth*). The predictions begin with a series of prophecies relating to the Anglo-Norman kings, foretelling the overthrow of the Norman power and promising the return of the traditional Welsh heroes, Cynan and Cadwaladr. The longest part of the prophecy is, however, in obscure symbolic language ending with a description of the end of the world expressed in astrological terms:

> The tail of the Scorpion shall breed lightning and the Crab shall fall at strife with the Sun. The Virgin shall forget her maiden shame and climb up on the back of the Sagittary. The chariot of the Moon shall disturb the Zodiac, and the Pleiades shall burst into tears and lamentations.

The prophecy is marked by a series of recurring motifs, for instance that of a struggle between a dragon and a man, periods of moral depravity, famine and pestilence and by the use of animal symbols.

The prophecy started a fashion in European literature for the use of animal symbolism in vaticination, a device long familiar in Celtic prophetic verse. This fashion was doubtless encouraged by the popularity of bestiary literature. In Wales, it started a fashion in prose prophecy; for earlier Welsh vaticination is all in verse. The *Prophetiae* were translated into Welsh at an early date and were included in the earliest Welsh translations of the *Brut*. Versions of the text also circulated independently during the fourteenth and fifteenth centuries. The popularity of the *Prophetiae* is further illustrated by the number of commentaries on it found in Welsh sources, ranging from the relatively simple one found in the thirteenth-century manuscript, Peniarth 16, to the elaborate commentary of Alanus de Insulis translated in the sixteenth century. Another of Geoffrey's prophecies which gained pre-eminence in Wales was *The Prophecy of the Eagle at Shaftesbury* known in Latin as *Prophetiae Merlini Silvestris*, a prophecy concerned with the struggle between the Red and White Dragons. It was referred to by the Welsh as *Y Broffwydoliaeth Fawr* (The Great Prophecy) as contrasted with *Y Broffwydoliaeth Fer* (The Short Prophecy).

Apart from these Gaufridian prophecies a great number of other prose prophecies became associated with Myrddin. Many of them derive from English sources. The fourteenth and fifteenth centuries were politically tempestuous times for the English throne. The uncertainty of the times shared by the Welsh was reflected in the political prophecy. There survive in Welsh prophecies which are adaptations of English and Scottish material like *The Prophecy of the Six Kings to follow King John*, which was a continuation of the *Prophetiae Merlini*. *The Prophecy of the Lily, the Lion and the Son of Man* was written around the French wars of Edward III. Another prophecy concerned a sacred ampulla which was sent to Richard II when he was a prisoner in the Tower of London. Some

Welsh prophecies seem comparatively free from English influence and continue native patterns in vaticination, preserving motifs which seem to be of considerable antiquity like the dragon struggle, or the names of traditional battles like the battle of Cors Fochno. A notable example of this kind of prophecy is the *Prophecy of the Eagle from Gwynedd is Conwy*. The prophecy is written in the form of a dialogue between Myrddin and Gwenddydd. The framework of the prophecy, its dialogue form, is taken from the *Cyfoesi*. There is mention of the battle of Cors Fochno and of the dragon struggle. Other features are the passages of rhetorical prose. At one juncture it is prophesied that a certain knight will appear,

> riding a pale-white horse with a red-gold saddle and a gown of red gold about the knight and azure eagles on the red and red eagles on the azure.

This prophecy is only one of a vast number preserved in the manuscripts of the period. Some consist entirely of passages of *araith* and a notable collection is found in the Glamorgan manuscript, *Y Cwta Cyfarwydd*. Their content and themes are echoed in the prophetic poetry and they were used as political propaganda by leaders like Owain Glyndŵr.

In Volume I a chapter was devoted to functional prose, namely religious, legal and miscellaneous technical and scientific texts. Traditions of prose-writing of this nature persisted during the latter part of the Middle Ages, sometimes showing interesting developments. One of the greatest treasures of the classical prose tradition of Wales is the prose of the lawyers. The Welsh law books show an almost unparalleled variety of styles. Although many of the law manuscripts were written before 1300, new law books continued to be compiled after that date to meet the needs of the hybrid legal situation that continued in Wales until 1536. Some of the important literary patrons of the later period, like Rhydderch ab Ieuan Llwyd, were authorities on the Law of Hywel. The later law compilations are interesting not only because they preserve stray archaisms, but also because they show a persistent tendency to fabricate and create anew using the patterns and formulae of the traditional law. One of these late fabrications is the so-called 'Charter of Hywel Dda' which fathers a series of rules, reflecting a struggle between Church and State, on the tenth-century Hywel Dda:

> When Howel the good, King of Wales, modified the laws of Wales, he permitted various privileges to various persons of his kingdom. And, the first place, he permitted every ecclesiastical lord, such as the archbishop of Menevia, or other bishops and abbots, royal privilege for holding pleas among their laics by the common law of Wales . . .

> Four things the king preserved in his own hand: one is making coin; the second is making law; the third is, maintaining the privilege of the croziers of the kingdom; the fourth is punishment of the person who commits illegality on the highways.

Outside the law-books, documents survive, showing an organic growth on the old stock of the laws suggesting that there were lawmen at work who were still using the old phraseology of the laws of Hywel to coin new compilations to meet the specific needs of the period. An example of this activity is to be seen in the texts called *cydfodau* which are treaties or indentures made between various local communities defining their rights and settling terms of peaceful co-existence between them. The need for these agreements sprang from a number of causes, the fundamental one being the fragmentary nature of Welsh political geography from time immemorial. One of these *cydfodau* was made between Presteigne, Gwerthrynion, Morton and the three commotes of Deuddwr six years after the war of Owain Glyndŵr. The *cydfod* is in the alliterative highly rhetorical style typical of those passages of the Law of Hywel which relate to Procedure:

> A hefyd o bydd neb ac esgus iddo, doed esgusodwr a'i wirio ar ei lw i'r esgus, sef ŷnt yr esgusodion gosodedig yn y gydfod hon: llif a llanw, briw a brath, clefyd gorweiddiog neu garchar cynnogn oddieithr am dda arglwydd, ac na bo i neb am dda brynu a gwerthu wedi dydd y gydfod hon, atebed ohono yn ôl y gydfod rhag llaw; am hynny cymered pawb a wertho da fach a goelio o'i wlad ei hun.

> [And also, if there be anyone with an essoign, let an essoigner come and affirm the essoign by his oath. These are the established essoigns: flow and tide, hurt and wound, prostrating illness or debtor's prison, save for a lord's goods, and lest anyone buy and sell for profit after the day of this covenant, let him answer according to the covenant forthwith; for that reason, let anyone who sells goods take a surety whom he may trust from his own country.]

A work which should be put in the same category as these late legal documents is one of the famous compositions connected with the bardic orders, the *Statute of Gruffudd ap Cynan*. Three versions survive, all from the sixteenth century. The statute defines the rights and duties of the various classes of poets and is attributed to the twelfth-century princes Gruffudd ap Cynan and Rhys ap Tewdwr. No scholar would claim that it derives from that period, though archaic elements in it suggest that some of the material in it is very ancient. It should be looked upon as a patchwork made up of older materials and as a prose type might be compared with legal documents such as the 'Charter of Hywel Dda'. It must be left to others to deal with its significance in the history of the bardic orders where it is probably the last bid of a declining order to state its rights in a rapidly changing society.

Other prose works and exercises remain as monuments to the poets' activities during this later period. Two chapters have been devoted to the grammars and mention has been made of numerical texts like the *Twenty-four Knights of Arthur's Court. Trioedd Ynys Prydain* had a cumulative history during this period. Other series of triads were also composed as indexes to facts, like the schematic numerical text *Trioedd Arbennig* listing scientific, biblical and apocryphal facts:

> The three special triads:
> The three 'personae' in heaven,
> The three kings who worshipped Christ, Jasper, Melchior,
> Balthazar, and
> The three divisions of the earth, Asia, Africa, Europe.

Series of gnomic triads were compiled which were fundamental exercises in style. The earliest text of triads of this kind is found in the *White Book of Rhydderch* but manuscripts of the fifteenth and sixteenth centuries contain increasing numbers of copies of these series. Like the *Areithiau Pros*, the triads are marked by the rhetorical devices of alliteration, compound words and collocation:

> Tri pheth i arddyrchafel gŵr,
> gwraig ddihun ddiwair,
> ac arglwydd diwyd cadarn,
> a difflais heddwch.

[Three things that exalt a man,
a wakeful, chaste wife,
a strong industrious lord,
and unflinching peace.]

Tri peth a ddarestwng gŵr,
dryctir,
a drygwraig,
a drygarglwydd.

[Three things that demote a man,
bad land,
and a bad wife,
and a bad lord.]

There are constant echoes of these triads in the *cywydd* poetry:

Tri pheth a gerir drwy'r byd
Gwraig a hinon ac iechyd.

[Three things are loved in the world
A wife and fair weather and health.]

and at a slightly later period they inspired various aspects of the style of humanists like William Salesbury, who included a text of them in his printed volume *Y Diarebion Camberaec*, and whose own predilection for the arranging of words in triplets: *dirvawr profit* (enormous profit), *budd anveidrawl* (immeasurable gain) and *lleshad afrifed* (countless benefit); *yn ddoethion* (wise), *yn ddyscedic* (learned) *ac yn gymen* (and fitting), reflect his familiarity with them.

The prose of the poets and that of the lawyers had its roots (with the exception of the bardic grammars) in what were primarily native traditions. Other *genres* of functional prose found in Welsh are foreign in their origin. Two types of writing deserve special mention, namely religious prose and miscellaneous scientific and philosophical texts. Of the latter it is the medical compilations that are in some ways the most interesting.

There existed in medieval Wales a fluid and continuous tradition of medical writing. This persisted until the seventeenth century. A reflection of the fluidity of the tradition can be seen in a brief note found in a manuscript which belonged to a copyist of the end of the sixteenth and early seventeenth centuries, Thomas Evans of Hendre-forfudd:

> This book was put together from various collections of the work of physicians and doctors, namely Rhiwallon the doctor and his sons, Cadwgan, Gruffydd and Einion. Some call them the doctors of Myddfai . . . also the work of Volvisianus, Aristotoles and others. Here is copied part of the book of Sir Gwytherin Bongam, Trawsfynydd, and others.

The basic stock of these medical collections consisted of lists of recipes, uroscopies, instructions for bloodletting and simple surgery and treatises on humoural science. The earliest manuscript collection stems from the mid-fourteenth century and many other subsequent collections were made containing the same matter arranged in very various ways. Two notable late collections were the so-called *Welsh Leechbook* which was copied in the sixteenth century and Sotheby MS.2, *Llyfr Bened Feddyg,* which belonged to a Flintshire family of doctors in the early sixteenth century. Although most of the matter of these collections was already old in Welsh by the fifteenth century, there were continual additions to the basic stock. A notable example of this is to be seen in Sotheby MS. 2 where sometime in the early sixteenth century Sir Thomas ab Ieuan ap Deicws added a translation of the foreword to an English version of the *Calendrier des Bergères*, a medieval encyclopaedic work which was known in a garbled English version as the *Compot of Ptolemy*, and was as such copied by Elis Gruffydd. Mostyn MS 88, Gutun Owain's manuscript, already mentioned, shows how medical material from a slightly different source was being absorbed into Welsh. The manuscript contains a calendar and medical drawings similar to those found in the stationers' copies which were usually available in University towns, such as Oxford and Cambridge. The stationer was usually appointed by the University to keep within its precincts all the manuscript books considered necessary for study, either for sale or for loan. The manuscript includes a figure of a bleeding man, showing the sites for venesections together with the relevant indications including one which is a hackneyed medieval medical joke:

> Bleeding from the two veins under the armpits causes death from laughing.

Another illustration in the same manuscript shows an incompletely coloured cycle of urines, a frequently used device for showing the diagnostic significance of urine colours. These descriptions have their origins in the Hippocratic literature. In Mostyn MS. 88 the illustration is accompanied by the text of a uroscopy.

Many other miscellaneous technical texts were constantly being absorbed into the Welsh tradition. There were miscellaneous charms; other works, like the hunting text, the *Naw Helwriaeth* (Nine Kinds of Hunting), perhaps mirror a fashion for works on hunting which prevailed in the fifteenth century in England: one technical text, a 'Treatise on the Management of Mills' (*Traethawd ar Felinyddiaeth*), employs the same numerical rhetorical patterns as distinguish the prose of the lawyers and poets:

> There are seven concealed things in a mill: freezing the small millrace and burning the shaft; breaking the sail or bags; losing water through the dam or some other place; the wedge breaking free from the top of the bridge; the nails of the cogs being free; the top being free in the hook; the miller missing the action.

Some texts represent translations of works of some importance in the contemporary European world. Such a text is the translation of Theophrastes's *Marriages*. This work, a fragment of a classical text, the *Aureolus*, preserved by Saint Jerome, influenced Juvenal's *Satire on Women* and medieval writers like Chaucer, and was translated by Boccaccio into Italian and by the priest Sir Huw Pennant into Welsh:

> This is the book of Theophrastes concerning marriages, in which the question is posed 'Should a wise scholar take a wife?' And if after posing the question, this was the answer given: 'If she be fair, if her habits be good, if she spring from gentle parents and if he be healthy and wealthy,' Theophrastes says, 'Perhaps it be more justified than otherwise.' The reason why a wise scholar should not marry is that it hinders the pursuit of wisdom and no one can serve equally books and a wife, because a wife must have many things, namely valuable clothes, gold and silver, gems, jewels, gilded seats and couches, great expenses and various furnishings.

Another technical work which reflects European fashions of the fourteenth and fifteenth centuries, but which is also deeply interlinked with the native Welsh tradition, is a treatise on heraldry, known by the Welsh title *Llyfr Arfau* (The Book of Arms) or *Dosbarth Arfau* (The Classification of Arms). Genealogy and later heraldry were subjects of primary interest to the Welsh bards and the earliest copy of this treatise is to be found in one of Gutun Owain's manuscripts. The work has been associated with the name of one Siôn Trefor, or John Trevor. The editor of the Welsh text, the late Professor E. J. Jones, maintained that the work should be compared with a Latin treatise on arms, the *Tractatus de Armis* (the oldest known work on heraldry by a native of Britain) attributed in one copy to a Johannes de Bado Aureo. Professor Jones argued that the title *de Bado Aureo* was in fact a pun on the Welsh name *Trefor* and that Siôn Trefor, alias Johannes de Bado Aureo, was an authority on heraldry who became bishop of St Asaph. If the identification of the author with the bishop of St Asaph be correct, Siôn Trefor had in fact in the 1380s taken part in an important heraldic case at the king's court involving families prominent on the Welsh border. He was also related to several well-known *cywydd-wyr*. The treatise, as it stands, is more than a description of arms, for it contains interesting references to works on natural history and reflects a wide knowledge of medieval law:

> And so every honourable man of rank can bear arms, even if they were not inherited. And if he had exalted in dignity by virtue of learning, knowledge, or wisdom and bravery or by graduation for, as Bartholus says, any man who had studied for twenty years is a dubbed knight—it is becoming that arms be granted to him and to anyone as he has risen in rank. And in the same place Bartholus asks a question: Can anyone bear another's arms? And he replies himself that he cannot, and that anyone who does this can be forbidden to do so: for any notary who uses the device of another notary is guilty of offence and in this the law agrees.

The *Llyfr Arfau* is important because for the first time a man of a cosmopolitan background records the general theories of heraldry in its own vernacular for a nation much preoccupied with matters of nobility and ancestry. Another text of the later Middle Ages has been attributed to Siôn Trefor, namely a translation of the *Life of Saint Martin*, a close rendering of a medieval *Vita* consisting of selections from the *Life* by Sulpicius Severus, from his *Epistulae* and *Dialogi*, and from the *Historia Regum Francorum* of Gregory of Tours. Like the *Llyfr Arfau*, it is also found in one of Gutun Owain's manuscripts.

As in the case of secular original works, the best-known religious texts in Welsh had already been translated at the beginning of the *cywydd* period. Copies of most of them are already to be found in *Llyfr yr Ancr*, which was written in 1346. The tradition of copying and circulating these texts did not however cease in 1346, and manuscripts of the fifteenth and sixteenth centuries contain many copies of old favourites like *Cysegrlan Fuchedd*. Some new texts were also translated like *Pymtheg Gweddi San Ffraid* (The Fifteen Prayers of Saint Birgitte). Reference has already been made to the *Life of Saint Martin*, and it is late in the period that the translations of saints' lives from the *Legenda Aurea* of Jacobus de Voragine, which are attributed to Sir Huw Pennant, were made. Many native saints' lives must also belong to this period, although the earliest manuscript copies, made by Roger Morris of Coed y Talwrn, spring from a period some century later. Included in his collection are the Lives of Saint Collen, of Saint Llawddog, of Ieuan gwas Padrig, and part of the Life of Saint Curig. These native lives preserve the traditional style of medieval religious *cyfarwyddyd*. I quote a translation of the opening passage of *Buchedd Collen* as an example; it opens with the traditional genealogy:

> Here is the story of Collen and his life. Collen ap Gwynog ap Cadebog ap Cawrdaf ap Caradog Freichfras. Caradog Freichfras struck his arm in the Battle of Hiraddug and from that hurt one arm became longer than the other. And for that reason he was called *Breichfras* ('Big Arm') son of King Lear, who was married to Margaret daughter of the Earl of Oxford. Saint Collen's mother was the Irish woman Eithinen daughter of Matholwch, Lord of Ireland.

Mention has already been made of the religious works attributed to the so-called Glamorgan school of translators. Most of these were translations of Catholic works belonging to the England of the fifteenth century: others by the early sixteenth century, like the contents of Hafod MS. 22, reveal signs of a new age and a new religion.

These, then, are the kinds of prose which were circulating in Wales between 1345 and 1546. They demonstrate the persistence of old fashions and the continuity of a tradition of copying and translating from other languages. Mention has been made time and again of the style and language of the prose of the Middle Ages and of the changes that came about in the sixteenth century. What exactly are the characteristics of the style and language of this prose and what changes, if any, can be seen in it during these two centuries? Linguistically the emergence of the *cywydd* used to be considered as marking the beginning of a new era in the history of the Welsh language. The work of Dafydd ap Gwilym has been regarded as beginning the period of Modern Welsh. Few definite statements can in fact be made about the linguistic features that mark his work. The earliest manuscripts that preserve it belong to a period about a century after the time of Dafydd so that they can hardly represent precisely the writing conventions of his time. The language of his poetry seems to have lost some of the archaic features of the generation of poets who preceded him; the old copula constructions have disappeared; the preverbal aspectual particle *ry–* has fallen into disuse; the fifteenth-century manuscript copies of his poems show some orthographical innovations. His greatest innovation however was the popularization of the *cywydd* metre. Dafydd ap Gwilym belonged to a class of poets writing in a formal idiom and in strict metres and the changes initiated in his work became the norm in the work of his successors. There is little difference between the language he used and the language of a sixteenth-century Glamorgan poet like Iorwerth Fynglwyd. What is the history of the language of prose in a society where Welsh was not the language of government or administration or of a professional class, where the themes dealt with were limited, where it had to compete with the Latin of the Church and the Norman French or English of the conqueror? When Hywel Fychan copied *The Red Book of Hergest* in about the year 1400, a task involving texts which on the whole belonged to a period some century earlier, the language he copied was fairly uniform and standard and his orthography was retrospective. It is difficult on linguistic grounds to localize almost any of the prose of the *Red Book*. By 1450 nearly all the manuscripts being copied show signs of dialect forms with little effort by the copyists to standardize the language. This is true of the prose texts copied by Gwilym Tew in Peniarth MS. 51 as well as of the language of Sir Thomas ab Ieuan ap Deicws and of the *cydfodau*. Elis Gruffydd coined his own peculiar orthographical conventions. The breakdown of a standard literary language and the growth of the influence of dialect is perhaps the saddest and most noteworthy linguistic feature of the prose of this period. It was left to the Protestant translation of the Welsh Bible to reintroduce a concept of standard form which then came not from law texts and story but from the literary bonds of the new religion.

Language is inseparable from style and much mention has been made within the compass of this chapter of the form of the prose of the Middle Ages. Professor T. J. Morgan and Sir Ifor Williams have analysed the style of medieval narrative prose. They have drawn attention to the comparatively short sentence, simple in form—a form which can be compared with the parataxis of medieval Latin prose. The short sentences are punctuated by temporal adverbs: the narrative is enlivened by passages of terse dialogue and purple passages of *araith* (rhythmic alliterative sentences), chiefly confined to descriptions. *Araith* is also a feature of technical prose like the law books or of some religious works like *Cysegrlan Fuchedd.* Early technical prose has however its own peculiar features. It shows a distinct predilection for triads and other numerical groupings. All these features are to be found in the prose of the earlier and later Middle Ages. The simple narrative style of the *Mabinogi* is paralleled in a story like *Ysgan ab asgo* or *Llywelyn and Cynwrig Goch.* The numerical schematicism of the law books is a feature of the later bardic texts. One component which becomes more evident in the prose as it develops is that of *araith.* Instead of being restricted to 'purple patches' it becomes a feature of whole works like the *Areithiau Pros* and the Prophecies. This may only represent the surfacing in a written form of something which earlier had been restricted to the oral tradition. Alternatively its development in the written literature may make it one of the distinguishing features of what is basically an undistinguished chapter in the history of Welsh prose, whose chief importance is that it shows a history of continuity and an awareness of contemporary English and European fashions. It was this continuity and awareness that enabled the University men of the next generation to create a limited Renaissance in Wales. That is, however, a topic for the next volume.

BIBLIOGRAPHY

Texts:

Thomas Jones, *Rhyddiaith Gymraeg, Y Gyfrol Gyntaf* (Caerdydd, 1954).

Idem, 'Disgrifiad Elis Gruffudd o'r cynadleddau a fu rhwng Harri VIII a'r ymherodr Siarl V a rhyngddo a Ffranses I, Brenin Ffrainc yn 1520', *Bulletin of the Board of Celtic Studies*, xviii (1958–60), 311–17.

Idem, 'Disgrifiad Elis Gruffudd o ymweliad y Cardinal Wolsey â Ffrainc', ibid., xxi (1964–6), 219–23.

Idem, 'Hanes Llywelyn ap Iorwerth a Chynwrig Goch o Drefriw', *National Library of Wales Journal*, iii (1943–4), 151–7.

Thomas Jones and J. E. Caerwyn Williams, 'Ystori Alexander a Lodwig', *Studia Celtica*, x/xi (1975–6), 261–311.

Henry Lewis, *Brut Dingestow* (Caerdydd, 1942).

Idem, *Chwedlau Seith Doethon Rufein o Lyfr Coch Hergest* (Caerdydd, 1958).

Idem, 'Darn o'r Ffestivalis', *Transactions of the Honourable Society of Cymmrodorion*, 1923–4, 18–70.

Idem, 'Proffwydoliaeth yr Eryr', *Bulletin of the Board of Celtic Studies*, ix (1937–9), 112–15.

J. J. Parry, *Brut y Brenhinedd, Cotton Cleopatra version* (Cambridge, Mass., 1937).

Brynley F. Roberts, *Brut y Brenhinedd, Llanstephan version* (Dublin, DIAS, 1971).

Idem, 'Ystori'r Llong Foel', *Bulletin of the Board of Celtic Studies*, xviii (1958–60), 337–62.

Idem, 'Rhai Swynion Cymraeg', ibid., xxi (1964–6), 198–213.

Idem, 'Pymtheg Gweddi San Ffraid a'r Pardwn', ibid., xvi (1954–6), 254.

Prys Morgan, 'Elis Gruffudd yng Nghalais', ibid., xxi, (1964–6), 214–18.

D. Silvan Evans, *Y Marchog Crwydrad* (1864).

J. E. Lloyd, *Owen Glendower* (Oxford, 1931).

Evan D. Jones, 'Ystoria Ysgan ap Asgo, Arglwydd Bodeugan', *Bulletin of the Board of Celtic Studies*, ix (1937–9), 219–21.

Graham C. G. Thomas, 'Chwedlau Tegau Eurfron a Thristfardd', ibid., xxiv (1970–2), 1–9.

Idem, *A Welsh Bestiary of Love* (Dublin, 1988).

Timothy Lewis, *A Welsh Leechbook, or Llyfr o Feddyginiaeth* (Liverpool, 1914).

J. Beverley Smith, 'Cydfodau o'r Bymthegfed Ganrif', *Bulletin of the Board of Celtic Studies*, xxi (1964–6), 309–24.

Thomas Parry, 'Statud Gruffudd ap Cynan', ibid., v (1929–31), 25–33.

Rachel Bromwich, *Trioedd Ynys Prydein* (Cardiff, 1961).

Morfydd E. Owen, 'Y Trioedd Arbennig', *Bulletin of the Board of Celtic Studies*, xxiv (1970–2), 434–50.

Nesta Lloyd and Morfydd E. Owen, *Drych yr Oesoedd Canol* (Caerdydd, 1986).
Theodore Chotzen, 'La "Querelle des Femmes" au Pays de Galles', *Revue Celtique*, xlviii (1931), 42–93.
E. J. Jones, *Medieval Heraldry*, 1943.
Idem, 'Buchedd Saint Martin', *Bulletin of the Board of Celtic Studies*, iv (1927–9), 189–207; 305–10.
Iorwerth Peate, 'Traethawd ar Felinyddiaeth', ibid., viii (1935–7), 295–301.
Idem, 'Y Naw Helwriaeth', ibid., vi (1931–2), 301–12.
R. Wallis Evans, 'Proffwydoliaeth y Fflowrddelis a Phroffwydoliaeth y Lili', ibid., xxi (1964–6), 327–33. 'Proffwydoliaeth y Disiau', ibid., 324–6.
Idem, 'Y Broffwydoliaeth Fawr a'r Broffwydoliaeth Fer', ibid., xxii (1966–8), 119–21.
Idem, 'Proffwydoliaeth Banastr o Brydain Fawr', ibid., 121–4.
Eurys I. Rowlands, *Poems of the Cywyddwyr* (Dublin, 1976).
J. H. Davies, 'A Welsh Version of the Birth of Arthur', *Y Cymmrodor*, xxiv, 247–64.
W. Gerallt Harries, 'Fersiwn Cymraeg o Ragair Cyntaf *The Kalender of Shepherdes*', *Bulletin of the Board of Celtic Studies*, xxvii (1976–8), 65–81.
Thomas Jones, *Ystoryaeu Seint Greal* (Caerdydd, 1992).
Patrick K. Ford, *Ystoria Taliesin* (Cardiff, 1992).
Patricia Williams, *Kedymdeithyas Amlyn ac Amig* (Caerdydd, 1982).

Critical Studies:

Geraint Bowen, *Y Drych Kristnogawl* (Caerdydd, 1996).
Brynley F. Roberts, 'Un o lawysgrifau Hopcyn ap Tomos o Ynys Dawy', *Bulletin of the Board of Celtic Studies*, xxiv (1970–2), 122–38.
Idem, 'Testunau hanes Cymraeg Canol', in Geraint Bowen (ed.), *Y Traddodiad Rhyddiaith yn yr Oesau Canol* (Llandysul, 1974), 274–302.
Thomas Roberts, 'Llawysgrifau Gutun Owain, a thymor ei oes', *Bulletin of the Board of Celtic Studies*, xv (1952–4), 99–109.
Thomas Jones, 'Syr Thomas ap Ieuan ap Deicws a'i gyfaddasiad Cymraeg o *Fasciculus Temporum* Werner Rolewinck', *Transactions of the Honourable Society of Cymmrodorion*', 1943, 35–61.
Idem, 'A Welsh Chronicler in Tudor England', *Welsh History Review*, i (1960–3), 1–17.
Edmund Reiss, 'The Welsh Versions of Geoffrey of Monmouth's *Historia*', ibid., iv (1968–9), 97–113.
Ifor Williams, *Chwedl Taliesin* (Caerdydd, 1957).
Margaret Enid Griffiths, *Early Vaticination in Welsh with English Parallels* (Cardiff, 1937).

A. O. H. Jarman, 'Cerdd Ysgolan', in J. E. Caerwyn Williams (ed.), *Ysgrifau Beirniadol X* (Dinbych, 1977), 51–79.

Gerallt Harries, 'Bened Feddyg', *Wales and Medicine*, (ed.) John Cule (Llandysul, 1975).

Morfydd E. Owen, 'Meddygon Myddfai: A Preliminary Survey of some Medieval Writing in Welsh', *Studia Celtica*, x/xi (1975–6), 210–34.

J. E. Caerwyn Williams, 'Bucheddau'r Saint', *Bulletin of the Board of Celtic Studies*, xi (1941–4), 149–57.

Idem, 'Medieval Welsh Religious Prose', *Proceedings of the Second International Congress of Celtic Studies, 1963* (Cardiff, 1966), 65–97.

G. J. Williams, *Traddodiad Llenyddol Morgannwg* (Caerdydd, 1949), 173–81.

R. Geraint Gruffydd, 'Dau destun Protestanaidd cynnar o lawysgrif Hafod 22', *Trivium*, i (1966), 56–68.

W. Alun Mathias, 'Rhai Sylwadau ar Robert Gwyn', *Llên Cymru*, 3 (1954–5), 63–74.

Glyn Roberts, 'Wales and England: Antipathy and Sympathy 1282–1485' in *Aspects of Welsh History. Selected papers of the late Glyn Roberts* (Cardiff, 1969), 295–319.

G. Charles Edwards, 'The Scribes of the Red Book of Hergest', *National Library of Wales Journal*, 21 (1979–80), 245–56.

Daniel Huws, 'Llyfr Gwyn Rhydderch', *Cambridge Medieval Celtic Studies*, 21 (Summer 1991), 1–37.

INDEX